SYNCHRONIC OR DIACHRONIC?

OUDTESTAMENTISCHE STUDIËN

NAMENS
HET OUDTESTAMENTISCH WERKGEZELSCHAP
IN NEDERLAND EN BELGIË

UITGEGEVEN DOOR

JOHANNES C. DE MOOR

KAMPEN

DEEL XXXIV

Participants in the Ninth Joint Meeting of the OTW and SOTS, Kampen, 28-30 August 1994

SYNCHRONIC OR DIACHRONIC?

A Debate on Method in Old Testament Exegesis

PAPERS READ AT THE NINTH
JOINT MEETING OF

HET OUDTESTAMENTISCH WERKGEZELSCHAP
IN NEDERLAND EN BELGIE

AND

THE SOCIETY FOR OLD TESTAMENT STUDY

HELD AT KAMPEN, 1994

EDITED BY

JOHANNES C. DE MOOR

E.J. BRILL
LEIDEN · NEW YORK · KÖLN
1995

The paper in this book meets the guidelines for permanence and durability of the Committee on Production Guidelines for Book Longevity of the Council on Library Resources.

Library of Congress Cataloging-in-Publication Data

Synchronic or diachronic? : a debate on method in Old Testament
    exegesis / [edited] by Johannes C. de Moor.
        p.   cm. — (Oudtestamentische studiën, ISSN 0169–7226 ; d. 34)
        Papers from the Ninth Joint Meeting of the "Oudtestamentisch
    Werkgezelschap in Nederland en België" and the British "Society for
    Old Testament Study", held at Kampen, Aug. 1994.
        Includes bibliographical references and index.
        ISBN 9004103422 (alk. paper)
        1. Bible, O.T.—Criticism, interpretation, etc.—Congresses.
    2. Bible. O.T.—Language, style—Congresses.   I. Moor, Johannes
    Cornelis de, 1935–   .   II. Series.
    BS1171.2.S86   1995
    221'.06—dc20   95–31344
                                                                  CIP

ISSN   0169-7226
ISBN   90 04 10342 2

PRINTED IN THE NETHERLANDS

Contents

This volume contains the papers read at the Ninth Joint Meeting of the 'Oudtestamentisch Werkgezelschap in Nederland en België' and the British 'Society for Old Testament Study', held at Kampen, 28th-30st August 1994.

The 'Oudtestamentisch Werkgezelschap' wants to express deep gratitude to

PROFESSOR A.S. VAN DER WOUDE

who has been Editor of the series *Oudtestamentische Studiën* for twenty-three years. Seventeen volumes appeared under his able guidance. As Editor Van der Woude exhibited an ecumenical broadness of mind, inviting representatives of many different denominations and schools to publish in the series provided their work met the high professional standards he set for himself. He took a most lively interest in every manuscript he was considering for publication and many an author remembers some significant improvement due to the attentive eyes and vast knowledge of Van der Woude. His great merits in the field of Old Testament scholarship found wide recognition, both in the Netherlands and abroad. This year Van der Woude received the Burkitt Medal in Biblical Studies of the British Academy.

Fortunately Van der Woude's retirement does not mean an abrupt end to his career as an outstanding scholar. Rather it testifies to his keen judgement that he decided to drop the burden of editorship in this electronic age in favour of his own research. May he enjoy his well-deserved freedom for many years to come!

J.C. DE MOOR, President OTW

Abbreviations

All abbreviations of series, handbooks and journals in this volume are according to: S.M. Schwertner, *Internationales Abkürzungsverzeichnis für Theologie und Grenzgebiete*, Berlin [2]1992. In addition the following abbreviations were used.

BiIntS   Biblical Interpretation Series (Leiden)
CBET   Contributions to Biblical Exegesis and Theology (Kampen)
OvBTh   Overtures to Biblical Theologie (Philadelphia)
PredOT   De Prediking van het Oude Testament (Nijkerk)
SHANE   Studies in the History of the Ancient Near East (Leiden)
WBC   World Biblical Commentary (Waco, Texas)

James Barr   *Nashville – Tennesee, USA*

The Synchronic, the Diachronic and the Historical: A Triangular Relationship?

It is now widely recognized that the distinction between the synchronic and the diachronic is an important one, and the credit for it goes back primarily to F. de Saussure and his *Cours de linguistique générale*, published in French in 1916 but in English only in 1959. Of Saussure, R.H. Robins wrote that "his influence on twentieth-century linguistics, which he could be said to have inaugurated, is unsurpassed" and that his "statement of the structural approach to language underlies virtually the whole of modern linguistics".[1] And it was on the synchronic axis that the emphasis of his thinking lay. Though both axes were legitimate and necessary, and though he himself had been distinguished in Indo-European historical philology, the interest in the synchronic was the newer, more original, and more creative element. The two, he wrote, "are not of equal importance ... the synchronic viewpoint predominates, for it is the true and only reality to the community of speakers" (*Course*, 90). The impression created was that synchronic linguistics was to be "regarded as methodologically prior".[2] In his lectures Saussure himself dealt with synchronic linguistics before he went on to the diachronic.

These ideas were slow to have any effect on biblical studies. People tended to look first at the history of linguistic elements, and this tendency was held in common by the language experts on the one side and by many of the theologians and philosophers on the other. In my first book, *The Semantics of Biblical Language* (London 1961), and in articles of about the same time,[3] I was the first, or one of the first, to make familiar the distinction between diachronic and synchronic as an element within biblical studies. On pp. 139-140 of that same book I wrote in Saussurean style that "Words can only

---

[1] R.H. Robins, *A Short History of Linguistics*, London 1967, 200-1.

[2] Wording of P. Mühlhäusler, article 'Linguistics: diachronic', in: R. Harré, R. Lamb (eds.), *The Encyclopedic Dictionary of Psychology*, Oxford 1983, 355.

[3] In *The Semantics of Biblical Language*, 220, n.2, I quoted Saussure himself for "the conception of language ... as a functional system of oppositions". In an article "Hypostatization of Linguistic Phenomena in Modern Theological Interpretation", *JSSt* 7 (1962), 85-94, written at about the same time, I said that "a greater emphasis on the distinction between synchronic and diachronic approaches to language" would be "helpful", because it would serve to prevent the misuse of etymology (quotation from p. 94).

be intelligibly interpreted by what they meant at the time of their use, within the language system used by the speaker or writer". This was written, of course, against the apparently diachronic method of etymology. Looking back on it, I can see that this was a rather easy case to establish, though this was not so evident to all readers at the time. But anyway it placed me firmly on the side of the synchronic.

Since that time however the interest in the synchronic approach has rapidly increased. Diachronic interests have come to be down-valued, and these tendencies have come to be associated with a more general anti-historical trend in modern culture – something that may have been quite absent from Saussure's own intention. Exegesis, it is now widely felt, should treat the text synchronically and largely leave aside historical matters. Thus the words of Saussure(*Course*, 81):

> "The linguist who wishes to understand a state must discard all knowledge of everything that produced it and ignore diachrony. He can enter the mind of speakers only by completely suppressing the past. The intervention of history can only falsify his judgement".

could be said to have been translated into something like this:

> The exegete who wishes to interpret a text must discard all knowledge of everything that produced it and ignore diachrony. He or she can enter the mind of the text only by completely suppressing the past. The intervention of history can only falsify his or her interpretation.

If so, then Saussure's principles have been carried more to an extreme in modern exegetical trends.

There are however several reasons why this understanding should be questioned. The first is this: that synchrony in the Saussurean sense, if one thinks about it, must support a historical approach, indeed must be a historical approach rather than an anti-historical one. This may sound surprising but one can quickly give examples to confirm it. I was already aware of this when I wrote the *Semantics* book. It struck me at the time, and puzzled me a little, that the synchronic meanings were also the historical meanings, in one sense of the word. If we could say that this was the meaning within (say) New Testament times, seen synchronically, then the same was obviously the historically correct and valid meaning. Historically it meant what it meant synchronically in the relevant biblical time.

Even in Saussurean terms, therefore, the synchronic cannot be absolutely opposed to the historical. A pure synchronic approach completely ignoring history, it would seem, would be logically possible only for a study of language in the present moment: as soon as one looks at the synchronic state of language in a past time, then one is entering into a historical investigation. Thus the synchronic can be as much a historical enterprise as the diachronic is. One way to think of this is by asking the question what we mean by a 'time'.

'Synchronic' is supposed to mean 'all at one time'. But how long, for this purpose, is a 'time'? This is a cardinal problem for the entire subject. In strict logic a Saussurean 'time' would seem to be a split second, a photographic instant in which no change in a language took place. But that works only as an abstract methodological principle: it does not work for the description of any language, dialect or idiolect. For actual work with languages or texts 'synchronic' might have to imply something like ten years. At the most one might extend it to a generation, say thirty years. To extend it to a lifetime or a century would scarcely be possible.

This is obviously relevant for a field like Old Testament, where the production of the texts plus the period of redaction and finalization, to say nothing of early interpretation, would last at least a thousand years. Of course Saussure did not have in mind anything like Old Testament exegesis; but his concept of the synchronic would natu- rally lead towards a historical reconstruction of several states of the language, as it was (say) in the ninth century, in the seventh, in the fourth and so on: in each of which the grammar and semantics of that time would have to be reconstituted. In this sense, perhaps surpris- ingly, synchrony in Saussure's sense naturally tends towards a reaffir- mation of a traditional 'historical-critical' approach. The sources for these different synchronic states would have to be distinguished. Syn- chrony would be achieved by separating out perhaps ten or a dozen synchronic states within the corpus of biblical texts.

It is of course possible to go another way and take synchrony to apply to the final text, say as the totality stood in Masoretic times, and quite a number of scholars have advocated this; I will say some- thing more about it in a moment, but for the present I just want to say that that approach is not the natural use of synchrony on Saussurean principles.

As we said, the question is how long a 'time' is. In order to achieve the absolute differentiation that Saussure makes between the syn- chronic and the diachronic approaches, one has to take synchronic time as a sort of photographic instant. Once we think of it as being thirty years or a hundred years or more, then of course change is going on within the synchronic state and the absoluteness of the difference breaks down. Saussure of course fully recognized the ubiquity of language change: see his pages on 'mutability of the sign' in *Course*, 74-78. But in his establishment of the synchronic axis he seemed to neglect this: at this cardinal point of his theory, change did not exist on the synchronic level.

Against his thinking therefore it may be objected, and in some recent linguistic thinking has been objected,[4] that normal use of language allows the language user to command a variety of language states through time – and also as differentiated by other factors, such as age, class, sex etc. Thus an English speaker of today can achieve a fair competence in a text of several centuries ago such as the King James Bible. We can understand a fair amount as far back as (say) Chaucer. Only beyond that time does English become for us opaque, more or less a different language which we have to learn just as we have to learn Dutch or German. And this factor may be significant for the point we just touched upon, namely the ability of a Hebrew speaker in late times to understand texts that were composed in a substantially different state of the language. One can thus think of taking the whole corpus as one, as seen and understood from the end of the process, with a grammar and semantics that includes within itself a partial but fairly adequate knowledge of the grammar and semantics of these earlier states. This might be a quite good approach. It might help those who want to take the Masoretic text 'in itself'. But, far from being a synchronic approach in the sense of Saussure's mind, it seems to be the opposite: it is more like the recent idea, associated with Labov and Bailey, of a "time-incorporating developmental linguistics",[5] which would actually *diminish* the opposition between diachronic and synchronic.

The Masoretic text does not give us direct and precise access to any one synchronic state of ancient Hebrew. The materials lie in layers which represent differing stages of analysis and registration over a long time.[6] If we were to follow a strictly Saussurean approach we would have to rewrite portions of text as we think they were realized

---

[4]For a brief overview see the articles "Language: Variation Theories", "Interlanguage" and others by P. Mühlhäusler in: Harré, Lamb (eds.), *The Encyclopedic Dictionary of Psychology*.

[5]Wording of Mühlhäusler, "Linguistics: Synchronic", *The Encyclopedic Dictionary of Psychology*, 355; on Labov and Bailey see also his "Language: Variation Theories", *ibid.*,332.

[6]As readers will recognize, this is part of the argument made familiar by E. Ullendorff in his article "Is Biblical Hebrew a Language?", in his collection with the same name (Wiesbaden 1977), 3-17; see especially his sentence "In any real sense of the term, BH in its Masoretic garb was scarcely a language which in that form was ever actually spoken" (p. 7).

in speech in the eighth century, the fourth, the first, the fourth AD
and so on. A familiar case is that of the passive qal, convincingly
recognized by scholars as such but in the tradition followed by the
Masoretic text revocalized as pual or hophal according to whether it
was perfect or imperfect. Another interesting case lies in the series
of verb forms like וְשִׁבַּר (2 Ki. 23:14), rather frequent in a key place
like the narrative of Josiah's reform, which must mean "and he broke"
but appears to contradict the normal waw-consecutive pattern. Is this
a sign of an early move toward the diachronic shift whereby in later
Hebrew the waw consecutive came to be disused? No, more probable is
the explanation recently given by Jeremy Hughes, namely that these
cases were infinitive absolutes used "as substitutes for the finite verb"
(GK § 113 y, z) but were later reclassified as ordinary perfects and
so vocalized, on the basis at least in part of Mishnaic Hebrew usage.[7]
Thus the taking of the Masoretic Text, "just as it stands", as a basis
cannot satisfy the criteria for synchrony on Saussure's own terms.
Strictly, it would be more accurate to follow J. Retsö in his learned
work *Diathesis in the Semitic Languages* when he writes that the
Masoretic text is "a veritable linguistic museum" giving evidence of
many centuries of diachronic change (p. 73).[8]

In saying this I do not imply that it is illogical or impossible to take
the Masoretic Text as it stands as basis: what I do say is that it does
not form the basis for a synchronic understanding on Saussure's terms.
To take the Masoretic text as basis in itself must depend on a principle
of its own finality, or of paucity of other comparable evidence, or of
sheer convention, or of religious authority. Even if we were to say that
it could be synchronic on the basis that we were studying the language
as it was for the Masoretes themselves, say in the period 600-900 AD,
it would still require a *historical* investigation in order for us to know
how the Masoretes in fact understood the text: for their text strictly
taken does not tell us this, it only provides partial evidence which if
taken along with other evidence may enable us historically to know
how they understood it.

Before going farther we have to say something about the diachronic
aspect. As I have already indicated, the synchronic should not be understood as an anti-historical aspect but as a deeply historical one.
What have we then to say about the diachronic? How does it differ?
For Saussure, at least in one of his formulations, the difference was
not between non-historical and historical, it was between system and
element:

---

[7]J. Hughes, "Post-Biblical Features of Biblical Hebrew Vocalization", in: S.E.
Balentine, J. Barton (eds.), *Language, Theology and the Bible*, Oxford 1994, 67-80.

[8]See the review of this work by J. Barr in *SOTS Book List* 1992.

"One is a relation between simultaneous elements, the
other the substitution of one element for another in time,
an event" (*Course*, 91).

The advantage secured by this distinction was that it overcame the
atomism of much of the older historical linguistics,[9] an aspect which
is well illustrated in the history of our own field, Semitic linguistics.
There was, however, a weakness in this formulation. It tended to
shift the ground from the difference between simultaneity and passing
time to another difference, that between system and discrete elements.
These may have connections but are certainly not the same thing.
Here again Saussure's thinking has been echoed and developed in
wide ranges of the modern discussion: people profess to want a holistic
approach and not an atomistic one.

But the change of ground introduced some possibility of confusion. On the one hand, it tended to eliminate the element of time and
change from the description of language as it now is: it meant that the
synchronic state was an abstract ideal rather than a holistic description of what was going on. Moreover, it suggested that the ultimate
and essential sort of change was a succession of states rather than one
taking place through discrete changes. But such a succession of states
is difficult to describe or comprehend. How can a state of language,
seen synchronically and holistically and containing no change, change
into another state which is quite different? In fact it seems to be
through many gradual and discrete changes, taking place all the time
but at different speeds, that changes of state take place. Moreover,
there seems to be no way of knowing a historically ancient synchronic
state of a language except through historical research which builds
upon the discrete diachronic changes. This is particularly true where
only limited or fragmentary texts and background information exist. All statements about the ancient synchronic state are subject to
modification on the ground of new diachronic information. Thus the
apparently clear and strict frontier between synchronic and diachronic
begins to come apart.

Finally, Saussure's formula suggested that diachronic change was
methodologically secondary to synchronic description. But it is not so
clear that this latter is right. The reverse can be argued: "development
can explain its endpoint or state but not vice versa".[10] Examples can

---

[9]C.-J. N. Bailey, *Variation and Linguistic Theory*, Arlington (Virginia) 1973,
13, writes that "Saussure ... began with the good intention of ridding linguistic
descriptions of an atomistic approach ..."

[10]Wording of Mühlhäusler, "Linguistics: Synchronic", *The Encyclopedic Dictionary of Psychology*, 355.

easily be suggested. Why is it that in German *Wort* is neuter but *Antwort* is feminine? No structural or systemic consideration seems to explain it. The answer is that *Antwort* had in older German an unstressed *e* ending and was a characteristic feminine form (*Antwürte*).[11] Thus the diachronic consideration explains the synchronic [modern] fact.

In Hebrew we do this a lot. Why is it that מֶלֶךְ generates מַלְכִי but דָּבָר generates דְּבָרִי? It is much the most economical explanation, and the one which most of us give to beginning students, to say that מֶלֶךְ and other such words came from a diachronically earlier form *malk-*. A strictly synchronic approach has simply no account of the facts to offer, or else it is a complicated, cumbrous and roundabout one.

Even, then, if synchronic states are the more important thing, as may well still be the case, it seems to me that synchronic states in the past are not accessible to us except through historical investigation and that involves diachronic study in Saussure's sense. Strictly synchronic study is available to us only for what is contemporary – and even then there are qualifications. Even in those synchronic studies that are strictly contemporary, it is probable that much evidence would be wrongly interpreted but for the influence of diachronic information. In this sense even fully contemporary synchronic description is dependent at many points on diachronic information. Part of the success of those who exclude diachronic information has come about because they already knew that same information. Once again therefore: the term 'history' comprises within itself both the synchronic and the diachronic.

This is relevant for the entire idea of what 'history' is. In some recent discussion there has been a tendency to talk about 'history' as if it was exclusively an account of changes, and in that sense diachronic. According to this viewpoint, it tells of events – battles, falls of governments, conquests, and so on – analogously to Saussure's idea of the diachronic, which handled only events and never states. But this seems to me to be wrong. It is simply untrue to say that history has been interested only in diachronic change. In the ancient history of Greece and Rome, for example, which before modern times was still the dominant area of historical work, it was always normal for historians to include at an early point a chapter on the constitutions of Athens, of Sparta, of Rome in the republican and/or in the imperial period. Of course these constitutions grew and changed somewhat in the course of time: but it was more economical to treat them basi-

---

[11]R. Priebsch, W.E. Collinson, *The German Language*, London 1962, 146.

cally as states, which from time to time underwent partial changes,
than to treat them as series of changes which would have left the description of the general underlying system unclear. Thus it is equally
a historical task to describe synchronic states or systems of the past
and to describe diachronic changes. That this is so is only confirmed
by the more modern styles in history, such as social history, economic
history, and - a notable example - the recent development in French
historiography, exemplified by Braudel's *La Méditerranée*, where the
basic presentation is more like a kind of geography, into which indications of things like wars, political changes, etc. are occasionally
inserted. Thus, to repeat, when applied to a past time, both the diachronic and the synchronic belong within the historical method and
are not in opposition to it. If the diachronic is to be down-valued, this
is not because it is historical, but because it is historically invalid –
as one can quickly see in the realm of language, if one reads those accounts of a language which are no more than catalogues of the known
phonological changes, or similarly in the case of etymology.

To summarize up to this point: the importance, seen from many
points of view, of the synchronic aspect in Saussure's linguistics does
not provide sufficient arguments in favour of a synchronic approach
to biblical exegesis or against a diachronic one. In application to an
ancient text like the Bible, or more correctly to its language, both
approaches would in fact necessarily be historical ones. Moreover there
are certain weaknesses in Saussure's conceptions which suggest that,
in spite of their importance for all modern linguistics, they require to
be modified in certain ways.

Saussure's conceptions were of course ideas for *linguistic description* and not for exegesis, and obviously no one would expect that,
even if they were completely correct, they would therefore on that
ground alone be definitive for questions of exegesis. Nevertheless it
is the importance of his ideas, and the association of them with the
entire current of anti-historical thinking that has become ideologically
so powerful in western culture, that forms the basis for the present
debate. It is proper therefore to observe that their relation to the
present exegetical problems is a very ambiguous one.

We thus pass to the question: whether the term 'synchronic', influ-
ential as it is because of its application to the description of languages,
is equally applicable to the matter of *exegesis*. How is synchronic exegesis supposed to differ from any other kind of exegesis? There seem
to be two areas affected. Firstly, some think that synchronic exegesis should concentrate on the text itself and ignore questions of the
historical background, what may have been thought previously, what

circumstances may have occasioned the creation of the text, and even in extreme cases what may have been the purpose and thinking of the writer or writers in creating the text. The text itself, and not the background or mode of its origin, should be central to exegesis. Second, and perhaps more prominent, is the question of putatively composite texts, where it is suggested that two or more sources have previously existed and have been combined with greater or less skill to form the existing text. In this case the idea of synchronic exegesis is that only the final text matters and that the existence of previous versions is irrelevant. The apparent difficulties and inconsistencies, the presence of which has led to the identification of previous versions, are in fact not difficulties or inconsistencies but are highly subtle evidences of the writer's skill and literary talent, qualities which the plodding minds of critical scholars were too lacking in insight to detect.

Of these two types, one may say, it is the question of composite texts that has been the more serious. No one would ever have made such a fuss over historical background, intentions of authors and the like, if these matters had not been linked with the separation of texts into different sources. Anyway, in both cases, it is customary to speak of a move from a 'historical' paradigm to a 'literary' one, and this seems to me to be right. The question belongs more to literary custom or theory than to the strictly *linguistic* theory from which the term 'synchronic' was derived. If the term 'synchronic' is used it is thus more as a sort of metaphor than as an exact account of the proposed shift of paradigm. I said "literary custom or theory" because I think there is a disparity here between the two sides. Traditional 'historical criticism' was on the whole rather lacking in theory. What one hears today as the theory of historical criticism is commonly a theory worked out for it by its enemies. Ideas that it claimed 'objectivity' or claimed to be the only valid method, and the like, are fictions imposed on it by modern opponents. In reality most criticism began with practice, and theory was worked out later, or rather was never properly worked out at all. Actual historical criticism worked in a rather empirical, trial-and-error, manner: if this piece was an older piece than that piece, and fitted with another old piece in another chapter, would that not be better? People came to accept critical approaches as effective practice, whether they troubled with the theory or not. To this day there does not exist any really clear and philosophically valid account of what traditional biblical criticism was doing.

The modern literary approach, by contrast, started much more from theory. Theory decided what was to be relevant and what not – take as a classic instance the influence of the attack on the 'intentional fallacy'.[12] Rather than starting from a body of practice in synchronic studies first built up, on the basis of which theoretical statements might later be made, on the contrary, the principle of synchrony seemed generally to be embraced *ab initio*, and it still today remains unclear what may come out of it as a body of widely accepted exegesis.

And here it is interesting to remember that attachment to a 'literary paradigm' is not peculiar to modern 'synchronic' exegesis but applies also to its supposed opposite, traditional historical criticism. Indeed, I well remember that, when I as a student began my acquaintance with these matters, the main currents of 'historical' criticism were commonly called 'literary criticism' and indeed were commonly attacked on these grounds, for example by Scandinavian scholars like Engnell with their emphasis on oral tradition.

What happens then is that, given a peculiar group of connections in the text, one scholar tends to think of traces of a previous version or of later redaction, while another tends to think of exquisite literary art on the part of the writer: the former is now deemed 'diachronic', the latter 'synchronic'. Where this is so my own reaction is that nothing can be solved by canonizing one of these contrary approaches: the only thing would be to set out, at every point, the full evidence and arguments in favour of both.

Moreover, there is a disparity between the two terms when so applied. Traditional 'historical criticism' was never purely 'diachronic'; indeed, it is probably impossible with texts to be purely diachronic. The historical critic started from the evidence of the existing text and used that evidence, 'synchronic' evidence therefore, as evidence for the preferability of a reading that involved composition from different versions, redactions etc. Far from it being the case that critics leapt at ideas of diverse sources, in some books such ideas were remarkably late to emerge: thus, in the familiar case of Ezekiel, Smend senior in 1880 still thought that the entire book was the well-considered work of one person and that "one could not take away any piece out of it

---

[12]Note for instance the immediate reference to this in the first paragraph of J.P. Fokkelman, *Narrative Art in Genesis*, 2nd ed., Sheffield 1991, vii; cf. J. Barr, "Reading the Bible as Literature", *BJRL* 56 (1973), 21-2, also *The Bible in the Modern World*, London 1973, Ch. 4, and the fine discussion in J. Barton, *Reading the Old Testament*, London 1984, 148ff. Incidentally, at a time when we are being told that authors as such are quite insignificant, it is odd that we are being urged to admire the incredible skill of these same authors in their placing chiasmus and such things – a practice which seems to me not to betoken a profound degree of skill!

without endangering the entirety", a highly holistic and 'synchronic' point of view.[13]

Further, if it is important to read texts holistically, this has to be balanced by the acknowledgement that historical study is also holistic in its own way. Historical comprehension of the Bible is fully synthetic and holistic and must be so. The work of historians, archaeologists and others creates and implies a holistic continuum in a respect in which the Bible itself, even taken as a whole, provides only a part.

We cannot avoid mention of another aspect: the supposed religious and theological values of synchronic and diachronic work. One of the main grounds for the turn of opinion against traditional historical criticism was that it was not religiously fruitful or theologically responsible. But this, whether a valid criticism or not, does not mean that a synchronic literary approach is in this respect any better. Indeed, the religious vacuity of some literary readings of the Bible is felt by many to be rather evident. I myself heard one of the leading practitioners of literary reading say that one of the advantages of his approach was that no clergyman or rabbi would ever raise any objection to it, since it made no connection, whether favourable or unfavourable, with religious concerns. Compare similarly the concluding pages of David M. Gunn and Danna Nolan Fewell's attractively written *Narrative in the Hebrew Bible*, London 1993, 204-5: the Bible has the many voices of many contradictory ideologies. It "shows us not merely patriarchy, élitism, and nationalism; it shows us the fragility of these ideologies through irony and counter-voices". Thus these texts "may be uncovering a world in need of redemption and healing and a world-view much in need of change. This is the kind of reading that can transform us. If we realize that the world of the Bible is a broken world, that its people are human and therefore limited, that its social system is flawed, then we might start to see more clearly our own broken world, our own human limitations, our own defective social systems. And who knows? Maybe we shall find ourselves called to be the agents of change". All this may possibly be quite true, but it is hardly a resounding claim for the religious centrality of the Bible: many of those anxious for a valid religious interpretation will regard it as vague, ambiguous and conspicuously lacking in direction. Considering the important positive function of historical criticism in the entire development of modern Old Testament theology, the failure of the newer literary paradigm to come anywhere near that achievement is striking.

---

[13] R. Smend, *Der Prophet Ezechiel* (KEH), Leipzig 1880, xxi, cited in O. Eissfeldt, *Einleitung in das Alte Testament*, Tübingen 1934, 413.

This point is by no means only my own impression. It is shared, at least in part, by the major pioneer in canonical exegesis, Professor Brevard Childs, and exactly on this point we see a certain change of direction in his thinking. One of the main arguments against traditional historical-critical scholarship has been that, even if justified as a matter of history, it was not theologically significant, since theology must depend on the final and canonical text of the whole. It is interesting therefore to see in Childs' *Biblical Theology of the Old and New Testaments*, London 1992, surely the culminating stage in the 'canonical approach', what seems to be a turn in the opposite direction. Looking back to the time when he wrote his *Introduction to the Old Testament as Scripture* (London 1979), Childs tells us (p. 722) that the major obstacle to serious theological reflection then seemed to him to be "the diachronic legacy of nineteenth-century historical criticism. Consequently I greeted as an ally the growing twentieth-century appeal to narrative theology as at least a move toward recovering a holistic reading of the Bible". Subsequent experience however has disproved this expectation. "The threat lies in divorcing the Bible when seen as literature from its theological reality to which scripture bears witness. When the focus of the analysis lies in the 'imaginative construal' of the reader, the text is robbed of all determinative meaning within various theories of reader response. The effect is to render the biblical text mute for theology and to deconstruct its tradition in a way equally destructive as the nineteenth-century historicists" (p. 723).

Elsewhere in the same volume we hear that the "move from history to language" (p. 204) has not been a success. Indeed, "the new focus on language in biblical studies has already run into profound problems, indeed far more quickly than the historical paradigm which it sought to replace" (p. 205). The emphasis on language can "domesticate the Bible theologically just as quickly as the excessive stress on history did". The danger of rendering the biblical text "mute for theological reflection" has not been diminished.

And thus, by contrast, we begin to hear of "the proper function of the diachronic" (p. 216). "In spite of the inadequacies of the use of the historical critical approach as an exegetical tool, I would strongly argue for the usefulness of recovering a depth dimension within the kerygma which does not fall victim to the persistent pitfalls of critical scholarship since the Enlightenment" (p. 216). "The recovery of the historical dimension within the kerygma can aid in correlating the witness to the concrete life of the early church", and similarly it "helps the interpreter understand the range of kerygmatic diversity as well

as establishing the nature of its unity" (p. 217). This leads on to
a positive section on "historical trajectories" (pp. 262ff.) within the
Gospels.

Thus Childs, after long and bitter opposition to the heritage of
historical critical work, an opposition which continues even as he now
seeks to play it down, now resists criticisms made on the ground that
the canonical approach "has no use for the diachronic dimension and
is basically a static handling of the biblical text" (p. 104). On the
contrary, the diachronic element is positively important. "It seems
obvious that this final form can be much better understood, especially in its crucial theological role as witness, if one studies carefully
those hundreds of decisions which shaped the whole. Thus it greatly
sharpens one's vision of the final form of the Pentateuch which is the
goal of exegesis if one first distinguishes between earlier and later levels within the witness ..." It is good (2) "if the various stages in the
growth of Israel's witness can be historically correlated ..." (3) "It
is theologically significant to see to what extent early stages of the
tradition became normative for particular groups ..." (4) "biblical
texts from different ages, even when given a subsequent normative
canonical form, continue to reflect a quality of their original life".

In other words, all has been said in favour of traditional historical criticism as an important theological resource is true. So we find
Childs actually producing arguments which use "careful historical
criticism" as a criterion. "Careful historical critical study of the legal
traditions in the Old Testament does not point to the covenant as a
late theological construct" (p. 136). It is a mistake, he goes on, "to
work without the needed sociological and historical dimension" – this
very surprisingly, since in the same work he shows stern opposition
to every attempt to use a sociological approach.

It would be surprising, however, if Childs has really become a late
convert to the values of the historical-critical approach. Where then is
the difference? According to Childs, the criterion is whether the Bible
is read "as source rather than as witness". As long as it is read as
witness, then the diachronic aspect is perfectly right and highly to be
welcomed. Here then is another novel twist in our already complicated
debate.

The "trajectories" of Childs' latest work are indeed a sign of some
measure of return towards the diachronic as an element that can be
valuable within the total perspectives of the canon and the final form
of the text. What is not clear to me is that these trajectories are
truly diachronic or historical. They seem to me to belong more to the
nature of the logical or theological: they are links which are theolog-

ically desirable within a particular theological system. There was, if
one thinks of it, no way of avoiding a certain 'diachronical' element
when constructing a theology of the two Testaments, for there is no
question that the Old Testament is diachronically earlier than the
New. The trajectories appear to be diachronical because they do make
connections over past stages; but because they are not subjected to
historical *criticism*, i.e. to questions whether things really developed
in this way or not, their diachronic character is only apparent. The use
of the text "as witness" is really a dogmatic argument rather than one
that belongs to biblical studies: within the many pages of his *Biblical
Theology*, no text ever 'witnesses' to anything other than what Childs
in his own personal theology believes to be right. 'Witness' is thus a
category which, while appearing to fit within a historical approach,
automatically cancels out any attempt to find any other meaning in
the text, because any suggestion of any other meaning would by its
own nature be using the text 'as a source'. The question is not whether
the text is used 'as a witness' or 'as a source', but how one decides
whether it 'witnesses' to theological reality X or theological reality Y.
Since for Childs the answer to this question is always theologically
presupposed there is no real historical or diachronic element in the
decision.

The sudden and surprising warmth of Childs towards the diachronic is thus only apparent and deceptive. Nevertheless it may be
an indication of a new turn in the current discussion.

In conclusion, I feel I ought to apologize for reading a paper which
has in it little or no detailed reference to the Old Testament. This
however is not an accident. The methodological discussions in which
biblical studies are now engaged seem to me to have rather little to do
with the Bible itself. They are not based on the Bible, nor can they
be settled by the Bible. Some works on hermeneutics contain only
a few pages that refer to the Bible at all – just as I heard recently
of a book about literary theory that contained no reference at all to
any author of any literary work. These discussions seem to me to be
discussions of our own modern experience and it is our own modern
experience in its many varied aspects that is the authority to which
we are appealing. Since these aspects are indeed very varied, we can
confidently expect that the answers to be produced will continue to
be varied also.

Willem A.M. Beuken   *Leuven – Belgium*

Isaiah 28:
Is It Only Schismatics That Drink Heavily?
Beyond the Synchronic Versus Diachronic Controversy

TRANSLATION OF ISAIAH 28
(basically according to RSV and NRSV)

1   *Woe to the haughty crown of the drunkards of Ephraim,*
        and to the fading flower of its glorious beauty,
    which is on the head of the fat valley,
        of those overcome with wine!
2   *Behold, the Lord has one who is strong and mighty:*
        like a storm of hail, a destroying tempest,
    like a storm of powerful, flooding waters,
        he will hurl down to the earth with (his) hand.
3   *Under foot will be trampled*
        the haughty crown of the drunkards of Ephraim;
4   *and the fading flower of its glorious beauty,*
        which is on the head of the fat valley,
    will be like a first-ripe fig before the summer:
        whoever sees it, swallows it
            while it is still in his palm.
5   *In that day*
    YHWH *of hosts will be a crown of beauty,*
        and a diadem of glory, to the remnant of his people;
6   *and a spirit of (right) judgment to the one who sits in judgment,*
        and valour to those who turn back the battle at the gate.
7   *These also reel with wine*
        and stagger with strong drink.
    Priest and prophet reel with strong drink,
        they are swallowed up by wine,
    they stagger with strong drink,
        they reel with the vision,
            they totter in giving a decision.
8   *Truly, all tables are full of vomit,*
        of filth with no (clean) place.
9   *"Whom will he teach knowledge,*
        whom will he make understand the message?
    Those who are weaned from the milk,

       those taken from the breast?

10   *Truly,* tsaw latsaw tsaw latsaw,
     qaw laqaw qaw laqaw,
       z^eʿer sham, z^eʿer sham".

11   *Truly, with a stammering lip*
     and with a foreign tongue
      he will speak to this people,

12   *he who has said to them:*
     "This is the resting-place; give rest to the weary;
   yes, this is your place of repose".
     Yet they have been unwilling to listen.

13   *So the word of* YHWH *to them will be:*
   "tsaw latsaw tsaw latsaw,
     qaw laqaw qaw laqaw,
       z^eʿer sham, z^eʿer sham",
   in order that they may go, stumble back, and be broken,
     and be snared, and taken.

14   *Therefore hear the word of* YHWH,
     you swaggerers,
   who rule this people
     in Jerusalem!

15   *Truly, you have said:*
   "We have concluded a covenant with death,
     and with sheol we have made an agreement.
   When the scourge of flooding passes through,
     it will not come upon us.
   Truly, we have made lies our refuge,
     and in falsehood we have hidden ourselves".

16   *Therefore thus says the Lord* YHWH:
   "Behold, I myself have laid in Zion for a foundation a stone,
     a tested stone,
   a cornerstone valuable for a foundation.
     One who trusts will not shake!

17   *I will make righteousness the line,*
     and justice the plummet.
   Hail will sweep away the refuge of lies,
     and waters will flood the hiding place.

18   *Your covenant with death will be annulled,*
     and your agreement with sheol will not stand.
   When the scourge of flooding passes through,
     you will be for it to trample on.

19   *As often as it passes through*

       it will take you;
     Truly, morning by morning it will pass through,
       by day and by night;
     and it will be sheer terror
       to be made understand the message".

20   *Truly, the bed is too short to stretch oneself out,*
       and the covering too narrow to wrap oneself up.

21   *Truly, as on Mount Perazim* YHWH *will stand up,*
       and as in the valley of Gibeon he will rage,
   to do his deed — strange is his doing!
       and to work his work — alien is his work!

22   *So now do not swagger,*
       lest your bonds be made strong.
   Truly, I have heard a decree of destruction
       from the Lord YHWH *of hosts upon the whole earth.*

23   *Give ear, and hear my voice;*
       pay attention, and hear my speech!

24   *Is it all day that the plower plows for sowing,*
       that he opens and harrows his ground?

25   *Does he not, when he has leveled its surface,*
       scatter dill and toss cumin,
   set wheat in rows,
       and barley in plots,
        and spelt at its border?

26   *Yes, he instructs him concerning the right order,*
       his God teaches him.

27   *Truly, dill is not threshed with a sledge,*
       nor is a cart wheel rolled over cumin.
   Truly, dill is beaten out with a stick,
       and cumin with a rod.

28   *Bread grain is crushed,*
       but not unceasingly does one thresh it.
   One drives one's cart wheel over it,
       but with one's horses one does not crush it.

29   *This also comes from* YHWH *of hosts;*
       he is wonderful in counsel, and great in wisdom.

1. Introduction to the Problem

Besides all the fundamental disagreements, the explanation of Isaiah
28 also reveals elements of agreement on a few important matters. On
this substratum, an approach can be based which crosses the dividing
line between a synchronic and a diachronic interpretation of the text.

A growing number of authors, basing themselves on the opening
'woe' of this section, have come to recognize the entire chapter as an
overarching unity, one of the six 'woe'-sections which make up Isaiah
28-33 (28; 29:1-14,15-24; 30; 31[-32]; 33). Nonetheless, it is only in
the most recent literature that this redactional arrangement has been
seen to have meaning at the level of content.[1]

Within the redactional context of this 'woe'-section, vv. 23-29 are
generally considered an original textual whole, and that on the basis
of their *mashal* character and the use of agricultural images. Most
authors also consider vv. 1-6 and vv. 14-22 to be relatively independent unities. Vv. 1-6 form a composite unity because the imagery of
the crown encompasses, next to an accusation, an announce18ent of
judgment and one of salvation which are connected to one another
by the stereotypical phrase and literary-historical seam 'in that day'
(vv. 1,2-4,5-6). Vv. 14-22 reveal in detail the classical pattern of an
accusation and an announcement of judgment (vv. 14-15,16-22), connected by the messenger formula in v. 16 and enclosed by the catch
word 'to swagger' (לוץ). Later on, we shall deal with the question of
the so-called authenticity of vv. 19-22.

The actual problem lies with vv. 7-13. According to some, these
verses form an original unity, existing of an accusation and an announcement of judgment (vv. 7-10, 11-13),[2] however, these subdivi-

---

[1]The earliest and strongest advocate is F. Delitzsch, *Commentar über das
Buch Jesaia* (BC, 3/1), Leipzig [4]1889, 311; further A. Penna, *Isaia* (SB[T]),
Torino 1958, 254; J.D.W. Watts, *Isaiah 1-33* (WBC, 24), Waco 1985, 352-3; J.N.
Oswalt, *The Book of Isaiah: Chapters 13-39* (NIC), Grand Rapids 1986, 504-5;
C.R. Seitz, *Isaiah 1-39* (Interpretation), Louisville 1993, 206; J.G. Williams, "The
Alas-Oracles of the Eight Century Prophets", *HUCA* 38 (1967), 75-91; W. Janzen,
Mourning Cry and Woe Oracle (BZAW, 125), Berlin & New York 1972, 54-62;
H.-J. Zobel, "הוי", in *ThWAT* II, 382-8 (386-8); J.Ch. Exum, "Whom Will He
Teach Knowledge? A Literary Approach to Isaiah 28", in: D.J.A. Clines *et al.*
(eds.), *Art and Meaning: Rhetoric in Biblical Literature*, Sheffield 1982, 108-139
(133ff.).

[2]B. Duhm, *Das Buch Jesaia* (HK), Göttingen [4]1922 (reprint Göttingen 1968);
A. Dillmann, *Der Prophet Jesaja*, herausgegeben und vielfach umgearbeitet von
R. Kittel (KEH), Leipzig [6]1898; E. König, *Das Buch Jesaja*, Gütersloh 1926; E.J.
Kissane, *The Book of Isaiah*, vol. 1, Dublin 1941; Penna, *Isaia*; O. Kaiser, *Der
Prophet Jesaja: Kapitel 13-39* (ATD, 18), Göttingen 1973; H. Wildberger, *Jesaja*,
3. Teilband: Jesaja 28-39 (BK X/3), Neukirchen 1982.

sions do not show any of the classical formal characteristics. Others take these verses with vv. 1-6, based, above all, on their common theme of drunkenness.[3] Still others include vv. 7-13 with vv. 14-22 because the boasting spoken of in v. 14 seems to refer to the quotation in vv. 9-10.[4]

The discussion continually runs in to the difficulty of the addressees. Strictly speaking only vv. 14-22 consist of a second person address: "You swaggerers, who rule this people in Jerusalem!" (v. 14) and "So now do not swagger" (v. 22). In vv. 23-29 an audience is indeed addressed, but who that audience is, is not said and is nowhere to be inferred. In the first text unit, vv. 1-6, no one is addressed, but these verses have, nevertheless, two intended groups (in the third person): 'the drunkards of Ephraim' (vv. 1-4) and 'the rest of his people' (vv. 5-6).

The problem here reaches a climax in the question: which group of people is the prophet setting out against in vv. 7-13? They are designated, in the first place, as 'These also', and subsequently referred to as 'priest and prophet'. Since the most ancient times the opinion has held sway that after 'Ephraim' (vv. 1,3), Benjamin and Judah are now being accused (Jerome,[5] Redak[6]). Traditionally, however, a minority of commentators has also been of the opinion that this group does not contrast in geographical terms but in social terms. Not only the rich and powerful of Ephraim but even the priests and prophets of the Northern kingdom have sinned by abusing alcohol (Rashi,[7] Cyril of Alexandria[8]). Even when historical-critical exegesis understands these words as a literary seam, the double explanation remains in effect.[9]

---

[3] A. Schoors, *Jesaja* (BOT, 9), Roermond 1972; Watts, *Isaiah 1-33*; Oswalt, *The Book of Isaiah: Chapters 13-39*.

[4] Delitzsch, *Commentar über das Buch Jesaia*; F. Feldmann, *Das Buch Isaias*, Bd. 1 (Kap.1-39) (EHAT, 14), Münster in Westfalen 1925; H. Barth, *Die Jesaja-Worte in der Josiazeit: Israel und Assur als Thema einer produktiven Neuinterpretation der Jesajaüberlieferung* (WMANT, 48), Neukirchen 1977, 10ff.

[5] *Commentariorum in Isaiam Prophetam* Liber IX, 373-374 (Migne, PL 24, 317).

[6] A.J. Rosenberg, *Isaiah*, vol. 1: Translation of Text, Rashi and Commentary (Miqra'ot Gedolot), New York 1982, 220, 255-6.

[7] Rashi (Rosenberg, *Isaiah*, vol. 1) integrates vv. 5-6 in this interpretation by identifying the priests and the prophets with "the one who sits in judgment" and "those who turn back the battle at the gate" (v. 6). This explanation recurs later on (E. Rosenmüller, *Scholia in Jesajae vaticinia in compendium redacta* (Scholia in Vetus Testamentum, 2), Lipsiae 1835; Oswalt, *The Book of Isaiah: Chapters 13-39*).

[8] *Commentariorum in Isaiam Prophetam* Liber III, I, 389 (Migne, PG 70, 620).

[9] V. Tanghe, "Dichtung und Ekel in Jes xxviii 7-13", *VT* 43 (1993), 235-260

This question is interesting from a hermeneutical point of view.
The text unmistakably leaves a sort of opening in v. 7 which the
readers feel called to fill, whether they read the text from a historical point of view or whether they find history irrelevant and consider
themselves as the addressees. Interest is focused from v.1 on Ephraim.
In the announcement of salvation this shifts to 'the remnant of his
people' (vv. 5-6). In the usage of the Scriptures, this implies all of
Israel in its post-exilic meaning,[10] but this change of perspective does
not exclude Ephraim, it simply broadens matters. Furthermore, traces
can be found in vv. 7-13 of a coloration which points to Jerusalem
(v. 12a) or Ephraim (vv. 11,12b), but these particulars are not decisive
for the purpose of the prophecy. The readers, both those synchronically and those diachronically inclined, have still turned their eyes
in Ephraim's direction and they share in the vision of the prophet
Isaiah ben Amoz, that is to say, they consider the Northern kingdom
to be an unfaithful part of Israel as well as a hostile neighbouring
nation, which will soon fall under God's judgment (Isa. 7:1-9; 8:6;
9:7-11,20; 10:9, 17:1-6).[11] Led by these presuppositions they proceed,
without further ado, to assume that the dreadful tableau of stagger-
ing, vomiting and stammering priests and prophets has its origin in
the Northern kingdom, perhaps even in Bethel. The scene must belong to that unfaithful Ephraim where people drink so disgustingly!
This judgment of affairs remains unchallenged up to the first explicit
address: "Therefore, hear the word of YHWH, you swaggerers, who
rule this people in Jerusalem!" (v. 14). At this point all eyes are open
to the misunderstanding. The accused are not to be found out there
in Ephraim but right here in Jerusalem, close to the readers themselves. It is the priests and prophets of Jerusalem who have behaved
so shamefully.

The phenomenon we encounter here is a kind of ambiguity of perspective. From the outset it is unclear whether vv. 7-13 have to do
with the religious leaders of the Northern kingdom or those of the
Southern kingdom. This ambiguity of perspective serves, from here
on, the steering of the readers. The ambiguity of the text takes a
chance on the bias of the readers against Ephraim and for Jerusalem.
This bias creates a temporary interpretation of the question where the
wayward priests and prophets should be localized. This interpretation

---

(240ff.).

[10] J. Hausmann, *Israels Rest: Studien zum Selbstverständnis der nachexilischen
Gemeinde* (BWANT, 124), Stuttgart 1987, 156ff., 199f.; R.E. Clements, "שאר",
in: *ThWAT*, Bd. 7, 933-50 (940-3).

[11] Wildberger, *Jesaja*, 3. Teilband: Jesaja 28-39, 1650.

is abruptly disarmed in v. 14. The readers have been mistaken: the tableau just painted does not take place in Ephraim but in Jerusalem. Their prejudice is now turned into an Achilles heal. The sudden disclosure that the scene of the crime is on their very doorstep, the place where they have committed themselves, must surely h·t them hard and move them to do something.

On the basis of this striking discovery the addressees of vv. 23-29 can be seen in a new light. This *mashal* contains a direct address by way of the so-called *Lehreröffnungsruf* (v. 23) and the interrogative sentences which follow (vv. 24f.), but the addressees are nowhere mentioned. The content of the verses does not help in clarifying matters. Literary-historical exegesis in general looks for the audience in the *Sitz im Leben* of a *mashal* or in the socio-political surroundings of the prophet and his 'school'.[12] Thus we meet such proposals as: the class of the wise men,[13] the pupils of Isaiah ben Amoz[14] and the post-exilic community in which the redactor of the Book of Isaiah (henceforth BI) lived.[15] A growing number of commentators determine the audience from the literary context of vv. 23-29. The *mashal* would then address the 'swaggerers' of vv. 14, 22 or precisely the opposite group,[16] who are indeed open to the message of the prophet,[17] perhaps the above named 'remnant of his people' (v. 5).[18] Seldom, however, is the opinion found that the primary addressees of the *mashal* are the readers of BI. This is the case in a conservative explanation which considers the entire chapter to be addressed to the same public. In this understanding, the followers of Isaiah and the readers of the book, are thrown together.[19] A consistent redaction-historical approach would deny that vv. 23-29 were ever intended for an audience of Isaiah ben Amoz. The *mashal* was designed to help the readers of BI to understand what precedes.[20]

---

[12]Surveys along with Wildberger, *Jesaja*, 3. Teilband: Jesaja 28-39, 1087-90, and N. Schuman, "Jesaja 28:23-29: Een boerengelijkenis als politieke profetie", in: T. Baarda (ed.), *Segmenten: Studies op het gebied van de theologie*, Amsterdam 1981, 83-141 (114-23).

[13]G. von Rad, *Weisheit in Israel*, Neukirchen 1970, 184-5; Schoors, *Jesaja*; G. Fohrer, *Das Buch Jesaja I* (ZBK), Zürich 1964; Watts, *Isaiah 1-33*.

[14]O. Procksch, *Jesaja*, Bd. 1 (KAT, 9), Leipzig 1930; Feldmann, *Das Buch Isaias*, Bd. 1; Wildberger, *Jesaja*, 3. Teilband: Jesaja 28-39.

[15]R. Kilian, *Jesaja*, Bd. 2: 13-39 (NEB.AT), Würzburg 1994.

[16]König, *Das Buch Jesaja*; Schuman, "Jesaja 28:23-29: Een boerengelijkenis als politieke profetie", 109,133f.

[17]Delitzsch, *Commentar über das Buch Jesaia*; Oswalt, *The Book of Isaiah: Chapters 13-39*; Seitz, *Isaiah 1-39*.

[18]J. Hirsch, *Das Buch Jesaia*, Frankfurt a. M. 1911.

[19]Rosenmüller, *Scholia in Jesajae vaticinia*.

The following image arises from the overview so far. Literary-historical exegesis has designated different addressees for the different oracles in Isaiah 28. It is also reasonable to suggest that at a variety of places in the text the readers themselves are being addressed, as part of the intention of the final redaction and, as it has been received, at the level of its rather shallow adaptation of the text.

The diachronic method, it is said, pays exclusive attention to the historically varied audience while the synchronic method focuses on the actual reader. The final redaction of the book, however, directs itself towards a public which stems from the contemporaries of the prophet and confers its fundamental contours on later generations, including the actual readers. In a nuclear way the actual readers also form part of the purview of a diachronic exegesis. Turned around, the actual readers, for an important part, are addressed alongside the various historical addressees of the prophetic oracles with whom they personally identify. The synchronic method, therefore, cannot avoid paying some attention to the historical audiences. In principle and in fact an absolute distinction between both methodical approaches is thereby denied.

The following scheme may clarify the hermeneutical situation (the sign - - -> means 'addresses', the sign ≫≫ means 'creates' or 'develops into'):[21]

Oral situation = preaching of the prophet:

Isaiah ben Amoz - - -> 8th century Judah

Written situation = scroll of prophecies / book of Isaiah:

---

[20]Kaiser, *Der Prophet Jesaja: Kapitel 13-39*, 207: "Über den Inhalt der Prophetenrolle bereits nachdenklich gewordene oder es beim kommenden Kapitel doch werdende Leser oder Hörer werden durch den Anruf eines Weisen aus ihren Gedanken gerissen, um dann im Licht der ihnen erteilten Belehrung weiterlesen oder weiterhören zu können".

[21]The present scheme is inspired by the well-known charts of S.B. Chatman, *Story and Discourse: Narrative Structure in Fiction and Film*, Ithaca & London 1978; M. Pfister, *Das Drama: Theorie und Analyse* (UTB, 580), München [6]1988 ([1]1977) and the corrections proposed by Sj. van Tilborg, *Al lezend stemmen horen*, Nijmegen 1994. It incorporates the diachronic dimension into the basically synchronic scheme.

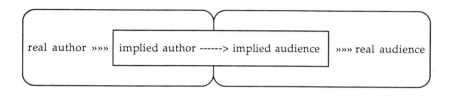

- Isaiah b. Amoz	- Isaiah of the	- 8th century Judah	- actual
- transmitters	scroll/book	- exilic community	readers
- Isaiah school		- future generations	

Measured against this schema we can characterize the one-sidedness of the two exegetical methods as far as it concerns the explanation of BI. The diachronic method tends to project the book onto the preaching of the prophet and to reduce the historical situation to one dimension. It neglects the fact that the Isaiah we meet in the book is a creation of the historical Isaiah ben Amoz and the transmitters together and that the addressees do not constitute a historical point in time but a continuum through time. The synchronic method tends to work in an ahistorical way and to neglect the fact that the actual readers can only accept the message of the writing prophet Isaiah when they identify with the historical, pluriform audience to which the original Isaiah and the tradition addressed themselves. For the reading process in itself creates time and again a changing perspective. The audience to which the text is addressed, or the group of people who are in the spotlight, changes continually.

Bearing this in mind we have given ourselves the task of explaining Isaiah 28 as a textual whole according to the schema outlined above.

2. The Function of the *Mashal* (vv. 23-29)

Historical exegesis has wrestled for a long time with the problem of how the primary prophetic genres of judgment, salvation and admonition come together in one meaningful perspective. In the situation of the oral preaching admonition and judgment can be conditionally related. Admonition can stem from the announcement of salvation, and after the announcement of judgment a perspective on salvation in the long term can follow. In the situation of the written word we run into different configurations. This is the case with Isaiah 28. The connection between salvation and doom in vv. 1-4 and vv. 5-6 can be explained as the transformation of an announcement of judgment over Ephraim into an announcement of salvation for the exilic community, 'the remnant of his people'. How is it possible, however, to follow up

an unconditional and absolute judgment over 'the swaggerers, who
rule in Jerusalem' (vv. 14-21) with a warning for the same group of
people (v. 22) and thereafter with an appeal to wonder at YHWH's
wise governance (vv. 23-29)? The situation of oral preaching does not
provide an explanatory framework. It is possible, perhaps, that in
the situation of the written text, the final redaction has transformed
the judgment that has fallen upon Israel into a topic which, against
the background of God's original plan of salvation, strongly urges a
change in lifestyle. Nowadays, such an insight is to be found among
exegetes in their attempts at answering the question of the purpose
of the *mashal* (vv. 23-29).

Opposite attempts to situate this comparison in the preaching of
Isaiah ben Amoz (see above) there are others which try to explain it
as a reflection on the three oracles in this chapter, a reflection of the
following purpose: the last word concerning God's actions is not the
downfall of his people, but his 'wonderful counsel and great wisdom'
(v. 29).[22] The passage links up with what precedes by means of some
topics and catch words. In this way, the 'wonderful counsel' stands in
one single line with the theme of God's strange actions (v. 21) and his
speaking in unintelligible language (v. 11). At this point the isotope
concerns precisely the relationship between coming judgment, past
salvation and admonition. Israel is used to the image of YHWH as
one who has given the land as a place of rest to which he has linked
the obligation to take care of the needy (v. 12a). According to the
transmitters of Isaiah, however, history teaches the following: should
God's people not comply with this task then YHWH will appear in a
new form, as one who speaks to Israel in the unintelligible language
of a hostile invader. If we take seriously the fact that the judgment,
in both its announcement and execution, has affected Israel's understanding of YHWH, including that of the exilic community who look
with hindsight upon the judgment, then a concluding passage is appropriate which points to the punishing action of God as 'the right
order' (v. 26: משפט), comparable with the right order in agriculture.
In recognizing this 'wonderful counsel and great wisdom' (v. 29) there
remains room, after the judgment, for admonition (v. 22).

The *mashal* serves this purpose of the entire chapter even in its
parts. The two stanzas, each with a conclusion, describe the process of
sowing and reaping (vv. 23-26, 27-29). Sowing consists of two actions,
plowing and planting, each of which must take place at the appro-

---

[22]Exum, "Whom Will He Teach Knowledge?", 130-134; D.L. Petersen, "Isaiah
28: A Redaction Critical Study", in: P. Achtemeier (ed.), *SBL 1979 Seminar
Papers II* (SBL.SPS, 16), Missoula 1979, 102-22 (115-9).

priate time (vv. 24-25). The manner of reaping or harvesting varies according to the type of crop: the use of too much strength is thereby avoided (vv. 27-28). Here also the aspect of time has a role to play (v. 28: "not unceasingly does one thresh it"). If we take account of the fact that the words 'to thresh' and 'to crush' elsewhere form images for the destruction of lands and peoples or horrifying acts of war (דוש: Isa. 21:10; 25:10; Judg. 8:7,16; 2 Kgs 8:12; 13:7; Amos 1:3ff.; Mic. 4:12f.;[23] דקק: 2 Sam. 22:43; Mic. 4:13) and even about God's judgment (Isa. 41:15; Hab. 3:12), then it becomes clear that the *mashal* does not only speak about agriculture but also refers metaphorically to the judgment over God's people. Time and manner of plowing, sowing and harvesting, comply with the 'right order' and serve the harvest. This is the way YHWH handles Israel. He gave her rest in the land (v. 12) and a solid foundation in Sion (v. 16), yet swept her away when she did not comply with the criteria of 'righteousness/justice' (vv. 17, 21). In the last analysis, however, he himself will be 'a spirit of (right) judgment' for 'the remnant of his people' (v. 6).

The thematic word 'to hear' (שמע) illustrates the position that a diachronic and a synchronic interpretation go together in showing the close semantic relationship between vv. 23-29 and what precedes.[24] The observation "they have been unwilling to listen" (v. 12) leads to the appeal to listen to the word of YHWH which announces downfall (vv. 14, 17-19). The following appeal to listen, in this case to a plea for God's 'counsel/wisdom' (vv. 23, 29) cannot be directed to the same audience. Therefore, the diachronic exegesis postulates a different public in the historical situation of Isaiah ben Amoz while the synchronic exegesis looks for another party within chapter 28, e.g. 'the remnant of his people' (v. 5; see above). If we combine both perspectives then in v. 23 the readers of the book, who identify themselves with the addressees in what precedes, are themselves addressed. For these people the whole course of accusation to judgment in vv. 1-22 does not simply consist of past events and meaning, it also has topical value, in the first place because it defines their situation and secondly because YHWH is a source therein of instruction for them and reveals himself to them as 'wonderful in counsel and great in wisdom' (v. 29). One can only agree with the remark: "The emphasis in vv. 23-29 is

---

[23]H.F. Fuhs, "דוש", in: *ThWAT*, Bd. 2, 195-9 (197-9).

[24]K.T. Aitken, "Hearing and Seeing: Metamorphoses of a Motif in Isaiah 1-39", in: Ph.R. Davies, D.J.A. Clines (eds.), *Among the Prophets: Language, Image and Structure in the Prophetic Writings* (JSOT.S, 144), Sheffield 1993, 12-41 (19-21, 26-8).

not only on YHWH's wisdom but also on YHWH's *teaching*."[25] The
passage is strongly affiliated with v. 9 where the adversaries reject 'the
teaching of knowledge' (ירה hiph'il; cf. v. 26) and 'the understanding
of the message' (שמועה; cf. v. 23).[26] The audience to which the *mashal*
addresses itself is called upon not to follow the way of the adversary
but to take the example of the farmer who lets himself be instructed
by God in 'the right order'.

If the *mashal* does indeed direct itself in this way to the readers of
BI, then to the farmer belongs a special meaning. He is more than a
necessary element in the 'vehicle' of the comparison. V. 26 calls attention to him too explicitly for that: "Yes, he instructs him concerning
the right order, his God teaches him". Between the farmer and '*his*
God' there is a relationship, he accepts instruction. A similar relationship is entirely lacking among the 'swaggerers' of vv. 14-22, and
also among the drunkards of vv. 7-13 for that matter. The farmer is
presented to the readers of BI as an example. He is a metaphor for
the writing prophet Isaiah, who allowed himself to be instructed by
'his God'.[27] Thus these people, the successors of those over whom the
judgment actually came, are able to learn God's 'wonderful counsel'
from the message of Isaiah, the prophet who himself has accompanied
this history.[28] This counsel comes just like 'the decree of destruction'
of 'YHWH of hosts'. (Via the words 'this also' and the repetition of
the divine title v. 29 points to v. 22).

3.   The Judgment Endures and Expands (vv. 19-22)

An examination of a classical question in the exegesis of vv. 14-22 may
contribute to our understanding of Isaiah 28 as a redactional unity,
addressed to the readers of BI. Vv. 19-22 are generally considered as
an insertion.[29] V. 19 broadens the effect of the punishment in time

---

[25]Exum, "Whom Will He Teach Knowledge?", 131-2. In this author's strictly
synchronic outlook v. 23 is addressed to 'all'. If by this she means 'all humans' or
'all nations' then the explanation is contrived since the passage lacks any reference
to the theme of universalism.

[26]I follow the traditional explanation at this point, not that according to which
God or the prophet is the speaker in v. 9. Cf. under 3.

[27]Fohrer, *Das Buch Jesaja*, Bd. 1, 69-70, has already pointed out the symbolic
function of the farmer but he sets the *mashal* in the last years of the historical
Isaiah.

[28]In this connection we can also point to the term משפט, which in its various
meanings (vv. 6, 17, 26) reflects the historical stratification of the audience in
chapter 28.

[29]J. Vermeylen, *Du prophète Isaïe à l'Apocalyptique: Isaïe, I–XXXV, miroir
d'un demi-millénaire d'expérience religieuse en Israël I* (EtB), Paris 1977, 396-9;

while this, according to vv. 17f., is already absolute and does not need repeating. Moreover, v. 20 contains a proverb which does not seem to continue the topics of vv. 15-19, and in v.21 God is referred to in the third person. In v. 22 ('do not swagger') we find the prophet again addressing the same audience which he has condemned to ruin (cf. v. 14: 'you, swaggerers'), but this time with an admonition which offers a new chance, and a resumé of his revelation which is very similar to 10:23.

Literary-historical exegesis extrapolates these verses as directed to a different audience than that of Isaiah ben Amoz. Synchronic exegesis tries to make it plausible that the same audience, both now and in the past, can conceive of the judgment both as a once-only event and as an on-going process. We prefer to interpret the phenomena mentioned in another way: the direction of speech, while continuing the plural address, enlarges in v. 19 to include the readers of BI of all ages and times. Here we touch upon a fundamental understanding of prophetic oracles as also valuable for the generations to come. In the view of the transmitters, the conflict between the prophet and the rulers of Jerusalem is not only an event worth being handed down for the sake of history only, but it is a paradigmatic event. It applies to God's people forever. The judgment which has come over the former generation still overshadows the generations to come. In v. 19, the perspective moves slightly towards apocalyptics in the sense that calamity simply swallows time. Existence and judgment, history and disaster are seen as coinciding. While v. 19a by itself may still be interpreted as a metaphoric exaggeration, v. 19b has certainly apocalyptic overtones ("morning by morning... by day and by night"). The task 'to make people to understand the message' cannot be performed by the prophets only, a disastrous course of history is necessary to that aim.[30] In this way, the judgment functions as a teaching authority and allows for an admonition to reform religious attitudes.

By means of some quite remarkable rhetorics the way to that admonition is paved. The announcement that the judgment will continue, opens with 'truly' (v. 19a": כי). It is followed by two statements (vv. 20-21) which also begin with 'truly' and serve as a confirmation

---

Wildberger, *Jesaja*, 3. Teilband: Jesaja 28-39, 1070, 1078; F.J. Gonçalves, *L'expédition de Sennachérib en Palestine dans la littérature hébraïque ancienne* (EtB), Paris 1986, 200; R.F. Melugin, "The Conventional and the Creative in Isaiah's Judgment Oracles", *CBQ* 36 (1974), 309-10, reckons v. 19 to be the original oracle and considers vv. 20-22 as an addition.

[30]Moreover, the term 'terror' (זועה) is at home in the later Jeremianic tradition: 15:4; 24:9; 29:18; 34:17; cf. H.Weippert, *Die Prosareden des Jeremiabuches* (BZAW, 132), Berlin & New York 1973, 187-91.

of the announcement. Thus, the three elements stand in one line.
The two statements, at the same time, challenge the audience since
the first contains an implicit comparison (v. 20), and the second an
explicit, but incomplete one (v. 21).

The first comparison (v. 20: "Truly, the bed is too short to stretch
oneself out, and the covering too narrow to wrap oneself up") proposes
an experience from daily life as can be found frequently in wisdom literature. It would be improper, however, to call this a proverb because
it deviates from the descriptive proverbs in that it does not draw out
or suggest a lesson (cf. Prov. 13:4; 14:28; 15:22; 17:8; 18:11; 20:14;
25:25; 26:13). It may be borrowed from a wisdom context but it is
made to fit this prophetic context in order to illustrate the nature
of the disaster. The association of 'bed' with 'night' (v.19) carries it
along. Formally, the text gives the vehicle of the comparison while the
tenor is to be invented by the audience, e.g.: "You will be looking for
rest, but the available means do not suffice" (cf. v. 12)[31] or: "You have
miscalculated the protection which your self-made hiding places offer
you" (cf. vv. 15,17).[32] The incompleteness of the comparison engages
the audience.

The second comparison (v. 21a: "Truly, as on Mount Perazim YH-
WH will stand up, and as in the valley of Gibeon he will rage")[33]
takes two connected episodes from Israel's history, both victories of
David over the Philistines, as examples to illustrate the nature of

---

[31]Duhm, *Das Buch Jesaia*; Kissane, *The Book of Isaiah*, vol. 1.

[32]Delitzsch, *Commentar über das Buch Jesaia*. Some commentators explain the
comparison as a dialectic aporia. If one stretches oneself the bed is too short, if
one puts up one's knees the covering is too narrow (A.B. Ehrlich, *Randglossen zur
hebräischen Bibel*, Bd. 4, Leipzig 1912, 101; Feldmann, *Das Buch Isaias*, Bd. 1).
A very different interpretation recognizes here the topic of the bed in sheol; cf.
Isa. 14:11; Ezek. 32:25; Job 17:13; Ps. 139:8 (N.J. Tromp, *Primitive Conceptions
of Death and the Nether World in the Old Testament* (BibOr, 21), Rome 1969,
156-7; W.H. Irwin, *Isaiah 28-33: Translation with Philological Notes* (BibOr 30],
Rome 1977, 34ff.). In view of the context of vv. 15,17, this interpretation seems
plausible, but the concomitant notion of wrapping oneself seems to contradict an
association with the underworld.

[33]Some scholars explain כעמק בגבעון/כהר פרצים not as adjuncts of place (P.
Joüon, T. Muraoka, *A Grammar of Biblical Hebrew*, Part 1-2 (SubBi 14/1), Roma
1991, § 133h: "After k^e the expected preposition – here b^e – is often omitted") but
as the vehicle of the comparison: "Like Mount Perazim YHWH will stand up, and
like the valley of Gibeon he will quake" (Hirsch, *Das Buch Jesaia*; Irwin, *Isaiah
28-33: Translation with Philological Notes*, 35: cf. Jer. 46:18; Exum, "Whom Will
He Teach Knowledge?", 123, 128). In this way, the cosmic dimension of God's
intervention, "the grandeur of Yahweh's action in terms of height and depth"
(Irwin) would come to the fore, but the reference to the two stories of 2 Samuel
5 would be distorted.

YHWH's immanent intervention (2 Sam. 5:17-20, 21-25).[34] They tes-
tify to YHWH's former willingness to strike down hostile armies in
order to rescue his people. Once again, YHWH will 'rise and rage'
(רגז/קום), i.e. he will take the initiative to appear (cf. 2 Sam. 5:24)
and reveal his sovereign might.[35] Against whom? In the same way as
the prophet left the application of the metaphor of the bed to the
audience (v. 20), so now too he leaves it to the audience to raise and
answer the question against whom YHWH will direct his attack.

V. 21b postpones the expected answer to that crucial question by
focusing on the exacerbating nature of YHWH's 'doing/work' (roots
עבד/עשׂה). The topic of what YHWH has done and will be doing (root
עשׂה) is extraordinarily important in BI. It covers what we call God's
rule over history. Only here, is it said that God's activity will be
'strange/alien' (נכרי/זר), but the basis for this statement lies in the
mashal of the vineyard. The baffling message regarding what the
owner 'will do' to his beloved plantation for which he 'has done' so
much, is that he will destroy it because of its poor vintage (5:4-6).
From this *mashal* on, the people are blamed for their lack of attention
for what YHWH, the 'Maker' of Israel (עשׂה: 17:7; 27:11; 29:16), 'is doing' (5:12; 22:11; 33:13), indeed for their challenging him to speed up
'his work' (5:19). In the announcement of judgment, YHWH is said to
use Assyria as his instrument in order to execute 'his work' of punishment (10:12, 23). It is only after this calamity which Israel deserves
so much, that YHWH will return to perform 'deeds' of salvation for
which his people will praise him (9:6; 12:5; 25:1,6; 29:23). Thus, if
vv. 19-21 are to be considered as stemming from the redaction, it is
of importance to realize that the theme of YHWH's 'doing' makes this
passage sound genuinely Isaianic.

The same holds true for the admonition of v. 22a: "So now do not
swagger". The verse line is wholly geared to what precedes by linking
up with the opening line: "Hear the word of YHWH, you swaggerers"
(v. 14). Moreover, it is neither exceptional for Proto-Isaiah (henceforth PI) to end an oracle by a conclusion with 'So now' (ועתה 5:3, 5;
16:14) nor are negative imperatives uncommon with him (6:9 [also followed by 'lest', פן]; 7:4; 10:24; 16:3; 22:4). Last but not least, v. 22a is

---

[34] According to some scholars, the second story referred to in v. 21a ("as in the
valley of Gibeon he will rage") is the defeat of the Amorites near Gibeon, when
YHWH came to rescue Joshua's army by hurling huge 'hail stones' on the enemy
(Josh. 10:11; cf. Isa. 28:17). It is more likely, however, that we are being reminded
here of David's second battle against the Philistines.

[35] רגז is a term of theophany both where God himself is the subject ('to rage':
Hab. 3:2; Job 37:2; Sir. 5:6) and where he makes others 'quake' (Isa. 13:13; 23:11;
Jer. 1:34; Job 9:6); cf. G. Vanoni, 'רגז", in: *ThWAT*, Bd. 7, 326-30 (330).

connected to the preceding verses by means of sophisticated rhetorics. The comparisons, as we have seen, are incomplete and form a challenge to the readers. V. 21 in particular leads up to the admonition. The readers have at their disposal the essential keys to interpret 'the strange work' which YHWH will perform as a threat to themselves, since they are familiar with the background of Isaiah's preaching with regard to God's 'working'. Yet, while it is left to their initiative to draw that perilous conclusion, the text goes on to explicitly invite them to turn away from their arrogance towards YHWH (v. 22a). In other words, before the theme of the on-going judgment has come to a natural end, it is superseded by another theme, that of conversion. From a one-dimensional historical point of view it is hard to understand that the announcement of judgment can be followed by a call to reform one's behaviour. However, against the background of the interpretation of the judgment as a lasting doom and in the light of the intricate rhetorics of the prophetic tradition, v. 22 does not contradict vv.16-19 but addresses itself to readers who are in symbiosis with the audience of the judgment passage.

In v. 22b ("Truly, I have heard"), the prophet is again explicitly presented as the speaker (prepared for by the third person reference to YHWH in v. 21). All that we have seen with regard to vv. 19-22a leads us to determine him as the Isaiah of the book, the prophetic figure created by the 8th century prophet and the transmitters together. He concludes his tirade by appealing to what he 'has heard' from God. In this way, he confirms his divine call and mission against those who contest against him (vv. 9, 12, 14, 19). It is not uncommon for the prophet to do this, mostly at the beginning of his oracles (5:9; 6:8-12; 8:11-18; 30:8-11), but also once at the end (22:14). In v. 22b, he summarizes his message as 'a decree of destruction' (כלה ונחרצה is a hendiadys). The Isaianic authenticity of this expression is discussed in connection with the authenticity of 10:23: "For the Lord YHWH of hosts will make a full end, as decreed, in all the earth". It seems defensible that this verse stems from the Isaiah tradition.[36] Again, however, the concept of 'to destroy' is so common to PI on all its literary-historical levels (כלה: 1:28; 10:18; 15:6; 16:4; 21:16; 24:13; 27:10; 29:20; 31:3; 32:10; 33:1) that we may consider it as a term used by transmitters to make Isaiah ben Amoz resound in the one who speaks in the book.

The speaking prophet traces his message back to 'the Lord, YHWH

---

[36]It builds on the previous verse, an authentic word of the prophet: "Destruction is decreed (כליון חרוץ) overflowing with righteousness" (10:22; cf. v. 25). The expression recurs in apocalyptic vocabulary (Dan. 9:27; 11:36).

of hosts'. This designation of God combines the titles already used in the chapter : 'the Lord' (v. 2), 'YHWH of hosts' (v. 5) and 'the Lord YHWH' (v. 16) so as to form a climax and to enclose vv. 16-22 as one divine oracle. Both epithets, 'the Lord' and 'YHWH of hosts', are characteristic of Isaiah ben Amoz (cf. vv. 1,5).[37] Whatever their origin may be, it is certain that this prophet has adopted them. By using them in formulaic and non-formulaic language, he has made them into important divine titles which embody his understanding of God. The full combination occurs at the beginning, in the midst and at the end of prophecies (1:24; 3:15; 10:23f.; 22:5,12,14f.). The way it is used here pleads again for the tradition's efforts to speak to the readers of BI in truly Isaianic terms.

The question of Isaianic authenticity comes up once again for the last words על כל הארץ in connection with the question whether this expression means 'upon the whole earth' or 'upon all the land'. (The former meaning is dominant in the Hebrew Bible, the latter is found in Gen. 13:9,15; Deut. 19:8; 34:1; *passim* in the books of Joshua, Judges, 1-2 Samuel, Jeremiah and Zecheriah.) In PI, the meaning 'the whole earth' is most frequent (6:3; 10:14,23; 12:5; 13:5; 14:7,26; 25:8; 'the whole land' is valid for 7:24). For this reason, and because of the serious hypothesis that the Isaiah tradition addresses the readers of the book, the same meaning is plausible here. However, the dynamics of chapter 28, in which the judgment moves from Ephraim (vv. 1-4) to Jerusalem (vv. 14-22), leave the way open for the other interpretation. Since v. 22b reflects the interest and the language of both Isaiah ben Amoz and the Isaianic tradition, intentional ambiguity may be at stake. The historical prophet has announced that the calamity will affect not only Ephraim but also Judah, in other words 'the whole land'. The tradition projects this judgment onto the course of history which it expects to be a judgment 'upon the whole earth'. In doing so, the Isaianic school does not deviate from the prophetic view, it only explicitates it. The judgment upon Israel signifies a radicalization of God's dealing with the world. It involves an ultimate reckoning with all the powers that oppose the realization of YHWH's counsel.[38]

4.   The Blurring of the Actants (vv.1-13)

It is a curious phenomenon in Isaiah 28 that some of the actants in the text are poorly defined. Their description lacks sufficient concrete characteristics. There is a suspicion of who they are but they are

---

[37]Wildberger, *Jesaja*, 3. Teilband: Jesaja 28-39, 1637-8 and 28, 1425-6, 1638.

[38]H. Wildberger, "Jesajas Verständnis der Geschichte", in: *Congress Volume Bonn 1962* (VT.S, 9), Leiden 1963, 83-117 (111-7).

not named. This brings about a blurring of their identity. The phenomenon of insufficient 'reference' is, of course, not unique, especially
in prophetic texts. Generally speaking we attribute this to our incomplete knowledge of the concrete situations referred to by the texts. It
is also thinkable, however, that the final redaction consciously employed the blurring to allow for a pluriform application. In this way
the oracles themselves could continue to function in later situations.

An example of this blurring in Isaiah 28 can be found in the absence of the name 'Samaria' in vv. 1-4. 'The haughty crown on the
head of the fat valley', 'the flower of glorious beauty', to be found indeed in Ephraim, a place, moreover, of luxuriant life, is a description
which can be applied to none other than the capital of the Northern
kingdom (cf. 1 Kgs 16:24,32; Jer. 23:13, Ezek. 23:4–7; 16:51; Hos. 7:1;
8:5f.; 10:5f.; Amos 3:9,12; 4:1ff.; 6:1ff.; Mic. 1:5ff.). Elsewhere in PI
the city is actually named (7:9; 8:4; 9:8; 10:9ff.; 36:19). A double effect arises from this 'concealment' (*aposiopesis*). In the first place, the
city is in this way strongly identified with the ruling class in Ephraim
(vv. 1, 3: 'crown') who have misused the riches of the land. In the second place, a contrast easily arises with the clearly different city which
is appealed to in vv. 5-6. The phenomenon is just the same here also.
From the promise of good administration of justice and spirited de-
fense (v. 6) it would seem to refer to a city, but its name, however,
is not given. At first sight we might think that the reference is to
the same city surmised from vv. 1-4, Samaria. The phrase 'the remnant of his people' is, however, such a stock phrase for the post-exilic
community, the descendants of all Israel who have escaped from the
destruction,[39] that it is difficult to read it as a reference to the capital of the Northern kingdom. In addition to this, the title 'YHWH of
hosts' belongs to the temple in Jerusalem. To name God as 'the crown'
of Samaria would be blasphemous from a religion-historical point of
view, even in an eschatological perspective. Furthermore, 'right judgment' (משפט) is Jerusalem's task and this characteristic is expected for
her as a gift of YHWH (Isa. 1:27; 2:3f.; 4:4; 28:16f.; 30:18f.; 33:5,14f.;
46:13; 51:3f.; Ps. 48:12; 97:8; 99:2ff.). Finally, the unique expression
'a diadem of glory' (v. 5),[40] which is absent from the description of
Samaria (vv. 1,3f.), underlines the unicity of this second city.

The second actant, 'one who is strong and mighty' (v. 2), is also
not named explicitly. He is presented as someone over whom YHWH
has authority ("the Lord has one who..."). The connection between

---

[39] Cf. note 10.

[40] The word occurs further in Ezek. 7:10 in the sense of a 'braided net'; cf. M.
Masson, "Sᵉ PĪRÂ (Ezéchiel VII 10)", *VT* 37 (1987), 301-11.

the terms 'strong' (חזק) and 'mighty' (אמץ) points in the direction of
military power and has the wars of YHWH as its background (Deut.
31:5f., 23; Josh. 1:6f., 9, 18; 10:25; Isa. 35:3; Amos 2:14ff.; 1 Chr. 22:13;
28:20; 2 Chr. 32:7f.).[41] The concrete shape of this figure, however, remains incomplete. In its place there immediately follows a comparison
with natural powers which makes our figure into an attendant phenomenon of God's coming ('storm', זרם: Isa. 4:6; 25:4; 30:30; 32:2;
Hab. 3:10; 'hail', ברד: Isa. 30:30; Ps. 18:13f.).[42] The metaphor and
terms 'powerful, overflowing waters' are used prior to this in PI for
the invading Assyrian army (8:6ff.; 17:12f.; cf. 30:28). Thus the nam-
ing of this figure is completely in line with the theme of God's use of
Assyria as an instrument in his policy concerning Israel (2:12; 5:25,30;
7:20; 8:5-8; 10:5f.,24f.; 22:5). The specific nature of this figure comes
to the fore just a little in the comparison with the fig: he has itchy
fingers and is greedy (v. 4). Nevertheless, on the whole he is lacking
the concreteness of a historical figure in a historical context.

The oracle of salvation in vv. 5-6 shares in the blurred description style. 'The remnant of his people' is broadly applicable to the
post-exilic community wherever it is to be found. The terms "the
one who sits in judgment" / "those who turn back the battle at the
gate" are lacking the concrete determining characteristics of a professional group, e.g. 'judges' (שפטים) or 'warriors' (גבורים). If, in this
formulation, Jerusalem should come to mind, then the text has been
unsuccessful in its task.

If we take everything together, then we must conclude that the
connection between the pre-exilic oracle against Ephraim (vv. 1-4)
and the post-exilic announcement of salvation (vv. 5-6) has undergone
a 'blurring of the actants' which allows the entire text to fit more
than one historical situation. The passage as a whole opposes the
tragic destiny of Ephraim to the felicitous perspective of those who
deserve the name of 'the remnant of God's people'.[43] This means that
vv. 1-4 in their present form do not necessarily stem from the eighth
century, the time of the confrontation with Assyria. They may have
undergone some adjustments at the time of the final redaction to make
them applicable to later generations. The original wording is hard to
recover although the text contains a good number of characteristically

---

[41]L. Laberge, "The Woe-Oracles of Isaiah 28-33", *EeT(O)* 13 (1982), 157-90
(164).

[42]Some other terms add to the suggestion of divine judgment: 'tempest', שער
(Ezek. 32:10; Nah. 1:3; Job 9:17) and 'destroying', קטב (Deut. 32:24; Hos. 13:14).

[43]J. Hausmann, *Israels Rest: Studien zum Selbstverständnis der nachexilischen
Gemeinde* (BWANT, 124), Stuttgart 1987, 156ff., 199-200.

Isaianic terms. In other words, the text itself invites the readers of BI
to look back upon a prophecy of Isaiah ben Amoz from the Assyrian
period which was originally destined for the people of the Northern
kingdom but is still valuable for the time in which they are living.
In other words, 'the blurring of the actants' has brought about an
actualization of the prophetic message *in the wording of the text itself.*

The technique we have been dealing with comes clearly to the
fore in vv. 7-13 which we partly discussed above. Are the priests and
prophets the same as 'the drunkards of Ephraim' or another section
of the population in the same Northern kingdom? Or are we talking about the religious leaders in Jerusalem at the time of Isaiah ben
Amoz, or about the religious leaders of 'the remnant of his people', the
post-exilic community? If the technique of 'blurring the actants' has
the purpose of partially obliterating the concrete historical characteristics of the people on stage in order to make it easier for the readers
of BI to identify themselves with them, then the answers we have
given are far too mutually exclusive. From a diachronic perspective
we should recognize in the opening words 'these also' a redactional
seam: there is still more drunkenness to complain about. This new
specimen of drunkenness, however, is not simply placed next to the
former without further ado. There is a movement towards a climax:
from the socially privileged (v. 1) to the religious leaders (vv. 7-10),
from a random moment to a dramatic scene in which the drunkards
seem to be neglecting their task, creating a nuisance and even having their say.[44] The description brings the readers of BI closer to this
event than is the case with the report of drunkenness in Ephraim.
These are the same readers of BI who have already heard the prophet
on a previous occasion erupt against his own people in Jerusalem for
abuse of alcohol, sometimes in connection with unjust legal judgments
(5:11, 22; 19:14; 22:13; 24:9, 11).

The question arises, of course, whether the 'blurring of the actants'
technique is also at the foundation of the serious lack of clarity which
holds sway in v. 9. It has to do with the very controversial question of
who is speaking in this verse, and who are the subject and the object
of the sentence: "Whom will he teach knowledge ?".[45]

There is much diversity of opinion:

---

[44]Other opinions, which we do not share, would have the prophet or God himself
speaking in v. 9.

[45]For surveys of opinions, cf. E. Rosenmüller, *Scholia in Jesajae vaticinia in
compendium redacta* (Scholia in Vetus Testamentum, 2), Lipsiae 1835, 419; J.A.
Alexander, *Commentary on the Prophecies of Isaiah* vol. 1, Philadelphia [2]1875
(reprint Grand Rapids 1976), 450-1.

(1) 'He' refers to Isaiah. The adversaries of the prophet, the denounced priests and prophets, are quoted as they protest against his sermonizing on the grounds that they are not little children. The word of God links up to this protest (v. 13). An opposition between a quotation of the addressees and a formal oracle of YHWH also occurs in 28:14-18 and in 30:15-17 (although here with a quotation formula). This interpretation is widely found. It was first proposed by Jerome and since Lowth[46] taken over by the critical exegesis.

(2) 'He' refers to God. The teaching of YHWH is an important theme by which the redactor has joined the separate prophetic oracles of the chapter and which culminates in vv. 23-29. In this case it would be Isaiah himself who is speaking here. He suggests either that the drunkards are like little children, unable to receive God's teaching, or that no one, other than the little children, are left to be taught by God. YHWH, therefore, will have to adapt his vocabulary to their mental grasp (v. 11) which he does in v. 13.[47] According to a variant interpretation, Isaiah mocks the incomprehensible utterings (v. 10) of his adversaries who claim to be the mouthpiece of their deity.[48]

(3) The first 'he' refers to the 'priest', the second to the 'prophet' both of whom have been mentioned in v. 7 (in the singular). The disjunction is argued on the basis of the fact that the objects, 'knowledge' and 'message', also refer to the specific tasks of the priests and the prophets. The inebriety of these officials renders them unfit to instruct even little children.[49]

The text itself does not give decisive indications. The suggestion of a confrontation between the prophet and those accused would be evident in the case of an address in the second person singular ("Whom will *you* teach?"), but this is not necessary. The passage as a whole avoids the impression of a direct clash between the prophet and his audience (v. 7 is also in the third person) whereas it announces God's speaking to 'this people' (vv. 11, 13) and reports an earlier direct contact between the same actants (v. 12). Furthermore the third person may express contempt.[50]

We opt for the first interpretation because the wickedness of those denounced is more salient if they not only lead a life of debauchery but also defy God's messenger. Moreover, the link between the verdict (v. 13) and the accusation (vv. [9-]10) is stronger if God repeats the obtuse words which Isaiah's adversaries have ascribed to the latter, and turns them into a announcement of disaster.

In the first instance, the 'blurring of the actants' does not seem to be

---

[46]R.Lowth, *De sacra poesi Hebraeorum praelectiones academicae*, Lipsiae 1815, 468-9.

[47]A. van Selms, "Isaiah 28:9-13: An Attempt to Give a New Interpretation", *ZAW* 85 (1973), 332-9 (332-3); Petersen, "Isaiah 28: A Redaction Critical Study", 109; Exum, "Whom Will He Teach Knowledge?", 111, 120-1, 131-5; S. Deck, *Die Gerichtsbotschaft Jesajas: Charakter und Begründung* (FzB, 67), Würzburg 1991, 87-8, but already C. Vitringa, *Commentarius in librum prophetiarum Jesaiae*, t. 2, Herbornae Nassaviorum 1722, 131.

[48]K. van der Toorn, "Echoes of Judaean Necromancy in Isaiah 28, 7-22", *ZAW* 100 (1988), 199-217 (205ff.).

[49]Dathius, quoted by Rosenmüller, *Scholia in Jesajae vaticinia*, 419; J.D.W. Watts, *Isaiah 1-33* (WBC, 24), Waco 1985, 363; V. Tanghe, "Dichtung und Ekel in Jes xxviii 7-13", *VT* 43 (1993), 236-9, 245-6.

[50]O. Procksch, *Jesaja*, Bd. 1 (KAT, 9), Leipzig 1930, 354.

relevant. The phenomenon is, in any case, the consequence of a technique which makes it possible for the readers of BI to define themselves in relation to the characters on stage in the text and the historical figures being addressed. The lack of clarity in v. 9 concerns the relationship between the actants *in* the text: the prophet and his adversaries (and perhaps God). At the same time, the unclear reference of subject and object in v. 9 indirectly contributes to the steering of the readers, helping them to identify themselves with the addressees in the text. First of all the vagueness gets the readers moving, forcing them to ask questions and look for answers. Subsequently, in the, in our opinion, most acceptable explanation, the drunken priests and prophets pose the question whether there is an audience for the prophet's instruction and what is its nature: "Whom will he teach knowledge, whom will he make understand the message? Those who are weaned from the milk, those taken from the breast?". In the historical situation of Isaiah ben Amoz, his preaching was written off in this way as something for mere children. In the situation of the readers of BI the same question returns at another level. Who are the ones to whom the prophet who speaks in the book can deliver his message? In this way the question of Isaiah's adversaries concerning his validity as a prophet is turned into a question concerning the interest his written prophecies have stirred: are there people who can accept the transmitted teaching and message of the writing prophet Isaiah?

In the passage against the leaders of Jerusalem, 'the blurring of the actants' gives way to the opposite: both place and actants are clearly defined (vv. 14-22). That this definition was prepared for in the previous prophecy (vv. 7-13) and then toned down at the end of the passage (v.22), witnesses to the literary quality of the redaction.

In vv. 7-13 terms with an implicit reference to all Israel and to Jerusalem are introduced gradually. The punishment for misbehaviour consists in that God will speak to 'this people' in the language of alien invaders (v. 11). In this way the judgment falls upon a broader group than the drunken priests and prophets, it also falls on the people they represent. The negative phrase 'this people', as far as the readers of BI are concerned, is aimed at the people of Judah (6:9f.; 8:6, 11f.; 10:15; 29:13f.). The expression prepares for the first explicit address in the chapter: "you swaggerers, who rule this people in Jerusalem" (v. 14). Furthermore, God is not named as such but is introduced in a way which focuses attention on all of Israel: "He who was said to them: 'This is the resting-place; give rest to the weary; yes, this is your place of repose' ". The reminder of God's former speaking and also of its content – the allotment of the land after Israel's entering it (Deut. 12:10; Josh. 21:44f.; 1Kgs 8:56) – includes the readers in the announcement of the coming speaking of God, uttered in hostile language. Finally, it would be difficult to understand the phrase: "This is the resting place (מנוחה)" without thinking of Jerusalem, where YHWH himself has entered in and thereby offers protection to his people.[51]

As far as the second section is concerned (vv. 14-22), we have already seen that 'the decree of destruction על כל הארץ' with intentional ambiguity can mean 'upon the whole land' or 'upon the whole earth' (see the end of 3). The first meaning fits in the orientation of vv. 14-22 towards Jerusalem, the second prepares for the undetermined address of the *mashal* (v. 23) which, in our opinion, is directed to the readers of BI.

Thus it appears that 'the blurring of actants' can also extend to the locations where the announced events have still to take place.

We conclude that the phenomenon we have outlined, 'the blurring of actants', finetunes the prophetic oracles of chapter 28 to each other with the purpose of turning the whole into a written prophecy in which the readers of BI can also consider themselves addressed.

5. Conclusion

The present study has moved along paths not entirely new in the research of BI.[52] We have tried to show in the case of one chapter, Isaiah 28, that the diachronic and synchronic approaches are not alternative methods, to be applied according to the specific skill of the exegete or the expected interest of the readers. The author of the final Isaiah text has neither confined himself to simply putting together in one frame four oracles which are addressed to four audiences divergent in time and place nor has he synthesized the speech direction of the

---

[51] Wildberger, *Jesaja*, 3. Teilband: Jesaja 28-39, 1061; H.D. Preuß, "נוח" in: *ThWAT*, Bd. 5, 297-307 (305-6).

[52] J.W. Groves, *Actualisation and Interpretation in the Old Testament* (SBL.DS, 86), Atlanta 1987; R. Liwak, "Literary Individuality as a Problem of Hermeneutics in the Hebrew Bible", in: B. Uffenheimer, H. Graf Reventlow (eds.), *Creative Biblical Exegesis: Christian and Jewish Hermeneutics through the Centuries* (JSOT.S, 59), Sheffield 1988, 89-102; C.R. Seitz, *Reading and Preaching the Book of Isaiah*, Philadelphia 1988; A. Pelletier, "Le livre d'Isaïe et le temps de l'histoire", *NRTh* 112 (1990), 30-43; B.G. Webb, "Zion in Transformation: A Literary Approach to Isaiah", in: D.J.A. Clines *et al.* (eds.), *The Bible in Three Dimensions: Essays in celebration of forty years of Biblical Studies in the University of Sheffield* (JSOT.S, 87), Sheffield 1990, 65-84; R.E. Clements, "The Prophet and his Editors", in: *ibidem*, 203-20; D. Carr, "Reaching for Unity in Isaiah", *JSOT* 57 (1993), 61-80; M.A. Sweeney, "On Multiple Settings in the Book of Isaiah", in: E.H. Lovering Jr. (ed.) *SBL 1993 Seminar Papers* (SBL.SPS, 32), Atlanta 1993, 267-73.

oracles while fully depriving them of their specifics with regard to personality, time and place. He has neither created one addressee of all times, a metahistorical customer of Isaianic prophecies, nor has he put the four addressees next to each other, four chance targets of Isaiah's preaching fire and brimstone. He has not left it to the readers of the book to find out whether the addressees have something in common and which oracle applies most to themselves. Instead, he has put the addressees on one line so as to allow the readers to perceive them in one perspective. Their outlines somehow flow into each other. They have been streamlined in order to make them resemble each other in terms of people addressed by the word of God. They have not entirely lost their historical and geographical identity, only so much of it as is necessary to convey the idea that their situation recurs in other generations. At the end of this line of perspective, the same readers should find themselves. The final redaction, in fact, has created a living chain of people through the centuries to whom the word of Isaiah is still directed, not as a deterministic fate ensuing from the ever impending judgment of YHWH, but as a chance to take the word of the prophet Isaiah, time and again, as the beginning of a new era.

Robert P. Carroll   *Glasgow – United Kingdom*

Synchronic Deconstructions of Jeremiah:
Diachrony to the Rescue?
Reflections on Some Reading Strategies for Understanding
Certain Problems in the Book of Jeremiah

> *There's a crack in everything.*
> *That's how the light gets in.*
> – Leonard Cohen[1]

The book of Jeremiah is a difficult book for post-Enlightenment scholars to read today. It is both untidy and repetitious, frequently eschewing chronological sequencing (except in chapters 26-29, 34-44), and
in chapters 2-20 there are insufficient rubrics to provide a narrative
framework for the book. The question of whether it is readable today had better be avoided as a negative answer would undermine all
contemporary scholarly operations. The question is better posed in
terms of "how is this book to be read today?". Following this formation of the question of reading allows for analyses of the book along
diachronic and synchronic lines as *one* approach to exploring possible
preferred readings of Jeremiah.[2]

In my opinion, the book of Jeremiah defies any easy reading operation. It is in many ways a book whose semantic substance is probably
easier to understand than the encyclopaedic Isaiah or the esoterical
Ezekiel. But these are relative matters and the book of Jeremiah raises
many problems for the *informed* reader. Some of these problems are
of an intertextual nature: the relationship of the book to Deuteronomy and the so-called Deuteronomic History, the different versions
of Jeremiah (MT and LXX). Some problems relate to the peculiar nature of the material in Jeremiah: the lament psalms in chapters 11-20,
the scroll-reflective aspects of Jer. 36. Other problems are raised by
the fact of the existence of a corpus of 'Jeremiah and Baruch' literature outside of and beyond the biblical book of Jeremiah.[3] The many

---

[1] 'Anthem' from 'The Future' in L. Cohen, *Stranger Music: Selected Poems and Songs*, London 1993, 373.

[2] Throughout this paper I will be discussing *preferred* readings. I can see no way out of producing a multiplicity of interpretative explorations of the text of Jeremiah and the commentaries of the past decade (especially those of Brueggemann, Carroll, Holladay, Jones and McKane) have demonstrated the inevitability of any reading being at best a preferred reading.

problems which make up the problematic of the book of Jeremiah may be left on one side in order to concentrate on reading certain aspects of Jeremiah in terms of diachronic and synchronic reading strategies.

Among the varying networks, interstices and labyrinths of reading Jeremiah (or of any book, biblical or otherwise), the presence in the text of contradictions, discrepancies, contrarieties or local difficulties is a godsend. They represent ruptures in the fabric of the text or seams in the material which allow, in Leonard Cohen's words (spoken of something different), the light to shine through. They are inherently interesting because they allow the modern (post-Enlightenment) reader a space in which to react and to operate.[4] A contradiction, contrariety or discrepancy forces the reader into having to make an act of interpretation.[5] It becomes a site of struggle, a place of contested readings, an opportunity for preferred readings. Forced by the text to opt for possibilities, contradictions make the reader do some work in the reading of texts. That is why in this paper I wish to focus on two sets of difficulties in the book of Jeremiah in order to bring the interpretative act to the fore and to offer some observations on these texts as a means to discussing diachrony and synchrony in the reading of Jeremiah.

---

[3] The beginnings of this corpus are in the book of Jeremiah (cf. chs. 36 and 44). The fact that later generations could produce books alternating the roles of Jeremiah and Baruch and making them witnesses to the two falls of Jerusalem (587 BCE and 70 CE) ought to be fair warning to scholars to avoid the trap of privileging the book of Jeremiah *as history* and all the other literature as legendary. I have tried to give due weight to this factor in my reading of the Jeremiah traditions as I think it is of great significance in any interpretation of the biblical Jeremiah; cf. R.P. Carroll, *Jeremiah: A Commentary* (OTL), London 1986, 55-64.

[4] In my abstract to this paper I focused on Baruch Spinoza's analysis of the bible in terms of commentators' reactions to the contradictions in the bible. It is out of his analysis that much of this paper was generated and here in the Netherlands I would like to recall how much the Academy owes to his sterling work in helping to break the ecclesiastical stranglehold over the bible of the pre-Enlightenment period which persisted for so long after the Enlightenment (and still persists as many an academic knows to personal cost in the modern world). See B. Spinoza, *A Theologico-Political Treatise*, in: R.H.M. Elwes, *The Chief Works of Benedict de Spinoza translated from the Latin, with an introduction*, vol. 1, New York 1951, 3-278.

[5] In spite of agreeing with much of what Susan Sontag has to say 'against interpretation' in her famous 1964 piece "Against interpretation", in: S. Sontag, *Against Interpretation and Other Essays*, London 1987, 3-14, I fear that in matters of ancient literature and the bible the need for interpretation is primary. Perhaps under the influence of feminism and other postmodernist readings of the bible it will become possible to move beyond hermeneutics to an erotics of biblical reading (to adapt Sontag's final point in "Against interpretation").

A diachronic reading of the book of Jeremiah keeps on bumping into repetitions and apparently misplaced pieces (the testimony of MT and LXX of Jeremiah indicates the non-absolute nature of the ordering of the text and the Qumran fragments confirm the fluidity of the text), whereas a synchronic reading attempts to do the impossible by rephrasing the book's representational levels into a coherent narratological account. In order to focus this discussion of diachrony and synchrony in reading Jeremiah I have opted to isolate two sets of texts which *in my opinion* afford ample opportunity for looking at discrepant material in relation to different kinds of explanatory explorations. The two foci used by me for this study are: Jer. 23:22 in conjunction with Jer. 25:3-7 and the two very different representations of the emperor Nebuchadrezzar as the servant/vassal of YHWH in Jer. 25:9; 27:6 and as the monster/dragon in Jer. 51:34.

One further introductory point may be made. It is assumed throughout this paper that these chosen texts do illustrate contradictions or discrepant material in the book of Jeremiah. It is, of course, an interpretative act which reads the texts as problematic at these points, but interpretation cannot be avoided in reading Jeremiah. I shall put forward the strong case for treating these texts as contradictory. Other commentators might prefer a weak case of contradiction or discrepancy or, *in practice*, seem to prefer not to treat them as raising any problems at all. I prefer to read the texts as reflecting conflicting value systems, partly because so few commentators are prepared to do so and partly because it is a much more interesting approach which generates greater interpretative possibilities than the conventional approaches. Beyond such general social reasons for reading Jeremiah differently from my academic confrères, there is a host of reasons for feeling (or intuiting) that the texts are inevitably contradictory or discrepant. Some of these reasons will become apparent by means of my exposition of the texts.

1.   Jer. 23:22 and 25:3-7

The long harangue against the prophets in Jer. 23:9-40 includes some material on the divine council (סוד יהוה) in which the prophets are effectively accused of not having stood in that council (vv. 18, 22). Proof of their absence from the council of YHWH is their failure to have turned the people from their evil way. The continuance of the people to do evil is in itself evidence of the prophets' failure to stand in the divine council. This charge is similar to the one which accuses the prophets of strengthening the hands of evildoers (23:14) in that it makes the prophets complicit in the social evils of their time. Both charges, while open to accusations of misrepresentation and prejudice, are coherent and unproblematic in their form.[6]

What raises serious problems for the claims of 23:16-22 is the presence of 25:3-7 in the book of Jeremiah. Elsewhere I have discussed some of these problems, though without convincing the major contemporary commentators on Jeremiah.[7] In 25:3-7 Jeremiah is represented as summing up twenty-three years of active preaching in terms of the people's failure to turn from their evil ways and wrong doings. Now if both Jeremiah and the other prophets failed to turn the people, why should the failure of the prophets to make the people turn be a serious offence and Jeremiah not come under condemnation for being no better than they were? What exempts Jeremiah from sharing the same failure as the prophets? Is 25:3-7 itself also evidence that Jeremiah too had not stood in the council of YHWH? When it comes to the question "who has stood in the council of YHWH?", the answer has to be neither Jeremiah nor the prophets! Is that a fair implicature of reading 23:22 and 25:3-7 together?

Readers of Jeremiah usually can avoid this reading of the texts together by modifying the sense of 'turn' in 23:22 to mean 'try to turn', so that the quarrel is between prophets who make no effort to change people's ways and prophets who try to turn the people even though they fail with their efforts. To me that looks like some form of rationalization driven by the need to 'save the appearances' and rescue the prophet from failure. I do not believe that the Hebrew word שוב includes the sense 'try to turn', nor would it have to if the problem of implicating Jeremiah in a failure similar to the other prophets was not entailed by the conjunction of the two sets of texts. Commentators are generally very loathe to recognize Jeremiah as a major failure in the prophetic traditions – no wonder the Deuteronomistic History does not include Jeremiah among its prophets! – and are equally reluctant to accept the logic of the shared failure of *all* the prophets to prevent the catastrophe which befell Jerusalem in 587. In my opinion, the logic of reading 23:22 and 25:3-7 together inevitably entails recognizing that

---

[6]There are textual difficulties in 23:l8, 22 (especially in comparison with the LXX text), but the curious reader may scrutinize BHS and the standard commentaries for further information. A more than adequate account of the text is provided in W. McKane, *A Critical and Exegetical Commentary on Jeremiah*, vol. 1: *Introduction and Commentary on Jeremiah I-XXV* (ICC), Edinburgh 1986, 576-84.

[7]See R.P. Carroll, "A Non-Cogent Argument in Jeremiah's Oracles against the Prophets", *StTh* 30 (1976), 43-51; cf. Carroll, *Jeremiah*, 463. McKane, *Jeremiah*, 584 dissents from my analysis, regarding my reading of 23:22 as a test of success on the prophets as 'improbable'.

whoever and whatever the prophets may have been all of them, including Jeremiah, failed in the task of saving Jerusalem (cf. the verdict of Lam. 2:14). In this sense, there is little to choose between success and failure, true and false, when it comes to prophets.[8] As for differentiating between 'true' and 'false' prophets that can only be done by support groups, common ideologies and canonizing frameworks.[9] It is the point of view perceiving or representing the prophet which determines whether that prophet is ideologically acceptable or otherwise. The textual legitimation of Jeremiah appears in the framework of the book of Jeremiah and in that context the prophets of 23:9-40 are deemed to be false and Jeremiah true. But the juxtaposition of 23:22 and 25:3-7 highlights the ideological controls on the material and effectively deconstructs the true/false dichotomy in the text.

Now it is arguable that the editor/writer of the Jeremiah text did not mean to represent Jeremiah as being a failure or as being equivalent to the prophets denounced in 23:9-40, but for the modern reader the intentions of that writer have limited interest.[10] My reading of the two texts together allows me to raise questions about how diachronic and synchronic reading strategies might address the issues involved in this discussion. The problem entailed in this reading of the text may be handled in different ways but, in my opinion, there is no escaping the deconstructive thrust of 25:3-7 *if* 23:22 is taken as a serious criticism of the prophets. If it were to be treated as a rhetorical gesture, scoring points off opponents, then it might be ignored or avoided

---

[8] On this point I think Martin Buber is correct in his assessment of the problems of success and failure among prophets; see his essay on Jer. 28 "False Prophets", in: M. Buber, *Israel and the World: Essays in a Time of Crisis*, New York 1948, 113-8.

[9] I stand by my opinions on the subject of prophets expressed in my *StTh* 30 article and also in R.P. Carroll, *From Chaos to Covenant: Uses of Prophecy in the Book of Jeremiah*, London 1981, 192-7. I see no reason to dissent from my previously expressed opinion (in *Chaos*, 196) "There is no such thing as a prophet recognized by all groups, because prophets are very much figures within their own group and speak solely to that group. One group's prophet is another group's deceiver, just as one group's messiah may be another group's magician (or antichrist)".

[10] This is not the place to raise the complex problem of authorial intention in biblical writing. While I think there is more to be said for author's intentions than has been maintained in recent literary theory (especially by the postwar New Criticism), here I am much more interested in the transformations caused by melding different texts together. For me the biblical text, especially that of Jeremiah, constantly deconstructs the coherence the reader would like to find in it. Modern reading strategies are more alert to the problematics of reading than traditional biblical studies have been and I would wish my work on Jeremiah to be regarded as modern rather than traditional.

when reading 25:3-7. It might be arguable from a diachronic reading
of the text that the two sections of material (23:9-40 and 25:1-14)
are quite discrete and should not be read together. That would allow
modern readers to isolate the sections and not read them together.
The diachronic approach could also separate the texts by seeing 23:9-
40 as hostile polemic characteristic of the prophet's earlier career and
then treat 25:3-7 as later reflection on how difficult effectively turning
the people had turned out to be as a way of prophetic activity. The
maturity of hindsight might then be allowed to inform 25:3-7 and
we could ignore the potential conflict between it and 23:22. Apart
from the lament psalms in Jer. 11-20, the book of Jeremiah is not
strong on reflective re-evaluations of Jeremiah's persistent failure to
achieve any of the things he set out to do. Even 25:3-7 shows no
sign of a reflective rethinking of things, only the same discourse of
blame directed at the community characteristic of the whole book.
Taking the book's representation of Jeremiah at face value I would
have to say that the prophet seems to have learned very little from his
many experiences of failure.[11] As a character apparently incapable of
learning from experience it is hardly surprising that there should be
considerable discrepancy between the position asserted in 23:22 and
the confession of defeat in 25:3-7. Diachronically speaking the gap
between the two texts is capable of various explanations.

I am less confident that I can provide equally satisfactory explanations from a synchronic reading of the text. Diachrony is the natural
way of reading any text of a linear nature (only musical scores of a
symphonic nature demand a synchronic reading at the same time as
a diachronic reading, books and scrolls elude an effective synchronic
reading simultaneously with a diachronic reading). Modern theories
of the composition of the book of Jeremiah inevitably follow a diachronic approach by arguing in terms of different sections, strands
or sources which have been linked together by redactional activities.
On the other hand, a synchronic reading of the book tends to ignore
detail by positing broad flows of narrative which have a coherent and
consistent story-line. Synchronic readings of the bible are often advocated by critics of the historical-critical approach to the text which
is inevitably seen as atomistic and excavative in its treatment of the
bible. While there is something to be said for such criticisms, the crit-

---

[11]Here I am reading the book of Jeremiah as I would read any book and the
Jeremiah referred to is the textual Jeremiah. It is the character Jeremiah as represented in the book which engages my attention and not any imagined connections
between this character and an equally imagined 'historical' Jeremiah. On this
latter 'character' I have nothing useful to say.

ical scrutiny has had such an eye for detail that I would be very loathe to dismiss it in favour of returning to an imagined pre-Enlightenment reading of the bible.[12] Ignoring the conflicting details in the text or eschewing a critical reading of the text may be ways of facilitating a synchronic reading. In that case, the synchronic approach to reading a biblical text sets out to follow a very different reading strategy and must inevitably produce a rather differently nuanced reading of the book of Jeremiah.

This paper is part of a discussion 'Workshop' on diachrony and synchrony in the bible, so I shall not attempt to produce exhaustive accounts of diachronic and synchronic readings of 23:22 and 25:3-7.[13] However, one synchronic reading approach to the problematic texts might take the following line. The overall representation of Jeremiah in the text is that of him as YHWH's (only) true prophet in the period before and after the fall of Jerusalem. All other prophets (with the obvious exception of Uriah in 26:20-23), in particular groups of prophets (often linked with priests), are *per definitionem* false. Anything said against prophets in the book of Jeremiah must necessarily be read as excluding Jeremiah himself, hence the critical remarks in 23:9-40 must in no circumstances be applied to Jeremiah. The perspective of 23:9-40, epitomized by the phrase '*against* the prophets' (23:9), must not be carried over to 25:1-7. The synchronic reading then takes 25:3-7 at face value and does not make any connections with 23:22.

---

[12]I do not wish here to engage with the very large issues involved in assessing medieval, modern and postmodern approaches to the bible. As a child of the Enlightenment and an admirer of Baruch Spinoza I am not in a position to renege on modernity or to deny my historical-critical heritage. At the same time I do not wish to denigrate the invaluable interpretative work done on the bible by literary critics who are hostile to traditional academic approaches to the bible (see the work of Robert Alter, Meir Sternberg and many of the writers associated with the 'Indiana Studies in Biblical Literature'). I am also very conscious of the profound readings of the bible undertaken by so many modern Jewish voices (George Steiner and Gabriel Josipovici come instantly to mind), readings which impinge on modern consciousness in important ways and which will contribute significantly to a powerful postmodern understanding of the bible. One such Jewish voice is Emmanuel Levinas; see his essay "The Strings and the Wood: On the Jewish Reading of the Bible" in: E. Levinas, *Outside the Subject*, transl. M.B. Smith, London 1993, 126-34.

[13]A real difficulty here is created by the fact that while this paper is being written *before* the meeting in Kampen, the discussion will only take place during the Workshops when actual diachronic and synchronic readings of the selected texts in Jeremiah will be constructed by the participants at the meeting. Not being a prophet, I cannot possibly anticipate how others will respond to my examples of diachronic/synchronic readings of Jeremiah. So like a good postmodernist work, this paper must be incomplete and even inchoate.

When the prophets of 23:9-40 fail to make the people turn, it is the prophets themselves who are to blame. When Jeremiah confesses to having failed to make the people turn throughout the duration of his twenty-three years of proclaiming YHWH's word, it is the people who are to blame. By not focusing on details it is possible to argue for a synchronic reading which removes the problematic raised by reading 23:22 and 25:3-7 together. Yet it looks more like a diachronic reading refusing a synchronic reading of the book!

2. Jer. 25:9/27:6 and 51:34

Nebuchadrezzar is a legendary figure in the bible. Apart from the role of the historical Nebuchadrezzar in the Babylonian hegemony over Palestine reflected in the biblical texts about the destruction of Jerusalem, his representation in biblical narratives appears to belong more to the legendary figure than to the historical character. Thus he knows about and is concerned for Jeremiah (39:11-12), is the great patron of Daniel (Dan. 2-4), and is compensated by YHWH with Egypt for his failure to take Tyre (Ezek. 26:7-14; 29:17-20). Later Jewish legends would portray him as being a son of King Solomon and the Queen of Sheba, so it is hardly surprising to find the beginnings of the mythicization process in the bible.[14] In my opinion, the representation of Nebuchadrezzar in Jer. 25:9/27:6; 51:34 belongs to this process of turning the historical figure into a mythic one. In 25:9/27:6 he is represented as the servant/vassal of YHWH (cf. the discourses on 'the servant' in Isa. 40-55), while in 51:34 he is represented as the dragon or monster (of chaos). These designations look like end-points on a spectrum, a merismus of loyalty and opposition to YHWH. Without extremely sophisticated ideological manipulation of the text it would be very difficult to imagine how one figure might be *both* vassal of YHWH and dragon of chaos and that is the central problem I wish to address in terms of diachronic and synchronic readings of the text.

The representation of Nebuchadrezzar as YHWH's vassal or servant (עַבְדִּי 'my servant' or possibly an abbreviated form of 'servant of YHWH') only appears in the MT, so it may reflect a development of the text in its second edition.[15] Whatever the reasons for such an expansion of the text may have been, I will simply treat the text here as it appears in the MT (without benefit of the LXX). The notion of

---

[14] On this see L. Ginzberg, "Nebuchadnezzar", in: L. Ginzberg, *Legends of the Bible*, Philadelphia 1992 (special one-volume edition), 625-6.

[15] See discussion of textual matters in McKane, *Jeremiah*, vol. 1, 623-33. Some of the issues are usefully set out and discussed in D.R. Jones, *Jeremiah* (NCBC), London 1992, 321-5.

YHWH's servant is too commonplace a phrase in the bible to excite attention and its application to the Babylonian imperial ruler here is on a par with the identification of the Persian emperor Cyrus as YHWH's messiah (מָשִׁיחַ) in Isa. 45:1.[16] Both uses reflect an ideology of subservience to the imperial emperors and belong to the second temple period (whenever that is imagined to have been). Much of the material in Jer. 25:1-14 and 27-29 represents a view of Babylon strikingly different from that represented by Jer. 50-51. So a diachronic reading of the two sets of texts would build on this difference and attribute them to distinctive origins and backgrounds in the construction of the book of Jeremiah.

The period of Babylonian hegemony over Judah is represented in 25:9/27:6 as a time when YHWH operates through his vassal Nebuchadrezzar, before abandoning that power in due course (three generations later). It is a benign view of Babylon, making a virtue of necessity and recognizing that living under diaspora conditions entails integrating the well-being of the community with the well-being of the imperial capital (29:7). Diasporic communities must live in harmony with their overlords or face destruction. The symbolic world of the diaspora shapes the notion of the emperor as YHWH's vassal, the overlord *as servant* tames the horror of such imperial power by domesticating it. From a different perspective, that of the Palestinian communities which had to live under the effect of the sword of the conqueror, the nature of the imperial power could not be seen in such a benevolent manner. For them the rhetoric of 25:9/27:6 was not possible. Nebuchadrezzar's destruction of Israel could never be domesticated by the discourse of conformity to political authority, but had to be recognized for what it was – the naked brutality of the beast! Hence the representation of Nebuchadrezzar in 51:34 as 'dragon'/'sea-monster' (כַּתַּנִּין). That allusion to chaos (cf. Isa. 27:1;51:9; Ezek. 29:3) is incompatible with the notion of Nebuchadrezzar as YHWH's servant because it identifies the emperor with everything that is anti-YHWH and because it focuses on the destructive nature of the Babylonian tyrant. I find in the two discrete metaphors (servant and monster) two rather different ways of representing the imperial power, though I have no difficulty reading the text diachronically.[17]

---

[16]For naive readers of the bible who believe in 'the plain meaning of the text' the answers to the often asked questions "who is the servant of YHWH?" and "who is YHWH's messiah?" are respectively Nebuchadrezzar and Cyrus.

[17]For some reflections on 'Babylon' in the biblical text, including Jer. 42:9-17 and 50:41-43, see W. Brueggemann, "At the Mercy of Babylon: A Subversive Rereading of the Empire", *JBL* 110 (1991), 3-22. Brueggemann does not address

I do not have any particular difficulties with the different representations of Babylon in Jeremiah. I would not expect the text to be consistent because it is too untidy and too massive a collection of discrete elements. Reading it diachronically I can detect the various symbolic worlds represented by these elements. The world of the diaspora differs from the world of Palestinian communities, so their writers view the imperium (or whatever is represented by it) differently. Source of shalom or identity with the beast: perspective determines values (and vice versa). However, when I attempt to read these different perspectives synchronically I have difficulties. How can Babylon, how can Nebuchadrezzar, be at one and the same time servant and beast? Is the dragon, that ancient sea-monster of chaos, also the servant of YHWH? Can the Chaos myth be so easily domesticated by religious discourse? Are there any grounds in the bible for making the equation servant = beast? Does the YHWH of the bible have such dealings with the chaos monster that the dragon rules by divine gift and authorization? The multiplicity of questions indicates the degree of difficulty in taking a synchronic view of the representations of Nebuchadrezzar in Jeremiah.

This difficulty provides an interesting perspective on the discussion of diachrony and synchrony in relation to reading the bible. It makes me wonder whether it is possible to provide an adequate synchronic reading of a book such as Jeremiah. Such a book appears to contain too many discrete elements to be reduced to a single, integrated synchronic reading, without considerable assistance from diachronic approaches to reading the text. Unless a synchronic account is prepared to recognize contradictions and discrepancies which cannot be incorporated into a synchronic reading it fails to take the text seriously. If it does make allowance for such problems then it cannot overcome the problem of the diachronic reading which focuses on the problems. The problematics of the text will not go away just because synchrony is substituted for diachrony. A mature, reflective reading of the text will have to transcend diachrony and synchrony, while recognizing that the biblical text is just too full of problems to be adequately represented by problem-free readings of it.

How might a synchronic reading attempt to resolve the problems inherent in the representations of Nebuchadrezzar as servant

---

the issue of Babylon as servant in his meditation on the empire; for his view on that see W. Brueggemann, *To Pluck Up, To Tear Down: A Commentary on the Book of Jeremiah 1-25* (ITC), Grand Rapids & Edinburgh 1988, 213. I guess the text with its notion of the emperor as YHWH's servant could be much more subversive for theologians than is usually allowed for by exegetes.

and dragon? Anticipating the discussion period, I shall offer a few observations on ways which might hold out some promise of producing a synchronic reading. If we take the book of Jeremiah as a totality (contradictions, discrepancies and contrarieties notwithstanding) we might try to read it as a narrative representation of the closing decades of the Judean state, with lengthy poetic discourses, in terms of the behaviour and utterances of the prophet Jeremiah (MT version). Within that narrative there is the recognition that Babylon had triumphed over all the nations for a specific period of time and that therefore the emperor Nebuchadnezzar must have been YHWH's servant/vassal in order to have been able to achieve that triumph. In the long run Babylon (like all empires) had collapsed and had been replaced by the next empire, so Babylon's true nature as the beast could be exposed in terms of its destructive attacks on Judah/Israel (Jer. 50-51). A prevailing ideology of triumphalist YHWHism might just about hold this explanation together, even though any post-Enlightenment reader would wish to ask many critical questions of such an imagined reading of the book. Perhaps a synchronic reading of Jeremiah can be sustained by postmodernist readers of the bible or by readers who resolutely refuse to recognize the Enlightenment as ever having happened in matters pertaining to reading the bible.

It might be possible to develop an argument for the equation servant = dragon, but it is not one made by the book of Jeremiah. Cities and emperors are symbolic in the bible — think of Sodom, Jerusalem, Babylon or Nineveh as symbolic cities or of David, Caesar (New Testament), the king of Tyre as symbolic kings. The equation Jerusalem = Sodom is almost a commonplace of the prophetic books (see also Rev. 11:8), so why not Babylon as servant/dragon? The biblical writers never make the equation Jerusalem = Babylon, so it is less easy to argue for an entity being both good and bad except as alternating possibilities. Entities can be ambiguous, poised on the edge of negative-positive factors. The servant in Isa. 42:19 is blind, which in the context of the book of Isaiah is a bad thing to be. But it is not a developed or articulated observation, so it may reflect paradoxical aspects of the servant's state rather than point to a sophisticated and ironizing awareness among the biblical writers of the deconstructive possibilities inherent in any representation of entities. I do not want to make the writers of the bible appear to be brilliant, postmodernist authors with a taste for irony, paradox and deconstruction, so I will not develop this line of argumentation. Modern readers of the bible may indulge such sophisticated imaginings in a context of reader-response exegesis, but in my opinion it is unlikely that the writer(s) of Jeremiah will have made the equation Nebuchadrezzar YHWH's servant is also the dragon. The LXX rather confirms that opinion.

My favouring of a diachronic reading over a synchronic one must be obvious from the above discussion. The only way I can rescue a synchronic reading is *to do it in a diachronic way!* I therefore have to choose the diachronic reading as my *preferred* reading for various reasons. It makes sense of the untidy book of Jeremiah, it allows me to incorporate my post-Enlightenment critically reflective perspective into my reading of the text, and it seems to make due allowances for the discrete and diverse interests operating in the production of the text.[18] It does not however overcome the problems of reading an ancient text such as Jeremiah. As a strategy of reading it raises as many problems as it solves. I do not believe that it is possible to produce a problem-free reading strategy of the bible. Nearly forty years of academic bible study have convinced me of the truth of that belief. If I recommend a diachronic reading approach to Jeremiah, with an eye on synchronic reading possibilities, that is the best I can hope for along the lines of a diachrony/synchrony approach to reading the bible. In my judgment, taking a synchronic approach to the text highlights the contradictions and discrepancies in it and makes them insoluble by way of explanation. Whereas taking a diachronic approach can explain them. Diachrony allows for explanations in terms of text construction, whereas synchrony insists on a holistic reading of the whole book as a performance and hence renders the contradictions and discrepancies stark and unresolvable.

That assessment is made from a post-Enlightenment point of view which treats contradictions and discrepancies as fundamentally important elements in the biblical text. From such a viewpoint it seems at times that the synchronic reading approach is an attempt to bypass the problems by ignoring them. The diachronic approach to reading the text as practised by historical-critical methods isolates contradictions and discrepancies by focusing on them and therefore appears to be an inherently deconstructive method of reading biblical texts. If that is really the case, then one must wonder whether the more modern demand for a synchronic reading approach is not a further attempt at saving the appearances by rendering the text less vulnerable to deconstructive modes of reading? In other words, is the synchronic approach inherently more conservative than diachronic readings of the bible? While I have called this paper "Synchronic deconstructions of

---

[18]On the interests served by the book of Jeremiah see my few comments in *Jeremiah*, 69-82. I owe the notion of critical reflexivity to the writings of the French sociologist Pierre Bourdieu (they are too numerous to list here).

Jeremiah: Diachrony to the rescue?", I suspect that whichever way we read the book of Jeremiah *now* it is inevitable that we shall only be able to deconstruct it. Neither reading approach holds out much promise of being able to avoid effectively the deconstructive turn. Of the difficulties in reading Jeremiah I have long experience and I have no wish to minimize those difficulties nor do I want to attempt to harmonize the contradictions and discrepancies in the book. Baruch Spinoza's analyses of the prophetic books as being compilations and fragmentary collections strike me as being a fair statement of the case.[19] This being so it is highly unlikely that either a diachronic approach or a synchronic approach will be able to overcome the problem of contradiction in any reading of Jeremiah. In fact I would go further and agree with Spinoza's general observation: "I do not hesitate to say that the true meaning of Scripture is in many places inexplicable, or at best mere subject for guesswork."[20]

---

[19]See his chapter on the prophetic books in *A Theologico-Political Treatise*, 146-56.

[20]*A Theologico-Political Treatise*, 112.

David Clines *Sheffield – United Kingdom*

Beyond Synchronic/Diachronic

The moment I heard of the topic for this conference I knew the title of the paper I wanted to propose for it. Ungraciously perhaps, it was a title that called into question the theme of the conference, perhaps the conference itself. But at the same time, it was a title that was parasitic upon the theme of the conference, that could not have been invented had it not been for the existence of the opposition synchronic/diachronic that had given rise to the conference, and moreover, would, in all probability, not have been invented had the conference itself not been arranged. So while I want to question, perhaps subvert or deconstruct the theme of the conference, I also want to thank its organizers for the stimulus of the theme, for posing the topic as a debate, and for accepting my *sachkritisch* paper for it.

There were two reasons why I felt inclined to question the theme of the conference. The first is a general view I now have of oppositional categories as such, especially binary oppositions, which I have come latterly to recognize as (1) an especially male, and therefore partisan and sectional, way of construing reality, and (2) a standing invitation to embark on a programme of deconstruction, that is, a testing to destruction of the adequacy of the logical coherence of the categories.

The second reason why I wanted to pose the possibility of a world 'beyond synchronic/diachronic' was a more practical conclusion I have come to: I have increasingly found that in exegesis and literary theory alike the distinction is, for me, constantly breaking down, that everything I most want to do myself is neither synchronic nor diachronic, neither one thing nor the other, but an indeterminate mixture of the two. Of course, the distinction could not possibly be 'breaking down' or 'open to question' or even 'deconstructible' if there was nothing in it in the first place that is to say, if it did not name certain apperceptions that are shared among us, certain working practices that have grown up among us, certain political parties and pressure groups indeed that earn their living and justify themselves to themselves on the basis of that very distinction. So I am far from denying the distinction or even arguing that it is a bad one. The worst I will say of it is that it is not good enough, and the most radical thing I will say about it is that it might be better to think of synchronic and diachronic as names for segments of a spectrum rather than the labels on the only two pigeonholes (or wastebaskets, if you prefer) for all that goes in the name of biblical scholarship.

The Concept of a Workshop

When the organizers of the conference asked me to transform my projected paper into the theme of a workshop, I agreed before giving it much thought, since I knew that it would be a quite different undertaking and the more I thought about the colder my feet would become. It was rather later that I also realized that the paper I could prepare for publication would need to be very different from a normal paper for a scholarly journal. This paper therefore has three elements in it: it is a brief account of the author's opinions on the subject (which you have now already read), a sketch of the principles and method of presentation used in the Kampen congress, and a report on the responses of participants.

In everyday teaching I make a distinction among four models of 'delivery' of a course. The models are: the lecture, the tutorial, the seminar, and the workshop. Some of the definitions are by no means universally accepted, and in particular, my understanding of a 'seminar' seems to differ from that of most European colleagues; so I shall ask for the reader's patience while I spell them out.

In a *lecture*, I am doing the talking. Perhaps I will accept comments and questions from the class, but if there are more than 50 or so students in the class I will not, because the chances of a really useful question, that is, useful to the class as a whole, is not very high, and I am not happy wasting the time of the whole class in order to solve the difficulty of an individual member of it.

In a *tutorial*, I expect to have from 5 to 10 students, on a theme that has been announced to them and for which they have done some preparation. I will expect to interrogate them about their understanding and to try to develop their own knowledge and skills through interacting with them, mainly on a Socratic model of question and answer, drawing out the implications and logical consequences of their responses. I will count on a great deal of student participation, but I will have goals of my own I will be trying to meet during the course of the hour.

In a *seminar*, I will be hearing a presentation from a student, a paper of ten minutes or an hour, which will at its conclusion be open for discussion and criticism from the class—and from me. The presenter will be 'sowing' (hence the term 'seminar') ideas in the class's mind and they, like good soil, will be growing those ideas. I for

my part will be sleeping silently—which is what men do while wheat
and weeds are growing (Matt. 13:25)—, and at the harvest, at the
end of the paper, will be encouraging the class as a whole to gather
the weeds and bind them in bundles to be burned, but to gather the
wheat into the barn.

In a *workshop*, which I understand on the model of the workshops
of the great painters, I will be attempting to have my pupils engage
in the same activities as I their teacher am undertaking. They will
be acquiring skills rather than knowledge, and the outcome of the
workshop will be pieces of work, of similar design to those of the
master, recognizably from the master's school even if not exactly of
the master's quality.

In our scholarly congresses, the model of the lecture, which I suppose is the most ancient model of teaching, still prevails. Often indeed
it seems as if the model of the lecture has been supplanted by that of
the article for the learned journal, and the idea that one is making an
oral presentation to a living audience seems not to have crossed the
paper-reader's mind. However, the model of the lecture is followed in
that the presenter has the lion's share of the time, and only one question, or peradventure a supplementary, is allowed from any member
of the audience.

The model of the lecture of course assumes a great disparity between the lecturer and the audience in ability and knowledge, which
is unrealistic, if not also a little offensive, at a congress of scholars.
So I greatly welcome the movement towards the democratization of
the scholarly meeting—for that is what it is—that is enshrined in
this word 'workshop'. The workshop with other scholars must be, of
course, very much more egalitarian than the workshops I set up with
my pupils, for none of the colleagues at the Kampen meeting is re-
motely a pupil of mine. So the key undertaking of this workshop, the
location of methods in biblical criticism on a synchronic/diachronic
grid (see p. 63 below), is conceived as essentially a collaborative
enterprise—one that I conceptualized, indeed, so perhaps to that extent I am the 'master', but one that I forswore even attempting myself
by way of practice before the meeting, so that I might experience the
difficulties of the task at the same time as colleagues.

The Workshops

In the original form of this paper, I set down my intentions and ambitions for the workshops before the meeting itself. Now that they have taken place, I have added short reports on the various elements of the programme.

The workshops are focused on several handouts, which put data in the hands of the participants, and enable all the participants to be on an equal footing, everyone in charge of their own learning.

1. The Notion of Workshop

I suspect that there are several different views around on what constitutes a workshop, and that my conception outlined above may be a novelty to some colleagues. So I am putting in their hands a handout with three items: 1. A quotation from a popular art-history book about the workshops of Renaissance artists; 2. A quotation from a more scholarly book about Florentine artists' workshops; 3. The article 'workshop' in the *Oxford English Dictionary*, which distinguishes the meaning 'room in which manual or industrial work is carried on' from the meaning 'a meeting for discussion, study', and provides numerous quotations from texts ranging from 1582 to 1984 CE.

Handout 1 **Workshops**

Please list three respects in which workshops described and referred to below might be parallel to what we can do in this workshop on synchrony/diachrony, and three respects in which they would differ.

An artist of the Renaissance who was well known and had more commissions than he could carry out alone would normally have a workshop of assistants to help him. They would prepare the surfaces and mix the colours; and sometimes, if they performed well, they might be allotted minor parts of a work to do or a design to execute ... Assistants would often graduate into pupils, who did more independent work reflecting that of their teacher. And in due course they would out from the studio and set up on their own, producing work that was individual in style and more clearly distinguishable from that of their master.

Mark Roskill, *What is Art History?*, London 1976, 55.

The rule for artistic practice in the Renaissance—and for the most part still in the Baroque—was a workshop organization corresponding to the artist's general position in the social and economic sphere of the artisan class. It appears most closely comparable to production procedure, work allocation, and work organization as we still meet with them today in any small artisan's workshop. The master, directing and producing the main work, is at the head, with two, three, or more apprentices and assistants who help him out and thus for their part undergo their gradually progressing training (p. 310).

[E]ven the great and famous master was still at the same time a craftsman, like all the more or less inferior colleagues who participated along with him as well as they could in the same artistic field. Sometimes ...many parts of the picture execution ...were also taken over from the master by the staff of pupils and assistants present in almost every workshop. Thus his personal achievement was confined to the truly essential and centered in the design process, the allocation and supervision of the assistants' work, the final retouching, and the finishing of the whole (p. 324).

Martin Wackernagel, *The World of the Florentine Renaissance Artist: Projects and Patrons, Workshop and Art Market*, transl. A. Luchs, Princeton 1981 (original, 1938).

workshop [f. WORK n. + SHOP n. 3.]
1. a. A room, apartment, or building in which manual or industrial work is carried on.
  1582 T. WATSON *Centurie of Love* Ep. Ded. (Arb.) 25 Alexander the Great, passing on a time by the workeshop of Apelles, curiouslie surueyed some of his doinges. **1775** JOHNSON *West. Isl.* 132 (Ostig) Supreme beauty is seldom found in cottages or work shops. **1813** CLARKSON *Mem. W. Penn* xviii. 335 All prisons were to be considered as workshops. **1865** DICKENS *Mut. Fr.* i. ii, What was observable in the furniture, was observable in the Veneerings—the surface smelt a little too much of the workshop and was a trifle sticky. **1901** *Act 1 Edw. VII*, c. 22 §149 The expression 'workshop' means ... any premises, room or place, not being a factory, in which ... or within the close or curtilage or precincts of which ... any manual labour is exercised.
  b. transf. and fig.
  1562 T. NORTON *Calvin's Inst.* Table s.v. *Supper of Lord*, The constitution which toke away from lay men the cup of the Lorde, came out of the deuells workshop. **1781** GIBBON *Decl. & F.* xvii. II. 62 *note*, Two accurate treatises, which come from the workshop of the Benedictines. **1814** SCOTT *Wav.* lii, Fergus's brain was a perpetual workshop of scheme and intrigue. **1838** DISRAELI *Sp.* 15 Mar. in *Hansard's Parl. Debates* XLI. 939/2 To suppose that ...the continent would suffer England to be the workshop for the world. **1878** GURNEY *Crystallogr.* 8 The workshop of Nature. **1900** W. P. KER *Ess. Dryden* Introd. p. xxi, If he cannot explain the secrets of the dramatic workshop.
  c. attrib.
  1869 J. G. WINTON (*title*) Modern Workshop Practice as applied to marine, land, and locomotive engines. **1873** SPON (*title*) Workshop Receipts, for the use of manufacturers, mechanics, and scientific amateurs. **1902** *Daily Chron.* 29 Apr. 3/5 The workshop system answers because the master works with his men, and gets the best out of them.
  2. a. A meeting for discussion, study, experiment, etc., orig. in educa-

tion or the arts, but now in any field; an organization or group established for this purpose.

1937 *N.Y. Times* 1 Aug. vi. 5/3 The major requirement for admission to this Summer workshop is an approved project for which the applicant seeks aid and advice. **1938** L. MAC-NEICE *Mod. Poetry* xi. 200 The communist poet, Maiakovski, established a 'word work-shop' ... to supply all revolutionaries with "any quantity of poetry desired". **1952** L. ROSS *Picture* (1953) 21 The elder Reinhardt ... came to Hollywood in 1934 ... For the next five years, he ran a Hollywood school known as Max Reinhardt's Workshop. **1959** *Ottawa Citizen* 14 Sept. 6/1 At a conference or 'workshop' on road safety sponsored by the Ontario Department of Transport recently, there was general agreement that much more must be done to improve driving standards. **1961** in *B.B.C. Handbk.* (1962) 36, I want to see a Television Workshop—a regular period in which everyone feels he can have a go without having to mind too much whether he is successful straight off. **1967** P. MCGIRR *Murder is Absurd* ii. 33 In college Kenny joined the ... drama workshop and began work on a play. **1972** *Computers & Humanities* VII. 96 The participants then divided into four workshops and, after five intensive meetings, reconvened to present their findings at the fourth and final plenary session. **1984** *Times* 17 Mar. 15/8 Priority bookings for their tastings, wine workshops and special dinners.

b. attrib.

1937 *N.Y. Times* 1 Aug. vi. 5/4 The importance of the workshop idea to American education. **1968** *Globe & Mail* (Toronto) 3 Feb. b 2/3 Local residents considered ... 17 consumer protection items suggested by workshop groups conducted on Thursday. **1976** S. BRETT *So much Blood* ii. 25 The Masonic Hall was not free for Charles to rehearse in ... Michael Vanderzee had just started a workshop session ... Charles ... had no objection to ... workshop techniques. They were useful exercises for actors. **1983** *National Trust* Spring 24/1 In the morning, group discussions were led by the Company's seven actor/teachers in a 'workshop' atmosphere concentrating on the social history of the early eighteenth century.

Oxford English Dictionary

Report. *Members of the groups noted as points of similarity with our intentions for our workshops the stress on production of a tangible result, the sense of co-operation and collaboration, the idea that a workshop is an occasion when "everyone feels he [sic] can have a go without having to mind too much whether he is successful straight off" (the BBC manual), and the consciousness that, as Samuel Johnson put it, "Supreme beauty is seldom found in cottages or work shops"—meaning that a workshop deals with imperfect and unfinished objects (as distinct from the more finished and polished character of a scholarly paper, for example). Some members especially noted the 'word work-shop' of Maiakovsky, reported on by Louis MacNeice, the intention of which was to supply all revolutionaries with "any quantity of poetry desired"; but we did not feel that our workshops were necessarily 'revolutionary' or that their aim should focus on quantity!*

Among the dissimilarities that were noted was the relation of the master to the pupils, especially in the Florentine artists' workshops, and the obvious economic aspects of the workshops of artisans. On the other hand, by attending a workshop even a scholar in some sense puts himself or herself in the position of a learner, and submits for the time being to the authority and instruction of a 'master' (no less than if one attends the reading of a learned paper). And although our Kampen workshops did not have an economic goal in view, it would be unfortunate if scholarship never had regard to the financial and socially useful aspects of its 'productions'. Finally, someone wondered aloud whether, since all prisons, according to the Oxford English Dictionary, *are to be considered workshops, it might also be true that all workshops are to be considered prisons.*

2. Constraints on Learning

It is widely recognized among teachers and educationalists that the learning process can easily be hindered by emotional factors, both in the learner and in the learning context. Individuals' capacity and speed of learning is not simply a reflex of their intellectual ability, but is to some extent determined by their readiness or otherwise for a learning experience.

My suspicion is that the topic 'synchrony/diachrony' carries, for some people at least, quite a lot of emotional freight, since it has been constructed as a set of oppositions that encode differing scholarly practices. People even define themselves as making methods enshrining one or other of these outlooks their life's work. So inevitably, very much personal investment attaches to any discussion of the topic.

Not much can be done in the context of a single collaborative session to allay fears, to dispel tensions, to reduce conflict, and so on; but one thing that can be done is to enable participants to recognize that they do have a prior personal and emotional relationship with the subject-matter (if they do) quite apart from, and underlying, the intellectual issues that are to be discussed. The hope is that by at least acknowledging to ourselves the non-cognitive aspects to the discussion they will have less power to intrude themselves into the discussion where they do not belong (no doubt they do belong in it at some points) and especially will not cripple the intellectual responses of participants.

In an attempt to uncover the feelings associated with this subject, I compiled a simple word-association test.

Handout 2 **Word Associations**

Which words, if any, do you associate with the term *synchronic*?

rigorous	fresh
easy	anxious
rigid	confrontational
loose	welcome
novel	cumbersome
free	trendy
dangerous	unnecessary
exciting	traditional
cautious	primary
controlled	subjective
authentic	uninteresting
orderly	pacifying
modern	left
legitimate	right
penetrating	old-fashioned

On the opposite side of the sheet, the list is repeated, but the rubric is different. It reads "Which words, if any, do you associate with the term *diachronic?*"

Participants in the workshop are asked to review these lists privately, *and tick any words that came into their minds as they thought of the concepts 'synchronic' and 'diachronic'. I told them that at the end of their review they would be told how to score their answers.*

Report. *The workshop members were remarkably docile in submitting to this exercise, which might not have seemed very 'scholarly'. I told them at the end that they should count the number of ticks they had written on each side of the sheet, and should add the two scores together. The scoring system was simple, I said. Any score higher than zero showed that one had an emotional relationship with the topic of the conference, and not just an intellectual interest in it. Their emotional investment in 'synchrony/diachrony' would almost certainly hinder their ability to deal with the subject intellectually. But it was too late, now that the congress had begun, to do anything much about it, since handling emotional conflicts and tensions can be a long process. All that could be done at this stage was to recognize the non-cognitive element in their approach to the subject.*

My announcement of the meaning of the scores was greeted with much surprise and mirth, but no one seemed to deny the force of the exercise!

3. Synchrony/Diachrony in Linguistics

Since the terms, and their opposition, were first developed by Ferdinand de Saussure in his work on language, I thought it would be helpful to consider the original senses of the terms. This is not because I think that original senses should be determinative for how the terms are later used (and we are now of course more than a hundred years on from Saussure's coinage). Nor do I think that a historical structure to a study or a lecture or a workshop is necessarily a good one. It is just that I thought it would be interesting in the present context to resurrect Saussure, and let him speak in his own words.

Handout 3 **Synchronic/diachronic in Saussure's linguistics**

The aim of general synchronic linguistics is to set up the fundamental principles of any idiosyncratic system, the constituents of any language state ...

To synchrony belongs everything called 'general grammar', for it is only through language-states that the different relations which are the province of grammar are established ...

The study of static linguistics is generally much more difficult than the study of historical linguistics. Evolutionary facts are more concrete and striking; their observable relations tie together successive terms that are easily grasped; it is easy, often even amusing, to follow a series of changes. But the linguistics that penetrates values and co-existing relations presents much greater difficulties.

In practice a language-state is not a point but rather a certain span of time during which the sum of the modifications that have supervened is minimal ...(p. 101).

[O]f all comparisons [to the distinction between synchrony and diachrony] that might be imagined, the most fruitful is the one that might be drawn between the functioning of language and a game of chess ...

First, a state of the set of chess-men corresponds closely to a state of language. The respective value of the pieces depends on their position on the chessboard just as each linguistic term derives its value from its opposition to all the other terms.

In the second place, the system is always momentary; it varies from one position to the next ...

Finally, to pass from one state of equilibrium to the next, or—according to our terminology—from one synchrony to the next, only one chesspiece has to be moved; there is no general rummage ...

In a game of chess any particular position has the unique characteristic of being freed from all antecedent positions; the route used in arriving there makes absolutely no difference; one who has followed the entire match has no advantage over the curious party who comes up a critical moment to inspect the state of the game; to describe this arrangement, it is perfectly useless to recall what had just happened ten seconds previously. All this is equally applicable to language and sharpens the radical distinction between diachrony and synchrony (pp. 88-89).

What diachronic linguistics studies is not relations between co-existing

terms of a language-state but rela- ...Phonetics—and all of phonetics—is
tions between successive terms that the prime object of diachronic linguis-
are substituted for each other in time tics ...(p. 140).

Ferdinand de Saussure, *Course in General Linguistics*, intr. Jonathan Culler,
ed. Charles Bally, Albert Sechehaye, transl. Wade Baskin,
Glasgow 1974 (original edition, 1915).

Participants in the workshop are asked to have a question in mind
as they read Saussure: If Saussure's concern is language, and ours
is the Hebrew Bible, what is it in our field that corresponds to his
field? They should also note any points at which they predict that the
Saussurean model will be especially relevant to Hebrew Bible studies,
and any at which it may not be.

Report. *I did not give much time for the discussion of this handout, but used it mainly to highlight the point that when we speak of
'synchrony/diachrony' in biblical studies, we are using Saussure's terminology in a transferred or metaphorical sense. And it is not self-
evident what it is in our subject that corresponds to the synchronic
state of a language in his usage. Perhaps we should say: it is a text
that should be regarded as constituting a system, and any study of
a text as a system is synchronic. Then study of the structure of the
text, or of its narrative shape, or of its logic or its ideas or its theology as a system would count as synchronic. It is not implicit in
the concept 'synchronic' that the result of such study must be that
the text is a unity; a synchronic approach—that is, regarding the text
as a system—could well lead to the conclusion that the text is poorly
organized and does not constitute a coherent system but manifests
unevennesses, contradictions and tensions.*

*If then we seek an explanation for such oddities in a text (though
we are not obliged to seek explanations, which are almost certainly going to be hypothetical), we might have recourse to diachrony. It might
be that the reason for a text's incoherence is that has evolved over
time without a strong unifying shaping. But this is by no means the
only, or even the most natural, way of accounting for unevennesses in
a text. A text may well be a literary unity in the sense of having been
composed by one person at one time, and yet manifest disorder and
contradictions to some extent (student essays and even papers submit-
ted for scholarly journals have been known to have such a character).
But, as a matter of fact, diachronic studies in biblical criticism often seem to have taken their rise from observed deficiencies in texts*

as systems—so much so that a plausible case can be made for say-
ing that synchronic study always comes first, whether logically or in
practice.

As for 'diachronic' in itself, a purist view might be that, since
'synchronic' studies systems at a given point in time, 'diachronic'
should compare systems across time. But it is very hard to envisage
how this could be done, whether we are speaking of language systems
or of texts. Saussure's formulation, that "What diachronic linguistics
studies is not relations between co-existing terms of a language-state
but relations between successive terms that are substituted for each
other in time", helpfully excuses us from the necessity of comparing
states or systems and authorizes a focus on terms—that is, elements
within systems that have undergone change over time. That is in fact
how diachronic studies in biblical criticism have been carried out.

4. A Synchronic/Diachronic Grid for Methods in Biblical Studies

The next, and major, element of the workshop is designed to test the
extent to which synchronic and diachronic procedures are implicit in
current methods in biblical criticism. Participants are provided with
a grid, having 'diachronic' and 'synchronic' as the two axes (see next
page).
The task here is to plot several critical methods and practices on this
grid according to the degree of importance diachronic aspects and
synchronic aspects are thought to have. Participants should consider
both the logical structure of a method or procedure such as textual
criticism or source criticism and the praxis of those who work with
such methods and procedures. Participants will work in groups of
three for this exercise, allowing themselves *a few* minutes to reach a
verdict on each method they review. See Handout 4 on the next page.

A checklist of critical methods and practices is provided with the grid.
It reads:

Methods and Practices

source criticism	textual criticism	psychoanalytic criticism
redaction criticism	stylistics	reader response
rhetorical criticism	new criticism	deconstruction
historiography	structuralism	theology
archaeology	feminist criticism	
lexicography	materialist criticism	other?

Handout 4 **The Synchronic/Diachronic Grid**

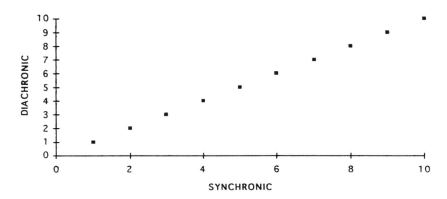

SYNCHRONY AND DIACHRONY IN METHODS IN BIBLICAL CRITICISM

Since some colleagues may not feel entirely conversant with some of the methods in this list, and since the scope of some of them may be controversial, I have provided a handout offering brief descriptions of some of the more recent methods in biblical criticism. These descriptions have of course no authority beyond that of the authors of the text on the handout, but it would be desirable for colleagues in the workshop to accept the definitions more or less at face value for the sake of the present exercise. Otherwise, the time of the workshop could be spent on agreeing a definition of 'reader-response criticism', for example—which is not the purpose of the present workshop.

Handout 5 **Methods in Biblical Criticism**

Literary Criticisms No Longer 'New'

New Criticism
New criticism stands for an attitude to texts that sees them as works of art in their own right, rather than as representations of the sensibilities of their authors. Against the romantic view of texts as giving immediate access to the ideas and feelings of great minds, the new criticism regards texts as coherent intelligible wholes more or less independent of their authors, creating meaning through the integration of their elements. And against a more positivistic scholarship of the historical-critical

kind, new criticism emphasizes the literariness of literary texts and tries to identify the characteristics of literary writing.

In biblical studies the term 'new criticism' has been rarely used, but most work that is known as 'literary'—whether it studies structure, themes, character, and the like, or whether it approaches the texts as unified wholes rather than the amalgam of sources, or whether it describes itself as 'synchronic' rather than 'diachronic', dealing with the text as it stands rather than with its prehistory—can properly be regarded as participating in this approach.

Rhetorical Criticism

Rhetorical criticism, sharing the outlook of new criticism about the primacy of the text in itself, and often operating under the banner of "the final form of the text", concerns itself with the way the language of texts is deployed to convey meaning. Its interests are in the devices of writing, in metaphor and parallelism, in narrative and poetic structures, in stylistic figures. In principle, but not often in practice in Hebrew Bible studies, it has regard to the rhetorical situation of the composition and promulgation of ancient texts and to their intended effect upon their audience. But, like new criticism, its primary focus is upon the texts and their own internal articulation rather then upon their historical setting.

Structuralism

Structuralist theory concerns itself with patterns of human organization and thought. In the social sciences, structuralism analyses the structures that underlie social and cultural phenomena, identifying basic mental patterns, especially the tendency to construct the world in terms of binary oppositions, as forming models for social behaviour. In literary criticism likewise, structuralism looks beneath the phenomena, in this case the texts, for the underlying patterns of thought that come to expression in them. Structuralism proper shades off on one side into semiotics and the structural relations of signs, and on the other into narratology and the systems of construction that underlie both traditional and literary narratives.

The New Literary Criticisms

Feminist Criticism

Feminist criticism can be seen as a paradigm for the new literary criticisms. For its focus is not upon texts in themselves but upon texts in relation to another intellectual or political issue; and that could be said to be true of all the literary criticisms represented in this volume. The starting point of feminist criticism is of course not the given texts but the issues and concerns of feminism as a world view and as a political enterprise. If we may characterize feminism in general as recognizing that in the history of civilization women have been marginalized by men and have been denied access both to social positions of authority and influence and to symbolic production (the creation of symbol systems, such as the making of texts), then a feminist literary criticism will be concerned with exposing strategies by which women's subordination is inscribed in and justified by texts. Feminist criticism uses a variety of approaches and encourages multiple readings, rejecting the notion that there is a 'proper way' to read a text as but another expression of male control of texts and male control of reading. It may concentrate on analysing the evidence contained in literary texts, and showing in detail the ways in which women's lives and voices have in fact been suppressed by texts. Or it may ask how, if at all, a woman's voice can be discovered in, or read into, an androcentric text. Or it may deploy those texts, with their evidence of the marginalization of women, in the service of a feminist agenda, with the hope that the exposing of male control of literature will in itself subvert the hierarchy that has dominated not only readers but also culture itself.

Materialist or Political Criticism

In a materialist criticism, texts are viewed principally as productions, as objects created, like other physical products, at a certain historical juncture within a social and economic matrix and existing still within definite ambits constituted by the politics and the economics of book production and of readerships. More narrowly, materialist criticism analyses texts in terms of their representation of power, especially as they represent, allude to or repress the conflicts of different social classes that stand behind their composition and reception.

Psychoanalytic Criticism

A psychoanalytic criticism can take as its focus the authors of texts, the texts themselves, or the readers of the texts. Since authors serve their own psychological needs and drives in writing texts, their own psyches are legitimate subjects of study. It is not often we have access to the psyche of a dead author, but even if little can be said about the interior life of real authors, there is plenty to be inferred about the psyches of the authors implied by the texts. Just as psychoanalytic theory has shown the power of the unconscious in human beings, so literary critics search for the un-

conscious drives embedded within texts. We can view texts as symptoms of narrative neuroses, treat them as overdetermined, and speak of their repressions, displacements, conflicts and desires. Alternatively, we can uncover the psychology of characters and their relationships within the texts, and ask what it is about the human condition in general that these texts reflect, psychologically speaking. Or we can turn our focus upon empirical readers, and examine the non-cognitive effects that reading our texts have upon them, and construct theoretical models of the nature of the reading process.

Reader Response

The critical strategies that may be grouped under the heading of reader response share a common focus on the reader as the creator of, or at the very least, an important contributor to, the meaning of texts. Rather than seeing 'meaning' as a property inherent in texts, whether put there by an author (as in traditional historical criticism) or somehow existing intrinsically in the shape, structure and wording of the texts (as in new criticism and rhetorical criticism), reader response criticism regards meaning as coming into being at the meeting point of text and reader— or, in a more extreme form, as being created by readers in the act of reading.

An obvious implication of a reader response position is that any quest for determinate meanings is invalidated; the idea of 'the' meaning of a text disappears and meaning becomes defined relative to the various readers who develop their own meanings. A text means whatever it means to its readers, no matter how strange or unacceptable some meanings may seem to other readers.

Reader response criticism further raises the question of validity in interpretation. If there are no determinate meanings, no intrinsically right or wrong interpretations, if the author or the text cannot give validation to meanings, the only source for validity in interpretation has to lie in 'interpretative communities'—groups that authorize certain meanings and disallow others. Validity in interpretation is then recognized as relative to the group that authorizes it.

Deconstruction

Deconstruction of a text signifies the identifying of the Achilles heel of texts, of their weak point that lets them down. As against the 'common sense' assumption that texts have more or less clear meanings and manage more or less successfully to convey those meanings to readers, deconstruction is an enterprise that exposes the inadequacies of texts, and shows how inexorably they undermine themselves. A text typically has a thesis to defend or a point of view to espouse; but inevitably texts falter and let slip evidence against their own cause. A text typically sets forth or takes for granted some set of oppositions, one term being privileged over its partner; but in so doing it cannot help allowing glimpses of the impossibility of sustaining those oppositions. In deconstruction it is not a matter of reversing the oppositions, of privileging the unprivileged and vice versa, but of rewriting, reinscribing, the structures that have previously been constructed. The deconstruction of texts relativizes the authority attributed to them, and makes it evident that much of the power that is felt to lie in texts is really the power of their sanctioning community.

David J.A. Clines, J. Cheryl Exum, "The New Literary Criticism", in: J. Cheryl Exum, David J.A. Clines (eds.), *The New Literary Criticism and the Hebrew Bible* (JSOT.S, 143), Sheffield 1993, 15-20.

Report. *This exercise, although somewhat artificial, proved both interesting and useful; working in groups of three or four was crucial to the success of this element of the workshop. Colleagues were at times surprised to find elements of the synchronic in procedures they typified as diachronic, and vice versa. One group, for example, had quickly designated 'archaeology' as 100% diachronic, but on reflection recognized that studying Hazor Stratum VII, the disposition of its buildings, its water system and the like, can be a clearly synchronic activity. Another group found it interesting to consider in what sense textual criticism, which in principle seems to be a strongly diachronic procedure, could be said to be synchronic, in that it could be said to take its rise from a synchronic state of affairs in which there are many texts of the same work, differing from one another in varying degrees. One group could not decide whether historiography was wholly diachronic or wholly synchronic. Others wondered if there was any method or procedure in biblical studies that was neither synchronic nor diachronic.*

I had not realized before the workshops that the method of scoring needed some further refinement. What was the difference between

*scoring a method as (a) 5 on the synchronic axis and 5 on the di-
achronic and (b) 10 synchronic and 10 diachronic? We managed to
convince ourselves that (a) means that half of the work in the method
is synchronic and half diachronic, while (b) means that everything
done in the method is both synchronic and diachronic.*

*All in all, I think that the exercise established the point I had set
out to make, that a great deal of what we all do in biblical criticism
has something of both diachronic and synchronic in it, and that consequently the idea of methodological tension in this regard is not a little
false.*

5. Synchrony/Diachrony as a Binary Opposition

Having now reviewed the functioning of the categories 'synchronic'
and 'diachronic' in the methodology and praxis of Hebrew Bible scholarship, and having found (as I think we must) that most of what we do
in biblical criticism has something of both elements in it, we next turn
to the question whether synchrony/diachrony has been constructed
(i.e. shaped in the scholarly consciousness) as a 'binary opposition'
and whether we should approach such an opposition with the tools of
a deconstructive criticism.

The next handout therefore offers some summary definitions of deconstruction, together with a checklist of some of the primary binary
oppositions that have come in for scrutiny by deconstructive critics.
By this stage in the workshop, some light relief is long overdue, so
the handout concludes with some lines from the brilliant and amusing book by the novelist Malcolm Bradbury, *My Strange Quest for
Mensonge,* where the concerns of poststructuralist and deconstructed
criticism are guyed in an affectionate (?) manner.

(*continued on next page*)

| Handout 6 **Synchrony/Diachrony and Deconstruction** |

Does synchrony/diachrony need deconstructing?

To deconstruct a discourse is to show how it undermines the philosophy it asserts, or the hierarchical oppositions on which it relies.

J. Culler, *On Deconstruction: Theory and Criticism after Structuralism*, London 1983, 86.

[D]econstruction is a dismantling of 'the binary oppositions of metaphysics' ... Of course, all oppositions are not created equal. "Each pair operates with very different stakes in the world", as Barbara Johnson has observed.

Stephen D. Moore, *Poststructuralism and the New Testament: Derrida and Foucault at the Foot of the Cross*, Philadelphia 1994, 45.

In a classical philosophical opposition we are not dealing with the peaceful coexistence of a vis-à-vis but rather with a violent hierarchy. One of the two terms governs the other ... or has the upper hand.

Jacques Derrida, *Positions*, transl. Alan Bass, Chicago 1981, 41.

Some classical binary oppositions:

mind/body
necessary/contingent
essence/accident
objective/subjective
reason/emotion
literal/metaphorical
precise/fuzzy
history/fiction
content/form
central/marginal
positive/negative

object/representation
text/interpretation
original/copy
text/context
conscious/unconscious
transcendent/immanent
presence/absence
male/female
white/black

Has synchronic/diachronic been 'constructed' as a binary opposition?

There can be no doubt that any bright student or intellectually active person of the 1980s who is at all alert to the major development in the humanities, philosophy and the social sciences, or is just getting more and more worried why so many way-out mint-flavoured green vegetables are showing up in a salad these days, is going sooner or later, and far better sooner than later, to have to come to terms with a pair of thought-movements that are making all the contemporary running ... Structuralism and Deconstruction ...

[T]his radical new spirit in intellectual life touches on every aspect of existence, social and cultural, literary and artistic, linguistic and anthropological. Indeed it has been so successful that it is capitalizing its resources and spreading out into totally new areas, including cheap home-loans and cut-price airlines. We all have colleagues in academic life ... who have tried to ignore the whole issue, keeping their heads in the sand and their noses high in the air ... [T]hey have chosen to believe that the whole issue will in die course disappear, and we will soon be back in the safety of empirical common sense again. I have to tell these people ... that they will have to think again ... As François Mitterand was heard to say the other day, teasing at a shrimp *vol-au-vent* at some Quai d'Orsay reception to do with either the building or the cancellation of the Channel Tunnel: "Aujourd'hui, mes amis, et aussi les anglais, nous sommes tous de nécessité structuralistes".

> Malcolm Bradbury, *My Strange Quest for Mensonge:*
> *Structuralism's Hidden Hero,*
> Harmondsworth 1987, 1, 3, 4.

Report. *Like the handout on Saussure, this collection of texts was intended to raise questions rather than to lead to a solution. There was a prima facie case for regarding synchrony/diachrony as a classical binary opposition, since for many people the opposition is a strict one, and one of the terms is privileged. On the other hand, synchrony/diachrony is unlike many of the binary oppositions mentioned above, in that it is by no means evident which is the privileged term in the dominant culture.*

Nevertheless, the effect of our attempts to locate synchrony/diachrony on a grid (§ 5 above) has certainly been to "undermine the hierarchical oppositions on which it [the critical discourse in biblical studies] relies", in Jonathan Culler's terms, and so it appears that the procedure of the workshop has been deconstructive in the formal sense.

6. Review of the Workshop: Task and Process

On the understanding that a cycle of learning is not complete until teachers and learners have reviewed what has taken place, participants are finally asked to consider the experience of the workshop with the categories of 'task' and 'process', and then to record their own initial evaluation of the workshop.

The following handout outlines the structure of this element of the workshop:

Handout 7 **Task and Process**

Task and Process

The learning cycle is not complete until the whole activity is reviewed.

For such a review, it can be helpful to distinguish task from process.

Task

What is the purpose of the 'debate' synchrony/diachrony?

What is the problem we were seeking a solution for in a workshop called 'beyond synchrony/diachrony'?

What conclusions could you say you have reached? In what ways have you performed the 'task'?

Process

What has been going on in this session apart from the achieving of the task?

Note three things that have happened to (or within) you or the group /three experiences you or the group have had — apart from working on the topic.

Evaluation

Please write any evaluative comments, positive or negative, on this workshop.

Report. *Members of the workshops seemed very open to the proposal that we should consider and evaluate the process as well as the task we had been engaged upon. Among the elements in the process that were identified were: the participation of all the members of the workshops* *(and not primarily of the older men, which is what generally happens in scholarly interchange); the cross-cultural work and relationships that resulted from the presence in each group of both OTW and SOTS members; the experience of group work which some found thought-provoking in the context of their own pedagogy; the sense of fun and the experience of laughter within a session of work (which seemed unfamiliar to some!).*

Meindert Dijkstra   *Utrecht – The Netherlands*

The Geography of the Story of Balaam:
Synchronic Reading as a Help to Date a Biblical Text

1. Introduction

The dating of a text seems almost exclusively to be the subject of a literary-critical Introduction to Old Testament Literature, the kind of a approach called 'diachronic' in the theme of this Joint Meeting as opposite to a synchronic approach to biblical literature. Synchronic reading on the other hand confines the question of date, if asked at all, to the final form of a text. For many narratives of the Pentateuch this implies they are as old as the presumed redaction of the Pentateuch itself, i.e. from exilic or post-exilic times at the earliest. Both approaches are often viewed and presented as antipodes.

However, any method of biblical exegesis which does not give attention to both the structural and historical aspects of a text remains a torso. As an interesting testcase for dating a text simultaneously from a synchronic-diachronic perspective, I would like to present an analysis of the geography used in the story of Balaam (Num. 22-24). Also places mentioned in a biblical narrative form an integral part of the plot, but it is often difficult to understand what part is played by toponyms because the narrator was addressing an audience which was familiar with them.[1] This audience was able to ascribe significance to those spots, which we cannot because of our inadequate knowledge of the biblical geography and also because tradition sometimes blurred topographical aspects in the course of its literary development.

In recent research the story of Balaam is taken as an independent literary composition which got its present place in the Pentateuch only at a rather late stage.[2] Mowinckel's and Eissfeldt's view that the first two oracles formed an integral part of the E-story, whereas the latter two oracles are older than the context of the J-saga, which was widely accepted, has since been thoroughly critized.[3] Also the

---

[1] Cf. Sh. Bar-Efrat, *Narrative Art in the Bible* (JSOT, 70), Sheffield [2]1984, 187.

[2] Cf. M. Wüst, *Untersuchungen zu den siedlungsgeographischen Texten des Alten Testaments: I .Ostjordanland* (BTAVO, B 9), Tübingen 1975, 217, n. 671; S. Tengström, *Die Hexateucherzählung: Eine Literaturgeschichtliche Studie* (CB.OT, 7), Uppsala 1976, 148; H. Rouillard, *La péricope de Balaam (Nombres 22-24): La prose et les "oracles"* (Études Bibliques, n.s. 4), Paris 1985, 479-80. This idea of a late insertion in the Pentateuch (or Hexateuch) goes together with rejection of its literary division and assignment to the old sources J and E (see below).

[3] Cf. S. Mowinckel, "Der Ursprung der Bil'āmsage", *ZAW* 48 (1930), 233-

often found assertion that the episode of the donkey (Num. 22:22-35) is the interpolation of a story older than the saga, has been refuted by Rofé, Rouillard and others who took it to be a burlesque on Balaam's prophetic faculties and as such a later interpolation reflecting a shift in Balaam's valuation in biblical tradition.[4] The classical division of the text in Jahwistic and Elohistic components has basically been given up,[5] because the alternative use of the divine names YHWH and Elohim cannot be explained in a satisfactory way by source-criticism. However, the cancellation of J and E as dating devices for the stratigraphy of the story of Balaam led to very divergent suggestions for its dating. Recent extremes of this diversity of opinion are on the one hand Grosz, Rost, Rouillard, Timm[6] and partly also Rofé, who assumed that the story of Balaam was invented after the period of classical prophecy – according to Rouillard inspired by the Transjordan

---

71; O.Eissfeldt, "Die Komposition der Bileams-Erzählung: Eine Nachprüfung von Rudolphs Beitrag zur Hexateuchkritik", *ZAW* 57 (1959), 213-41= *Kleine Schriften*, Bd. 2, Tübingen 1963, 189-226; see L. Rost, "Fragen um Bileam", in: H. Donner *et al.*, *Beiträge zur alttestamentlichen Theologie: Festschrift für Walther Zimmerli zum 70. Geburtstag*, Göttingen 1977, 377-87, esp. 382-7, who assumes unity of action in chs. 22-24 though he admits that the oracles (מְשָׁלִים) might derive from two (?) earlier poets. Rouillard, *La péricope de Balaam*, 386ff., 468-9, 484-5 dates the prose part 23:27-24:20 (formerly ascribed to J) and the last two poems in or after the Exile.

[4] A. Rofé, עִיוּנִים בְּמִקְרָא וּבִתְקוּפָתוֹ) סֵפֶר בִּלְעָם, 1) [*The Book of Balaam (Numbers 22:2-24:25): A Study in Methods of Criticism and the History of Biblical Literature and Religion*, with an Appendix: Balaam in the Deir 'Alla Inscription], Jerusalem 1979, 49-57; Rouillard, *La péricope de Balaam*, 116, 480.

[5] Mainly the work of W. Grosz, *Bileam: Literar- und formkritische Untersuchung der Prosa in Num 22-24* (StANT, 38), München 1974, 243, 328-30; cf. K. Seybold, *BZ* 22 (1978), 144-5 (review); H. Donner, "Balaam pseudopropheta", in: H. Donner *et al.*, *Beiträge zur alttestamentlichen Theologie: Festschrift für Walther Zimmerli zum 70. Geburtstag*, Göttingen 1977, 112-23, esp. 116, n. 18; Rofé, *The Book of Balaam*, 37-40; R. Rendtorf, *Das Alte Testament: Eine Einführung*, Neukirchen-Vluyn ³1988, 158; Rouillard, *La péricope de Balaam*, 486-7; though L. Schmidt, "Die alttestamentliche Bileamüberlieferung", *BZ* 23 (1979), 254ff. again distinguishes between two parallel narrative strands ascribing them to J and E.

[6] Cf. Rost, "Fragen um Bileam", 384-5 "sehr spät in der Königszeit ... in die Zeit Josias"; Grosz, *Bileam*, 289-91, 328-30 (E 2+3 "späteren Königszeit"); Rouillard, *La péricope de Balaam*, 484-5, **1**. 22:2-21, 36-41, 23:1-26, 24:25 (about 650); **2**. 22:22-32 (donkey – Exile); **3**. 23, 27-24, 1-19 (during Exile and shortly after); **4**. 24:20-22 (Ezra/ Nehemiah); **5**. 24:23-24 (Seleucid era); S. Timm, *Moab zwischen den Mächten: Studien zu historischen Denkmälern und Texten* (ÄAT, 17), Wiesbaden 1990, 97-158 (late monarchic or even exilic period). Like Rouillard's view Timm's dating is mainly based on stylistic evidence and semi-statistical word comparisons. The question whether the present text rests on older literary traditions or not is not posed, cf. also B. Becking, *BiOr* 49 (1992), col. 821 (review).

Balaam-tradition as reflected in the Deir 'Alla plaster inscription[7] –,
dating the basic form of the story as low as the Exile, whereas on the
other hand Cross/Freedman – the Albright school in general – Vetter,
Boling, De Moor, Lemaire etc. favour the early, pre-monarchic dating of at the least the personality[8] and the oracles of Balaam.[9] The
extremes may be exemplified by noting that De Moor discovers in Balaam's final oracle (Num. 24:23 - sic! = 24:23b-24) a reference to the
Sea Peoples' invasion of Transjordan ca. 1190 B.C., whereas Rouillard
considers the same text Num. 24:23-24 to be a *vaticinium ex eventu*
from the Seleucid era and consequently as the latest addition to the
pericope of Balaam.

After having indicated some of the problems regarding the date
of the Balaam story and in particular the complexity of the literary
traditions about this non-Israelite seer, I could follow this lead of recent research. This would mean: to go once more over the arguments
tracing the proces of oral and literary tradition and testing the his-
toricity of persons and events. One established fact would make such
a search somewhat less speculative than it used to be in the past.
Balaam, son of Beor, is indeed confirmed to be a historical person in
the independent Transjordan Balaam-tradition preserved in the plaster text from Deir 'Alla. Beside the biblical "Book of Balaam" we
know now of the existence of another Sefer Balaam which completely
or partly was copied on the wall of a sanctuary or cenotaph at Deir
'Alla early in the eighth century B.C.[10] It was most probably copied

[7]Cf. Rouillard, *La péricope de Balaam*, 483-4.

[8]This view fits in with the identification of Balaam with the Edomite king
Bela', son of Be'or cf. Th. Nöldeke, *Untersuchungen zur Kritik des alten Testaments*, Kiel 1869, 87-8, n. 1; H. Gressmann, *Mose und seine Zeit* (FRLANT NF,
1), Göttingen 1913, 318ff.; Mowinckel, *ZAW* 48 (1930), 235ff. and other references
with Grosz, *Bileam*, 96-7; Lemaire, *ZAW* 102 (1990), 184; Lemaire now defends
Balaam's Aramean origin (Num 23:7) assuming that Gen. 36:31-39 represents a
primitive list of Aramean kings identifying Dinhaba with *Danabu/Dhouneibe* in
the Aramean kingdom of Hazael, Lemaire, *ZAW* 102 (1990), 185-6.

[9]Cf. F.M. Cross & D.N. Freedman, *Studies in Ancient Yahwistic Poetry*, Missoula 1975, 47ff., 65; F.M. Cross, "Reuben, First-Born of Jacob", *ZAWSuppl*
10 (1988), 55, 57ff.; D. Vetter, *Seherspruch und Segenschilderung* (CThM, 4),
Stuttgart 1974; R.G. Boling, *The Early Biblical Community in Transjordan*, Missoula 1988, 57ff.; J.C. de Moor, *The Rise of Yahwism: The Roots of Israelite
Monotheism* (BEThL, 91), Leuven 1990, 151ff. with references.

[10]For recent treatments, dating and bibliographies see J. Hoftijzer & G. Van
der Kooij (eds.), *The Balaam Text from Deir 'Alla Re-evaluated: Proceedings of
the International Symposion held at Leiden 21-24 August 1989*, Leiden 1991; G.
van der Kooij & M.M. Ibrahim, *Picking up the Threads...: A Continuing Review
of Excavations at Deir Alla, Jordan*, Leiden 1989; M. Dijkstra, "Is Bileam ook
onder de Profeten", *GThT* 90 (1990), 159-85; idem, "Is Balaam Also Among the

from an existing document. One may safely say that in recent years the biblical tradition about Balaam received much attention because of this Transjordan extrabiblical text, found in a next to Israelite geographic context. An area by biblical and extrabiblical texts ascribed to the tribal territory of Gad which in the ninth century B.C. also included by and large parts of the western tableland of the Mishor as far as the northern tributary of the Arnon (*Wādî walā*)[11]. It is this area between the Jabbok (*nahr az-zerqā*) and the Arnon (*Wādî el-mugīb*) which centres around the main stage of the Balaam-story, the spur of the Pisgah, also known as the mountain of Nebo.

2. The City of Nebo, Mt Nebo and the Top of the Pisgah

It appears that the biblical Balaam-tradition focuses around the same mountain ridge of Nebo where biblical tradition also surmises Moses' tomb. The identity of place is remarkable and is certainly more than a coincidence. In its present position the story of Balaam marks within the Pentateuch the end of Israels itinerary from Egypt to the fields of Moab (Num. 22:1 // 33:48-49). One may even ask whether this common localization around the slopes of the Pisgah once had a different historical origin and background than Pentateuchal tradition suggests: the settlement of the Israelites in the former kingdom of Sihon. In spite of Balak's and Moab's fears (Num. 22:2-4a), it is hard to understand why king Balak only took action after the Israelites had crossed his country – according to one itinerary passing unopposed along the King's Highway and Dibon-Gad(!) (Num. 33)[12] according to another partly circumventing it (Num. 21:10-30; Deut. 2) – had defeated king Sihon, had taken his country and had arrived safely in the plains of Moab across Jericho. On the other hand it strikes the

Prophets", *JBL* 114 (1995), 43-64.

[11]Cf. M. Noth, *Geschichte Israels*, Göttingen [6]1966,145; Z. Kallai, *Historical Geography of the Bible: The Tribal Territories of Israel*, Jerusalem/Leiden 1986, 85, 320-1; 440-1; E.A. Knauf, *Midian: Untersuchungen zur Geschichte Palästinas und Nord-Arabiens am Ende des 2. Jahrtausends v.Chr.* (ADPV), Wiesbaden 1988, 162; J.A. Dearman, "Historical Reconstruction and the Mesha' Inscription", in: J.A. Dearman (ed.), *Studies in the Mesha Inscription and Moab* (ABSt, 2), Atlanta 1989, 190-1.

[12]Consult about these problems: M. Noth, "Nu 21 als Glied der 'Hexateuch'-Erzählung", *ZAW* 58 (1940/41), 161-89 (= *Aufsätze zur biblischen Landes- und Altertumskunde*, ed. H.W. Wolff, Bd. 1, 75-101); J. Maxwell Miller, "The Israelite Journey Through (Around) Moab and Moabite Toponomy", *JBL* 108 (1989), 577-95; idem, "Moab and the Moabites", in: Dearman (ed.), *Studies*, 28-31; W. Zwickel, "Der Durchzug der Israeliten durch das Ostjordanland", *UF* 22 (1990), 475-95.

eye of the observer that Balak himself crosses freely the area of Sihon north of the Arnon (Num. 21:24) which is said to be conquered and settled by Israel in the mean time. No need to say that such a state of affairs creates some historical problems which are difficult to solve.

Noth once called the tradition of Moses' death and tomb in the fields of Moab (Num. 27:12-14 // Deut. 32:48-52 (P); 34:1-8) in the valley opposite Beth Peor "das Urgestein eines nicht mehr ableitbaren geschichtlichen Sachverhaltes."[13] Though for some unknown reason knowledge about the exact position of Moses' tomb got lost, in early days his tomb was shown in the valley opposite Beth Peor. An original connection between this tradition of Moses' tomb and the existence of an early Israelite, perhaps Gadite or Reubenite sanctuary at Nebo, also mentioned in the Mesha-stela (KAI, 181:14-18) may be assumed.[14] Biblical tradition also hints at this connection. Usually the pair of toponyms הר נבו and ראש הפסגה mentioned in the introduction of the story of Moses' death are thought to be alternative names applied to the same ridge, or the top of Pisgah is taken as the specification of a particular peak in the mountain range of Nebo. Though topographically distinguished in early Christian tradition and at present as rās eṣ-ṣiyāḡah and gebel en-nebā only 3 km separated from one another by no more than a depression in the ridge (see map),[15] it is also plausible that הר נבו identifies the ראש הפסגה to be the mountain ridge belonging to the city of Nebo. There cannot be any doubt that Nebo was a city in Transjordan (Num. 32:3, 38; 33:47;[16] Isa. 15:2; Jer. 48:1, 22; 1 Chr. 5:8.) and also that it possesed a sanctuary of Yahweh. Both city and sanctuary of Yahweh are mentioned in the Mesha-stela (KAI, 181:14-18.): w'qḥ mšm '[t k](18)ly YHWH w'sḥb hm lpny kmš "I took from there th[e ves]sels of Yahweh and dragged them before Kemosh."[17] From that time onwards Nebo was a Moabite town (Isa. 15:2).[18]

---

[13]M. Noth, Überlieferungsgeschichte des Pentateuchs, Stuttgart [3]1969, 190.

[14]Cross, ZAWSuppl 100 (1988), 52, n. 19.

[15]Cf. F.-M Abel, Géographie de la Palestine, t.1: Géographie physique et historique, Paris 1933, [3]1967, 379-84; S.J. Saller & B. Bagatti, The Town of Nebo (Khirbet el-Mekhayyat), Jerusalem 1949, 9, fig. 3; B. Bagatti, "Phasga", DBS, t. 7, 1115-41; Rouillard, La péricope de Balaam, 268, n. 8.

[16]Zwickel, UF 22 (1990), 487.

[17]The usual restoration '[t k](18)ly yhwh is not completely secured, but other proposals are hardly plausible, cf K.P. Jackson & J.A. Dearman, "The Text of the Mesha' Inscription", in: Dearman (ed.), Studies, 94, 180-1.

[18]Isa. 15:2 and also Jer. 48:1, 22 know Nebo as a Moabite city, presumably still existing in the era of Tiglat Pileser (end of 8th c. B.C.), cf. H.Wildberger, Jesaja, 2.Teilband: Jesaja 13-27 (BKAT, 10/2), Neukirchen-Vluyn 1978, 597-8, 609.

Where exactly Nebo was located is as unknown as the exact location of Moses' tomb which, presumably, once was associated with Nebo. Usually, Nebo is identified with *Ḥirbet el-muḥayyiṭ* because Iron Age tombs and pottery associated with the *tell* have been excavated.[19] The name of the city is mentioned in the Copper Scroll from Qumran: קול המים הקרובין לכפר נבו (IX,11) 'the resounding waters (waterfall) near the village of Nebo'. Cross[20] identifies Nebo with *Ḥirbet 'ayūn mūsā* because of this description, but though there might have been an Iron Age fortress near to the springs, there was presumably no city.[21] Nebo is mentioned in Eusebius' *Onomastics* (16, 24),[22] and also other early Christian sources.[23]. An exact location awaits still further archaeological evidence, but *Ḥirbet el-muḥayyaṭ* is a very plausible candidate, because it seems to have been the only walled Iron Age city of considerable size in the area.[24] Perhaps, it served as a religious

---

[19] Cf. Abel, *Géographie*, t.1, 382, n. 1; *HAL*, 623; Dearman, "Historical Reconstruction", 180-1; Saller & Bagatti, *The Town of Nebo*, 1-31; S.J. Saller, "Iron Age Tombs at Nebo, Jordan", *LASBF* 16 (1966), 165-298; M. Piccirillo, "Campagna archeologica a Khirbet al-Mukhayyet (Citta del Nebo)", *LASBF* 23 (1973), 322-58; Wildberger, *Jesaja 13-27*, 612; Bagatti, *DBS*, t. 7, 1137-8; E.D. Grohman, "Nebo", *IDB* vol. 3, 528-9; W. Zwickel, *Eisenzeitlichen Anlagen im Ostjordanland* (BTAVO, B 81), Wiesbaden 1990, 157.

[20] Cross, *ZAWSuppl* 100 (1988), 51-2.

[21] Milik, *DJD*, vol. 3, 294-5 sticks to the identification with *Ḥirbet el-muḥayyaṭ*, see further N. Glueck, "Explorations in Eastern Palestine II", *AASOR* 15 (1935), 110; M.Piccirillo, "Archaeological Excavations at 'Ayun Mousa, Mount Nebo 1984-1987," *ADAJ* 32 (1988), 197-8.

[22] Eusebius, *Das Onomastikon* der biblischen Ortsnamen, ed. by E. Klostermann, Leipzig 1904 (repr. Hildesheim 1960), between *Livias* and *'Esbous* (Hesbon, *ḥesbān*), though he makes a distinction between the mountain of Nebo and the city of Nebo (*Naboor*) eight miles south of Hesbon, cf. Grohman, *IDB*, vol. 3, 528; Bagatti, *DBS*, t. 7, 1115.

[23] The site of mount Nebo is described in early Christian sources, like the Life of Peter, the Iberian, *Peregrinatio ad loca sancta*, ed. by Gamurrinni, Roma 1888, 23, and the pelgrimage of the nun Egeria (february 384), *Itinarium Egeriae, editio critcia et studio*, ed. by A. Franceschini & R. Weber, Turnhout 1958, X.49-54; cf. Saller & Bagatti, *The Town of Nebo*, 3; Bagatti, *DBS*, t. 7, 1115-6, 1133-4. The Targum Onqelos has in Num. 32:3 in some of the manuscripts the addition סיעת בית קברתא דמשה "Si'ath, the house of Moses' tomb" (B. Grossfeld, *The Targum Onqelos to Leviticus and Numbers* (The Aramaic Bible, 8), Edinburgh 1988, 154, n. h), which some would connect to the present name *rās eṣ-ṣiyaǧā*, cf. Bagatti, *DBS*, t.7, 1113; for Talmudic sources and second century Samaritan inscriptions found at Nebo, cf. *ibid.*, 1129-33.

[24] Knauf, *Midian*, 162; Dearman, "Historical Reconstruction", 180-1. As yet no architectural remains of the Iron period have been identified, but the place is replete of Iron II and perhaps some Iron I ceramics, cf. Bagatti, *DBS*, t. 7, 1137; M. Piccirillo, "La capella del Prete Giovanni di Khirbet El-Mukhayyat (Villaggio di Nebo)", *LASBF* 38 (1988), 297-315, esp. 312; A. Alliati, "La ceramica dello

and administrative centre for "seven thousand" Israelites in the area
(Mesha-stela, KAI 181:14-18) and is as such comparable to the early
Iron Age city and sanctuary of Shilo.[25] I accept here the identification
Nebo=ḥirbet el-muḥayyaṭ.

3. Analysis of the Geographic Structure of the Balaam-Story

Is there a connection between Nebo and the story of Balaam? Does
the story focus on Israel living on and around the top of Pisgah not
only overlooking the valley of the Jordan, but also lodging on one of
its slopes this ancient central sanctuary of the Transjordanian tribes?
Before I attempt to answer this question with the help of diachronic
argumentation, it seems advisable to get more hold on the structure
and composition of the story. Before answering the question of its
Sitz im Leben, a synchronic approach to the story should help us to
discover what exactly the narrator intended to tell us and by what
narrative means he achieved his end. Of course, I cannot present here
an exhaustive structural analysis of the story. Neither is it possible to
clarify all textual problems posited by these chapters,[26] nor to discuss
at length the delimitation of the pericope. Jagersma, for instance, let
the Balaam-story start with Num. 21:21 indicating that Num. 22:21-
24:25 is defined as a unity by two *petuḥot*.[27] It looks indeed as if early

Scavo dello cappela de prete Giovanni a Kh. el Mukhayyat", *LASBF* 38 (1988),
317-60, esp. 323; Zwickel, *Eisenzeitlichen Anlagen im Ostjordanland*, 157.

[25]Cross' objections against the identification Nebo=*Ḥirbet el-muḥayyiṭ* because
it must have been a large city with 7000 inhabitants applies similarly to his own
suggestion *Ḥirbet ʿayūn mūsā* (*ZAWSuppl* 100 (1988), 51). A city of that size
would be exceptional in the Iron Age, cf. A. Mazar, *Archaeology of the Land of
the Bible: 10.000-586 BCS*, New York 1990, 463-4. More probably the site was
an administrative center and therefore of strategic significance for Mesha. For
the regional function of Shilo, cf. I. Finkelstein, "Excavations at Shilo 1981-1984:
Preliminary Report", *Tel Aviv* 12 (1985), 123-80; *Shiloh*, Tel Aviv 1993, 383-8.

[26]The Balaam-pericope contains also quite a lot of textual problems, compare
for instance the corrupt text of Num. 24:23-24 (see note 49). Comparison of the
use of divine names in the *versiones antiquae* hardly supports the literary analysis
of former source criticism (*pace* Mowinckel, *ZAW* 48 (1930), 233ff.; Schmidt, *BZ*
23 (1979), 234-5, etc.). The Masoretic text used 29 times יהוה, 11 times אלהים and
5 times אל, whereas the Septuagint has 11 times κύριος and 34 times (ὁ) θεός,
but the reason for this inversion is perplexing. Twice the Samaritan has אלהים
for יהוה (Num 23:3, 26b), but once יהוה for אלהים (22:22 harmonization? Compare
Num. 22:28,31!). יהוה is basically used in direct speeches and אלהים in the strictly
narrative parts (cf. Grosz, *Bileam*, 243, 329). The parallellistic structure of the
three sacrificial actions (22:41-23:12 // 23:13-26 // 23:17-24:9) is strongly in favour
of the suggested replacement of 23:4b after 23:2 (cf. app. *BHS*). Other textual
problems I will discuss in connection with the geographic-structural analysis.

[27]H.Jagersma, *Numeri*, dl. 3, Nijkerk 1988, 98; C.L. Labuschagne, "The Pat-

Jewish exegesis thought of a textual unity, but it runs counter to the liturgical division which starts a *seder/parash* at Num. 22:2 after the *setumah* dividing the two *petuḥot*. Another problem with Jagersma's scheme is that Num. 22:1 parallel to Num. 33:48-49 forms the end of the wilderness-itinerary. The usual delimitation 22:2-24:25 conform the Masoretic text seems still the best and as I hope to show is also confirmed by my geographical analysis.

The story of Balaam is built up of a number of seven episodes. At first sight most clearly to dinstinguish are, of course, the three times repeated action of sacrifice and attempted cursing of Israel: 1) 22:41-23:12; 2) 23:13-26; 3) 23:27-24:9. They are preceded by an episode narrating the encounter of Balak and Balaam 22:36-40 and followed by the dismissal of Balaam by Balak and a final non-asked for oracle spoken on the initiative of Balaam (24:10-19+25). This set of five episodes in which Balak and Balaam play their part together is preceded by the twofold sending of an embassy to Balaam by Balak requesting him to come and curse Israel (22:4b-21). All these episodes are marked by the initiative of king Balak:

1. So Balak, son of Sippor, who was king of Moab at that time, sent messengers to summon Balaam, son of Beor ... (22:4b-5)

2. Then Balak sent other princes ... (22:15)

3. When Balak heard that Balaam was coming, he went out to meet him ... (22:36)

4. And it happened the following morning that Balak took Balaam (22:41)

5. Then Balak said to him: "Come with me to another place ..." (23:13)

6. Then Balak said to Balaam: "Come let me take you to another place ..." (23:27)

7. Then Balak's anger burned against Balaam ... (24:10)

An deviation from this pattern, and therefore a difficult structural problem, is the donkey-episode. Balaam is the chief actor of this

---

tern of the Divine Speech Formulas in the Pentateuch: The Key to its Literary Structure", *VT* 32 (1982), 268-96, esp. 272-4 suggested that the Balaam-story comprised Num. 21:31-24:25 because of two groups of seven divine speech formulas, see also Rouillard, *La péricope de Balaam*, 479, n. 2.

episode situated "on the road" (Num. 22:22-23, 32) between his home-
country and Moab. Scholars differ strongly about the origin and nature of the donkey-tale. In general, the story is considered to be
secondary to the original composition, be it an older, independent
Balaam-tradition[28] or a primitive folktale inserted into the Balak-
Balaam-tale, be it a product of a later, prophetic reinterpretation,[29] or
even a burlesque playing on Balaam's so-called prophetic faculties.[30]
It cannot be denied that the episode on the one hand forms a kind
of intermezzo and is marked as such by a so-called 'Wiederaufnahme'
(22:20-21 // 35), but on the other hand it is stylistically so well-
integrated into its present narrative context that it forms clearly the
story 'on te road' introduced by 22:21. We find no special introduction of the chief actor. His name is not mentioned again before the
end of 22:23. The episode of the donkey is so smoothly connected to
the previous episode, that sometimes 22:21 is considered to be its first
sentence.[31] Again the final verses 34-35 create a fluent transition from
the donkey-interlude to the mainstream of the tale. Balaam is ready
to go back, but the angel of the Lord confines himself to repeat the
instruction before Balaam sets out on his journey: "Go, but speak
only what I tell you." In my opinion the episode of the donkey was
deliberately incorporated into the composition of the original story.
Whether the narrator knew it as part of the Balaam-tradition, or clev-
erly used an orginally anonymous folk-tale of the motive 'the smart
animal' saving its owner from a calamity,[32] is a question of secondary
nature. Though perhaps originally not his own story, the story-teller
used it for his own purposes, as an intermezzo "on the road" somewhere between Balaam's country and Balak's country. There is no
room to turn either to the right or to the left, there is no escape
from the divine instruction either. From a structural point of view,
the donkey-interlude is a well-integrated part of the second episode
which sees Balaam on the move.[33] As a full-blown story within the

---

[28]Cf. Mowinckel, *ZAW* 48 (1930), 258; Noth, *Numeri*, 157; Rost, "Fragen um
Bileam", 383-4.

[29]Cf. H.Rouillard, "L'ânesse de Balaam", *RB* 87 (1980), 5-36, 211-41; idem, *La
péricope de Balaam*, 115ff. (summary).

[30]Cf. Rofé, *The Book of Balaam*, 21-8, 49-52.

[31]Cf. Noth, *Numeri*, 156; G.J. Wenham, *Numbers* (TOTC), Leicester 1981, 170;
Jagersma, *Numeri*, 125, but see the objections of Rouillard, *RB* 87 (1980), 22-4;
idem, *La péricope de Balaam*, 108-11.

[32]Cf. Gressmann, *Mose*, 327; Mowinckel, *ZAW* 48 (1930), 257-8; Grosz, *Bileam*,
368-9.

[33]Cf. Mowinckel, *ZAW* 48 (1930), 256-9; R. Alter, *The Art of Biblical Narrative*, New York 1981, 105-7; J. van Dorp, "Het ezelinneverhaal in Numeri 22-24",

main story it has a predicting value for the latter. The familiar folk-
tale pattern telling three times the same incident will be repeated in
the main story: "The parallel between the two halves of the story is
emphasized by the fact that in Balaam's prophecies there are again
three symmetrically arranged occurences of the same incident, each
time with greater discomfort to Balak."[34] The impotent fury of Balak
dismissing his hired magician (seemingly on a 'no cure no pay' con-
tract), reflects Balaam's blind rage against his donkey and marks
the transition to what Balaam and Balak really should see. There
is certainly a lot of humour presented in the way the famous seer is
outwitted by his old stalwart donkey,[35] but it is not a burlesque, let
alone a negative portrait marking the beginnings of Balaam's later
revilement, as some scholars would have it.[36]

4. The Periphery and the Centre of the Story
4.1 The Periphery

Including the donkey-interlude, all seven episodes are marked by particular geographic codes functioning as narrative parameters to which
I would like to draw your attention. Particularly, these changes of time
and place mark the episodes as different scenes of the composition.
Synchronic reading of the story reveals a set of geographic circles
which clearly focus the narrative around a centre. One may ask the
question whether the narrator intended to convey a message by his
rather detailed geography, what perception he had of Transjordan topography, and why of all places the efforts of Balak and Balaam to
curse Israel were concentrated around the top of the Pisgah. The outer
circle of the story is immediately drawn in the opening-sentences of
the story. The southern periphery is Moab and Midian, the northern
one Petor on the River Euphrates.[37] In an exhaustive study of Num.
22:5 Layton again suggested to explain פְּתוֹרָה as an Aramaic *nomen
agentis* 'diviener'. This is not impossible, though linguistically problematic. Beside the vocational designation הַקֹּסֵם 'soothsayer' (Josh.
13:22) it could be another word for Balaam's suspected mantic abili-

---

ACEBT 5 (1984), 110-7.

[34] Alter, *The Art of Narrative*, 106; Van Dorp, *ACEBT* 5 (1984), 114-6.

[35] Alter, *The Art of Biblical Narrative*, 105-6.

[36] Grosz, *Bileam*, 366; Rofé, *The Book of Balaam*, 49-57; Rouillard, *La péricope
de Balaam*, 480.

[37] The efforts to find here an a different river indicated are unconvincing, cf. J.
Simons, *The Geographical and Topographical Texts of the Old Testament*, Leiden
1959, § 445 and lately S.C. Layton, "Whence Comes Balaam? Num 22,5 Revis-
ited", *Bib.* 73 (1992), 42-3; tradition thought clearly of the Euphrates, the river
par excelllence, in Mesopotamia, cf. Deut. 23:5.

ties. Exegetical tradition deemed the vocable ambiguous.[38] This does
not mean, however, that the geographical explanation of פתורה is as
secondary as Layton suggests. On the contrary, the geographical exegesis is clearly predominant in older textual tradition. The Masoretic
tradition concurs with this dominant geographical interpretation of
פתורה in Mesopotamia.[39] All movements of the characters within the
borderlines of the story take place between these two geographically
opposite countries and cities. The embassies, the journeys and other
movements create a sense of space in a world which shows at its hori-
zon the nations and in its center Israel.[40]

Why Moab approaches Midian in this situation is unclear. Some
would refer to close historical and cultural relations between Moab
and Midian,[41] but the connection seems to be more literary than historical. It is rather conspicuous that the Midianite involvement suddenly disappears after vs. 7 and that the messengers of Balak appear
overnight as the people they apparently were in the original story:
the Moabite princes (22:8, 14, 21). Many scholars consider these references to Midian (22:4, 7) to be late interpolations[42], but this leaves
us still with a question to ask from a synchronic perspective: why
did the literary tradition make the Midianites partners in crime? It
may be noted that the Balaam-story is followed immediately by the
affair with the Baal of Peor in which the Midianites are also associated with Moab. This story is in turn closely related to the story
of the vengeance on the Midianites (Num. 31), in which Balaam is
said to be killed together with the kings of Midian (Num. 31:8 //

---

[38] Cf. Grosz, *Bileam*, 96-115; Rouillard, *La péricope de Balaam*, 43-53, esp. 48ff.;
Layton, *Bib.* 73 (1992), 34-50; the geographical names פתורה אשר על הנהר and
ארץ בני עמו[ן] (cf. app. *BHS*) are mutually exclusive in the light of Deut. 23:5.
The present text may be a textual and geographical compromise, see Rouillard,
La péricope de Balaam, 48ff. and below § 6.

[39] Samaritan Pentateuch: פתרה (Deut. 23:5); Septuagint: Φαθουρὰ (lacks in
Deut. 23:5); Targum Onqelos: לפתור ארם, idem in Deut. 23:5; Vulgate/Peshitta
translate: *ariolum*/ܐ, cf. about the versiones and ancient Jewish exegesis of
Num. 22:5 exhaustively, Grosz, *Bileam*, 101-3; Rouillard, *La péricope de Balaam*,
43-5; Layton, *Bib.* 73 (1992), 35-42. Rouillard (*ibid.*, 52-3) rightly stresses that
the Masoretic text opposes the reading בני ארץ עמון because of its Mesopotamian
explanation of Petor.

[40] Cf. about the shaping of space in biblical narrative, Sh. Bar-Efrat, *Narrative
Art in the Bible*, (JSOT.S, 70), Sheffield ²1984, 184ff.

[41] Cf. Noth, *Geschichte Israels*, 144, 149, n. 3; idem, *Überlieferungsgeschichte*,
80, 83, n. 220; De Vaux, *Histoire*, 526; Rouillard, *La péricope de Balaam*, 38-9,
who even speaks of "l'un des rares cas où affleurerait, dans ce récit éminemment
littéraire, un peu de réalité."

[42] Cf. Noth, *Numeri*, 198; Grosz, *Bileam*, 373; but see on the contrary Rouillard,
La péricope de Balaam, 38-9; Jagersma, *Numeri*, 111-2.

Josh. 13:21-22) [43]. There exists a strand in the Pentateuchal narrative inside and outside the Balaam-story associating Moab and the 'evil' Midianites,[44] a literary strand especially marked by a negative assessment of Balaam's personality (Num. 31:16; Rev. 2:14).[45]

Perhaps we can make some progress if we look at the beginning of the story from its end, because in Hebrew narrative art the story often returns to the outset after the accomplishment of the narrative program. The last sentence sounds so self-evident –the chief actors return home– that it hardly draws the attention, particularly because its effectiness has been weakened by some 'stop-press' inserted prophecies. The final sentence of the Balaam-story is significant and meaningfull in its shortness and abruptness: "Then Balaam got up, he went on and returned home and also Balak went his own way" (24:25). Then Balaam got up, that is: once more, as he did twice before early in the morning (22:13, 21), the last time to go with the Moabite princes. He went on after a long and tiresome day, but this time no longer with the Moabite princes or king Balak (22:21, 35, 39), and he returned to his place (וישׁב למקומו). The narrator reminds us that he returned with nothing achieved as he suggested to do after the incident "on the road", but only after he willy-nilly had spoken the word of the Lord as announced in his last oracle to Balak (24:1, 14, cf. Deut. 23:5).[46] And also Balak went his own way ... Certainly the narrator means the way he came. The chief characters part like they met before the confrontation and leave the central stage of their meeting (Num. 22:36). Balak is clearly going back to his home-country Moab which infers that he did not accomplish his goal. On the contrary, Balaam's final word addressed to Balak announces the utter destruction of Moab (24:17). In the present context the מקום of Balaam must be Petor on the River in the land of his people.

But what happened to the Midianites? It may be of interest that

---

[43] Also Donner, "Balaam pseudopropheta", 122, n. 26; Rost, "Fragen um Bileam", 383; Grosz, *Bileam*, 373 and Knauf, *Midian*, 167 indicate redactional relationship between Num. 22:2-4a,7 and Num. 31:8, Josh. 13:22.

[44] Cf. concerning the change of imagery between the 'good' and 'evil' Midianites, Knauf, *Midian*, 150ff, esp. 160-8 (Num. 25,6-18;31).

[45] Cf. Donner, "Balaam pseudopropheta", 119-20 who suggest that later tradition of Balaam's revilement (Philo, Revelation, Jude) already started within the Old Testament in a literary-exegetical way; Knauf, *Midian*, 167.

[46] The comment of Deut. 23:5 seems to me completely in line with the narrator's message in Num. 22-24: Balaam is not converted to be a prophet of Yahweh, but becomes –as the donkey-interlude stresses– nilly-willy the powerfull instrument of Gods blessing, cf. also Donner, "Balaam pseudopropheta", 121; Schmidt, *BZ* 23 (1979), 258.

Balaam, from a narrative point of view unexpectedly, carries on to
prophesy after his anouncement of doom for Moab. First he said *ex-
pressis verbis* to Balak: "Now I am going back to my people, but
come let me warn you – give you an oracle(?)[47] – of what this people will do to *your* people in days to come." But his final words are
not only about Moab. Not only is in the fourth מָשָׁל Edom included,
but three other מְשָׁלִים are added to the Moab-prophecy: the first set
against the Amalekites and the Kenites,[48] who will be taken captive
by Ashur, and presumably the final one against the Ishmaelites and
the Kittiyim together,[49] who will subdue Ashur and Eber,[50] but also
will come to ruin in the end ... I cannot deal here with all the textual
and geographical names found in these final oracles and their rami-
fications (see the notes). From a structural perspective, however, it
cannot be accidental that twice mentioned Ashur refers again to the
area, where also Petor on the River is located according to Assyrian
sources and Hebrew tradition: Mesopotamia. In the final version of

---

[47]Cf. L. Ruppert, יעץ, *ThWAT*, Bd. 3, 721; W. Werner, *Studien zur alttestamentlichen Vorstellung vom Plan Jahwes* (BZAW, 173), Berlin 1987, 2-3; M.
Dijkstra, "Is Balaam Also Among the Prophets?", 58.

[48]Rouillard considers them to be a literary unity, cf. *La péricope de Balaam*,
448ff.

[49]I would like to suggest to read this enigmatic text Num. 24:23b-24:

ויצא(!) מיד כתים || אוי מי יחיה משׁמואל
וגם־הוא עדי אבד || וענו אשׁור וענו־עבר

Ah, who can live because of Sumu'el
and escape from the hand of the Kittiyim?
they will subdue Ashur and they will subdue Eber,
but it will end in ruin!

Many manuscripts read משׁמואל as one word (cf. app. *BHS*). Greek: καὶ ἐξελεύσεται;
Sam. Pent. יוצאים suggest a form or verb יצא (cf. De Moor, *Rise of Yahwism*, 154, n.
240). Parallel to מיד כתים the vocable משׁמואל is most probably another geographic
name. I take שׁמואל to be an 'Assyrian' spelled form of ישׁמעאל = ᵏᵘʳ*Su-mu-il*(AN)
= *Šumu'il*, cf. about the connection between the Šumu'il and the Ishmaelites, E.A.
Knauf, *Ismael: Untersuchungen zur Geschichte Palästinas und Nord Arabiens im
1. Jahrtausend v.Chr.*, Wiesbaden 1985, 1-9, 38-40, n. 170; M. Dijkstra, "Ishmael",
in: *Dictionary of Deities and Demons*, ed. by B.E.J.H. Becking, P.W. van der
Horst & K. van der Toorn, Leiden (forthcoming).

[50]As a geographic name opposite Ashur, Eber can hardly mean the Hebrews
or be an abbreviation for עבר הירדן (e.g. De Moor, *Rise of Yahwism*, 177, n.
333). More probably administrative Assyrian/Persian עבר הנהר = *eber nāri* = עבר
נהרא is intended: the Syrian, Levantine side of the river Euphrates, cf. *HAL*, 739;
Rouillard, *La péricope de Balaam*, 464; Jagersma, *Numeri*, 170 etc. Understood
this way the oracle forebodes an apocalyptic invasion from the West and East
into the fertile Crescent!

the Balaam-story the announcement of the 'Assyrian' captivity closes the narrative circle by disclosing another name of the area where the seer came from. If so, the involvement of the Midianites becomes only meaningfull in the light of the oracle about the Amalekites and Kenites and possibly the Ishmaelites. On a synchronic level we find in the beginning and end of the Balaam-story a delicate and intricate network of topographic references which add to the story in its present context a definite apocalyptic ring. The vision of Assyrian captivity and Ashur's downfall offer interesting clues to date at the least the narrative framework of the Balaam-story.

I will return to this later on. What I wanted to establish at this point is that the involvement of Midianites was intended to prepare this apocalyptic message. I may repeat again: I am not talking about probable historical relations, but about possible theological and literary lines of thought in the narrative perception and perspective of the Balaam's story in its present form. In this final perception no longer direct historical knowledge of second or early first millenium Midian, Amalek and the Kenites should be detected. At this stage topographical names have become mere nicknames to name the 'Arabian' threat from the East.[51] We may compare it to the stories of Ehud and Gideon, where respectively the Moabite and Midianite threat in the deuteronomistic framework is easily extended to the Amalekites and all other peoples of the East (Judg. 3:13; 6:3, 33; 7:12; 8:10).[52]

4.2 The Centre

All places mentioned in a narrative contribute to the construction of the arena in which the events occur helping the listener to focus on the central plot and spot. We leave now the periphery of the story and follow Balaam to the centre of the story where he meets Balak. This happens after the incident "on the road" in Num. 22:36 where it is told that Balak went out to meet Balaam: אל עיר מואב [אשר על גבול ארנון] אשר בקצה הגבול "at a city of Moab [which is on the Arnon border], at the edge of his territory."[53] It is an obscure double statement which seems to be redactionally influenced by the description of Reuben's territory (Josh. 13:16) and the preceding Sihon-episode

---

[51] Cf. Knauf, *Ismael*, 45-9, 104-6; idem, *Midian*, 160-1.

[52] In the archaeological remark of Judg. 8:24 they are even identified as Ishmaelites.

[53] Cf. Simons, *GTT*, § 441, n. 229, 446; Noth, *Numeri*, 147; Jagersma, *Numeri*, 132; Josh. 13:16 mentions העיר 'the city' in the middle of the valley of the Arnon (Wādî muġib). Some would think of Ar-Moab (Num. 21:15, 28), cf. however Maxwell Miller, in: Dearman, *Studies*, 33, n. 85.

(21:26), glossing over the rather non-descript meeting-point at the
edge of his territory.[54] From the narrative perspective of the Pentateuch it is clear that the encouter should take place on the border the
Arnon, that is: after what has been told in Num. 21:26+31 about Israels settlement in Sihon's kingdom, irrespective of what the original
narrator told. It is possible that the story itself was less specific about
this city near the central stage of the story. For the development of the
narrative program of the story it may suffice to know that king Balak,
like Balaam, starts on his way in order to meet his honoured guest
on the border of his territory. He does so in order to take him close
to the border of the people of Israel the next morning (22:41;23:13).
After their meeting they enter the city of Kiriath Huzoth (22:39).
The location of this city or village is unknown. Simons[55] presumed
that Qir Hareseth (el-Kerak), the capital in central Moab, was meant.
It is tempting to assume that Kiriath Huzoth and the city of Moab
on the border mentioned in 22:36 are one and same meeting-point
where the chief characters of our story met. Whether the narrator
had an existing city in mind, or not, is difficult to say. Some scholars
would identify Kiriath Huzoth "city of streets/market town"[56] with
Kiryathaim (Hirbet el-qureiye = Qiryatayim/Qrytn, Mesha-stela KAI
181:10, Ezek. 25:9, Jer. 48:1 etc.).[57] Spots mentioned in the narrative
are an intergral part of the plot[58] and though the author seems to
have had an intimate knowledge of the area (see below), he does according to the spirit of his story more than locate the different scenes
of his tale at well-known cities. There is often a 'double entendre' or a
little word-play with a known toponym. I wonder whether the narrator wanted us to hear in this name the geographical pun: *קִרְיַת חַצּוֹת
'Middletown', or 'the Village of Half-way."[59] This is not a joke. Cities

---

[54]Cf. Noth, Numeri, 158; Grosz, Bileam, 123-5, 373; a different, opposite meaning with Rouillard, La péricope de Balaam, 123-7.

[55]Simons, GTT, §§ 447-448.

[56]Cf. Rouillard, La péricope de Balaam, 145.

[57]Cf. Simons, GTT, § 298, a twin ruin 10 km north west of Diban, south of
Ataroth = Hirbet 'atārūs, cf. Y. Aharoni, The Land of the Bible. A Historical
Geography, London ²1979, 337=Hirbet el-muhayyat; however, A. Kuschke, "Das
KRJTN der Mesa-Stele", ZDPV 77 (1961), 24-31; idem, "Horonaim and Qiry-
athaim. Remarks on a Recent Contribution to the Topography of Moab", PEQ
99 (1967), 104-105; Wüst, Untersuchungen, 148, n. 495, 156-63 map 3; Maxwell
Miller, in: Dearman, Studies, 2; Dearman, in: Dearman, Studies, 176-7 identify it
with Hirbet el-qureiye near 'Ayūn el-dib 10 km West of Medeba, where the descent
to the Jordan Valley begins, and 5.5 km south-south-west of Hirbet el-muhayyat
on the Iron Age road from Mā'in to the Jordan Valley.

[58]Cf. also Bar-Efrat, Narrative Art in the Bible, 187.

[59]Cf. Ugaritic: hṣt KTU 1.39:10; 1.136:11; 4.131:5; Hebrew: חצות (ה)לילה, HAL,

of such names can still be found in my *Reader's Digest Road-book of Europe*. Identification of this city 'Half-way' with Kiryathaim on the edge of the tableland is possible then, but not really crucial in order to follow Balaam's and Balak's itinerary. In the geographical framework of the story it indicates only the meeting-place halfway down the road from where both Balaam and Balak enter the central scene of action. In a city half-way down king Balak prepares a sacrificial banquet for his foreign guest and his princes.

The next morning Balak takes Balaam to a place called Bamoth Baal. It is within the narrative program of the story not only a detestable high place,[60] where Balaam orders Balak to built seven altars, but also the counterpart of the top of Peor. This place, however, is also mentioned as a real toponym in Josh. 13:17, belonging to the tribal territory of Reuben. It is perhaps the first real toponym in the story. If the place called Bamoth in Num. 21:19-20 is identical with Bamoth Baal,[61] it is one of the last stations of Israel's itinerary before it enters the valley where the top of the Pisgah overlooks the road into the Jeshimon and the "fields of Moab", i.e. most probably the present *Wādî ʿayūn mūsā*, also known as "the valley opposite Beth-Peor" (Deut. 3:29, 34:6).[62] An exact identification with an archaeological site is again not possible in this case, but we may certainly imagine the spot of Bamoth Baal somewhere south of the Pisgah and

---

330 'midnight'. One might consider a translation "Then Balaam went with Balak and they arrived in Qiryat at midnight/noon(?)." But compare also חצי in expressions found in Josh. 10:13; 1 Sam. 14:14. It is certainly a whim of history that close to the scene of our narrative somewhat north of Medeba a village *Kefeir al-Wusṭā* (hamlet of the middle) is found (see map).

[60] Cf. the Septuagint thinks even of a cenotaph of Baal (במה בעל = ἐπὶ τὴν στήλην τοῦ Βαὰλ), see also 22:39 εἰς πόλεις ἐπαύλεων = קרית חצות and 23:14 εἰς ἀγροῦ σκοπιὰν = שדה צפים; the Septuagint shows a tendency to translate the toponyms.

[61] Compare e.g. Simons, *GTT*, § 441; the place is presumably not identical with Beth Bamoth of the Mesha-stela. Simons, *GTT*, § 449; Zwickel, *UF* 22 (1990), 491 *et al.* identify it with *Ḥirbet el-Queiqiyeh* a few km south of *Gebel en-Nebā*; see however Aharoni, *Land of the Bible*, 339; Dearman, "Historical Reconstruction", 185-6, who locate it in the environment of *dibān/mādabā*; Noth, "Nu 21 als Glied der 'Hexateuch'-Erzählung", 89-90, n. 49, doubted the equation of Bamoth = Bamoth Baal = Beth-Bamoth. Bet Bamoth of the Mesha-stela was located somewhere in the Mishor north of the Arnon together with Beser, Medeba, Beth Diblaten and Beth Baal Maon.

[62] Simons, *GTT*, § 441, Grollenberg, *Atlas van de Bijbel*, nrs. 158-160; Cross, *ZAWSuppl* 100 (1988), 50-1; Maxwell Miller, in: Dearman, *Studies*, 28. The שדה מואב = ארץ מואב = גבול מואב (Num. 33:44), names for the land of Moab (Simons, *GTT*, § 441) should be distinguished from "the fields of Moab" in the Jordan-Valley (Num. 22:1, 33:48f etc. Simons, *GTT*, §§ 137, 170, 441).

the *Wādî ʿayūn mūsā* on a mountain ridge,[63] overlooking the main road which descends into this valley to the Jordan (see map).

The next place where king Balak takes the seer is called שֹׂדה צפים אל־ראש הפסגה (Num. 23:14). The location of the top of Pisgah (*rās eṣ-ṣiyāġā*) on the mountain ridge south of the *Wādî ʿayūn mūsā* is generally accepted, but again the first part שֹׂדה צפים is an unknown toponym.[64] Its interpretation, however, is of decisive significance for the understanding of the course of events. The basic problem seems to be that tradition and exegesis thinks of a locality on top of, or on the slopes of the Pisgah.[65] Traditional exegesis was certainly influenced by Moses' ascent of the top of mount Nebo (Num. 27:12; Deut. 32:19, 34:1). Presumably, the narrator again did not mean to indicate an existing toponym, but a general description of an area in the neighbourhood of the top of the Pisgah, from where an unobstructed view on the Israelite people is permitted (Num. 23:13). It may be noted that the parallel structure of the three sacrificial scenes also applies to the geographic parameters. The first time Balaam was taken up to Bamoth Baal from where he looks down on the edge of the people. The third time Balak will take Balaam to the top of Peor overlooking the Jeshimon. From this perspective, the top of Pisgah is not meant to be the observation-post, but the locality observed from the second place where Balak took Balaam in order to curse Israel: the field or tableland looking out on the top or mountain ridge of which the Pisgah is the spur.[66] Not the Pisgah itself, but a position higher up into the Mishor of Moab is described, where Balak put watch-posts to spy on Israel.[67] The verb צפה usually has the meaning of being on the look-out, spying on someone or something.[68] Compare, for instance

---

[63]Compare ראש צרים paralel to גבעות in Num. 23:9.

[64]Its relation with *talaʿat aṣ-ṣafā* suggested by Simons, *GTT*, § 451, Bagatti, *DBS* t.7, 1136-7, a steep valley north of Ḥirbet el-muḫayyaṭ (see map) is rather tenuous. Arabic *ṣafā* means 'stone, rock' and the toponym something like 'rocky hillside', cf. also Rouillard, *La péricope de Balaam*, 269. To assume a relationship with מצפה מואב (1 Sam. 22:3) does not help further, for, though it is a residence of a king of Moab, its location is unknown, cf. Simons, *GTT*, § 699.

[65]Cf. Septuagint: ἀγροῦ σκοπιὰν ἐπὶ κορυφὴν λελαξευμένου; Vulgate: *in locum sublimem super verticem montis Phasga*; Abel, *Géographie*, t.1, 383; De Vaux, *Histoire*, 525; Bagatti, *DBS*, t.7, 1136: "le Champ des Guetteurs au sommet du Pisgah" because of the fact that the top dominates the whole area north of the Dead Sea.

[66]For this meaning of ראש 'projecting end, cape, promontory', cf. *HAL*, 1087; particularly cognate is Arabic *rās* 'promontory, headland, cape'.

[67]Cf. Hebrew Sir. 37:14 משבעה צפים על מצפה "more than seven watch-posts on a watch-tower"; Hab. 2:1 etc.

[68]צפה אל, Lam 4:17; with ל, Ps. 37:32; also Ps. 10:8 (cj); with accusative, e.g.

the מגדל הלבנון צופה פני דמשק, "a tower on the Lebanon, looking out at the side of Damascus" (Cant. 7:5). In an enveloping movement, Balak takes Balaam around the east end of the mountain ridge of Nebo which is dominated by the top of the Pisgah.

The third time Balak completes this flanking manoeuvre by taking Balaam to the ראש הפעור הנשקף על־פני הישימן (Num. 23:28) "the top of Peor overlooking the Jeshimon", the wasteland of the Aravah north of the Dead Sea.[69] A similar description is given of the ראש הפסגה in Num. 21:20. Though this geographical expression is only found here, Peor was most probably the name of the mountain ridge or spur north of the *Wadî 'ayūn mūsā* which gave his name to the deity Baal of Peor and the city which accommodated his sanctuary Beth Peor (= Beth Baal Peor*).[70] The exact location of this sanctuary is disputed. Some would find it near modern *(Serabit el-)mušaqqar* or *Muhatta*, others in *Ḥirbet 'ayūn mūsā*.[71] Whether the sacrifice took place at the sanctuary or not, is irrelevant for the understanding of the story. Probably not, because the narrator stresses that at every occasion a new set of seven altars is built. What is inferred by Balak's movements is that the Israelites who live around the Pisgah on the mountain ridge, in the valleys and the Jeshimon are the target of Balaam's curses. This time Balaam does not longer resort to his mantic abilities and sorcery,[72] but turns his face to the מדבר and humbly awaits the inspiration of Gods Spirit. The meaning of המדבר in this context is enigmatic, but considering what follows, this desert is located somewhere in the direction of Palestine. One could think of the Desert of Judah, or otherwise of a synonym for the Jeshimon.[73] It is of interest that only

---

דרך, Jer. 48:19; Nah. 2:20, cf. Rouillard, *La péricope de Balaam*, 264ff. who rightly points to the 'double entendre' of צפה 'watch-post' = 'prophet'.

[69] Cf. Simons, *GTT* §§ 61, 705; the geographic name seems to be related to Bet-Jeshimoth (Num. 33:49; Josh. 12:3,13:20; Ezek. 25:9) a village in "fields of Moab".

[70] The mountain gave its name to the deity and not vice versa, cf. M.J. Mulder, *Ba'al in het Oude Testament*, 's Gravenhage 1962, 132-3; idem, *ThWAT*, Bd. 1, 720.

[71] *Ḥirbet muhatta*: Cross, *ZAWSuppl* 100 (1988), 50; Dearman, "Historical Reconstruction", 180-1; S.D. Waterhouse & R. Ibach, "Heshbon 73 – The Topographical Survey", *AUSS* 13 (1975), 217-25. *Ḥirbet eš-šēh gayil* (cf. A. Musil, *Arabia Petraea*, Bd. 1, Vienna 1907, 344, 348) does not exist, see Donner, "Balaam pseudopropheta", 116, n. 17; Simons, *GTT*, § 443; De Vaux, *Histoire*, 525. As for the localization at *Ḥirbet 'ayūn mūsā*, cf. O. Henke, "Zur Lage von Beth Peor", *ZDPV* 75 (1959), 155-63, the city Cross identified as Nebo (*ZAWSuppl* 100 (1988), 51-2; Dearman, "Historical Reconstruction", 181).

[72] Cf. Rost, "Fragen um Bileam", 377-82.

[73] Num. 23:28; see also the parallellism of מדבר || ישמון in Isa. 43:19-20.

this time Balaam is permitted an unobstructed view of Israel, like Moses, who got it from the top of Pisgah (24:2, cf. Deut. 34:1). One wonders whether this tradition of Moses' death was already known to the narrator. From a narrative perspective it is certainly significant that Balaam was not allowed a full view of Israel from the same place where Moses stood.

We are able to reconstruct to a certain degree the itinerary of the Balaam-story. Before we try to relate this itinerary to the different synchronic levels of the story's stratigraphy, I summarize the most significant topographical data. Balaam enters the central stage of the story from the north, coming either from a city in Aram Naharayim at the Euphrates, or from his native land (variant: the Land of the Ammonites). Balak comes from his kingdom Moab in the south. They meet most probably somewhere in a city of Moab half-way down the road between their respective starting points. An exact localization does not seem to be intended by the narrator. The narrative becomes only more specific in the area around the mountain ridge of the Pisgah. Three attempts are made to curse Israel from three different geographical points. They are told in three narrative units with slight stylistic variations. I would like to stress again that these scenes form together a structural unity in the original program and plot of the Balaam-story.[74] The first attempt at cursing Israel takes place at a site called Bamoth Baal where a view on Nebo from the south is possible. Following the watershed (roads usually follow the watershed or go through the valleys), Balak surrounds the spur of the Pisgah and takes Balaam for a second attempt to a place east of Nebo. Finally, a spot on the watershed between *Wādî ʿayūn mūsā* en *Wādî ḥesbān* is reached on the spur of the Peor from where one overlooks the other side of *Wādî ʿayūn mūsā* from the north. If really a view on the city and sanctuary of Nebo should be intended by the narrator from all three sides, this would be in favour of Cross' identification of Nebo = *Ḥirbet ʿayūn mūsā*. Presumably, the story suggested only an 'encirclement' of the mountain ridge commanding the road into the Jeshimon, including the city and sanctuary of Nebo. De Vaux and others may be right after all that at the time that this story of Balaam at Nebo originated, the edge of the Mishor was the actual border between Moab and Israel and that the Pisgah and the city of Nebo were still Israelite.

---

[74] *Pace* literary-critical and other theories, ancient and modern, which ascribe the third scene either to the Yahwist (Mowinckel, Eissfeldt etc.) or to a later stage in tradition, cf. e.g. Grosz, *Bileam*, 295ff.; Rouillard, *La péricope de Balaam*, 484-5.

5. Was the Biblical Balaam-Story Created and Told at Nebo?

This brings us finally to some deliberations about the origin and date of the Balaam-story, and also the origins and whereabouts of this Transjordan saint. This seems the proper moment to turn to the dia-chronic aspects of the story with the help of some form-criticism and some *Überlieferungsgeschichte*. It will not come as a surprise that I start with Noth. In his earliest study of the Balaam-traditions Noth, following Mowinckel,[75] situated the person and tradition at the Trans-jordanian sanctuary of Beth-Peor, where Midianites, Moabites and Israelites met. Contrary to their late literary context he thought that Num. 31:8, 16; Josh. 13:22 which relate the death of Balaam among the chieftains of Midian, represented the oldest stage of oral Balaam-tradition.[76] This tradition of the evil magician is also the source of the later negative Balaam-image. Contrary to this negative tradition the Israelites in Transjordan developed a positive tradition. Via the stage found in Deut 23:5b, 6 (reversal of the curses in blessings), the story of a foreign magician was invented who was called to support Moabite territorial claims, but became a quasi-Israelite prophet instead.[77] Not only Noth himself revised his earlier views considerably,[78] when he ac-knowledged that Num. 22-24 contained the earliest and only source of the Balaam-tradition. Also Grosz, Donner and Schmidt proved con-vincingly that Noth's original reconstruction was too complicated. Both Donner and Schmidt showed how the revision of the image of Balaam was gradually achieved through literary reinterpretation in-fluenced by deuteronomistic theology.[79] Such a redactionally devel-oped exegesis renders it impossible to assume that a positive image of Balaam was the product of a negative one. The negative image of Balaam is the redactionally developed exegetical product of the Balaam-image found in Num. 22-24 and perhaps Micah 6:5.

Equally, the assumption that the central sanctuary of Beth Peor was the place where the Balaam-story originated is most improbable. If our topographical analysis of the story is acceptable and Balak's 'encirclement' of the Israelites points the faces of the audience de-liberatedly into a certain direction, the story centers around the top of the Pisgah and therefore most probably the Transjordan sanctu-

---

[75] Mowinckel, *ZAW* 48 (1930), 233-71.

[76] Noth, *Überlieferungsgeschichte*, 80-6, esp. 82-3.

[77] Cf. Donner, "Balaam pseudopropheta", 114-5; see, however, Noth, *Überliefe-rungsgeschichte*, 84, n. 223.

[78] Noth, *Numeri*, 151-69, esp. 152-4.

[79] Donner, "Balaam pseudopropheta", 119ff.; Schmidt, *BZ* 23 (1979), 247ff.

ary at Nebo. Without being mentioned itself, this central place of
worship plays a key-role in the Balaam-tradition. One could imagine
how such a story of a foreign magician called to curse Israel, presumably in preparation of a military campaign, was told at Nebo for the
greater honour and glory of YHWH. As noted above, the floruit of
this sanctuary came suddenly to an end after its conquest and destruction by king Mesha, presumably during the reign of Jehoram of
Israel (shortly before 841 B.C.).[80] This provides us with a *terminus
ante quem* for the story which complies basically with the date of the
Deir 'Alla plaster inscription (ca. 800 B.C.). But even if its location
at the sanctuary of Nebo is thought to be too speculative, it is hard to
understand how such a narrative plot encircling the top of the Pisgah
in the former tribal area of Gad, could have been developed after the
time that Nebo and its surroundings were lost to Israel and became
a Moabite province, as *is* confirmed by Isa. 15:2.

If the different Balaam-traditions originated in the ninth century B.C., this leaves enough time for the development of a negative
Balaam-image which certainly also affected the redaction of Num. 22-
24 and which finally made the seer the instigator of the affair at the
sanctuary of Beth Peor (Num. 25:1-5, 31:16). In the final form of the
story as it was incorporated in the Pentateuch, Balaam's itinerary
is marked by a starting-point at Petor on the River Euphrates and
ends with the vision of Assyrian captivity and beyond. In this form
it also became a so-called ישראל כל-story, in stead of the limited
number of Transjordan tribes encamped around its central sanctuary at Nebo (Num. 24:2, 6-7). We found that the involvement of
Midian in the opening-sentences corresponded to the judgment of the
Amalekites, Kenites and Ismaelites in the last oracles. These oracles
about the peoples of the East belong to the apocalyptic re-lecture of
the Balaam-story after the Exile, in which also the star out of Jacob
was reinterpreted as an announcement of the future Messiah. Agag
in 24:7 and the Amalekites in 24:20 gradually assumed apocalyptic
features. He was either identified with Gog of Magog (Ezek. 38-39) or
associated with Haman, the Agagite from the book of Esther (Esth.
3:1, 10 etc.).[81] Whether this stage of the story can also be associ-

---

[80]Cf. on possibilities and suggestions of dating the events in the Mesha-stela
see Dearman, "Historical Reconstruction", 164ff., with references.

[81]Cf. *HAL*, 10; G.Gerleman, *Esther* (BK, 21), Neukirchen-Vluyn 1973, 91;
H. Bardtke, *Das Buch Esther* (KAT, 17/5), Gütersloh 1963, 315; Rouillard,
La péricope de Balaam, 370-1. Gog according to the Samaritan Pentateuch and
the Septuagint is certainly not original, but reveals an interesting strand in the
apocalyptic-messianic interpretation of the Balaam-story. As such the variant is
significant for the history of interpretation which already started within the Old

ated with Balaam's origins in Petor on the Euphrates or not, remains unclear. The tradition is already known in Deut 23:5 and if a relocation of the magician, it may derive from deuteronomistic circles like the announcement of the Assyrian captivity. Another possibility is that this relocation was the product of a too literal interpretation of מן־ארם and the hill-country of Qedem (Num. 23:7).[82] Some would even strongly defend the Aramean origin of the seer without resorting to Petor as the city of Balaam's origin.[83] It was the younger biblical tradition which relocated Balaam in Petor on the Euphrates-river in Mesopotamia and promoted him to be an Aramean diviner.[84] When all evidence is taken together, it is more feasible that Balaam's origin lies somewhere in the northern Transjordan mountains in the direction of Aram. That is what the narrator let him suggest in his own

---

Testament. This interpretation went into two directions: 1) Agag as the ancestor of Haman, the Agagite (cf. e.g. Jos, *Antt.*, XI, 6, 5) and 2) the rendering of the name Gog instead of Agag, the mythic enemy from the North (Ezek. 38-39), presumably called after the legendaric Lydian king Gugu/Gyges (ca. 687-652 B.C.). This last interpretation is also reflected in the Septuagint's rendering of Esther 3:1 etc. אגגי = Βουγαῖος/Γωγαῖος, see also ὁ Μαχεδῶν Greek Esther 8:12k; 9:24. The Gog-interpretation is certainly post-exilic, see also the comment in Targum Pseudo-Jonathan on Num. 24:17 דגוג משיריתיה דשת בנוי "the sons of Shet, the armies of Gog".

[82] Mowinckel, *ZAW* 48 (1938), 237; Simons, *GTT*, § 445 suggest therefore to emend the Hebrew text in Num. 22:4 to נהר ארץ בני קדם; Qedem is often connected with Egyptian *qdmy* (Sinuhe etc., cf. review in: Grosz, *Bileam*, 98-100) limiting the original topograhic range of Egyptian Qedem to the wooden hinterland of Byblos in the Libanon or Transjordan (e.g. the Hauran mountains), cf. S. Aḥituv, *Canaanite Toponyms in Ancient Egyptian Documents*, Jerusalem/Leiden 1984, 158. An Ugaritic incantation mentions Horon's city *Mṣd* as *'r dqdm* (KTU 1.100:61) "city of Qedem". It might be noted that in Ezek. 25:2-4, 10 Qedem borders upon the territory of Ammon and Moab.

[83] Cf. review Grosz, *Bileam*, 96-7 and lately Lemaire, *ZAW* 102 (1990), 180-7; idem, "Les incriptions sur plâtre de Deir 'Alla et leur signification historique et culturelle", in: Hoftijzer & Van der Kooij (eds.), *The Balaam Text from Deir 'Alla Re-evaluated*, 51; for Balaam as an Aramean foreigner at Deir 'Alla, see A. Wolters, "The Balaamites of Deir 'Alla as Aramean Deportees", *HUCA* 59 (1988), 101-13; Layton, *Biblica* 73 (1992), 60, but Wolters' reconstruction has been rendered out of date by the earlier dating of the inscription ca. 800 B.C. (cf. Dijkstra, *GThT* 90 (1990), 178, n. 73).

[84] Petor is usually identified with Pitru about 20 km south of Kargemish (Tell Ahmar) at the mouth of the Irgamri or Saguri tributary into the Euphrates, cf. S. Parpola, *Neo-Assyrian Toponyms* (AOAT, 6), Neukirchen-Vluyn 1970, 279; K. Kessler, *Untersuchungen zur historischen Topographie Mesopotamiens nach keilschriftlichen Quellen des 1. Jahrtausends v.Chr.*, Wiesbaden 1980, 107, 191-2, for the exact location, see the annals of Shalmanessar III, Monolith-Inscription, II,78ff (cf. *ANET*, 278b); Layton, *Biblica* 73 (1992), 37, n. 22, though some still think a location of Petor at the Jabboq (*nahr ez-zerqā*) or Jordan possible.

words and the text from Deir 'Alla confirms that he was a locally ven-
erated saint עבר הירדן whose floruit may be dated at least in the ninth
century B.C. but probably earlier. Whether this was in the valley of
Succoth, or in the land of the Ammonites, is a secondary matter.[85]
The variant reading (!) בני עמון ארץ in a large part of the textual tradition (BHS on Num. 22:5[c]) is in my opinion strongly supported by
the topography which underlies the narrative program of the story.
Unlike later tradition, the original narrator did not suppose Balaam
to travel greater distances than one or two days.[86] Even if one maintains the Masoretic text ארץ בני־עמו "in his native land" as the *lectio
difficilior*,[87] in the original plot of the narrative this native land was
hardly farther away from the centre of our story than the land of
Moab. Balaam's relocation at Petor (also מפתור ארם נהרים, Deut. 23:5)
was part of the re-evaluation of his person which moved him both
theologically and geographically out of the sight of Israel.

6.   Dating the Bibical Balaam-Story

Both the biblical and extra-biblical literary texts and traditions
strongly suggest for their origin a *terminus ante quem* in the second
half of the ninth century B.C. Is it also possible to indicate a *terminus
post quem*? Of course, I cannot present here a full discussion of all the
problems concerning Moabite and Israelite relations in history. Balak
is not attested as a Moabite king outside the Balaam-story itself. The
obscure remark in Judg. 11:25 is clearly a part of a deuteronomisti-
cally styled review of Israels history laid in the mouth of Jephtah. If
originally a relation did exist between the tradition of Moses' tomb in
the valley opposite Beth Peor and the sanctuary of Nebo, one could
think of a period of several centuries extending from about 850 B.C.
into the pre-monarchic period. De Vaux thought it possible that the
tradition rested on a real historical conflict between Moab and Israel
"après l'installation des tribus et avant le règne de David", but did

---

[85] The Ammonite origin is defended by J. Lust, "Balaam, an Ammonite", *ETL*
54 (1978), 60-1; M. Delcor, "Le texte de Deir 'Alla et les oracles bibliques de
Bala'am", *SVT* 32 (1981), 71-2; Rouillard, *La péricope de Balaam*, 48, 53.

[86] *Pace* Jagersma, *Numeri*, 114. Actually, the scheme of narrated time could be
interpreted in this way that Balak and Balaam met on the same day on which the
donkey-incident happened (22:21, 41). But because of the fact that Balak received
the message that Balaam was coming, some more real time seems to be suggested
than the narrated time.

[87] See a comparable idiom in Gen. 23:11; Judg. 14:16; Lev. 19:18, 20:17 etc. and
Balaam's own words בני עמו (24:14) and לעמי (24:14) recall the kinsfolk of the seer
(עמה) mentioned in the Deir 'Alla text line 4! The theological argument which
makes the expression a *hapax* in Num. 22:5 according to Rouillard, *La péricope
de Balaam*, 46, is rather tenuous.

not specify further.[88] It is however very doubtfull whether there ever existed a pre-monarchic Balaam-tradition. As said above, the story was clearly adapted to its context when incorporated in its present place in the Pentateuch. This incorporation of Num. 22-24 among the settlement-traditions was probably caused both by the redactional process of Balaam's denigration as the evil 'moving spirit' among the peoples of the East and on the understanding that the story concerned all Israel. Presumably, the original story served a different purpose when it was created in Israelite circles at Nebo. It is again the plaster text of Deir 'Alla which offers an interesting example of how and why a document telling the story of a seer is copied and posted on the wall of a tomb or sanctuary. This could happen in memory of the tomb-owner, but also for apologetic reasons. I would like to suggest here that the story of Balaam in its older stage (without the elaborations in 22:1-4a, 7*, 36*; 24:18-25) carried on propaganda for Israel, its king and its God in the confrontation between Israel and Moab. The historical cornerstone for the *terminus post quem* in the early period of the monarchy is the mentioning of Agag, king of Amalek (Num. 24:7). To suggest here a tribal name or to assume the existence of more than one king with this name is unwarranted and unnecessary. The war between king Saul of Israel and Agag, king of Amalek, related in 1 Sam. 15, rests notwithstanding its deuteronomistic revision most probably on a historical base.[89] The question whether it involved the tribe of the Amalekites in Southern Palestine and Transjordan or a Canaanite kingdom at the North-Western edge of the hill-country of Ephraim is now of minor importance. In any case, later interpretation associated Agag and Amalek with the Midianites, the Kenites and other peoples of the East (Num. 24:20-22, like Judg. 6-8). Historically a 'Canaanite' Amalek seems more probable, but conclusive

---

[88]De Vaux, *Histoire*, 525; Jagersma, *Geschiedenis*, 97; similarly Noth, *Geschichte*, 144, n. 2; De Moor following Albright, Bright, *History*, 117, 126 etc. supposes that the oracles may contain authentic information about the time of Moses' arrival in Transjordan, see: *Rise of Yahwism*, 151ff.

[89]See also 1 Sam. 14:47-48, H.J. Stoebe, *Das erste Buch Samuelis* (KAT), Bd. 8/1, Gütersloh 1973, 281-2; Noth, *Geschichte*, 162, J.H. Hayes & J.M. Miller, *Israelite & Judaean History*, London 1990³, 328, J. Alberto Soggin, *A History of Israel: From the Beginnings to the Bar Kochba Revolt A.D. 135*, London 1985, 48; Schmidt, *BZ* 23 (1979), 253-4. Probably the original event was not about the nomadic Amalekites, but about an autochtonous Canaanite people settled in the north-western region of the hill-country of Ephraim (near פרעה = *far'atah* 10 km south-west of Nablus, 1 Sam. 15:6; Judg. 5:14, 12:15), cf. H. Cazelles, "Deborah (Jug V 14), Amaleq et Makir", *VT* 24 (1974), 235-8; J. Alberto Soggin, "Amalek und Ephraim", *ZDPV* 98 (1982), 58-62; Soggin, *History*, 48.

evidence is lacking.[90] A date after the beginning of the first millenium B.C. for the oldest poems in Num. 23:3-9; 24:15-17 comports
best with all the evidence in my opinion. It remains uncertain whether
these poems are about the rise of Saul's or David's kingdom, but they
clearly reflect the emergence of the monarchy in Israel which in itself
is a hard to neglect *terminus post quem* for the origin of the Balaam-
traditions. Presumably, the victory over king Agag was remembered
and celebrated like the day of Midian's defeat in Isaiah's times (Isa.
9:4). Origin and use of the poems as royal propaganda to celebrate
David's wars and dynasty is a reasonable possibility.[91] There is, however, also the possibility that the text of the poems with the names
of Israel and Jacob only refers to the kingdom of Israel. The story of
the curses which were turned into blessings could in such a case have
its background in another confrontation between Israel and Moab at
the start of Omri's reign and dynasty (early 9th century B.C.). But
this brings us within the realm of speculation. If for instance 'the star
out of Jacob' orginally was quoted as an oracle of Balaam to refer to
Omri's rise to power, it infers that Balaam and Balak were already
figures of the past and that they were cited and told about as willy-
nilly witnesses of Israel's expansion in Transjordan. Mesha informs us
that his father reigned thirty years (KAI 181:2). If we assume that
Mesha became king shortly after Achab's death (about 853 B.C.),
this refers us again to a period before the beginning of the Omride
dynasty, i.e. most probably to the tenth century as the floruit of Balaam. A probable date for the origin and early development of the
biblical Balaam-tradition itself is then the period of Israelite political expansion in Transjordan in the ninth century under the Omride
dynasty.

---

[90]The name Agag could be Canaanite (CIS I, 3196:3), or Hurrian: **ag-** 'to
give, take' with augment **-(a)ga**, cf. names like Šawušga, Šimige; nouns: **ašta-ga**,
taḫa-ga.
[91]Schmidt, *BZ* 23 (1979), 253-4.

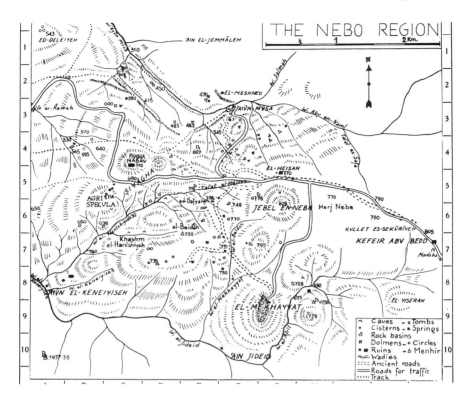

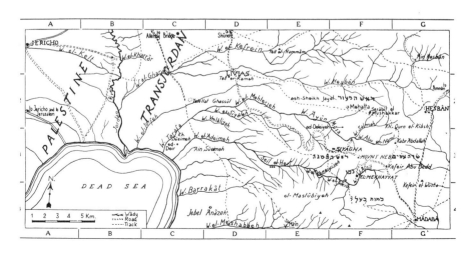

Adapted maps of the Nebo region.

Jacob Hoftijzer *Leiden – The Netherlands*

Holistic or Compositional Approach?
Linguistic Remarks to the Problem[1]

Dedicated to the memory of Martin J. Mulder

Among the many legitimate scholarly approaches to the texts of the
Hebrew Bible there are two we are especially concerned with during this meeting. The first approach tries to define and describe the
possible compositional/redactional history of each of these texts. The
second approach tries to define and describe the structure of each of
these texts and the insight afforded by the definition of this structure
into the meaning of the relevant text. On purpose I avoid here the
use of the terms 'diachronic' and 'synchronic' which in literary studies
can be used in a completely different way and for this reason could
be ambiguous.[2] I shall use the terms 'compositional/redactional' and
'structural'. There are some scholars who attempt to combine both
approaches, while there are others who avoid such a combination.[3]

---

[1] I wish to thank my colleagues C. van Bree, J.P. Fokkelman, E.C. García, J.G.
Kooy and I. Tieken-Boon van Ostade for helping me to find scholarly literature
outside my special field. I feel greatly indebted to them.

[2] Generally the terms 'synchronic' and 'diachronic' are used in modern literary
structural studies to indicate respectively: 1) the approach which aims at the definition and description of the structure of a text in the final form in which it is
handed down to us – 2) the approach which aims at the definition and description
of the compositional/redactional history of this text. To mention but a few examples, cf. A. Berlin, *Poetics and Interpretation of Biblical Narrative* (BiLiSe, 9),
Sheffield 1983, 111; D.J.A. Clines, J.Ch. Exum, "The New Literary Criticism", in:
J.Ch. Exum, D.J.A. Clines (eds.), *The New Literary Criticism and the Hebrew
Bible* (JSOT.S, 143), Sheffield 1993, 11-25 (16); E. Talstra, *Solomon's Prayer:
Synchrony and Diachrony in the Composition of 1 Kings 8,14-61* (Contributions
to Biblical Exegesis and Theology, 3), Kampen 1993, 81-2. (See also the title of
J.P. Fokkelman's article, "Structural Reading between Synchrony and Diachrony"
JEOL 30 (1989), 123-36).
   However, there is also another way to use both terms, namely as indicating respectively: 1) the approach by which one tries by comparing literary texts of the
same period to come to the definition and description of a literary system valid
for that period – 2) the approach which aims by comparing the literary systems
of different periods to come to a definition and description of the development of
these systems in the course of time. This is the way the terms are used by, for
example, W. Richter, *Exegese als Literaturwissenschaft: Entwurf einer alttestamentlichen Literaturtheorie und Methodologie*, Göttingen 1971, 35ff., 70ff., 121ff.
Personally I would prefer the latter use of the terms which is more parallel to the
way they are used in linguistics.

[3] On this subject, see the description given in n. 42.

The question I want to put before this meeting is whether or not the two approaches ought to be interrelated? In particular I wish to ask what contribution linguistics can make in answering such a question.

However, before starting with this subject, I would like to make some general remarks indicating the presuppositions from which I proceed. I agree that every text is an entity which can have its own special character. But this does not mean, in my opinion, that this entity can be considered as completely independent from its *Umwelt*. It is written in a certain language (in our case Classical Hebrew)[4] which it shares with other texts, and it (normally) accepts the system of that language and in consequence the modes of expression implied by the use of that system.[5] In other words, a text presupposes a competence common to the author and the readers/hearers of his text. This competence is not only one of a linguistic nature, it also includes a non-linguistic knowledge presupposed to be common to the author and his readers/hearers. The presence of such a knowledge becomes particularly clear to us in those cases where it is no longer available anymore to the modern reader. To give an example: the meaning of בית המרחק in 2 Sam. 15:17 must have been clear to the original readers/hearers without further commentary, but it is not clear to us.[6] And, as already implied in the preceding lines, the text presupposes a certain author/redactor who, writing/composing it, consciously or unconsciously had a certain readership in mind. The text is influenced

---

[4]The term 'Classical Hebrew' does not indicate a uniform language. Besides the different language levels discussed below, there are within the text corpus handed down to us also clear signs of a diachronic development. To mention only some studies on this point, cf. e.g. R. Polzin, *Late Biblical Hebrew: Toward a Historical Typology of Biblical Hebrew Prose* (HSM, 12), Missoula, 1976; A. Hurvitz, *A Linguistic Study of the Relationship between the Priestly Code and the Book of Ezekiel: A New Approach to an Old Problem* (CRB, 20), Paris 1982; M.F. Rooker, *Biblical Hebrew in Transition* (JSOT.S, 90), Sheffield 1990.

[5]On this point, see the interesting remarks made by W. Richter, *Exegese als Literaturwissenschaft*, 42, 78 (cf. also M. Sternberg, *The Poetics of Biblical Narrative: Ideological Literature and the Drama of Reading*, Bloomington 1985, 11-2). As to the structure of the language, I adhere to an approach which considers the language structure to exceed the limits of the sentence; on this point, cf. Chr. Hardmeyer, *Texttheorie und Biblische Exegese: Zur rhetorischen Funktion der Trauermetaphorik in der Prophetie* (BEvTh, 79), München 1978, 30ff. (cf. also e.g. K. Koch, *Was ist Formgeschichte? Methoden der Bibelexegese*, Neukirchen-Vluyn ³1974, 307.

[6]Cf. C.J. Goslinga, *Het tweede Boek Samuel verklaard*, Kampen 1962, 278; R.P. Gordon, *1 & 2 Samuel: A Commentary*, Exeter 1986, 272-3; A. Caquot, Ph. de Robert, *Les Livres de Samuel*, Genève 1994, 530. For the relation of a text with its historical context, cf. also Sternberg, *The Poetics of Biblical Narrative*, 16-7.

by both factors[7] (see below). Moreover the text usually belongs to a certain type of medium and will be influenced to a greater or lesser degree by the rules valid for that medium in the time and *Umwelt* in which it was written[8] (see also below).

The first question one has to ask when discussing the relationship between the structural and compositional/redactional approaches, is how to decide whether there is reason to think of a compositional/redactional history of the text in question. In our case the question is which linguistic facts could be considered to be valid indicators of such a history.

One can approach the problem from a grammatical angle and a lexematic semantic one. In this lecture, however, both approaches will be used. When we look for grammatical and lexematic semantic differences which allow us to conclude that a text has a compositional/redactional history, it would be completely inadequate to establish the fact that grammatical forms/constructions or lexemes/lexeme combinations are attested for one presumed 'source' and not for other(s). To give an example. In his book on the Hexateuch Simpson gives "lists of Hebrew words and forms characteristic of documents".[9] As a lexeme characteristic for JE he mentions the noun בכירה.[10] Although בכירה is attested five times for those parts of the Hexateuch which are considered to be JE and not for other parts, this cannot be considered to be a decisive linguistic argument for source analysis. In the other parts of the Hexateuch there is no mention of 'first-born daughters', so we do not know whether the author(s) of these parts would have used

---

[7] Cf. the remarks of Sternberg, *The Poetics of Biblical Narrative*, 11, 58. For the importance of our knowledge of the so-called 'Partnerkonstellationen', cf. Hardmeyer, *Texttheorie und Biblische Exegese*, 89ff. See also the linguistic side of the problem as discussed below. Sternberg, *The Poetics of Biblical Narrative*, 69-70, distinguishes between "the writer as the historical man" and "the writer as the authorial figure reflected in the writing" (respectively the person and the persona), who are "two faces of the same entity". The knowledge of the person can help to understand the persona and the text he wrote. The fact that we do not know much (and in a number of instances nothing) of the person of Biblical authors (see below) does not change the fact that the knowledge of the person of an author can help to understand the text, the author being part of the text's context. This has nothing to do with an approach which has "the romantic view of texts as giving immediate access to the ideas and feelings of great minds" (cf. Clines, Exum, *The New Literary Criticism*, 15). Cf. also n. 22.

[8] A clear example of a medium with its own rules (or set of rules) is poetry. On the subject, cf. also e.g. Koch, *Was ist Formgeschichte?*, 89.

[9] Cf. C.A. Simpson, *The Early Traditions of Israel: A Critical Analysis of the Predeuteronomic Narrative of the Hexateuch*, Oxford 1948, 403ff.

[10] Cf. Simpson, *The Early Traditions of Israel*, 403. Outside the Hexateuch the lexeme בכירה is attested in 1 Sam. 14:49.

this lexeme, or whether there was a lexeme (group) that was inter-changeable with it or has replaced it, or was perhaps replaced by it. In this lecture I want to approach this subject from this last-mentioned angle. I shall not speak, however, about indications of changes in the structure of the language within one text. In my opinion *proofs* of such a change in one text (which in that case must be composite and the parts of which must be written in different phases of the language) is very difficult to give, if it is possible at all. Even if an author only uses an 'older' form/lexeme (or a 'younger' form/lexeme) this does not prove that the other form(s)/lexeme(s) were not used anymore (or not yet used at that time). It is also possible that both were used in the language, but that the author in question only uses one of the possible forms/lexemes in his idiolect. This problem can only be solved if one has outside knowledge about the language phase in question, which for Classical Hebrew is not the case. This means that I shall direct my attention only to interchangeable elements. In the case of these elements we have to ask whether in a particular part of the text the use of one of the possible forms/constructions/lexemes is significantly higher than in the other(s).[11] But we must not do this indiscriminately. Such interchangeability may be dependent on contextual circumstances. Drawing from the work of four different Spanish authors, García has studied the occurrence of the deictic *él* and the personal pronoun *sí* which are interchangeable. She showed that under certain contextual circumstances only *sí* is used.[12] More-

---

[11] For a method of determining under which circumstances one percentage is significantly higher or lower than an other percentage, cf. J. Hoftijzer, *A Search for Method: A Study in the Syntactic Use of the h-locale in Classical Hebrew* (SStLL, 12), Leiden 1981, 16-7, 186ff.

The fact that two forms/constructions or lexemes are interchangeable does not necessarily mean they either have the same function or are synonymous, cf. e.g. J. Lyons, *Introduction to Theoretical Linguistics*, Cambridge 1968, 451ff. For a good example, cf. E.C. García, "Quantity into Quality: Synchronic Indeterminacy and Language Change", *Lingua* 65 (1985), 275-306 (285ff.) who discusses the interchangeability of *sí* and *él*.

In my opinion this method of determining the frequency of interchangeable elements is preferable for our aims to the method of determining the relative frequency of certain linguistic discriminants, as described by e.g. Y.T. Radday, H. Shore, "The Definite Article: A Type and/or Author-Specifying Discriminant in the Hebrew Bible", *Bulletin of the Association for Literary and Linguistic Computing* 4 (1976), 23-31, and Y.T. Radday *et al.*, "The Book of Judges Examined by Statistical Linguistics", *Bib.* 58 (1977), 469-99. In the last-mentioned method instances where the discriminant in question could not have been used (or could not have been used without changing the meaning of the text essentially) have also been considered.

[12] Cf. García, *Lingua* 65, 293 table 7.

over, the frequency of *sí* is different for each of the other four context types which she distinguishes.[13] A comparable situation is shown by Tieken for the use of the auxiliary *do* in her study on this verb in 18th-century English.[14] For Classical Hebrew one may compare the fact that the frequency of the use of the ה-locale can be dependent on the (type of) lexeme it is attached to.[15]

Before we draw any conclusion from the frequency of an inter-changeable grammatical form/construction or lexeme about the possible compositional/redactional history of a text, we also have to consider another problem. A language is no unity on a synchronic level. It can be subdivided into different language levels which may exhibit corresponding differences in grammar and vocabulary.[16] Such a level may be determined by the speaker/author and the hearer(s)/reader(s), and

---

[13] Cf. García, *Lingua* 65, 293 table 7.

[14] Cf. e.g. I. Tieken-Boon van Ostade, *The Auxiliary* do *in Eighteenth Century English: A Sociohistorical-Linguistic Approach*, Leiden 1987, 136 table 10. For many authors treated here the frequency of the use of the auxiliary *do* in negative sentences and in questions differs considerably. For example, in informative prose Defoe did not use this *do* in respectively 45.24% and 5.00% of the relevant instances, Richardson in 52.94% and 11.11%, Fielding in 22.22% and 0.00%.

[15] To give only two examples. In Ezekiel there are 9 instances attested of שׁמּה with local-terminative function against 11 instances without the ending ה- (45%). In the same book there are 4 instances attested of שׁמה with locative function against 43 instances without the ending ה- (8.5%). Cf. Hoftijzer, *A Search for Method*, 142-143. In the prose parts of Jeremiah there are no instances attested where בֵיתה is *nomen regens* and the *nomen rectum* is the name of a deity or a person against 7 instances without the ending ה- (0.00%). In the same text there are 15 instances attested of בבל with the ending ה- against 9 without this ending (62.5%). Cf. Hoftijzer, *A Search for Method*, 68, 118. In both these cases the differences in frequency are significant.

[16] Cf. J. Lyons, *Semantics* (2 volumes), Cambridge, etc. 1977, 580-1, (and context), cf. also P. Trudgill, *Sociolinguistics: An Introduction to Language and Society* (Penguin Books), London 1983, for example on 100ff., and Hardmeyer, *Text-theorie und Biblische Exegese*, 137ff. (see also pp. 89ff.). The survey of the problem in E.C. Traugott, S. Romaine, "Some Questions for the Definition of 'Style' in Socio-Historical Linguistics", *Folia Linguistica Historica* 6 (1985), 7-39, is most interesting. I. Zatelli, *Il campo lessicale degli aggettivi di purità in Ebraico Biblico* (QuSem, 7), Firenze 1978, 9ff., uses the term 'functional language' to indicate the different synchronic language levels.

I have avoided the use of the term 'style' (used e.g. by Traugott, Romaine, *Folia Linguisica Historica* 6, because it is ambiguous; the term is not only used by scholars in a sociolectic context (formal style, informal style, etc.), but it is also used by some in an idiolectic context (the style of Dickens or Hemingway, cf. G. Leech, *Semantics: The Study of Meaning* (Penguin Books), Hammondsworth [2]1981, 14, cf. also the use of the term by, for example, M. Riffaterre, "Critères pour l'analyse du style", in: M. Riffaterre, *Essais de stylistique structurale* (présentation et traductions de D. Delas), Paris 1971, 27-63 (29)).

their relation, and by the medium chosen for the contact. To give an example. In her study concerning the use of the auxiliary *do* in 18th century English, Tieken shows that in the work of the same author the frequency in the use of this auxiliary within the same context type can differ considerably from literary genre to literary genre.[17] The clearest example in Classical Hebrew (evidently it is not typical for this language) is the difference in grammar and semantics between poetic texts and prose texts.[18] But even within Classical Hebrew prose one also has to reckon with this type of difference. To give an example from my own research on the ה-locale. In Judg. 21:19 one finds two instances of respectively a less common ה-morpheme and a ה-morpheme with deviating meaning; this verse gives the description of a geographical situation. In the relatively short list of Solomon's taxation districts one finds two comparable instances, in 1 Kgs. 4:12 and 14. At these points both Judg. 21:19 and the list of districts differ from their contexts. The texts Num. 33-35 and Josh. 13-21 which for the major part consist of geographical descriptions and an itinerary show a much higher frequency of less common ה-morphemes or of a less frequent use of them, compared with their context.[19] It seems probable that these grammatical differences do not necessarily indicate that these parts are written by a different author than their context. It seems more probable that (at least for a certain phase of Classical Hebrew)[20] for geographical description (in a broad sense of the word) a different language level was used.[21] Unfortunately there

---

[17] In his informative prose Steele uses 6 times the auxiliary *do* in negative sentences (with a form of to know) against 1 instance where this auxiliary was not used (a frequency of 85.7%). In his epistolary prose he uses in the same context type 3 times *do* against 6 instances where the auxiliary was not used (a frequency of 33.3%). Cf. Tieken-Boon van Ostade, *The Auxiliary* do, 130, 159.

In his informative prose Richardson uses 8 times the auxiliary *do* in questions against 1 instance where this auxiliary was not used (a frequency of 88.8%). In his epistolary prose he uses in the same context type 19 times the auxiliary *do* against 8 instances where the auxiliary was not used (a frequency of 70%). Cf. Tieken-Boon van Ostade, *The Auxiliary* do, 132, 161.

For this phenomenon, cf. also, for example, the lexematic examples given by Leech, *Semantics*, 14-5.

[18] See e.g. Hoftijzer, *A Search for Method*, 248 (conclusion 1); J. Hoftijzer, *The Function and Use of the Imperfect Forms with Nun Paragogicum in Classical Hebrew* (SSN, 21) Assen & Maastricht 1985, 94 (conclusion 6).

[19] See Hoftijzer, *A Search for Method*, 245.

[20] This conclusion is not valid for a type of Classical Hebrew such as that found in the Book Ezekiel. Cf. Hoftijzer, *A Search for Method*, 246.

[21] Possibly one can in this connection also refer to a single case of 'deviant' use of the so-called *nun*-paragogicum in Josh. 17:10 in the geographic context Josh. 13-21; on this case, cf. Hoftijzer, *The Function and Use*, 57.

is no clear, more or less generally accepted, system for this type of subdivision of Classical Hebrew prose.[22] But one must constantly be aware of these possibilities.

In their studies García and Tieken have shown that in the work of different, more or less contemporaneous authors, the frequency of interchangeable grammatical forms/constructions and lexemes can vary significantly, even where the same type of context and medium is concerned.[23] Does this fact also justify the reverse conclusion that a significant difference in frequency of this type for different text parts is a probable indication of different (original) authors? In my opinion it does. This would not be so if authors showed a complete freedom in deciding which grammatical element or lexeme to use at any particular moment. But this does not seem to be the case. Let me explain.

In Dutch hypotactic clauses there are two possibilities to place forms of the auxiliary *hebben* (= *to have*), before or after the past participle. So *the book I have read* can be expressed as *het boek dat ik heb gelezen* and as *het boek dat ik gelezen heb*, a clear case of interchangeability. Speaking about this phenomenon Sassen refers to the use of both construction types by the Dutch historian Huizinga. Sassen has counted the instances of both of these types of word order in the works of this author for the years 1906, 1914, 1927, 1943. The use of the second construction type has a frequency of 12.5% in 1906, 18.25% in 1914, 35.5% in 1927 and 48.5% in 1943. Sassen justly concludes that there is an increase in the use of the second construction

---

[22]Zatelli, *Il campo lessicale*, 17 proposes the distinction between poetic language, historical-narrative language and juridic-cultic language. It would be worthwhile to experiment further with this proposal. The circumstance that for many Classical Hebrew texts we do not know much (if anything at all) about the author, or about the type of readers/hearers intended, renders it more difficult for us to make divisions and subdivisions in language levels.

[23]For frequency differences in the use of *sí* and *él* (in the same context type and the same type of text) by different more or less contemporaneous authors, cf. García, *Lingua* 65, 293 table 7. In informative prose Steele uses the auxiliary *do* 6 times in negative sentences against 1 instance where the auxiliary was not used (a frequency of 85.7%). In the same type of prose and context Swift never uses the auxiliary *do* against 9 instances where the auxiliary was not used (a frequency of 0.0%). Cf. Tieken-Boon van Ostade, *The Auxiliary* do, 130. In epistolary prose Addison uses the auxiliary *do* 5 times in negative sentences (with a form of the verb *to know*) against 1 instance where this auxiliary was not used (a frequency of 83.3%). In the same type of prose and context Steele uses 3 times the auxiliary *do* against 6 instances where this auxiliary was not used (a frequency of 33.3%) and Swift uses 4 times the auxiliary *do* against 10 instances where this auxiliary was not used (a frequency of 21.4%). Cf. Tieken-Boon van Ostade, *The Auxiliary* do, 159. This type of example can be multiplied.

type in the historical work of Huizinga during his lifetime.[24] This type of example can easily be multiplied.[25] This picture of increase or decrease in the use of an interchangeable form/construction or lexeme during one's lifetime suggests that at a certain moment of someone's life the frequency in the use of an interchangeable element will, to a certain degree, be fixed, provided we are dealing with the same context type and medium, whatever the reason for such a conditioning may be.[26]

This also means that significant differences in the frequency of this type of word order can be used as an indicator that certain text parts were not written by the same author or at least not by one author at a particular moment in his life. For our specific field, this conclusion is confirmed by what we know of the Books of Chronicles.

It is a well known fact that the Books of Chronicles have a compositional history.[27] In this case a *Vorlage* is known, a text which, though not completely identical, was at least virtually identical with the texts we know from, for example, the Books of Samuel and Kings. When we divide the Books of Chronicles into two parts, those parts which have been borrowed from the *Vorlage* known to us and those parts which have not, but which have been combined with them at a later date, we can observe many of the frequency differences mentioned above. To give an example. The Classical Hebrew lexeme ממלכה

---

[24]Cf. A. Sassen, "Endogeen en exogeen taalgebruik", *De Nieuwe Taalgids* 56 (1963), 10-21 (14).

[25]To give some other examples. One may compare a quite abrupt change in the frequency of these constructions in the prose work of the Dutch author Potgieter, mentioned by Sassen, "Endogeen en exogeen taalgebruik", 14. See also the remarks of I. Tieken-Boon van Ostade, "Do-Support in the Writings of Lady Mary Montagu: A Change in Progress", *Folia Linguistica Historica* 6 (1985), 127-51 (135ff.) about the change in the frequency of the use of the auxiliary *do* in the epistolary prose of Lady Montagu. These examples can be multiplied.

[26]This type of more or less fixed frequency and conditioned use of language at a certain phase of the work of one person (and a possible change in the course of time) must have a cause. Sassen, "Endogeen en exogeen taalgebruik", 14, tries to give an explanation for it in the case of Huizinga. But even if the explanation of the phenomenon escapes us for the moment, the phenomenon itself is undeniable. Because our information about most Biblical authors is scanty (to say the least) it will not be possible to give an explanation for comparable phenomena in Classical Hebrew texts.

[27]Cf. e.g. O. Eissfeldt, *The Old Testament: An Introduction: Including the Apocrypha and Pseudepigrapha and also the Works of Similar Type from Qumran. The History of the Formation of the Old Testament*, transl. P.R. Ackroyd, Oxford 1966, 531ff.; B.S. Childs, *Introduction to the Old Testament as Scripture*, Philadelphia 1979, 645ff.

is over the course of time replaced by the lexeme מלכות.[28] At a certain time they were used interchangeably. So we find in those parts of the Books of Chronicles which have been borrowed from the *Vorlage* mentioned above 4 instances of ממלכה (2 Chr. 9:19; 11:1; 22:10; 25:3)[29] against 4 instances of מלכות (1 Chr. 14:2; 17:11, 14; 2 Chr. 7:18).[30] In the other parts of the Books of Chronicles (added texts and additions in borrowed texts) 11 instances of ממלכה are attested (1 Chr. 29:11; 2 Chr. 13:5, 8; 14:4; 17:5; 21:3, 4; 22:9; 23:20; 29:21; 32:15) against 24 instances of מלכות (1 Chr. 11:10; 12:24; 22:10; 26:31; 28:5, 7; 29:25, 30; 2 Chr. 1:1, 18; 2:11; 3:2; 11:17; 12:1; 15:1, 19; 16:1, 12, 13; 20:30; 29:19; 35:19; 36:20, 22). The difference in frequency of ממלכה in the two parts of the Books of Chronicles is significant: 50% in the borrowed part, 31.4% in the other part. This means that the fact that both parts are not originally from the same author is still reflected in the frequency of the interchangeable lexemes ממלכה and מלכות. This conclusion stands notwithstanding the fact that the redactor has made changes in the text of the *Vorlage*: the 4 instances of מלכות in 1 Chr. 14:2; 17:11, 14; 2 Chr. 7:18 are not attested in the parallel texts in the Books of Samuel and Kings, where forms of ממלכה are attested (cf. respectively 2 Sam. 5:12; 7:12, 16; 1 Kgs. 9:5).[31] This type of examples could be multiplied.[32]

---

[28] On the subject of the replacement of ממלכה by מלכות in the course of time, cf. e.g. Rooker, *Biblical Hebrew*, 56-7.

[29] I did not use here one instance where ממלכה is used, namely 1 Chr. 16:10 (cf. Ps. 105:13), because it stands in a poetic context and not in a prose context as is the case with the other instances.

[30] I have only treated here singular instances of ממלכה and מלכות because, in my opinion, the frequency of the singular of ממלכה in these two types of Chronicler texts is different from that of the plural. For the plural there are no instances attested in the parts borrowed from a *Vorlage* known to us, but in the other parts 6 instances ממלכה occur (1 Chr. 29:30; 2 Chr. 12:8; 17:10; 20:6, 29; 36:23) against none of מלכות. (The only instance where the plural of מלכות is attested in the Hebrew Bible is in Dan. 8:22).

[31] In the parts of the Books of the Chronicles borrowed from a *Vorlage* known to us ממלכה appears in two instances where in the *Vorlage* also a form of the singular of ממלכה is used (2 Chr. 22:10; 25:3; cf. 2 Kgs. 11:1; 14:5). The parallel of 2 Chr. 9:19 (1 Kgs. 10:20) has the plural of ממלכה. In the *Vorlage* of 2 Chr. 11:1 (1 Kgs. 12:21) one finds מלוכה, which is changed into ממלכה. This also proves that the author who composed the text of the Books of Chronicles still used this last-mentioned word. See also in this connection the remarks of J.H. Tigay, "The Stylistic Criterion of Source Criticism in the Light of Ancient Near Eastern and Postbiblical Literature", in: J.H. Tigay (ed.), *Empirical Models for Biblical Criticism*, Philadelphia 1985, 149-73 (150, 172).

[32] One has only to think of the examples given by A. Kropat, *Die Syntax des Autors der Chronik verglichen mit der seiner Quellen: Ein Beitrag zur historischen Syntax des Hebräischen* (BZAW, 16), Leipzig 1909.

The circumstance that a text is preserved which is virtually identical with its *Vorlage*, makes it indisputable that the Books of Chronicles have a compositional history. For other prose texts of the Hebrew Bible the situation is more complex. Although it is often contended for much of this material that there is also a compositional/redactional history, no *Vorlagen* have been preserved which provide the same type of indisputable proof as is given by the *Vorlage* of the Books of Chronicles. Moreover, a comparison of the text of the Books of Chronicles with that of their *Vorlage* must make it clear, that had we not possessed this last-mentioned text, it would have been impossible for us to determine exactly which part of the text belonged to that *Vorlage*, where the redactor had changed its *Wortlaut*, and in what instances this did not happen. This also implies that, if we can prove that other prose texts in the Hebrew Bible also had a compositional/redactional history, it will be impossible to define and describe in all details their whole compositional/redactional process, unless one wants to indulge in sheer speculation. Unfortunately there is much scholarly literature on the subject which does not show the necessary restraint. However, this does not mean that it is undesirable for scholars to ask themselves whether these texts show signs of a compositional history and to which extent this history can be defined and described.[33]

From a linguistic standpoint there are signs that there has been a compositional history. To give an example. In the books of Judges up to and including Kings there is a considerable internal difference in the frequency of the use of the ה-locale with the adverb שׁם with local-terminative function. Thus, in the Eliah-stories שׁמה is never used,

---

[33] On the situation in the scholarly research on this subject, cf. for example R. Alter, *The Art of Biblical Narrative*, New York 1981, 13-4; J.H. Tigay, "Introduction", in: J.H. Tigay (ed.), *Empirical Models for Biblical Criticism*, Philadelphia 1985, 1-20 (2). J.P. Fokkelman, "Is the Literary Approach to the Bible a New Paradigm?", in: E.G.L. Schrijver *et al.* (eds.), *The Literary Analysis of Hebrew Texts: Papers read at a Symposium held at the Juda Palache Institute, University of Amsterdam, 15 February 1990*, Amsterdam 1992, 11-34 (15-6) has drawn the inference from this situation that this type "is doomed to fail". R. Polzin, *Moses and the Deuteronomist: A Literary Study of the Deuteronomic History*, Part 1: Deuteronomy, Joshua, Judges, New York (1980), 13 and Berlin, *Poetics and Interpretation*, 134 are very pessimistic about the results which can be reached by the application of this approach. In my opinion this approach has to be continued, although it is quite possible that the number of reasonably valid results reached may be limited. (See also the remarks of Sternberg, *The Poetics of Biblical Narrative*, 13, 22). Moreover, we have have to distinguish between the indication(s) that a certain text has a compositional/redactional history and the definition and description of this history. Even if this definition and description may turn out to be only possible in a (very) limited way, this does not disprove the first mentioned fact.

against 6 instances of שׁם (0.0%); in the Elisha-stories, however, 9 instances of שׁמה are attested against 2 instances of שׁם (81.8%).[34] This is
a significant difference which clearly points to a compositional history.

A way of looking for possible differences of the above-mentioned
type could also be the provisional use of the outcome of the traditional
source analysis to see whether this idea of a compositional history of,
for example, the Hexateuch can be confirmed by linguistic arguments
or not.[35] Let me give some examples which in my opinion point to a
compositional history of the text.

In the text parts traditionally considered to belong to JE one finds
18 instances where the ה-locale is attached to the noun ארץ, against
no examples where an interchangeable construction with this noun
is used (100%). In the parts considered to be D one finds 1 parallel
instance with ה-locale against 3 examples with an interchangeable
construction (25.0%).[36] In the text traditionally considered to belong
to P no instance of the n-paragogicum is attested, against at least
34 instances where an interchangeable form is used (0.0%). In JE one
finds 17 n-forms against 14 instances where an interchangeable form
has been used and in D 27 n-forms against 27 interchangeable forms.[37]

I shall also give some lexematic semantic examples. There are
various semantic ways to express the idea of 'to be/become angry'. In
the Hexateuch one finds the Qal of חרה + ל, the Qal of חרה with אף
as subject, the Hitpael of the root אנף and the Qal of the root קצף.
Because the instances with the Hitpael of אנף (which play a central
role in this example) have only God as the subject, I shall restrict
myself to instances which speak of the anger of God. In JE one finds
two instances of חרה ל (Gen. 18:30, 32, 13.33%), 13 instances of חרה אף
(Exod. 4:14; 32:10, 11; Num. 11:1, 10, 33; 12:9; 22:22; 25:3; 32:10, 13;
Deut. 31:17; Josh. 7:1, 86.67%), and no instances of the Qal of קצף or
the Hitpael of אנף. In P one finds only two instances of the Qal of קצף

---

[34]Cf. Hoftijzer, *A Search for Method*, 225.

[35]As a provisional basis one could use for example O. Eissfeldt, *Hexateuch-
Synopse: Die Erzählung der fünf Bücher Mose und des Buches Josua mit dem
Anfange des Richterbuches in ihre vier Quellen zerlegt ...*, Leipzig 1922. For a
way to do this, cf. Hoftijzer, *A Search for Method*, 4. I have proposed to take
the texts Num. 33-35 and Josh. 13-21 as a separate part (*siglum* L, not to be
confounded with Eissfeldt's *Laienquelle*). The possibility has to be considered
that one is not dealing here with a special source, but with a text written on a
language level different from that of its context (see above).

[36]Cf. Hoftijzer, *A Search for Method*, 41. There is no comparable material attested from P. The instances of ארץ mentioned here concern only those instances
where ארץ is not a *nomen regens*.

[37]Cf. Hoftijzer, *The Function and Use*, 23ff.

(Lev. 10:6; Num. 16:22) and in D one finds 5 instances of חרה אף (Deut. 6:15; 7:4; 11:17; 29:26; Josh. 23:16, 45.4%), 2 instances of the Qal of קצף (Dt. 1:34; 9:19, 18.2%) and 4 instances of the Hitpael of אנף (Dt. 1:37; 4:21; 9:8, 20, 36.4%). There are significant differences between JE and D (respectively 86.67% and 45.4% for חרה אף and respectively 0.0% and 36.4% for the Hitpael of אנף).[38] Another significant fact is that in P there is only one instance of the personal pronoun אנכי against 130 instances of אני, whereas אנכי is very frequently used in the other parts of the Hexateuch.[39]

It goes without saying that for deciding (in as far as that is possible) which parts of, for example, the Hexateuch could be of the same author/redactor and which parts could be attributed to different authors/redactors, single examples such as those given above are insufficient, they should be seen as –more or less convincing– indicators of a possible compositional/redactional history of the text. A number of these examples used cumulatively are needed before a firm conclusion can be reached.[40] If possible they ought to be combined with potential indications of non-linguistic differences within a text. One cannot avoid the idea that, where this type of indications is concerned, the question "what is a valid indication?" has to be reconsidered.[41]

---

[38] Cf. also M. Weinfeld, *Deuteronomy and the Deuteronomic School*, Oxford 1972, 346.

[39] Cf. Polzin, *Late Biblical Hebrew*, 127-8.

[40] For lists of grammatical constructions and/or lexemes/lexeme strings considered as characteristic for certain texts/sources, cf. Simpson, *The Early Traditions of Israel*, 403ff.; Weinfeld, *Deuteronomy*, 320ff.; H.-D. Hoffmann, *Reform und Reformen; Untersuchungen zu einem Grundthema der deuteronomistischen Geschichtsschreibung*, Zürich 1980, 325ff. One can also refer to the relevant material treated in for example Kropat, *Die Syntax*; Polzin, *Late Biblical Hebrew*; A. Hurvitz, *A Linguistic Study*, and Rooker, *Biblical Hebrew in Transition*. This list does not imply that I agree with every example or conclusion found in these studies. On this subject, cf. also the remarks of Tigay, *Empirical Models*, 170.

In this article I have not discussed the partly related problem of determining whether two texts are written by the same author, cf. e.g. the survey of M.A. Throntveit, "Linguistic Analysis and the Question of Authorship in Chronicles, Ezra and Nehemiah", *VT* 32 (1982), 201-16.

[41] The non-linguistic indications mentioned here are outside the province of this article. For this reason I shall not discuss them here. A reconsideration of the validity of the argumentation used in deciding whether one has to do with such a non-linguistic indication would not be superfluous in my opinion. Thus, for example, the question which type of contradiction makes the decision unavoidable that we are dealing with different sources within one text, ought to be methodologically reconsidered (in this connection, see the remarks of Fokkelman, "A Lie Born of Truth, Too Weak to Contain It: A Structural Reading of 2 Sam. 1-16", in: A.S. van der Woude (ed.), *Prophets, Worship and Theodicy: Studies in Prophetism, Biblical Theology and Structural/Rhetorical Analysis and on the Place of Music*

From the foregoing it will be clear that, in my opinion, it is possible to prove linguistically that certain texts besides the Books of Chronicles have a compositional/redactional history. This means that we are confronted with the next question: "should this conviction have an influence upon one's attitude towards the way a structural description of the complete text is realized, and, if so, which influence?". The answer to this question concerns a subject about which there is no *communis opinio* in the more recent scholarly literature, to say the least. The relevant proposals range from the idea that the definition and description of the structure of a text with a compositional/redactional history is only possible on the basis of the knowledge of this history, to the idea that this structure can be defined and described without any reference to such history, or if so, only as a last resort in extreme circumstances. In between there are those scholars who want both a structural and a compositional/redactional approach to such a text with the understanding that the first approach has priority.[42]

---

in *Worship: Papers read at the Joint British-Dutch Old Testament Conference held at Woudschoten 1982* (OTS, 23), Leiden 1984, 39-55). On this point, cf. also Alter, *The Art*, 21.

[42] One of the most well-known representatives of the opinion that the definition of the structure of a text with a compositional/redactional history is only possible on the basis of the knowledge of this history, is Richter, *Exegese als Literaturwissenschaft*, 68ff., 165ff. Cf. e.g. also K. Koch, *Was ist Formgeschichte?*, 72-3; J. Van Seters, *In Search of History: Historiography in the Ancient World and the Origins of Biblical History*, New Haven & London 1983, 16ff., 51ff.; J.H. Tigay, "Summary and Conclusions", in: J.H. Tigay (ed.), *Empirical Models for Biblical Criticism*, Philadelphia 1985, 239-41 (241). Needless to say the approach of these authors to the problem shows considerable differences among them.

For authors who adhere to the idea that the structure of a text (also if it has a compositional/redactional history) can (normally) be defined and described without any reference to such history, cf. for example Berlin, *Poetics and Interpretation*, 111-112, 122-123; L.M. Eslinger, *Kingship of God in Crisis; A Close Reading of 1 Samuel 1-12*, Sheffield 1985, 36ff.; Fokkelman, *JEOL* 30, 134ff.; Fokkelman, *The Literary Analysis*, 11ff.; E.J. van Wolde, *A Semiotic Analysis of Genesis 2-3: A Semiotic Theory and Method of Analysis applied to the Story of the Garden of Eden* (SSN, 25), Assen & Maastricht 1989, 3ff. Eslinger is one of those authors who want to fall back on compositional/redactional history as a last resort (Eslinger, *Kingship of God in Crisis*, 38-9). Needless to say that the approach of these authors to the problem can show considerable variety too.

An author who stands in the middle ground is Talstra, *Solomon's Prayer*. His opinion is that one "needs to analyze a text twice" (Talstra, *Solomon's Prayer*, 20). One has to analyze it on a synchronic level (this means one has to analyze the structure of the text itself) and on a diachronic level, with the understanding that the first-mentioned approach has priority (cf. for example Talstra, *Solomon's Prayer*, 81-82, 257, 261-262). In his study the first-mentioned approach is executed first (Talstra, *Solomon's Prayer*, 83ff.), the second one only subsequently (Talstra, *Solomon's Prayer*, 171ff.). Talstra's approach corresponds to that of the

It goes without saying that any answer I shall give, will only be a partial one, because I am speaking only about the linguistic side of the problem and shall leave the possible non-linguistic aspects out.

In the foregoing I have spoken of the language as such, and I have also spoken of different levels in the language which are dependent on who the speaker/author is, on who is the hearer/reader and on the medium used. In the last instance we came into the field of sociolects.[43] But we have gone further. In trying to decide whether parts from a text were by the same author or by different ones, we have occupied ourselves with the question which linguistic pecularities are typical of *one* author, in other words with the problem of idiolects.[44] I came to the conclusion that in his choice between interchangeable forms/constructions or lexemes an author is more or less conditioned, although this choice may be influenced by the medium used and the hearer he has in mind. (In the last mentioned case one has to do with an idiolect within a sociolect.) In those instances where we are dealing with indications that parts of a text are by different authors, we find in such a text more than one idiolect. A text which is written by one author during a certain phase of his life will be written in his more or less conditioned idiolect and this will show its own internal coherence. Such a type of coherence is absent in a text where one finds more than one idiolect. This conclusion means that for the definition and description of the structure of a text one cannot avoid the linguistic indications of a compositional/redactional history, unless one wants simply to ignore certain facts. A situation which, in my opinion, would be less than desirable. This also means that I partly disagree with Talstra, *Solomon's Prayer*, (1993), 264 when he speaks of the " 'linguistic layer' of the text" which (in a synchronic approach)

---

preceding group of scholars in that their approach to the description of the text's structure is not (essentially) influenced by the outcome of the study of the text's possible compositional/redactional history. With the method of Talstra one may compare the remarks made by Polzin, *Moses and the Deuteronomist*, who says that both methods of analyzing the text have "a complementary relationship" (Polzin, *Moses and the Deuteronomist*, 2), but the literary analysis of the text itself has priority with him ("not in rank, but only in operation", cf. Polzin, *Moses and the Deuteronomist*, 6).

[43]With the term 'sociolects' I indicate in this study the different synchronic language levels the grammatical and lexematic structures of which are dependent on who speaks/writes to/for whom and on what is the medium used.

[44]Talstra, *Solomon's Prayer*, 19 says that linguists "tend to reduce the linguistic data to the general langue". This is true about much linguistic work. However, this description is not the right one for the way I have approached the problem (the description of idiolectic features). This approach could be more suitable for the description of single (literary) texts.

is the "real object of study". Such a layer exists in as far as the parts
of the text reflect the same language/sociolect phase, but does not
exist on the idiolectic level.

There are, however, other sides to this problem. The linguistic
distinction of idiolects as described above, is based on significantly
different frequencies in the use of interchangeable elements. We have
to be aware, however, that not every grammatical form/construction
or lexeme is interchangeable.[45] To give only a few lexematic examples.
In prose at least, lexemes such as אב, אם, כלב, and the Qal of הרה
are not interchangeable. Moreover, two different idiolects need show
significant differences on every point where interchangeability is
possible. To give one example. In the prose parts of Ezekiel one finds 4
instances in which the ה-locale is attached to שם with locative function
against 43 instances where this is not the case. In the parts of the
Books of Chronicles not borrowed from a *Vorlage* known to us we find
1 corresponding instance with ה-locale against 17 instances without
this ending. There is no significant difference between both idiolects
on this specific point.[46] So, the number of significant differences of
the above mentioned type between two idiolects can as such be quite
divergent.[47] This means that, speaking about the absence of internal
linguistic coherence (as meant above) it is better to speak of grades
of absence and not to describe this absence (necessarily) in absolute
terms.[48]

It goes without saying that the internal coherence within a text is
not only dependent on linguistic factors, there are many factors which
contribute to it.[49] A clear example are the Books of Chronicles. It

---

[45]For this approach, cf. already Hurvitz, *A Linguistic Study*, 14, who provides
lexematic examples different from those given by me.

[46]Cf. Hoftijzer, *A Search for Method*, 143. There is a difference in percentages
(respectively 8.5% and 5.55%), but this difference cannot be considered significant.

[47]Moreover a redactor can have more or less adapted on certain points the
language of an older text which he uses to his own use of language. Cf. for example
n. 31.

[48]This does not essentially change my conclusion, that if one finds in a text signs
of two or more idiolects, the text does not show a complete internal coherence
on the linguistic level. This remains also true, if there are only few indications of
such a difference.

[49]The discussion of the non-linguistic factors which contribute to the internal structure of a text lies outside the framework of this study. For an interesting
proposal for the description of all factors (organized in different levels), cf. Fokkelman, *Prophets, Worship and Theodicy*, 53-4; J.P. Fokkelman, *Narrative Art and
Poetry in the Books of Samuel: A Full Interpretation Based on Stylistic and Structural Analyses*, vol. 2, The Crossing Fates (1 Sam. 13-31 & 2 Sam. 1) (SSN, 23),
Assen & Maastricht, 4ff. The different levels described by Richter, *Exegese als*

cannot be denied that they have a compositional/redactional history. On the other hand, their great internal coherence cannot be refuted.[50] The conclusion must be that there are many factors which determine an internal structural coherence, the linguistic factor is only one of them. Moreover, it is not necessary for a text to have an absolute coherence on all levels (in our case on the linguistic level), to show a strong internal coherence. A too absolute and one-sided use of terms such as 'unity', 'holistic', etc., must not make us blind to this truth.[51]

Literaturwissenschaft, 31, 80 are of a more methodological nature.

[50] For the internal cohesion of the Books of Chronicles (notwithstanding the fact that it has a compositional/redactional history), cf. also Fokkelman, *The Literary Analysis*, 16.

[51] There is a great danger that in speaking about the cohesion and coherence of texts one uses a terminology which (unwittingly) implies that no real cohesion/coherence is possible unless it is a cohesion/coherence that exists in every factor on all levels and that it is impossible that there is real cohesion/coherence in any other way. Cf. for example Berlin, *Poetics and Interpretation*, 117 who says: "What is the status of the present text, is it fundamentally a unity or is its unity *artificial*?" (my italics); R. Polzin, *Samuel and the Deuteronomist: A Literary Study of the Deuteronomic History*, Part two: 1 Samuel, San Francisco & New York, etc. 1989, 10-1 speaking about the '*real* text' against the '*pre-text*' (my italics); Fokkelman, *The Literary Analysis*, 19: "a literary artefact is a *monument* not a document. It ... deserves to have its *full* say" (my italics); Talstra, *Solomon's Prayer*, 21 who (in his synchronic approach) considers the text a "*unique creation* which it is", "as a unity, as a meaningful whole to which *all* textual elements contribute" (my italics). The possibility is not considered here that there can be a strong cohesion/coherence in a text without all factors on every level being involved. Neither is the possibility considered that an author in composing a text in such a way that there is no cohesion/coherence on every point still does creative work (cf. also Richter, *Exegese als Literaturwissenschaft*, 114; Polzin, *Moses and the Deuteronomist*, 17; Tigay, *Empirical Models*, 240-1). In my opinion these possibilities have to be considered seriously and it would be worthwhile to describe the ways in which a real cohesion/coherence could be attained. I agree with A. Rofé, "Joshua 20: Historico-Literary Criticism Illustrated", in: J.H. Tigay (ed.), *Empirical Models for Biblical Criticism*, Philadelphia 1985, 131-47 (134), who warns against seeing all texts as "hermetic units formed by single authors". Cf. also Tigay, *Empirical Models*, 151 who says that "since the message a redactor wished to convey was usually not impaired by differences in vocabulary, formulas and style these were normally left untouched".

There is also the attitude described by Clines and Exum, "The New Literary Criticism", 11-25 (11) which sees the text as "an object, a product, not as a window upon historical actuality". This is a view in which it is (unwittingly) implied that knowledge of the text's history can have no value whatever for the description of the present text, there being no discussion possible on the relevant point.

It goes without saying that what one expects of the structure of a text with (or without) a compositional/redactional history in the world of the Hebrew Bible may be completely different from historical reality. See in this connection the

Hopefully this study will contribute to the discussion on the relation between redactional/compositional and structural approaches to
Classical Hebrew texts. I have tried to show that linguistics can contribute to it and how this may be done. This contribution can only
be a partial one. Not only because language structure and linguistics
are merely some of the factors that determine the discussion. But because we must always be aware that our competence in the Classical
Hebrew language can never be on the level (and in my opinion is often
far below the level) of the original native speakers. The circumstance
that we are dealing in our relatively small corpus with texts from
different periods and language levels and with a variety of context
types can only add to this problem. It goes without saying that this
competence problem does not only exist on the language level and
that in our endeavour to give an as complete as possible structural
description and definition of Classical Hebrew texts we will always be
hampered by this fact.[52]

---

interesting suggestions of Van Seters, *In Search of History*, 16ff., 51ff.

[52] Cf. J. Hoftijzer, "Überlegungen zum System der Stammesmodifikationen im
klassischen Hebräisch", *ZAH* 5 (1992), 117-34 (131). Cf. also nn. 7, 22 of the
present article. Fokkelman, *The Literary Analysis*, 13 sees the danger that in
underlining these facts one makes the Hebrew Bible "a remote body of texts".
There is the danger of the student being "prone to despair" and being "inclined
to find the text more obscure than is necessary". I agree that all exaggeration
must be avoided, but I still find it necessary that every student has a realistic
view on the situation and that he/she knows the limits of what we, on the basis
of the material preserved, can reasonably know.

Paul M. Joyce   *Oxford – United Kingdom*

Synchronic and Diachronic Perspectives on Ezekiel

The distinction between synchronic and diachronic perspectives has become commonplace in biblical studies over recent years, but it goes back, of course, much further than its currency in these circles. It was the great Swiss scholar Ferdinand de Saussure (1857–1913), generally regarded as the founder of modern linguistics, who first established the distinction.[1] His major work was reconstructed (just how faithfully is disputed) from the lecture-notes of his students after his death; it is quite an irony then that conferences should be devoted to this theme more than three quarters of a century later.

The work of Saussure marked the shift from traditional philology to modern linguistics. Up until his time the study of these matters was predominantly historical or evolutionary, tracing the origin and development of words through time (hence the term 'diachronic'). It was characteristically concerned with ancient written languages (often studied comparatively), and the tendency was to be prescriptive, attempting to distil and codify standard forms. Modern linguistics since Saussure, on the other hand, has been more concerned with the static (or, better, 'synchronic') picture; it has aimed to describe actual usage and practice in all its diversity, rather than presuming to prescribe. Saussure gave priority to synchronic linguistics: one must, he argued, adopt the user's point of view (rather than that of the antiquarian) if one is to understand language as a coherently organized structure. Structure is a key word here, for it is important to acknowledge the structuralist nature of Saussure's work: for him, language was about the structural relations between words. The linguistic sign does not exist independently of a complex system of contrasts; being intrinsically arbitrary rather than having an inherent meaning, the linguistic sign can be identified only by contrast with coexisting signs of the same nature, which together constitute a structured system of language.

Typically, modern linguistics has concerned itself overwhelmingly with living, spoken languages, but many of its insights can be and have been applied to the study of ancient languages and literatures. Thus it is that synchronic studies of the Hebrew Bible have found a place over

---

[1]F. de Saussure, *Cours de linguistique générale*, Paris 1916. Eng. Tr.: *Course in General Linguistics*, eds. C. Bally & A. Sechehaye, London 1983, 79-98. See J. Lyons, *Introduction to Theoretical Linguistics*, Cambridge 1968, 38-52.

recent decades. All too often biblical scholars have been rather slow in taking on board the insights of other disciplines, and even then they have frequently done so in a piecemeal fashion and in a somewhat diluted form. This has certainly been the case, for the most part, of structuralism in general,[2] and it is also true, in large measure, of the adaptation of the language of synchrony and diachrony. In biblical studies, the words 'synchronic' and 'diachronic' have tended to be used without all their broader connotations being in view, primarily in relation to questions concerning the unity and analysis of texts. The typical contrast has, of course, been between studies which attempt to trace the development of texts through time (diachronic) and those which deal with texts as holistic units (synchronic).

Whilst today we tend to think of diachronic approaches yielding the stage to synchronic ones, in the longer term of course synchronic readings of Ezekiel preceded diachronic analysis. Although one can observe isolated diachronic elements even in some rabbinic exegesis,[3] in general traditional readings, both Jewish and Christian, are characterized by synchronic assumptions. The rise of historical biblical criticism, in the wake of the Reformation and the Enlightenment, brought a readiness to ask questions about the unity of texts and about their development. However, it was for a long time widely believed that the book of Ezekiel was largely free of the kind of problems of unity and authorship which had been recognized by modern scholars in the case of the other major prophetic books. The distinctively orderly appearance of Ezekiel, with its thematic sections, was an important factor in sustaining this view. R. Smend wrote: "The whole book is ... the logical development of a series of ideas in accordance with a well thought-out, and in part quite schematic, plan. We cannot remove any part without disturbing the whole structure".[4] In the case of Isaiah and Jeremiah, modern scholars acknowledged at a relatively early date that certain parts of the books might well be from hands other than those of the prophets after whom they were named. However, matters seemed rather different with regard to the book of Ezekiel. Gunkel was able to describe Ezekiel as "the first prophet who wrote a book"[5] and G.B. Gray could write that "No other book of the Old Testament is distinguished by such decisive marks of unity of

---

[2]See J. Barton, *Reading the Old Testament: Method in Biblical Study*, London 1984, 121-39.

[3]E.g. Rashi's commentary (11th century CE) in *Mikra'ot Gedolot*, Lublin 1911.

[4]R. Smend, *Der Prophet Ezechiel* (KEH), 2nd ed., Leipzig 1880, xxi.

[5]H. Gunkel, "Die israelitische Literatur", in: P. Hinneberg (ed.), *Die Kultur der Gegenwart*, Berlin & Leipzig 1906, 90.

authorship and integrity as this".[6]

However, this scholarly consensus was not to remain unchallenged. There were hints of an alternative approach already in the works of R. Kraetzschmar[7] and J. Herrmann.[8] But it was Gustav Hölscher who in 1924 first articulated a more critical view of the unity of the book of Ezekiel.[9] He proposed that only one seventh of the book actually came from the prophet; the bulk he attributed to a Zadokite redactor in Jerusalem in the early fifth century. Hölscher's work marked an important turning-point in the history of Ezekiel scholarship: the unity and integrity of the book could never again be taken for granted. A decade or so later G.A. Cooke, though himself relatively conservative on such questions, had to acknowledge that Ezekiel studies had undergone "something like a revolution ... It is no longer possible to treat the Book as the product of a single mind and a single age".[10] Hölscher opened the way for others to embark on the difficult task of attempting to distinguish between those parts of the book which could with some certainty be traced back to the prophet himself and those which should be regarded as secondary additions.

A range of criteria has been employed in the diachronic study of Ezekiel. The distinction between prose and poetry has played an important part, indeed this had a major role in Hölscher's analysis, prose in general being regarded as secondary. The occurrence of apparently priestly vocabulary has been another widely-employed indicator of secondary material, albeit a complex one, given that Ezekiel is himself presented as a priest. The similar but distinct criterion of apparently deuteronomistic vocabulary should also be mentioned here. Repetition and alleged redundancy have been seen as evidence of later hands (e.g. by Wevers). Consistency of grammar and motif have also played their part, and textual criticism has been important too in the exploration of the editorial process, as for example in the work of Johan Lust.[11] One of the most difficult criteria to apply is that of consistency of theological content; for example, a number of schol-

---

[6]G.B. Gray, *A Critical Introduction to the Old Testament*, London 1913, 198.

[7]R. Kraetzschmar, *Das Buch Ezechiel* (HK), Göttingen 1900.

[8]J. Herrmann, *Ezechielstudien* (BWANT), Leipzig 1908.

[9]G. Hölscher, *Hesekiel, der Dichter und das Buch* (BZAW, 39), Giessen 1924.

[10]G.A. Cooke, *A Critical and Exegetical Commentary on the Book of Ezekiel* (ICC), Edinburgh 1936, preface, v.

[11]J. Lust, "The Use of Textual Witnesses for the Establishment of the Text: The Shorter and Longer Texts of Ezekiel, An Example: Ez 7", and "The Final Text and Textual Criticism: Ez 39,28", in: J. Lust (ed.), *Ezekiel and his Book: Textual and Literary Criticism and their Interrelation* (BETL, 74), Leuven 1986, 7-20 and 48-54.

ars have judged as secondary some of the more optimistic passages
in the book (such as 17:22-24) on the ground, in part at least, that
they are alleged to be inconsistent with the prophet's own theology.
Here as more generally, it is very problematic to decide what really
does constitute evidence of secondary addition. The danger of built-
in assumptions dictating results is all too evident, especially where
theology is involved. As with the discussion of any prophetic book,
an important safeguard has been to draw upon a broad range of evidence, employing, where possible, different criteria side by side, but
even then the quest for 'assured results' in the diachronic study of
Ezekiel has been a frustrating one.[12]

A distinctive feature of the book of Ezekiel made things especially difficult. For this book has proved notoriously resistant to any
straightforward division between primary and secondary material.
The particular complexity of questions of unity and authorship in
the book of Ezekiel is owed especially to the marked homogeneity of
the Ezekiel tradition, in which secondary material (even where it can
be identified) bears an ususually close 'family resemblance' to primary. Such a situation has often been contrasted with that in Isaiah
and Jeremiah, where (rightly or wrongly) the distinctions between
primary and secondary material have often been judged to be more
clear-cut.

Some examples will help illustrate the phenomenon which we have
called the homogeneity of the Ezekiel tradition. In Ezekiel there is often real difficulty in discerning whether a certain distinctive feature
is a characteristic of the prophet Ezekiel himself or of some subsequent stage in the tradition. For example, are repetitions the result
of accretions or do they represent an important feature of Ezekiel's
own style? Wevers has characteristically sought to trim the text,[13]
whereas Boadt regards such repetition as one of the distinctive features of the prophet himself.[14] Such questions do not permit of a
straightforward solution; answers may often be of the 'both/and' variety. We may well here be dealing with genuine features of the words
of the prophet Ezekiel which have nevertheless been heightened in
the course of redaction, and so have become more characteristic of
the finished book than of the primary material. Another example of
this phenomenon is provided by the priestly affinities of much of the

---

[12]For a fuller discussion of criteria, see P.M. Joyce, *Divine Initiative and Human
Response in Ezekiel* (JSOT.S, 51), Sheffield 1989, 22-7.

[13]J.W. Wevers, *Ezekiel* (NCeB), London 1969.

[14]L. Boadt, "Textual Problems in Ezekiel and Poetic Analysis of Paired Words",
JBL 97 (1978), 489-99.

material: there seems little reason to doubt the witness of the book that Ezekiel was himself a priest and one would therefore expect his own style to reflect this; on the other hand, such features may well have been heightened in the course of transmission.

There had emerged something of a consensus position by the 1960s, according to which much material in Ezekiel was judged to be from the prophet or his immediate disciples, but the book was acknowledged to be the product of a long tradition. Such a position was represented by, for example, Fohrer[15] and Eichrodt,[16] and – above all – by Zimmerli, whose work will long remain a major landmark in Ezekiel studies.[17] Zimmerli developed the theory of an Ezekiel 'School' and posited a long process of accretion and redaction. For Zimmerli the 'School' hypothesis served to explain the marked homogeneity of the Ezekiel tradition. For all the additions and elaborations, the process is essentially one of continuity, for in Zimmerli's view the complex redactional history nevertheless "preserves for us on the whole the peculiar characteristics of the prophet".[18] And so we could describe this critical consensus as in many respects a conservative one.

The homogeneous nature of the Ezekiel tradition has been the key determining factor in the shaping of Ezekiel studies over recent years, much depending on how scholars react to this phenomenon. Many of those who have chosen to pursue the diachronic quest have felt the need to resort to increasingly refined stratification of the book, reconstructing its redactional history in minute detail. The work of J. Garscha affords a good example of this approach, and its appearance in 1974 was symptomatic of the breakdown of the critical consensus described above. Garscha attributed only about 30 verses of the entire book to Ezekiel himself (17:2-10, the riddle of the two eagles and the vine, and 23:2-25, the story of the two sisters, Oholah and Oholibah).[19] He believed that the basic structure of the book and its uniformity of style are the result of the work of a redactor active either in about 485 or in about 460. Garscha went on to discern a layer for which he used the term 'Deutero-Ezekiel'. This he dated between 400 and 350; it is marked by a sharp polemic against the non-exiles

---

[15]G. Fohrer (with K. Galling), *Ezechiel* (HAT, 13), Tübingen 1955.

[16]W. Eichrodt, *Der Prophet Hesekiel* (ATD, 22), 3rd ed., Göttingen 1968; Eng. Tr.: *Ezekiel* (OTL), London 1970.

[17]W. Zimmerli, *Ezechiel* (BK, 13), 2 vols, 2nd ed., Neukirchen-Vluyn 1979; Eng. Tr.: *Ezekiel 1*, Philadelphia 1979; *Ezekiel 2*, Philadelphia 1983.

[18]W. Zimmerli, "The Special Form- and Traditio-Historical Character of Ezekiel", *VT* 15 (1965), 515.

[19]J. Garscha, *Studien zum Ezechielbuch: Eine redaktionskritische Untersuchung von Ez 1–39* (Europäische Hochschulschriften, 23/23), Bern & Frankfurt 1974.

and by the use of the formula "You shall know that I am Yahweh" and its variants. Next (that is, fourth), he isolated a 'Sacral law stratum', from around 300, and to this he assigned the bulk of the priestly language of the book. Even later than this fourth stage, a range of further elements were added, the book being completed in about 200 BCE. One cannot help feeling that Garscha's stratifications have to be so minutely detailed (if they are to have any plausibility at all) precisely because there is no clear-cut distinction between the style and theology of Ezekiel and those who followed him.

H. Schulz, whose major work appeared a little earlier, in 1969,[20] represents a rather similar radical attempt at stratification. We see the diachronic nature of these approaches clearly in the tendency of Schulz and Garscha to make a sharp distinction between the prophetic and the priestly, in marked contrast to the tendency of many earlier scholars to see the integration of the prophetic and the priestly as one of the distinctive features of Ezekiel himself. Schulz and Garscha each assign the priestly material to a secondary stratum. It may be acknowledged that this represents one coherent way of dealing with this tension within Ezekiel; it is, however, less encouraging when one discovers that each of the two scholars assigns the priestly material to a different stratum and a different period! Comparable theses discerning numerous layers within the text have been presented over recent decades by many others, including H. Simian,[21] F.L. Hossfeld[22] and G. Bettenzoli.[23] We see these diachronic concerns still very much alive and well today in the work of, for example, K.-F. Pohlmann.[24]

All of these scholars claim to discern late material in the book of Ezekiel. And so we might reasonably locate at the far end of this scholarly spectrum the extreme views of those such as C.C. Torrey,[25] J. Smith,[26] and, much more recently, J. Becker.[27] These scholars trace

---

[20]H. Schulz, *Das Todesrecht im Alten Testament* (BZAW, 114), Berlin 1969.

[21]H. Simian, *Die theologische Nachgeschichte der Prophetie Ezechiels: Form- und traditions-kritische Untersuchung zu Ez. 6; 35 ; 36* (FzB, 14), Würzburg 1974.

[22]F.L. Hossfeld, *Untersuchungen zu Komposition und Theologie des Ezechielbuches* (FzB, 20), 2nd ed., Würzburg 1983.

[23]G. Bettenzoli, *Geist der Heiligkeit: Traditionsgeschichtliche Untersuchung des QDŠ-Begriffes im Buch Ezechiel* (QuSem, 8), Florence 1979.

[24]K.-F. Pohlmann, *Ezechielstudien: Zur Redaktionsgeschichte des Buches und zur Frage nach den ältesten Texten* (BZAW, 202), Berlin & New York 1992.

[25]C.C. Torrey, *Pseudo-Ezekiel and the Original Prophecy*, New Haven 1930.

[26]J. Smith, *The Book of the Prophet Ezekiel: A New Interpretation*, London 1931.

[27]J. Becker, "Erwägungen zur ezechielischen Frage", in: L. Ruppert, P. Weimar and E. Zenger (eds.), *Künder des Wortes: Fs J. Schreiner*, Würzburg 1982, 137-

no material at all to a historical Ezekiel living in the early sixth century, but rather, in their varying ways, judge the book to be a pseude-pigraphical work from the second temple period. But, paradoxically, at this extreme of late dating theories we encounter approaches to Ezekiel which in some respects share features of synchronic readings - of which more in a moment.[28]

The Ezekiel Colloquium in Leuven in 1985, under the direction of Johan Lust, provided an invaluable opportunity for taking stock of the state of scholarly discussion on these matters, and the collected papers of that gathering provide an important resource.[29] Already, alongside much refinement of the diachronic task, we find contributions working, in their various ways, towards a very different, synchronic approach to the problems of the book of Ezekiel, wishing to analyse the text in its present form rather than speculate about possible earlier forms or posit a hypothetical history of the development of the text. This position is by no means necessarily a flight to naïve conservatism; its proponents are generally skilled in the use of historical methods but believe them no longer adequate to the task. M. Greenberg's contribution combines features of rabbinic scholarship and the influence of literary studies.[30] His 'holistic' approach, developed at length in his commentary,[31] could be described as a conservative or even agnostic approach to diachronic analysis rather than a fully developed synchronic approach, but there are important synchronic features to his position. He writes: "There is only one way that gives any hope of eliciting the innate conventions and literary formations of a piece of ancient literature, and that is by listening to it patiently and humbly".[32] Greenberg deduces that the book is "the product of art and intelligent design ... A consistent trend of thought expressed in a distinctive style has emerged, giving the impression of an individual mind of powerful and passionate proclivities".[33] There is an interesting irony here, related to the phenomenon of homogeneity described earlier: the very feature of Ezekiel which led others to

---

49; J. Becker, "Ez 8-11 als einheitliche Komposition in einem pseudepigraphischen Ezechielbuch", in: J. Lust (ed.), *Ezekiel and his Book: Textual and Literary Criticism and their Interrelation* (BETL, 74), Leuven 1986, 136-50.

[28] Most scholars who have favoured the theory of a late pseudepigraphical work have posited a unified piece of writing.

[29] The volume was cited in notes 11 and 27.

[30] M. Greenberg, "What Are Valid Criteria for Determining Inauthentic Matter in Ezekiel?", in: J. Lust (ed.), *Ezekiel and his Book*, 123-35.

[31] M. Greenberg, *Ezekiel 1-20* (AncB, 22), Garden City 1983.

[32] Greenberg, *Ezekiel 1-20*, 21.

[33] Greenberg, *Ezekiel 1-20*, 26.

stratify the text ever more finely has led Greenberg to abandon the quest for layers altogether. Indeed, it is what we have called the 'family resemblance' between primary and allegedly secondary material in Ezekiel which leads Greenberg to espouse his 'holistic' interpretation.

One can quite see why scepticism about the diachronic task has grown in many quarters. As Muilenburg pointed out many years ago, the very variety of the conclusions arrived at by the more radical scholars of Ezekiel is itself sufficient to counsel greater caution with regard to such attempts at stratification.[34] Consider, for example, the confusion caused by Schulz and Garscha each using the term 'Deutero-Ezekiel' of different strata within the book! Their excesses have done much to give the diachronic enterprise a bad name. However, not all features of the reaction to this are entirely healthy either. It was suggested earlier that synchronic reading by no means necessarily represents a flight to naïve conservatism. However, one has to be wary of an implicit assumption on Greenberg's part of Ezekiel's authorship of the book as a whole. His position all too easily slides from a healthy agnosticism about editorial layers into an attribution of authorship to the prophet himself. He writes: "The assumption grows on one as piece after piece falls into the established patterns and ideas that a coherent world of vision is emerging, contemporary with the sixth-century prophet and decisively shaped by him, if not the very words of the prophet himself".[35] This assumption is never fully explored or defended directly, it is simply implied with the help of some seductive rhetoric, calculated, it would seem, to tempt those who think it would be nice if Ezekiel wrote the whole book himself after all.

A major catalyst in the development of synchronic readings of Ezekiel has been the impact of literary studies in English, French, Italian and other modern languages. Synchronic concerns characterize the work of Lawrence Boadt, who reflects the influence of rhetorical criticism; he has done much to show that features (such as repetition and apparent redundancy) which many have regarded as lending weight to diachronic theories are often more plausibly explained as features of rhetorical skill. Boadt certainly establishes very effectively the methodological principle that even a scholar given to diachronic analysis should not resort to such hypotheses before other possibilities have been fully tested.[36] Mention should also be made in this con-

---

[34] J. Muilenburg, "Ezekiel", in: M. Black & H.H. Rowley (eds.), *Peake's Commentary on the Bible*, London & Edinburgh 1962, 569.

[35] Greenberg, *Ezekiel 1-20*, 27.

[36] L. Boadt, "Rhetorical Strategies in Ezekiel's Oracles of Judgment", in: J. Lust (ed.), *Ezekiel and his Book*, 182-200. Similar concerns mark Boadt's other

text of the symbolic-structuralist reading of Ezekiel offered by Marco Nobile[37] and also the semiotic approach of Nicholas J. Tromp.[38] All three of these contributed to the 1985 Leuven Colloquium and the subsequent volume, as well as publishing important studies elsewhere. Also of importance have been the structural studies of H. Van Dyke Parunak.[39]

There is now a wide range of contributions to the study of Ezekiel from literary, feminist, psychological and other perspectives, many of them emerging from North America, including the work of Julie Galambush, who draws upon literary, feminist and psychological insights in her stimulating treatment of the city of Jerusalem as Yahweh's wife, whilst giving very little attention to questions about the history of the text. She locates herself and her work among "a number of scholars" who "have reasserted the substantial literary unity of Ezekiel, and have therefore been free to focus on (among other aspects) Ezekiel's literary style".[40]

Carol A. Newsom provides a most perceptive reading of Ezekiel's oracles against Tyre within the conventions of literary criticism. Her primary dialogue partners are those literary critics who have explored the nature of metaphor. She concludes that "Analysis of the rhetoric of metaphor is an essential part of critical exegetical method".[41] Questions concerning possible secondary additions to the oracles are acknowledged briefly in a couple of footnotes; otherwise Newsom seems to assume Ezekiel as the creative author, and speaks not only of Ezekiel's rhetorical strategies but even at one point - with apparent comfort - of Ezekiel's "purpose".[42] Reference should be made here to the work of the late Fokkelein Van Dijk-Hemmes. In her essay on "The Metaphorization of Woman in Prophetic Speech",[43] she takes

---

published contributions on Ezekiel, e.g. "Textual Problems in Ezekiel and Poetic Analysis of Paired Words", *JBL* 97 (1978), 489-99.

[37] M. Nobile, *Una lettura simbolico-strutturalistica di Ezechiele*, Rome 1982.

[38] N.J. Tromp, "The Paradox of Ezekiel's Prophetic Mission: Towards a Semiotic Approach of Ezekiel 3, 22-27", in: J. Lust (ed.), *Ezekiel and his Book*, 201-13.

[39] H. Van Dyke Parunak, *Structural Studies in Ezekiel*, PhD Dissertation, Harvard University 1978; "The Literary Architecture of Ezekiel's Mar'ot Elohim", *JBL* 99 (1980), 61-74.

[40] J. Galambush, *Jerusalem in the Book of Ezekiel: The City as Yahweh's Wife* (SBL.DS, 130), Atlanta, Georgia 1992, 16.

[41] C.A. Newsom, "A Maker of Metaphors: Ezekiel's Oracles Against Tyre", *Interp.* 38 (1984), 151-64. Reprinted in J.L. Mays, P.J. Achtemeier (eds.), *Interpreting the Prophets*, Philadelphia 1987, 188-99.

[42] Newsom, "A Maker of Metaphors", *Interpreting the Prophets*, 195.

[43] F. van Dijk-Hemmes, "The Metaphorization of Woman in Prophetic Speech: An Analysis of Ezekiel xxiii", *VT* 43 (1993), 162-70. Another version appears in:

Carol Newsom's article as her point of departure for an analysis of
Ezekiel 23. She brings a radical feminist critique to bear, exposing
what she describes as the "androcentric-pornographic character of
this metaphorical language". She is more thoroughgoingly synchronic
in her approach than Newsom, writing, for example, that: "The literary strategy deployed in the text appears to be successful".[44] She
does, however, add a diachronic note, considering the possibility that
if the final verses of chapter 23 are secondary (as some have judged),
then they may reflect the response of male readers. She refers here
especially to the words of 23:48 ("...so that all women may take
warning"), which narrow the condemnation of the nation to focus
specifically upon women. This would be an interesting case of reader
response incorporated into a text!

David J. Halperin presents a psychological interpretation of Ezekiel. His recent book, *Seeking Ezekiel: Text and Psychology*, represents
something of a paradox. For his is a reductionistic work of psychoanal-
ysis (all theology is reinterpreted in psychoanalytical terms), which
is nevertheless based on a conservative approach to the text which
amounts to a holistic or synchronic reading of the book as a unified body of evidence for the prophet's inner mental life.[45] Halperin
is reluctant ever to countenance textual emendations and he resists
proposals to reorder the text or to stratify it into "primary" or "secondary" levels. But here we have a synchronic reading which has
apparently learned nothing from literary studies: in using the text
rather crudely as a historical source, Halperin fails completely to do
justice to it as literature. It is vital to acknowledge that prophetic
texts are literary artefacts, and not to make naïve historical assumptions about them. To take an example from what might be described
as the mainstream of Ezekiel studies rather than their margins, Zimmerli attached great importance to the speeches in the first person
which characterize the book, taking this feature as suggesting at least
the probability that they derive in large part from the prophet himself, albeit couched in traditional language.[46] Terence Collins, on the
other hand, has rightly argued that we should not in any simplistic

A. Brenner, F. van Dijk-Hemmes (eds.), *On Gendering Texts: Female and Male
Voices in the Hebrew Bible* (Biblical Interpretation series, 1), Leiden 1993, 167-76.

[44]Van Dijk-Hemmes, "The Metaphorization of Woman", *VT* 43 (1993), 167.

[45]D.J. Halperin, *Seeking Ezekiel: Text and Psychology*, University Park, Penn-
sylvania 1993. For further discussion of Halperin's work, see P.M. Joyce, "Reading
the Bible within the Public Domain", in: F.M. Young (ed.), *Can we Speak of God
in Public? The Cadbury Lectures 1994*, London 1995.

[46]W. Zimmerli, "The Special Form- and Traditio-Historical Character of
Ezekiel", *VT* 15 (1965), 516.

way regard these as straightforward reports of personal experiences. They have clearly been "worked on" and he shows from comparative literary studies that the use of an artificial first person singular was as well known to the ancients as it is to modern novelists.[47]

It is important to understand that synchronic readings frequently represent much more than mere conservatism or agnosticism about the diachronic task. For some a synchronic or holistic approach amounts to a reading strategy, which need in no way rest upon historical judgements about how our text became our text. Such thoroughgoing synchronic styles of reading most often characterize those from or most heavily influenced by the world of non-biblical literary studies, of whom Gabriel Josipovici may be cited as an example.[48]

A special case cannot go unmentioned in our review of synchronic studies, namely the canonical approach of Brevard Childs.[49] His position shares much with literary approaches, but is part of a bold theological project with far-reaching implications (which cannot be explored here). In practice, Childs' handling of Ezekiel is essentially synchronic. Even though he acknowledges a long process of collection and shaping, he criticizes Zimmerli for resting "his interpretation on a critically reconstructed pre-canonical form of the book".[50] "To divide a passage historically into stages often destroys the synchronic dimension of the text", he argues, "A literary entity has an integrity of its own which is not to be identified with the sum of its parts. Zimmerli's method is vulnerable to the criticism of mishandling the text as literature".[51]

It is time to take stock. It seems to me that we have to do justice to two things. The book of Ezekiel has its integrity as a work of literature read synchronically, and an approach to the book which fails to do justice to this and to learn from the wealth of recent studies of this kind would be sadly impoverished. And yet we must also take seriously the evidence of redactional activity which is to be discerned within the book of Ezekiel. The diachronic task is difficult but that does not mean that it is impossible, or that it is invalid. The fact that consensus is rarely achieved rightly makes one all the more aware of the partial nature of our evidence and of the subjective nature of

---

[47]T. Collins, *The Mantle of Elijah: The Redaction Criticism of the Prophetical Books* (The Biblical Seminar, 20), Sheffield 1993, 156.

[48]G. Josipovici, *The Book of God: A Response to the Bible*, New Haven & London 1988.

[49]B.S. Childs, *Introduction to the Old Testament as Scripture*, Philadelphia & London 1979.

[50]Childs, *Introduction to the Old Testament as Scripture*, 360.

[51]Childs, *Introduction to the Old Testament as Scripture*, 370.

our judgements. But this calls for a sober and modest recognition of constraints, not a pessimistic retreat from or casual abandonment of such a task.

As Collins puts it, "We can say that the book Ezekiel is characterized at one and the same time by both literary unity and literary complexity".[52] Here we again encounter the homogeneity of this tradition, which seems to me to be the key to our problem. Redactional material has kept close to what went before, both in style and in content. An analogy may help here. In a city or village of historical and architectural importance, the local authorities may decree that all new building should be at least coherent with the old, indeed it may be stipulated that the very same building materials be used, whether granite or Cotswold Stone. Modern additions may reflect many new needs and technological developments, but an unmistakable 'family resemblance' unites the architecture. In some cases one can never be absolutely sure how much goes right back to the earliest times; indeed sometimes a 'classic' status may be achieved by something which is in reality a relatively late stylized version. So with the book of Ezekiel, there is much evidence to suggest a tenacious continuity of tradition, with regard both to content and to style. Although the completed book results from a long and complex history, I believe that it probably reflects much of the prophet Ezekiel and his teaching; and yet one must beware the easy assumption and (for some, at least) attractive idea that one is dealing with the very words of the prophet. One may often have to be content with a proper agnosticism about this. Because of the distinctive continuity which characterizes both the book of Ezekiel and the tradition which stands behind it, it is essential to employ both diachronic and synchronic tools in its study.

But what is to be said about the relationship between diachronic and synchronic approaches? Must one not opt for one, and reject the other? I suggest not. Provided that different approaches are distinguished carefully and not confused, much of value is to be learned from both diachronic and synchronic approaches to the book of Ezekiel. The work of Mark Brett has made a clear case for careful methodological pluralism in biblical studies, within which a range of strategies

---

[52]T. Collins, *The Mantle of Elijah*, 91. Whilst valuing much in Collins' presentation, I do not share his view that Ezekiel himself can plausibly be described as "an author in the modern sense of the word" and "the pioneer of the new post-exilic genre 'the prophetical book'" (*op.cit.*, 93-4). His position here is comparable with that adopted by E.F. Davis in her: *Swallowing the Scroll: Textuality and the Dynamics of Discourse in Ezekiel's Prophecy* (JSOT.S,78; Bible and Literature Series, 21), Sheffield 1989.

may be seen as serving distinct but (potentially) equally legitimate interpretative interests.[53] It is vital to maintain distinctions clearly. Saussure was absolutely insistent upon this: "The contrast between the two points of view – synchronic and diachronic – is absolute and admits no compromise".[54] And again, "In studying a language from either point of view, it is of the utmost importance to assign each fact to its appropriate sphere, and not to confuse the two methods".[55] Within the context of biblical studies such clarity is equally important. This said, I favour an equality between these distinct tasks. It was part of Saussure's polemical thesis to give priority to synchronic linguistics, but I wish to assign an equal place to diachronic and synchronic tasks within biblical studies. To value one thing need not always be to diminish another. We can ask – and learn from – both kinds of question.

Eep Talstra has done valuable detailed work in considering how one may combine a synchronic with a diachronic approach to 1 Kings 8.[56] Within Ezekiel studies, Gordon Matties has explicitly adopted an eclectic or pluralist method, favouring a synchronic analysis, while recognizing the possibility of diachronic development: "Perhaps we can combine a holistic approach (Greenberg) with an awareness of a complex process of formation (Zimmerli)", he writes, and again, "The literary-historical study of chap. 18 will provide the necessary diachronic facets in a study which might otherwise tend toward the synchronic".[57] It is not clear to me that Matties has fully worked through the implications of his pluralist method, but the attempt is to be welcomed.

A clearly articulated pluralism can be wonderfully liberating. One is freed of the danger of the misunderstanding that by valuing one thing one is necessarily rejecting another. I for one do not share Walter Wink's famous judgement that "historical biblical criticism is bankrupt".[58] I wish to retain a place for historical concerns, al-

---

[53]M.G. Brett, *Biblical Criticism in Crisis?*, Cambridge 1991, especially 5-6, 11-26. See also M.G. Brett, "Four or Five Things to do with Texts: A Taxonomy of Interpretative Interests", in: D.J.A. Clines, S.E. Fowl and S.E. Porter (eds.), *The Bible in Three Dimensions* (JSOT.S, 87), Sheffield 1990, 357-77.

[54]F. de Saussure, *Cours de linguistique générale*, Paris 1916. Eng. Tr.: *Course in General Linguistics*, eds. C. Bally & A. Sechehaye, London 1983, 83.

[55]F. de Saussure, *Course in General Linguistics*, London 1983, 98.

[56]E. Talstra, *Solomon's Prayer: Synchrony and Diachrony in the Composition of 1 Kings 8, 14-61* (Contributions to Biblical Exegesis and Theology, 3), Kampen 1993.

[57]G.H. Matties, *Ezekiel 18 and the Rhetoric of Moral Discourse* (SBL.DS, 126), Atlanta, Georgia 1990, 4-5.

[58]W. Wink, *The Bible in Human Transformation: Towards a New Paradigm*

beit a carefully circumscribed place.[59] But once that is clearly understood, I can be freed to explore all kinds of exciting ways of reading
the text of Ezekiel, including some far removed from the familiar
shores of the diachronic approach, and perhaps even some imaginative flights of fancy reading the text of Ezekiel synchronically in the
light of Postmodernism.[60] The ancient tradition of Merkabah mys-
ticism provides plenty of stimulus for such liberated reading, whilst
from a very modern source the allusions to the same Ezekiel 1 chariot
imagery in the cinema film *Close Encounters of the Third Kind* offer
further encouragement. The history of interpretation (understood in
the broadest sense) provides much other food for thought too – including the remarkable scene conjured by William Blake in his *The
Marriage of Heaven and Hell*, where the prophets Isaiah and Ezekiel
join the author for dinner!

In summary, let us at every point be as clear as possible about
what we are doing in interpretation, but – that said – let a thousand
blooms flourish.

---

for Biblical Study, Philadelphia 1973, 1.

[59] P.M. Joyce, "First Among Equals? The Historical-Critical Approach in the
Marketplace of Methods", in: S.E. Porter, P.M. Joyce and D.E. Orton (eds.),
*Crossing the Boundaries: Essays in Biblical Interpretation in Honour of Michael
D. Goulder*, Leiden 1994, 17-27.

[60] Cf. W. Brueggemann, *The Bible and Postmodern Imagination: Texts under
Negotiation*, London 1993; M. Sarup, *An Introductory Guide to Post-Structuralism
and Postmodernism*, 2nd ed., New York & London, etc. 1993.

Edward Noort *Groningen – The Netherlands*

'Land' in the Deuteronomistic Tradition
Genesis 15: The Historical and Theological Necessity of a Diachronic Approach[1]

1. General remarks

Diachronic approaches have a bad name outside the specific historical questions in modern exegesis. Both methods and results are under heavy fire from many sides. The classical historical-critical approach has lost a lot of its reputation and even in the heartland of diachronic exegesis, protestant Germany, new and other voices can be heard. On the other hand many synchronic victories were not won by better positive arguments or by a better and convincing exegesis but by demonstrating the weakness of the diachronic positions, mostly as they were held in the beginning of the century.

Therefore I will now have a look at some developments inside the field of historical-critical exegesis.[2] What disappeared and which new questions arose?

– First the automatism of dating by absolute chronology has disappeared. It was not so long ago that we knew the exact date of the Jahwist[3], where to locate the Elohist[4], and when we still believed in

---

[1] Paper read as an introduction to a workshop during the Joint Meeting.

[2] H.J. Kraus, *Geschichte der historisch-kritischen Erforschung des Alten Testaments*, Neukirchen & Vluyn ³1982; R. Smend, *Deutsche Alttestamentler in drei Jahrhunderten*, Göttingen 1989; R. Smend, *Epochen der Bibelkritik*, (Gesammelte Studien 3; BEvTh, 109), München 1991; D.A. Knight, G.M. Tucker (eds.), *The Hebrew Bible and Its Modern Interpreters*, Philadelphia 1985; C. Houtman, *Inleiding in de Pentateuch: Een beschrijving van de geschiedenis van het onderzoek naar het ontstaan en de compositie van de eerste vijf boeken van het Oude Testament met een terugblik en een evaluatie*, Kampen 1980 = C. Houtman, *Der Pentateuch: Die Geschichte seiner Erforschung neben einer Auswertung* (CBET, 9), Kampen 1994; A. de Pury, *Le Pentateuque en question: Les origines et la composition des cinq premiers livres de la Bible à la lumière des recherches récentes*, Genève 1989.

[3] Traditional: W.H. Schmidt, *Einführung in das Alte Testament*, Berlin & New York ⁴1989. Careful: R. Smend, *Die Entstehung des Alten Testaments*, Stuttgart & Berlin, etc. 1978, 86-94.

[4] H. Klein, "Ort und Zeit des Elohisten", *EvTh* (37) 1977, 247-72. More careful: R. Smend, *Die Entstehung des Alten Testaments*, Stuttgart & Berlin, etc. 1978, 82-6 (Die elohistischen Fragmente [sic!]); O. Kaiser, *Grundriß der Einleitung in die kanonischen und deuterokanonischen Schriften des Alten Testaments*, Bd. 1: Die erzählenden Werke, Gütersloh 1992, 70-7.

one deuteronomistic author[5] it was not difficult to date him in the exilic period. The single scholar who dared to speak of a pre-exilic Priestly Code received a friendly smile but was not taken seriously.[6] All that has now changed. The existence of an Elohist corpus was already questioned in the thirties.[7] In the sixties and seventies the date of the Jahwist was lowered[8] and the Deuteronomistic History was split up into redaction levels or blocks.[9]

[5]M. Noth, *Überlieferungsgeschichtliche Studien*, Bd. 1: Die sammelnden und bearbeitenden Geschichtswerke im Alten Testament, Halle 1943, 3-110; E. Jenni, "Zwei Jahrzehnte Forschung an den Büchern Josua bis Könige", *ThR* (27) 1961, 1-32, 97-146; A.N. Radjawane, "Das deuteronomistische Geschichtswerk", *ThR* (38) 1974, 177-216.

[6]Y. Kaufmann, *The Religion of Israel: From Its Beginnings to the Babylonian Exile*, transl. M. Greenberg, Chicago 1960, 175-200; Th.M. Krapf, *Die Priesterschrift und die vorexilische Zeit: Yehezkel Kaufmanns vernachlässigter Beitrag zur Geschichte der biblischen Religion* (OBO, 119), Freiburg & Zürich 1992.

[7]P.Volz, W. Rudolph, *Der Elohist als Erzähler – ein Irrweg der Pentateuchkritik?* (BZAW, 63), Berlin 1933; W. Rudolph, *Der "Elohist" von Exodus bis Josua* (BZAW, 68), Berlin 1938.

[8]H.H. Schmid, *Der sogenannte Jahwist: Beobachtungen und Fragen zur Pentateuchforschung*, Zürich 1976; M. Rose, *Deuteronomist and Jahwist: Untersuchungen zu den Berührungspunkten beider Literaturwerke* (AThANT, 67), Zürich 1981; O. Kaiser, *Grundriß*, Bd. 1, 63-70; C. Levin, *Der Jahwist* (FRLANT, 157), Göttingen 1993; J. van Seters, *Prologue to History: The Yahwist as Historian in Genesis*, Louisville & Zürich 1992; J. van Seters, *The Life of Moses: The Yahwist as Historian in Exodus-Numbers* (CBET, 10), Kampen 1994.

[9]R. Smend, "Das Gesetz und die Völker: Ein Beitrag zur deuteronomistischen Redaktionsgeschichte", in: *Probleme biblischer Theologie*, Fs. G. von Rad, München 1971, 494-509; W. Dietrich, *Prophetie und Geschichte* (FRLANT, 108), Göttingen 1972; T. Veijola, *Die ewige Dynastie: David und die Entstehung seiner Dynastie nach der deuteronomistischen Darstellung* (AASF, 193), Helsinki 1975; T. Veijola, *Das Königtum in der Beurteilung der deuteronomistischen Historiographie: Eine redaktionsgeschichtliche Untersuchung* (AASF, 198), Helsinki 1977; T. Veijola, *Verheißung in der Krise: Studien zur Literatur und Theologie der Exilszeit anhand des 89. Psalms* (AASF, 220), Helsinki 1982; W. Roth, "Deuteronomistisches Geschichtswerk, Deuteronomistische Schule", in: *TRE*, Bd. 7/4.5, Berlin 1981, 543-52; F.M. Cross, *Canaanite Myth and Hebrew Epic*, Cambridge & Mass. 1973, 274-89; R.E. Friedman, *The Exile and Biblical Narrative: The Formation of the Deuteronomistic and Priestly Works* (HSM, 22), Chico 1981; R.D. Nelson, *The Double Redaction of the Deuteronomistic History* (JSOT.S, 18), Sheffield 1981; B. Peckham, *The Composition of the Deuteronomistic History* (HSM, 35), Atlanta 1985; A.D.H. Mayes, *The Story of Israel between Settlement and Exile: A Redactional Study of the Deuteronomistic History*, London 1983; H. Weippert, "Das deuteronomistische Geschichtswerk: Sein Ziel und Ende in der neueren Forschung", in: *ThR* (50) 1985, 213-49; M.A. O'Brien, *The Deuteronomistic History Hypothesis: A Reassessment* (OBO, 92), Freiburg & Göttingen 1989; H.D. Preuß, "Zum deuteronomistischen Geschichtswerk", *ThR* (58) 1993, 229-64, 341-95.

The character of the Priestly Code – redaction or source – was challenged and the dating now ranges from the pre-exilic and exilic to the post-exilic period.[10]

The general tendency is to lower dates. In addition to the field of Old Testament exegesis we also have a good seismograph in the 'genre' 'History of Israel'. Israelite historiography was always based on interpretations of the text. The 'Histories of Israel', therefore, usually mirrored contemporary exegesis. This is illustrated by J. Bright who still let Israelite history begin with the 'Age of the Patriarchs' in the beginning of the second millennium[11], whereas Soggin began his Israelite history only in the time of the kings.[12] A similar picture can be given of the latest attempts to understand the Old Testament as a Hellenistic book. It is charming to note that also some academic positions have been completely reversed. Forty years ago, in the discussion about the early history of Israel, the positions of M. Noth and A. Alt were called 'nihilistic' by W.F. Albright, G.E. Wright and J. Bright[13], whereas only recently Alt's last assistant, the German scholar and historian S. Herrmann, criticized the new views about the settlement period proposed by N.K. Gottwald[14], N.P. Lemche[15] and C.H.J. de Geus[16] in the very same way. He would probably pass

---

[10]F.M. Cross, *Canaanite Myth*, 293-325; S. Tengström, *Die Toledotformel und die literarische Struktur der priesterlichen Erweiterungsschicht im Pentateuch* (CB.OT, 17), Uppsala 1981; J.L. Ska, "La place d'Ex. 6:2-8 dans la narration de l'exode", *ZAW* 94 (1982), 530-48; A. Hurvitz, *A Linguistic Study of the Relationship Between the Priestly Source and the Book of Ezekiel: A New Approach to an Old Problem* (CRB, 20), Paris 1982; R. Rendtorff, *Das Alte Testament: Eine Einführung*, Neukirchen 1983, 146ff.; E. Zenger, *Gottes Bogen in den Wolken: Untersuchungen zu Komposition und Theologie der priesterschriftlichen Urgeschichte* (SBS, 112), Stuttgart 1983, 27-49; A. Hurvitz, "Dating the Priestly Source in Light of the Historical Study of Biblical Hebrew A Century after Wellhausen", *BZAW* 100 (1988), 88-100.

[11]J. Bright, *A History of Israel*, London ³1981, 67-87.

[12]J.A. Soggin, *A History of Israel: From the Beginnings to the Bar Kochba Revolt AD 135*, London 1984, 41ff.; J.A. Soggin, *Einführung in die Geschichte Israels und Judas: Von den Ursprungen bis zum Aufstand Bar Kochbas*, Darmstadt 1991 (problem-orientated).

[13]See the samples collected by M. Noth, "Der Beitrag der Archäologie zur Geschichte Israels", in: M. Noth, *Aufsätze zur biblischen Landes– und Altertumskunde*, Bd. 1: Archäologische, exegetische und topographische Untersuchungen zur Geschichte Israels, Neukirchen-Vluyn 1971, 33-51 (35, n.2).

[14]N.K.Gottwald, *The Tribes of Yahweh: A Sociology of the Religion of Liberated Israel, 1250-1050 B.C.E.*, Maryknoll & New York 1979.

[15]N.P. Lemche, *Early Israel: Anthropological and Historical Studies on the Israelite Society Before the Monarchy* (SVTP, 38), Leiden 1985.

[16]C.H.J. de Geus, *The Tribes of Israel: An Investigation into Some of the Presuppositions of Martin Noth's Amphictyony Hypothesis* (SSN, 18), Assen 1976.

the same judgement, if not even a more severe one, on the new books
of T.L. Thompson[17] and Davies.[18] In this way old frontiers were broken through and new ones emerged.

Clearly absolute chronology has become a weapon which should
be used only very carefully. The automatic dating of a text by showing
its belonging to a particular group or school no longer works. In many
ways we find ourselves at a new startingpoint again.

This does not mean that the tool of relative chronology has to be
abandoned. Theology in the Old Testament, the meaning of smaller
and larger units, is often found in the background of a reaction to
former texts. We all know the famous example of Jes. 19:25b where
the MT reads: "Blessed be my people Egypt, Assyria my creation
and Israel my heritage", but the LXX translates: "εὐλογημένος ὁ λαός
μου ὁ ἐν Αἰγύπτῳ καὶ ὁ ἐν Ασσυρίοις καὶ ἡ κληρονομία μου Ισραηλ.".
In the translation the meaning of MT has been turned upside down
by adding only two prepositions. In the LXX it is the blessed Israel
which was in Egypt and was exiled to the Assyrians instead of the
blessing of Egypt itself and Assyria itself in the MT.[19] In this case
we know about this radical change because we have the two versions
in different languages. It would be very strange though, if we would
be unable to detect this kind of processes within the Hebrew text
itself. We do have the phenomenon of "Fortschreibung" in the Old
Testament. Texts have a history and looking for a relative chronology
within that history helps to understand the process in which texts
were actualized in a new context.

– Secondly, within the historical-critical exegesis the support of
classical source-criticism is crumbling. Because of their specific language and themes, the separation of the Priestly Code[20] and deuteronomistic texts[21] experienced the greatest acceptance. But even in
those sources there is no agreement about the beginning of the Deu-

---

[17]T.L. Thompson, *The Early History of the Israelite People: From the written
and archaeological sources* (SHANE, 4), Leiden 1992.

[18]Ph.R. Davies, *In Search of 'Ancient Israel'* (JSOT.S, 148), Sheffield 1992.

[19]The same translation technique was employed by the Targum and the Peshitta
on this verse, cf. P. Churgin, *Targum Jonathan to the Prophets*, Baltimore 1928,
99; L. Smolar, M. Aberbach, *Studies in Targum Jonathan to the Prophets*, New
York & Baltimore 1983, 327.

[20]S.E. McEvenue, *The Narrative Style of the Priestly Writer* (AnBib, 50), Rome
1971

[21]M.Weinfeld, *Deuteronomy and the Deuteronomic School*, Oxford 1972;
E.Talstra, *Het gebed van Salomo: Synchronie en diachronie in de kompositie van
I Kon. 8,14-61*, Amsterdam 1987.

teronomistic History up till now.[22] and the end of the Priestly Code.[23]
Moreover, every text which does not belong to these two corpora cannot that easily be assigned to either a Jahwist or Elohist or JE group,
since the old criteria are no longer valid. On the other hand, however,
it has proved to be possible to understand the expansion of the Pentateuch in a diachronic way without falling back on the old boundaries
of the classical sources.[24]

– A third change concerns the criteria for looking at the texts. In the
classical historical-critical exegesis, the student was trained to make
observations about the (dis)unity of the text. He had to look for dou-
blets, discrepancies, antitheses, changes of subject etc.[25] Here too we
have learned to be more careful with the criteria. A better understanding and a better knowledge of Ancient Near Eastern literature
suggests that a lot of irregularities were not as irregular as many exegetes always thought. Synthetic analysis showed the possibility of a
unity despite signals of disunity. In many cases it seemed possible to
separate some parts from each other, but the possibility of linking
them as a redactional layer to form greater unities could be proved
only a few times. For instance, R. Smend and his pupils started to
analyze different layers within the Deuteronomistic History,[26] but it
soon became clear that the presupposed nomistic Redactor (DtrN)
could not be only one author because the materials attributed to him
differed too much. In this case a choice has to be made. The first possibility is to maintain a strict vocabulary and a limited field of thoughts.
The result will be to accept X other deuteronomistic nomists. The second possibility is to accept the differences within one group, but this
entails the loss of the newly postulated criteria.[27] Thisproblem is not

---

[22]Houtman, *Inleiding in de Pentateuch*, 247f.

[23]L.Perlitt, "Priesterschrift in Deuteronomium?", *BZAW* 100 (1988), 65-88 ;
E.Aurelius, *Der Fürbitter Israels: Eine Studie zum Mosebild im Alten Testament*
(CB.OT, 27), Stockholm 1988.

[24]E.Blum, *Die Komposition der Vätergeschichte* (WMANT, 57), Neukirchen-
Vluyn 1984; idem , *Studien zur Komposition des Pentateuch* (BZAW, 189), Berlin
& New York 1990; idem, "Israël à la montagne de Dieu: Remarques sur Ex 19-24;
32-4 et sur le contexte littéraire et historique de sa composition", in: A. de Pury,
Le Pentateuque, 271-95, 297-300.

[25]O.H. Steck, *Exegese des Alten Testaments: Leitfaden der Methodik. Ein
Arbeitsbuch fur Proseminare, Seminare und Vorlesungen*, Neukirchen & Vluyn
[12]1989, 52ff.

[26]R. Smend, "Das Gesetz und die Völker"; W. Dietrich, *Prophetie und
Geschichte*; T. Veijola, *op. cit.*

[27]R. Smend, *op. cit.*, 123ff.

only limited to diachronic exegesis, but I admit that it is a serious one in our field.

– A fourth change refers to a new emphasis on redaction-criticism. The aim of explaining the text is no longer to reach the oldest stage, where the 'real text arises', but to understand why and how texts grew together into their canonical shape, i.e. to understand texts as a grown unity and to trace their reactions to their own tradition.

2. Land with the Deuteronomists and the Priestly Writers

When we now return to the title of the subject of our study group: " 'Land' in the Deuteronom(ist)ic Tradition: Genesis 15: The Historicial and Theological Necessity of a Diachronic Approach", we realize that this title is of course itself a thesis. To begin with, the use of the word 'land' implies a theology of the land of Israel in the deuteronomic/deuteronomistic traditions.[28] A land that can be found on a map, a land with boundaries, towns, roads and people. Land in the vison of the Deuteronomist does not only mean space as such, but a space rooted in the soil of Palestine.

The second assumption is that there exists something like a deuteronomic/deuteronomistic tradition about the land, while the third one assumes that at least in some of its parts Gen. 15 has something to do with it. And last but not least, the two adjectives to 'necessity' in the subtitle demonstrate that these texts and their traditions are rooted in history and theology. In no part of the tradition thinking about the land was noncommittal. It always was connected with political circumstances, the economic frame, and geographical conditions. 'Theological' means that we can negate only at our own cost the processes and the various opinions in the struggle of thinking about the land in the different parts of history. But to ask questions in such a way presumes the existence of different opinions concerning the land. Do we have such a starting point for a diachronic quest?

---

[28]P. Diepold, *Israels Land* (BWANT, 95), Stuttgart 1972; G.C. Macholz, *Israel und das Land: Vorarbeiten zu einem Vergleich zwischen Priesterschrift und deuteronomistischem Geschichtswerk*, Diss. habil. Heidelberg 1969; W. Brueggemann, *The Land: Place as Gift, Promise and Challenge in Biblical Faith* (OvBTh, 1), Philadelphia 1977; A. Ohler, *Israel, Volk und Land: Zur Geschichte der wechselseitigen Beziehung*, Stuttgart 1979; W.D. Davies, *The Territorial Dimension of Judaism*, Los Angeles & London 1982. More Literature: E. Noort, *Een plek om te zijn: Over de theologie van het land aan de hand van Jozua 8:30-35*, Kampen 1993, 26f., n. 30.

Maybe we can start with two extremes: the deuteronomic/deuteronomistic texts at one side and the late post-exilic prophecy at the other. In the deuteronom(ist)ic texts the promised land has boundaries. These boundaries differ at several stages and in several parts of the textunits. In general the promised land is the land west of the Jordan.[29] Sometimes Transjordan is included too in the concept[30] and only a few texts dream of 'Euphratic' Israel.[31] Those boundaries and the size of the land they implicate may be idealistic, they may represent the country which is endangered by the threat of the occupying military powers in the seventh and sixth century, they may be a blue print for a return to the land after the exile – and all these positions have their own right –, but the land (with the exception of 'Euphratic' Israel) is concrete. From the endangering of the country in the seventh century in the deuteronomic tradition to the reflection about the loss of the land in the deuteronomistic parts a concrete place is meant. We may differ with the Deuteronomists about the reality of their concepts, but they speak of a land they can map!

In the late post-exilic prophecy a change can be observed.[32] Isa. 27:9-11 speaks about the destruction of the holy city, the town which is hostile to YHWH: "... the fortified city is abandoned now, it lies deserted, forsaken as a wilderness ... " This hostile, punished town will not be restored as in Isa. 1:21-26, but a heavenly, eternal Jerusalem will appear[33]: "A strong city is given to us, his redemption he has set as a wall and a rampart about us."[34] Jerusalem on earth is transformed into a heavenly city, and the land, which after the exile can be called the holy land[35] becomes the symbol for the whole world. These voices understand the land as a symbol for the suffering, guilty world and their eschatological hope is the delivered land as a symbol for the delivered world, the whole creation.[36] So the understanding of אֶרֶץ in the meaning of land disappears behind the wideness of אֶרֶץ in the meaning of world. Nowhere can this change be better seen than in the reflection of this view in Jewish-Hellenistic texts. For example in Testamentum Iobi Job speaks to his friends: "Be silent ... ἐμοὶ δὲ ὁ θρόνος ὑπάρχει ἐν τῇ ἁγίᾳ γῇ ... for ... ἐμοι δὲ ἡ βασιλεία εἰς αἰῶνας

---

[29]Deut. 12:10; Josh. 3 & 4, etc.

[30]Deut. 4:45-49.

[31]Gen. 15:18; Ex. 23:31; Deut. 1:7, 11:24; Josh. 1:3f.

[32]R. Hanhart, "Das Land in der spätnachexilischen Prophetie", in: G. Strecker (ed.), *Das Land Israel in biblischer Zeit* (GTA, 25), Göttingen 1983, 126-40.

[33]R. Hanhart, "Das Land", 130.

[34]Isa. 26:1.

[35]Zech. 2:16.

[36]R. Hanhart, "Das Land", 131.

αἰώνων is given."[37] This heavenly holy land of Job is identified with the βασιλεία, the Kingdom of God.[38]

So we have two different views, both closely connected with the challenges of their time. Real land and land as a symbol. But they are not only opposing each other. The connecting factor between the two is the law. Where law and land correlate, as happens in the deutero-nomic/deuteronomistic tradition, the development of the tradition reaches a point where the codification of the law and the change of the prophetical voice to a congregation gathered around the written Torah opens up the possibility of spiritualizing the land.[39]

The first example showed something about the changes caused by the challenges in different times, but such differences can also be discovered in groups of texts which react to each other more directly.

In the deuteronomic texts land and covenant are connected. But this covenant which opens the way into the land regulates the life of Israel in the promised land in several ways. The promise of the land and the settlement there are linked with the stipulations of the covenant. But differences can be observed here too. Some texts for-mulate the commands following the fact of entering and settling in the land: "Now these are the laws and customs that you must keep and observe, in the land that YHWH the God of your fathers has granted you to possess, for as long as you live in that land."[40] But it is necessary to look very closely here. Early deuteronomic theology was aware of the fact that the land was endangered. Therefore their interest was in the promises to the patriarchs. This theology knows many formulas of God giving the land. And here the law comes into view. Living according that law shall show Israel's gratitude to their God who keeps his oath. So Deut. 6:10ff. opens: "When YHWH has brought you into the land which he swore to your fathers Abraham, Isaac and Jacob that he would give you, with great and prosperous cities not of your building, houses full of good things not furnished by you, wells you did not dig, vineyards and olives you did not plant, when you have eaten this and had your fill, then take care you do not forget YHWH who brought you out of the land of Egypt, out of the house of slavery." This is original deuteronomic thinking. The bless-ings and the gifts are central. YHWH will bring his people into the land and they will rejoice the gifts of the land. What is asked of Israel

---

[37] Test. Iobi 33:5, 9.
[38] R. Hanhart, "Das Land", 136.
[39] Noort, *Een plek om te zijn*, 19ff.
[40] Deut. 12:1.

is 'not to forget'. But the gift of the land and enjoying living there is not put into question.[41]

The later deuteronomistic authors were not able to speak in the same way. They experienced the loss of the land but did not want to give up speaking of God keeping his promises now formulated as an oath to the fathers. Now the gift of the land becomes conditional, as in the same chapter Deut. 6:17 illustrates: "Keep the commandments of YHWH your God and his decrees and laws that he has laid down for you and do what is right and good in the eyes of YHWH so that you may prosper and take possession of the rich land which YHWH swore to give to your fathers." Keeping the law here is the only possibility to enter the land. Keeping the law is put in between the promise of YHWH and taking possession of the land. Or in the words of Perlitt: "Landbesitz (ist) nicht mehr Erfüllung von Verheißung, sondern Lohn für die Erfüllung von Gebot. Damit ist das Land zu einer Funktion des Gesetzes geworden. Ohne Gesetzesgehorsam kommt man jetzt nicht nur aus dem Lande wieder heraus, sondern gar nicht erst in das Land hinein."[42] In this new relationship between Torah and land, the thinking about the covenant changes: ברית becomes conditional too. Not only in the deuteronomistic parts of Deuteronomy and the Early Prophets, but also in the deuteronomistic Jeremiah 'to obey the law' can be synonymous with 'to obey the covenant'. So Jer. 11:6 reads: "Listen to the words of this covenant and obey them!" This line of deuteronomistic thinking comes to an end with the famous words of the new covenant, Jer. 31:33, "But this is the covenant which I will make with the house of Israel after those days, says YHWH: I will put my law within them, and I will write it upon their hearts; and I will be their God and they shall be my people." The connection between covenant and law is maintained. Without the law there will be no life. But YHWH himself will be the guarantee that man cannot fail. The law will be written in man's heart. So even the great promise of the new covenant confirms the importance of the law. As we go back to the deuteronomistic texts where the authors tried to find a way between the believed fidelity of God and the reality of the lost land, we observe that they opted for a choice, in which the land became a function of the law, became the space where Torah could be lived and where without Torah there would be no land. So land and the possession of land became a standard for the way in which Israel lived with the Torah.

---

[41]L. Perlitt, "Motive und Schichten der Landtheologie im Deuteronomium", in: G. Strecker (ed.), *Das Land Israel*, 46-58 (55).

[42]L. Perlitt, "Motive und Schichten ", 54.

Let us now have a short look at another opinion about the land, the covenant and the law than occurs in the deuteronomic/deuteronomistic way of thinking.

The covenant at Sinai, described in Ex. 24, became so important to later Israel, that during the growth of traditions any important law had to be given at Sinai and received by Moses. In the same way everybody who became important in the early history of Israel afterwards grew into a position of having been present at Sinai. Suddenly Joshua appears as the servant of Moses in Ex. 24:13 and climbs the mountain with him. This contradicts Ex. 24:1 where only Aaron, Nadab and Abihu (and the seventy elders) are allowed to come with Moses. But Joshua's presence here is quite understandable. The successor of Moses cannot be missed at Sinai. So we have some glimpses of the importance of the covenant at Sinai.

But when we ask whether and in which way the Priestly Code is represented here, we only have the verses 15-18 at our disposal: Moses climbing the mountain, the six days of waiting and the call of God at the seventh day, the presence of God in his כבוד, the fire on the top of the mountain. Here the whole terminology speaking about the presence of God in the priestly tradition is visible. But only here. This is remarkable, because the Priestly Code emphasizes the points where in its view of history a covenant is concluded: after the flood the covenant with Noah[43] and in Gen. 27 the one with Abraham. It would indeed then be remarkable, if a covenant at Sinai was missing in the priestly tradition. W. Zimmerli, who noticed this[44] suggested, that it was a knowing omission showing something of the theology of the Priestly Code. His arguments were the promissional, unconditional character of the Abraham covenant in Gen. 17 and, more importantly, the character of Ex. 25ff., which also belongs to the Priestly Code. Everything here focusses on the presence of God in the sanctuary. No laws how to live in the promised land, with the exception of the law of the Sabbath[45] and a short communication of handing out the "tables of testimony, inscribed by the finger of God".[46] No communication at all about making a covenant appears here. The central figure is the promise of God to dwell among Israel: "And they shall build me a sanctuary (מקדש) so that I may dwell (שכן)

---

[43] Gen. 9:8ff.

[44] W. Zimmerli, "Sinaibund und Abrahambund: Ein Beitrag zum Verständnis der Priesterschrift", in: W. Zimmerli, *Gottes Offenbarung: Gesammelte Aufsätze* (TB, 19), München 1963, 205-16.

[45] Ex. 31:12-17.

[46] Ex. 31:18.

among them."[47] The structural connections of this central promise can be seen at two points in the Priestly Code. At first this promise at Sinai is the fulfillment of the covenant of Gen. 17 between God and Abraham: "I will give to you and to your descendants after you the land you are living in, the whole land of Canaan, to own in perpetuity, and I will be your God." This means that the Priestly Code needs no new covenant at Sinai. At Sinai Israel is still standing in the covenant of promise with Abraham,[48] and this promise will be fullfilled after the building of the sanctuary.

The second point is the importance of this promise in the whole structure of the Priestly Code. There is not only a connection with the covenant with Abraham, but first and foremost with the priestly story about creation, blessing and Flood.[49] The building of the sanctuary[50] and the end of the creation are both concluded with the same כלה pi., they are both approved: "God saw all he had made and indeed it was very good"[51] and "Moses examined the whole work, and he could see they had done it as YHWH had directed him".[52] Both the workers at the sanctuary and the creation are blessed.[53] The scheme 'six days / seventh day'[54] relates the two stories with each other.[55] B. Janowski showed that not only these well known relationships between creation and Sinai existed, but that in the overall structure of the Priestly Code these two parts are correlated in a most stringent way.[56] Not in the way that the creation was unfinished and that only after Sinai it was completed,[57] but in the aim of creation as the dwelling of

---

[47] Ex. 25:8.

[48] W. Zimmerli, "Sinaibund und Abrahambund", 213.

[49] B. Janowski, *Sühne als Heilsgeschehen: Studien zur Sühnetheologie der Priesterschrift und zur Wurzel KPR im Alten Orient und im Alten Testament* (WMANT, 55), Neukirchen & Vluyn 1982, 295-313; P. Weimar, "Sinai und Schöpfung: Komposition und Theologie der priesterschriftlichen Sinaigeschichte", *RB* 95 (1988), 337-85; B. Janowski, "Tempel und Schöpfung: Schöpfungstheologische Aspekte der priesterschriftlichen Heiligtumskonzeption", *JBTh* 5, Neukirchen & Vluyn 1990, 37-69 = B. Janowski, *Gottes Gegenwart in Israel: Beiträge zur Theologie des Alten Testaments*, Neukirchen & Vluyn 1993, 214-96.

[50] Ex. 39:32a; 40:33b

[51] Gen. 1:31a.

[52] Ex. 39:43a.

[53] Gen. 2:3a; Ex. 29:43b.

[54] Gen. 1:3-31; 2:2f. and Ex. 24:15b-17

[55] B. Janowski, "Tempel und Schöpfung", 46.

[56] B. Janowski, "Temple und Schöpfung", 47-63.

[57] For the Jewish traditions about the relation between creation and Sinai, see B. Janowski, "Temple und Schöpfung", 37-38.

God among mankind.[58] In the view of the Priestly Code this aim
was reached by building the sanctuary at Sinai and this confirms the
importance of the priestly view of the events on the mountain. With
that structure the Priestly Code developed a competing view of the
covenant, Sinai and the land. The priestly authors had another point
of view than the Deuteronomists. They negated the strong relation
between covenant and law. Sinai was not the place where the law
was given, but where God fullfilled his promise of dwelling among the
people. The realisation of the aim of creation and the revelation of
the secret meaning of the seventh day in the scheme of creation even
changed the position of the land.

Land was no longer a function of the law as it had been in the
deuteronomistic thought. Land was the place where God was present.

Of course these two conceptions are not in absolute opposition to
each other, but the deuteronomists related land and law in a different
way than the priestly writers. That this really is a different conception
is shown by the peculiar role the land has in the Priestly Code. How
important is the land for the Priestly Code if we do not have a priestly
narrative about the settlement of Israel in Kanaan? K. Elliger stressed
the function of the land as the aim of the priestly writers,[59] but G.C.
Macholz[60] denied it, since in his view every concrete reminiscence
disappeared behind the beginning of cult and the presence of God.
Both alternatives are wrong.[61] The sanctuary is in the land, at first
moveable, later on Mount Zion. This is the direction of thought in
the Priestly Code. But surely the concrete land pales in view of the
possibility to meet YHWH in his sanctuary. Following the priestly
writers the land is a circle with a moving centre. Where the centre is,
there is the land.

If we look back, we have two axes in relation to the land. From
concrete to symbolic in the change from the deuteronom(ist)ic texts
to the late prophets after the exile. And from the connection between
conditional covenant, law and land with the deuteronomists to the
connection between covenant of promise, presence of God and land of
the priestly writers. Different concepts, different opinions and different
times. Considering this background we can now have a look at the role
of the land in Gen. 15.

---

[58]B. Janowski, "Temple und Schöpfung", 67.

[59]K. Elliger, "Sinn und Ursprung der priesterschriftlichen Geschichtserzäh-
lung", *ZThK* 49 (1952), 121-43 = K. Elliger, *Kleine Schriften zum Alten Testament* (TB, 32), München 1966, 174-98.

[60]G.C. Macholz, *Israel und das Land*, 142ff.

[61]B. Janowski, *Sühne als Heilsgeschehen*, 324, n.278; B. Janowski, "Tempel und
Schöpfung", 66, n.130.

3. Genesis 15

The problems of Old Testament research with the covenant, the promises of progeny and of land in Gen. 15 are well known. A few years ago they were impressively demonstrated by J. Ha in the part about the history of research in his study of Gen. 15.[62] Some exegetes understood Gen. 15 as the starting point for the Elohistic work, but since Wellhausen the chapter was mostly divided between Jahwist, Elohist and several other redactions. During a long time v. 1-6 and 7-21 were understood as belonging to different sources.[63] But from the fifties J. Hoftijzer,[64] followed by N. Lohfink[65] and J. van Seters,[66] defended the unity of the chapter and O. Kaiser,[67] L. Perlitt,[68] J. van Seters,[69] again, and H.H. Schmid[70] stressed the deuteronomistic character of Gen. 15. Even in recent times the thesis of one author who had the whole Pentateuch in front of him,[71] has been advocated, but at the same time a proposal for a partition in three layers could also be defended.[72] A history of research up to now would include many more names and positions, so I limit myself to a few points within the framework of the questions about the land I mentioned above.

1. A comparison between the two big chapters about the covenant of God with Abraham in Gen. 15 and 17 shows that the author of Gen. 17 reworked the account of Gen. 15 and 18. The main points, worked out by S. McEvenue[73] and confirmed by E. Blum,[74] are the paral-

---

[62] J. Ha, *Genesis 15: A Theological Compendium of Pentateuchal History* (BZAW, 181), Berlin & New York 1989, 30-8; O. Kaiser, "Traditionsgeschichtliche Untersuchung von Gen. 15", *ZAW* 70 (1958), 107-26 (108, n.4).

[63] J. Ha, *Genesis 15*, table between p. 29 and p. 30.

[64] J. Hoftijzer, *Die Verheißungen an die Erzväter*, Leiden 1956, 17ff.

[65] N. Lohfink, *Die Landverheißung als Eid: Eine Studie zu Gen. 15* (SBS, 28), Stuttgart 1967, 35ff., 45ff.

[66] J. van Seters, *Abraham in History and Tradition*, New Haven & London 1975, 249ff.

[67] O. Kaiser, "Traditionsgeschichtliche Untersuchung ", 107-26.

[68] L. Perlitt, *Bundestheologie im Alten Testament* (WMANT, 36), Neukirchen & Vluyn 1969, 69ff.

[69] J. van Seters, *Abraham*, 249ff.

[70] H.H. Schmid, *Der sogenannte Jahwist*, Zürich 1976, 121ff.

[71] J. Ha, *Genesis 15*, 91-2; see T. Römer, "Genesis 15 und Genesis 17: Beobachtungen und Anfragen zu einem Dogma der 'neueren' und 'neuesten' Pentateuchkritik", *DBAT* 26 (1989/90 [ersch. 1992]), 32-47.

[72] H. Mölle, *Genesis 15: Eine Erwählung von den Anfangen Israels* (FzB, 62), Würzburg 1988.

[73] S. McEvenue, *The Narrative Style of the Priestly Writer* (AnBib, 50), Rome 1971, 152-3.

[74] E. Blum, *Die Komposition der Vätergeschichte*, 422-3.

lelisms between Gen. 15 and 17 such as the introductory promise,[75] the reaction of Abraham,[76] the promise of an heir and large progeny,[77] God taking an oath with Abraham and his seed,[78] and the possession of the land promised to the descendants.[79] S. McEvenue listed the following changes by the author of Gen. 17:

1. He largely eliminated the dialogue character of Gen. 15.

2. He uses the ברית as a startingpoint, contradictory to Gen. 15 where it appears only at the end as an explanation of the scene with YHWH taking an oath.

3. First, Gen. 15 promises a son, thereafter a large progeny, whereas in Gen. 17 the large progeny appears first and the direct promise of a son is told in v. 16, the whole scene taken from Gen. 18.

4. In Gen. 15:18 the land will belong to the descendants but in Gen. 17 to Abraham and the descendants.[80] Gen. 17 took up the material from Gen. 15 and Gen. 18, but the chapter itself is a unity,[81] so the movement can only be from 15 and 18 to 17 and not in reverse. The first conclusion then is the relative chronology between Gen. 15 and 17, Gen. 17 reacting to Gen. 15.

2. The second point is the deuteronomistic character of Gen. 15 or rather its belonging to the D-Composition as proposed by E. Blum. For the first part 15:1-6 this can be demonstrated by the parallelisms between Gen. 15:1-6, 17:15-18 and 26:3bβ-5,[82] There is a small difference between these two textual units and Gen. 15. Gen. 15:1-6 is developed as a narrative scene whereby הרבה is lacking, but this belongs to

---

[75]Gen. 15:1 // 17:1f.

[76]Gen. 15:2f. // 17:3a

[77]Gen. 15:4f. // 17:4-6

[78]Gen. 15: 7-12, 17f. // 17:4-8

[79]Gen. 15:18 // 17:7-8

[80]McEvenue, *The Narrative Style*, 152-3.

[81]S. McEvenue, *The Narrative Style*, 156.

[82]E. Blum, *Die Komposition der Vätergeschichte*, 362 ff. He sums up the following points:

1. The promise as an oath taken by YHWH: Gen. 22:16; 26:3.

2. The promise of progeny constructed with זרעך and הרבה: Gen. 22:17; 26:4; Deut. 7:13; 13:18.

3. The comparison of the promise of progeny with ככוכבי השמים: Gen. 22:17; 26:4. The blessing.

the specific character of Gen. 15. The promise of land in Gen. 15:7ff. is characterized by the oath of YHWH (נִשְׁבַּע). A comparison with all the נִשְׁבַּע-texts shows that these formulations do not belong to a proto-deuteronomic group. They are related to the later deuteronomistic texts.[83] It is therefore possible to conclude with E. Blum: "Die Gestaltung der Landverheißung und vor allem die erzählerische Entfaltungen der Verheißungen in V.5 und in der Szenerie des 'Bundesschlusses' erweisen Gen. 15 insgesamt als *den Basistext für die Mehrungs- und Landverheißung im Kontext der D-Überlieferungen.* Offenbar ist er auch für diese Funktion konzipiert worden."[84] Consequently Gen. 15 is the central text of the D-composition in the Tetrateuch, as the most important narrative about the promise of the land and progeny.

3. The third point is the secondary character of Gen. 15:13-16. The narrative sequence of Gen. 15:8-18 is interrupted by a speech of YHWH in which the whole salvation history from the stay in Egypt, the slavery and the Exodus is foretold. The real possession of the land will only begin after the sojourn in Egypt. This weakens the promise of v. 18. Here, clearly, a later voice is heard which reminds of the slavery and the Exodus. But a double meaning cannot be excluded: reminding of Egypt is reminding of Babylon. For the history of redaction it is important that here not only post-deuteronomistic schemes are used, but that priestly terminology is present too.[85]

These points give us only a glimpse of the problems in Gen. 15. But how do these points fit together with the axes about the land I mentioned above? If it is true that the whole chapter Gen. 15 belongs to the D-composition and if this D-composition as it was worked out by Blum for the Pentateuch has in view the Deuteronomistic History, then we are with these texts in early post-exilic time. At Sinai, Israel was constituted by covenant and law following the deuteronomists and in parts of the Deuteronomistic History this connection has not been abandoned. But with the return to the land and confronted with losses in the south to Edom, in the west to the people of the coastal plain and threatened by a hostile Samaria the question arises: "who will possess the country?" The answer is clear: to the (real) descendants of Abraham. This could be the background of the question of Abraham for a sign: "אֲדֹנָי יהוה בַּמָּה אֵדַע כִּי אִירָשֶׁנָּה?" It is the key sentence with its

---

[83] E. Blum, *Die Komposition der Vätergeschichte*, 373ff.

[84] E. Blum, *Die Komposition der Vätergeschichte*, 382.

[85] Blum, *Die Komposition der Vätergeschichte*, 379: The 400 years in Egypte are a rounding off deriving from the 430 years in Ex. 12:40. The four generations can be explained with Levi, Kehat, Amram and Aaron/Moses from Ex. 6:14ff. Gen. 15:15 is fullfilled in Gen. 25:8.

anxious search for certainty and the old verb of all the deuteronomistic views about the conquest of the land ירש. The divine answer gives a sign: an oath by YHWH himself connected with a curse for the taker of the oath if he breaks it. It is an answer distant from the views of the priestly circles, yet both have one thing in common: the guarantee of the land lies in the hand of YHWH.

Looking for the diversity and the similarity between these views among different groups and in different times, a diachronic, redaction-historical approach cannot be missed.

John W. Rogerson   *Sheffield – United Kingdom*

Synchrony and Diachrony in the Work of De Wette and Its Importance for Today

W.M.L. De Wette died in 1849.[1] The terms 'synchronic' and 'diachronic' were introduced to the general public in F. de Saussure's posthumous *Cours de linguistique générale* in 1916.[2] How, then, does it make sense to speak of De Wette's use of the notions of 'synchronic' and 'diachronic'? The obvious answer is that although Saussure coined these words the concepts that they denoted can be traced at least well back into the nineteenth century. Thus John Lyons remarks, in connection with Saussure, that his structuralism can be traced back as far as Herder, Wilhelm von Humboldt, and even Leibniz.[3] E.F.K. Koerner, among others, has undertaken a specific enquiry into the antecedents of Saussure's work.[4] He finds many anticipations of various aspects of Saussure's thought in the nineteenth century, and notes the verdict of Leonard Bloomfield in 1924 "that most of what Saussure had put forward had long been 'in the air' but only fragmentarily expressed until then".[5]

In what follows, I intend to re-examine some aspects of De Wette's work in the light of nineteenth and twentieth century discussions of literary theory. This will help to fill one of the gaps in my biography of De Wette, namely, the lack of a complete discussion of De Wette's aesthetics. However, this will not be a discussion of De Wette for its own sake. I hope that it will also show that methods in Biblical Studies cannot be seen in isolation from the circumstances and interests of the scholars who used or use them, and that literary theory should not be considered apart from aesthetic theory. Finally, I shall suggest something that I believe that De Wette would have endorsed, that literary and aesthetic theory must be anchored in social theory.

There is one part of this contribution about which I feel uncertain, if not confused, although I seem not to be alone in this judging from what I have read. The question is, how are the terms synchronic and diachronic to be applied to the study of literary texts? The view that

---

[1] See J.W. Rogerson, *W.M.L. de Wette, Founder of Modern Biblical Criticism: An Intellectual Biography* (JSOT.S, 126), Sheffield 1992.

[2] F. de Saussure, *Cours de linguistique général*, Paris [3]1971, 117.

[3] J. Lyons, *Semantics*, vol. 1, Cambridge 1977, 231.

[4] E.F.K. Koerner, *Ferdinand de Saussure: Origin and Development of his Linguistic Thought in Western Studies of Language*, Braunschweig 1973.

[5] Koerner, *Ferdinand de Saussure*, 37.

I shall take here is that a synchronic study of a literary text is a study of its form or content independently of its historical setting, authorship or literary origins; while a diachronic study takes into account factors such as sources and redactions. I accept that, while it is often useful to conduct synchronic investigation separately from diachronic considerations, and vice versa, in practice this is not always easy, and ultimately it may not be desirable.[6]

That De Wette was one of the founders of modern biblical criticism has been recognised at least since the time that Wellhausen acknowledged his indebtedness to De Wette.[7] However, early assessments of De Wette divided his work into two phases: an early critical phase and a later pietistic phase, with the later phase seen as not living up to the promise of the early criticism.[8] I have attempted to see things quite otherwise; and in what follows now I shall concentrate on the early so-called critical phase, arguing that it was profoundly affected by literary and aesthetic, as well as personal factors.

Few, if any, biblical scholars can have had as much exposure to and interest in literature and aesthetics as De Wette. In his last years at the gymnasium in Weimar he was taught by Herder.[9] As a student in Jena he heard Schelling's lectures on the philosophy of art in the winter semester of 1802 and the summer semester of 1803. Just prior to this, in 1801, he read W.H. Wackenroder's *Phantasien über die Kunst* which Ludwig Tieck had published in 1799, a year after Wackenroder's early death. Wackenroder's text inspired De Wette to write his *Eine Idee über das Studium der Theologie* in the summer of 1801, in which De Wette declared that the study of theology should begin with the study of art (*Kunst*). Also while a student in Jena De Wette walked the thirteen miles to Weimar to see first performances of Schiller's plays *Maria Stuart* and *Die Jungfrau von Orleans*. From 1807, as a professor in Heidelberg, he began to embrace the post-Kantian philosophy of J.F. Fries, and especially its aesthetics. As if this were not enough, De Wette wrote two novels, a quantity of poetry, a play and an opera libretto in verse, of which the latter was highly praised by Goethe.

From the standpoint of the history of biblical criticism, De Wette

---

[6]Note the careful remarks in Lyons, *Semantics*, vol. 1, 243-4.

[7]See J. Wellhausen's description of De Wette as "der epochmachende Eröffner der historischen Kritik auf diesem Gebiete" in *Prolegomena zur Geschichte Israels*, Berlin 1883, 4.

[8]The matter is discussed in R. Smend's *Wilhelm Martin Leberecht de Wettes Arbeit am Alten und am Neuen Testament*, Basel 1958, 106-12.

[9]For this and other details that follow see Rogerson, *De Wette*.

introduced diachrony into the discipline in a way that has had consequences ever since. He was not, of course, the first to argue that there were sources or 'unauthentic' material in biblical books.[10] His contribution was much more far reaching. Up to 1804 Old Testament history had acted as a synchronic framework in terms of which everything else was studied and understood. The story of the Hebrews from Abraham to Nehemiah was a set of inter-locking fixed points which provided the setting for the study of priestly or prophetic traditions, or other biblical writings. Scholars could and did argue about the dates and authors of biblical books, but this was still in the context of the fixed framework provided by the overall story.

De Wette changed all this. A footnote in his 1804 doctoral dissertation foreshadows the 1806 first volume of his *Beiträge zur Einleitung in das Alte Testament* in which he first disposed of Chronicles as a reliable source for Israel's history, and then read Samuel and Kings against the view implied in Exodus to Numbers, in order to dispute the claim of those books that Moses had instituted a fully-developed system of sacrifice and priesthood. With an eye on the analogy of the chess match in Saussure's *Cours*,[11] we can say that De Wette removed one piece from the inter-locking structure and this altered everything. For Biblical Studies ever since, there has been no overall agreed historical framework providing the context for other discussions. Continually shifting sands have replaced the firm ground once thought to exist, and this may be one reason why firmer ground has been sought through the synchronic study of biblical texts.

However, I now propose to argue that what we might broadly call synchronic concerns were behind De Wette's attempt to undermine the coherent story of the Hebrews that had hitherto provided the framework for Biblical Studies. Among De Wette's teachers at Jena were J.P. Gabler and H.E.G. Paulus who, in their different ways, were trying to strip the supernatural trappings from biblical narratives in order to get to the 'real history' that they contained.[12] But for De Wette, history was unimportant compared with art (*Kunst*). Art, as De Wette wrote in his *Eine Idee über das Studium der Theologie*

> present(s) to limited vision the beauty and harmony that
> is not to be perceived in the infinite universe. You (*Kunst*)
> bring down to us from heaven the divine in earthly form,

---

[10] For further details see J.W. Rogerson, *Old Testament Criticism in the Nineteenth Century: England and Germany*, London 1984, 15-27.

[11] Saussure, *Cours*, 125-6.

[12] For further details see J.W. Rogerson, *Myth in Old Testament Interpretation* (BZAW, 134), Berlin 1974, 4-8 and Rogerson, *De Wette*, 31.

and bringing it into our view you move the cold and narrow heart to accept feelings that are divine and mediate
harmony.[13]

History could not do this, in De Wette's view, and therefore he wanted
to undermine attempts to read the Old Testament as real history mi-
nus the supernatural, and he wanted instead to promote an aesthetic
approach to its literature.

In the case of the Pentateuch, De Wette rejected the documentary
theory of its composition as advocated by Eichhorn and embraced the
fragmentary theory.[14] Because the stories of the Ancestors (Abraham
etc.) were made up of fragments which reflected the outlook of later
periods there was little or no history to be found in them. Instead,
each fragment had to be treated on its own, and the task of interpretation was to see how it expressed ancient Israelite piety. But further,
this ancient piety was not just a religious attitude of the past; it
was a genuine, even if imperfect, grasping or sensing of something of
ultimate value.

How this could be was clarified further in De Wette's *Beytrag zur
Charakteristik des Hebraismus* which he published in 1807.[15] This remarkable work was undoubtedly affected by the two terrible tragedies
that De Wette had experienced the previous year. These were the
death of his wife Eberhardine in childbirth in the February, and the
plundering of his possessions by the victorious French after the battle
of Jena in the October. These tragedies greatly sharpened De Wette's
attempt to gain some sense of the purpose of life from art and philosophy, but they did not change his basic approach. The *Beytrag* deals
with the Psalms, Job and Ecclesiastes and asks how these writings
deal with the problem of contradiction (*Zweckwidrigkeit*), that is, the
contradiction involved in the suffering of innocent people; or, to put
it differently, the contradiction that individuals believe that they are

---

[13]W.M.L. De Wette, *Eine Idee über das Studium der Theologie*, Leipzig 1850.
The whole passage, p. 20, reads: "Heilige Kunst, du vermagst es allein, mir den
Sinn für das Göttliche aufzuschliessen und das Herz bessere, hörere Gefühle zu
lehren! In deinen zauberischen Schöpfungen, wie in einem klaren, schönen Spiegel,
stellst du dem beschränkten Auge die Schönheit, die Harmonie dar, die es im
unendlichen Universum nicht zu finden, nicht zu fassen vermag; du bringst uns
das Göttliche in irdischer Gestalt vom Himmel herab, rückst es näher hin vor
unsern Blick und zwingst das kalte, enge Herz, göttliche, harmonische Gefühle
aufzunehmen".
[14]See further Rogerson, *De Wette*, 51-5.
[15]The work was published in C. Daub and F. Creuzer's *Studien* 3/2, Heidelberg
1807.

free while they are at the same time buffeted by the constraints and unfairnesses of life.

There is, in fact, no answer to these questions at the level of understanding (*Verstand*). According to De Wette, we must take account of our moral conviction that we are free and responsible agents, as well as of our aesthetic feelings of an ultimate reality that is harmonious and purposeful. We can then face, even if we cannot explain, the tragedies of life. This is where the Psalms, Job and Ecclesiastes are instructive. The book of Job wrestles profoundly with the question of suffering but does not provide an explanation. Instead it provides a theophany that enables Job to come to terms with his plight as he appreciates his weakness and nothingness. Ecclesiastes reflects in depth on the apparent purposelessness or futility of life, but does not give in to cynicism or scepticism. The Psalms of ill fortune, the *Unglückspsalmen*, of which there are many in the Bible, give expression to feelings of hurt and injustice, but do so within the continuing life of a believing community. De Wette does not claim that the Psalms, Job and Ecclesiastes attain the insights of the German philosophy of his own day; but he does claim that if these texts are read in the light of that philosophy they can be seen to be wrestling with questions of ultimate concern, and can be interpreted accordingly. For our purposes, we can describe this approach as essentially synchronic.

De Wette followed up the *Beytrag* with his commentary on the Psalms of 1811, and in this work we find the same antipathy to diachrony and advocacy of synchrony that I believe underlies his earlier work.[16] The two main ways of taking the Psalms among critically-minded scholars immediately prior to 1811 were the historical and the cultic, which sought to place them in either a reconstructed historical or cultic setting. I would call these approaches diachronic. De Wette did not entirely reject these methods of interpretation; but in the majority of cases he advocated a synchronic, aesthetic approach. This point needs to be stressed so that De Wette can be rescued from the place to which he has been assigned by the history of interpretation in regard to the Psalms. He divided the Psalms into various main classes or *Gattungen*, including individual and national laments. In this regard he can be, and has been, described as having anticipated Gunkel and the form-critical study of the Psalms.[17] However, it must be stressed that De Wette was not a form critic. His classification of

---

[16] W.M.L. De Wette, *Commentar über die Psalmen*, Heidelberg 1811. For further details see Rogerson, *De Wette*, 72-7.

[17] See H.-J. Kraus, *Geschichte der historisch-kritischen Erforschung des Alten Testaments*, Neukirchen ²1969, 181.

the Psalms was done as much on aesthetic grounds as anything else. Already in 1806 he had declared:

> the only criticism of the Psalms that is possible, and which can only be fully satisfactory for us, is the aesthetic.[18]

De Wette's reason for dividing the Psalms into classes was in order to link them with aesthetic theory about the relation between literary forms and human experience of life. For him, literary forms such as tragedy and comedy were ways of grappling with and overcoming the human experience of apparent purposelessness in life or the tragic fate of free people who were, however, overcome by external forces or situations that they could not control. At its best, a tragedy showed that the power of a vanquished spirit had an intrinsic value; that self-sacrifice for the sake of honour and justice exhibited supreme faith in the existence of eternal values. Comedy, on the other hand, enabled contradictions to be overcome by ridiculing them. He did not, of course, find comedy in the Psalms; but in the laments he found tragic-like expressions of the spirit of resignation (*Entsagung*) that enabled a person to maintain faith in eternal values in the face of uncertainty or danger. De Wette's view of the metaphysical nature of literary genres reflected, of course, the general thinking about this subject in the late eighteenth and early nineteenth centuries;[19] what is noteworthy, however, is that he maintained that the methods of literary aesthetics were the only appropriate ones for dealing satisfactorily with the Psalms.

I have tried, then, to show that De Wette was much more interested in synchrony than diachrony. He was not only sceptical about how much history could be reconstructed from the Hebrew Bible; he did not see history as a useful artefact for anyone who was trying to understand the tragedies of life. His main interest in the Bible was in its literature which he treated synchronically whenever he could. In the case of Hebrew poetry, he was also interested in the structure of the mode of expression – what Hjelmslev called the expression plane. Otherwise, his concern was with content as displaying features

---

[18]W.M.L. De Wette, *Beiträge zur Einleitung in das Alte Testament*, Bd. 1, Halle 1806, 158: "Die einzige Kritik, die über die Psalmen möglich ist, die uns aber auch vollkommen hinreichend seyn kann, ist die des Aesthetiker".

[19]See further R. Wellek, *A History of Modern Criticism: 1750-1950*, vol. 2, London 1955, *passim*. De Wette's views were greatly influenced on this matter by J.F. Fries. See Fries's novel *Julius und Evagorus*, Göttingen 1910, especially p. 100 (English translation in J.F. Fries, *Dialogues on Morality and Religion*, Oxford 1982, 76).

that identified genres, which were then treated in accordance with the aesthetic theory that De Wette embraced.

I now propose to relect further on De Wette's aesthetics, using the material in Peter Zima's recent book, *Literarische Ästhetik*.[20] Zima reviews modern literary theory from Kant and Hegel through to deconstruction, in the light of the differing views of aesthetics proposed by Kant and Hegel. Zima does not argue that Kant and Hegel directly influenced subsequent literary theory (although Hegel certainly was very important); rather, that useful insights can be gained from reflecting on literary theory in the light of the differences between Kant and Hegel.

Zima sees these differences as follows.[21] Kant argued for the autonomy of aesthetics because it is impossible to subsume aesthetic judgements under the concepts (*Begriffe*) governing pure or practical reason. The Kantian antinomy of aesthetic judgement draws attention to the apparent contradiction that judgements of taste (*Geschmacksurteile*) must be based upon concepts (*Begriffe*) otherwise it would be impossible for people to discuss such matters and reach agreement on them. However, it is impossible to find concepts (*Begriffe*) in terms of which a science of aesthetic judgement could be articulated.[22] The beautiful thus relates to a concept that is not like other concepts. This concept, in relation to an object, cannot be known or proved, yet it can have universal validity. Thus an aesthetic judgement is not cognitive and is essentially subjective, for all that it can also be inter-subjective. Kant elsewhere sums up the paradox by describing a work of art as *Zweckmäßigkeit ohne Zweck* (purposiveness without a purpose).[23]

In contrast to Kant, Hegel was a realist who sought to overcome the dualism between subject and object in Kant's thought. He did this by seeing the whole of human history as the dialectical process in which absolute spirit came to complete self-consciousness in its highest achievement, idealist philosophy. The Kantian antinomies were evidence for the essentially dialectical nature of reality. Whereas Kant resolved the antinomies statically, by analysing them into different modes of judgement, Hegel resolved them dynamically by seeing them as stages in the process by which absolute spirit reached its perfection. Thus, for Hegel, art (including literature) was not an au-

---

[20] P. Zima, *Literarische Ästhetik*, Tübingen 1991.

[21] Zima, *Literarische Ästhetik*, 17-31.

[22] The antinomy is stated in I. Kant, *Kritik der Urteilskraft*, in: *Kants Werke* (Akademie Textausgabe, 5), Berlin 1968, 339-40.

[23] Kant, *Kritik der Urteilskraft*, 228.

tonomous sphere but part of a larger process; and to that extent art could be described in terms of concepts (*Begriffe*). In fact, Hegel distinguished literature and especially poetry from other forms of art such as music and architecture, because literature, like philosophy, was expressed in words. He also subordinated art to religion and philosophy (philosophy being the highest form), judging the value of art, and especially literarature, according to its ability to anticipate the ultimate expression of absolute spirit in philosophy. Zima quotes the following passage from Hegel's *Vorlesungen über die Ästhetik* in relation to poetry in which the latter is evaluated as "that particular manifestation of art in which art both begins to dissolve itself and constitutes for philosophical thought its transition to religious notions as such as well as to the prose of scientific thought".[24]

The contrast between Kant and Hegel then, according to Zima, is a contrast between the untranslatability of art on the one hand, and the necessity of describing it in terms of an overall view of reality on the other; between an undefinable but not entirely uncertain view of art best summed up in the phrase *Zweckmäßigkeit ohne Zweck*, and a realist view that sees art as a presentation (*Darstellung*) of an aspect of reality.

Shortly, I shall indicate how Zima reflects on literary theory from this perpective. First, however, I want to consider where De Wette is to be placed in regard to it. De Wette was certainly much more of a Kantian than a Hegelian (De Wette and Hegel were briefly colleagues in Berlin) but in important respects he differed from both, while at the same time grasping important elements from both. Following his friend and philosophical mentor J.F. Fries, De Wette agreed with Kant in dividing human knowing into pure, practical and aesthetic judgement, each with its own subject matter and procedures.[25] However, he rejected Kant's view that we cannot know the *Ding-an-sich*. Admittedly, human knowing was limited by our subjectivity, but what was known was the object itself. In the case of aesthetic judgement, the faculty of knowing was called *Ahnung* (or *Ahndung*) by Fries and De Wette, and this was an intuitive grasping of the values of harmony and purposiveness that lay at the heart of reality.

---

[24] Zima, *Literarische Ästhetik*, 29: "die Poesie wird in den Vorlesungen 'als diejenige besondere Kunst' definiert, 'an welcher zugleich die Kunst selbst sich aufzulösen beginnt und für das philosophische Erkennen ihren Übergangspunkt zur religiösen Vorstellung als solcher sowie zur Prosa des wissenschaftlichen Denkens erhält'" (quoting G.W.F. Hegel's *Vorlesungen über die Ästhetik*, Bd. 3, Frankfurt 1970, 234).

[25] See Rogerson, *De Wette*, 98-103.

Although De Wette would have agreed with Kant that art (including literature) is autonomous in the sense that it cannot be described in concepts taken from pure or practical reason, he also wanted to integrate aesthetic judgements closely into religion and morality. Indeed, religion, for De Wette, is an aesthetic intuition of ultimate values. Aesthetic experience gives warmth and feeling to religion and morality, and the intuitions of ultimate value are themselves expressed by religions in the aesthetic forms of myths, symbols, ceremonies, architecture, art and literature. Thus De Wette could not have accepted Kant's view that art was *Zweckmäßigkeit ohne Zweck*. Art had a purpose, for De Wette, and this purpose was to mediate, via aesthetic experience, the conviction that reality was ultimately purposeful and harmonious. In this respect, De Wette stood slightly closer to Hegel than to Kant, although he entirely rejected Hegel's view of reality as that of the unfolding dialectic of absolute spirit.

Standing, as he did, somewhere between Kant and Hegel, and asserting both the autonomy of art and literature and yet its articulation of something real, De Wette's work becomes fascinating when considered in the light of Zima's reflections, only some moments of which can be picked out here. Zima begins, as we would expect, with the young hegelians who, in the turmoils of the revolutionary Europe of the mid-nineteenth century could no longer accept the optimistic hegelian view of reality.[26] They developed what we might call a dialectic without resolution (my phrase) in which they emphasised the contradictions inherent in life without looking for a resolution. In the the field of art and literature they valued literary forms for their own sake, and saw them as necessary complements to each other if the contadictoriness of reality was to be recognised. Thus tragedy needed to be complemented by comedy, and the beautiful needed to be complemented by the ugly. Zima's discussion of comedy is particularly interesting. Hegel had dismissed comedy as a degenerate form of classical art. Friedrich Vischer, on the other hand, put comedy on the same level as the sublime (*Erhaben*) and the serious (*Ernst*) because together they expressed the ambivalence of reality. Further, comedy, especially when it is satire or parody, shows how even serious and sublime matters can be presented in quite different, comic, ways, thus denying that reality is a harmonious whole. Comedy also has political implications in that it is much more a form which is at home among ordinary people, as opposed to the more elitist tragedy. Thus, comedy is the literature of the people and of democracy. The young heglian

---

[26] Zima, *Literarische Ästhetik*, 31-41.

tendencies reach an extreme, according to Zima, with Nietzsche, who uses the dialectical process as a destructive force, subverting all standards and ideals. The main purpose of art is to show that reality is only appearance (*Schein*).[27]

On the other side of the hegelian movement Zima discusses the materialists, especially Marx and his faithful follower in these matters in the twentieth century, Georg Lukács.[28] Marx examined the material and social conditions in which literature is produced in order to see how literature was related to scientific and technological progress. This is an approach which has since become more widespread, including in Biblical Studies. I doubt whether Von Rad was an enthusiastic Marxist. However, his view that the 'Solomonic Enlightenment' and the conditions of tenth-century Israel made possible the collecting and writing of Israelite traditions seems to me to echo Marx's interest, as do other similiar theories in Biblical Studies.

Another point of interest is the way that Marx developed Hegel's view that a work of art is a presentation (*Darstellung*) of the idea. If, for the metaphysical notion of idea you substitute the concrete and material ideal of a classless or other kind of hoped-for society, you can say that art and literature should attempt to capture or portray aspects of the ideal society and the processes that might lead to it from the present situation. We are deep into art and literature as ideology here, with obvious implications for the literature of the Hebrew Bible. However, the point that I wish to emphasize is Zima's discussion of how Lukács developed Hegel's ideas so that art and literature become the means whereby a plea is made on behalf of humanity in the face of scientific and technological processes that threaten to dehumanise us.

One of the key concepts in the thought of Lukács is *Verdinglichung*, variously translated as reification or objectification.[29] What is meant is the way in which modern industrial and economic needs tend to turn workers into objects, depriving them of their dignity as human beings. In the face of this, the task of art and literature, for Lukács, is to preserve and articulate human values that have been forgotten in industrial and economic life. What interests me here is that this can be compared with De Wette's position. De Wette was not, of course, familiar with an industrialising society and its effects on human lives;

---

[27]For the treatment of Nietzsche see Zima, *Literarische Ästhetik*, 41-8.

[28]See Zima, *Literarische Ästhetik*, 60-77.

[29]See, for example, G. Lukács, "Die Verdinglichung und das Bewußtsein des Proletariats" in G. Lukács, *Georg Lukács Werke*, Frühschriften II, Bd. 2, Berlin 1968, 257-397.

but he was caught up in war and in political upheavals, and lived at a time when empirical knowledge swept all before it. He appealed to the aesthetic, and to its expression in religion, art and literature, as an element in human self-understanding without which humanity would have no sense of the ultimate values of harmony and purpose which, according to De Wette, alone made sense of self-sacrifice and service to others.

It also seems to me that the same kind of approach can be found in Charles Taylor's recent book *Sources of the Self*.[30] After a discussion of the conflict between human reason regarded as an instrument with which humanity must conquer and control nature, and human reason seen as part of nature and designed to act in harmony with it, Taylor appeals to the work of art as a human product which nevertheless points beyond itself and which imparts a kind of vision that can inspire humanity to treat each other and the natural world graciously.[31]

To return to Zima, his many other discussions touch on Brecht's disagreement with Lukács, the formalist-realist debate in Soviet Russia and the way in which political circumstances there affected literary and aesthetic theory, the appeal of M. Bakhtin to varieties of interpretation and especially to the grotesque in art as a way of opposing Soviet attempts to enforce a particular view of the aesthetic, and the work of critical theorists, especialy Adorno and Benjamin.[32] In Zima's view the approaches known as New Criticism and Deconstruction can be seen in terms of the Kantian view of the autonomy of the work of art and its irreducability to other modes of description.

Zima's ultimate aim, and this is why I have referred to him in the context of this conference, is to define literary theory as a process of dialogue or debate designed to seek consensus.[33] The work of people such as Habermas can be seen behind this aim. But Zima modifies

---

[30] C. Taylor, *Sources of the Self: The Making of the Modern Identity*, Cambridge 1989.

[31] Taylor, *Sources of the Self*, 419: "There are many strong continuities from the Romantic period, through the Symbolists and many strands of what was loosely called 'modernism', right up to the present day. What remains central is the notion of the work of art as issuing from or realizing an 'epiphany' ... What I want to capture with this term is just this notion of a work of art as the locus of a manifestation which brings us into the presence of something which is otherwise inaccessible, and which is of the highest moral or spiritual significance; a manifestation, moreover, which also defines or completes something, even as it reveals".

[32] See Zima, *Literarische Ästhetik*, 72 for discussion of Lukács and Brecht. A much fuller treatment is found in D. Pike, *German Writers in Soviet Exile, 1933-1945*, Chapel Hill 1982. See Zima, *Literarische Ästhetik*, 100-73 for discussion of the Soviet debates, Bakhtin, and Adorno and Benjamin.

[33] Zima, *Literarische Ästhetik*, 364-407.

Habermas in one important respect. Whereas Habermas is concerned
with communicative interaction among individuals, Zima is concerned
with dialogue among groups. As applied to literary theory, this means
that groups or schools that have distinctive views (Zima uses the term
Soziolekt) should engage in a type of discussion in which the interests of the groups – the social, class, gender, political, psychological
factors that affect their positions – should be clarified and examined.
The outcome will not necessarily be unanimity; indeed, Zima regards
variety of interpretation as a fundamental characteristic of the creation and use of art and literature, and his sympathies do not lie
with those trends in literary theory such as New Criticism and Deconstruction which, in his view, tend towards what he calls monosemy
as opposed to his preferred polysemy. He also believes that literary
theory must be part of social theory if the dialogue between different
types of literary theory is to be most fruitful.

All that I have said may seem to be a long way from De Wette
and synchrony and diachrony, and so I must explain and justify what
I have been trying to do. I have tried to show that, although De
Wette was a scholar who worked diachronically, his primary motiva-
tion was synchronic. His treatment of the fragments that he believed
made up much of the Pentateuch, and above all his treatment of the
Psalms, Job and Ecclesiastes was synchronic. He was interested in
the time of composition and the sources of these works; but he was
more interested in their aesthetic content. Further, his concern with
their aesthetic content was part of his philosophical position which
was an attempt to understand the nature of human existence. Thus,
although he accepted the Kantian view of the autonomy of art he assigned to it a vital place in the human perception of ultimate values.
The synchronic study of biblical literature was therefore not an end in
itself, but rather an end that provided the means whereby life could
be coped with and self-sacrifice and service of others could be valued.

The purpose of describing Zima's discussion was to show that De
Wette's concerns, if rare among biblical scholars, can be set in a wider
context of debate about purpose or otherwise of art and literature.[34]
Although one of the welcome features of recent Biblical Studies is
that such matters have become a subject of interest in the discpline,
I wanted to ensure that at this conference, diachrony and sychrony
were not simply discussed as ends in themselves.

This brings me to my final point, the need, as I see it, for literary

---

[34]An excellent modern example of what I would call an aesthetic literary discussion of the Bible is in J.C. Exum's *Tragedy and Biblical Narrative*, Cambridge
1992.

theory to be part of social theory. De Wette wrote two sets of lectures on ethics, and he was a fervent democrat at a time of increasing suppression of democratic freedom in Prussia, because he believed, on moral and aesthetic grounds, in the essential freedom of individuals. Indeed, one of the reasons for his dismissal from his post in Berlin in 1819 was because of his contacts with politically-active people, including memers of the *Burschenschaften*, the politically-active student unions. I have no doubt that De Wette would have avidly studied social theory had he known of it, and would have modified his philosophy accordingly.

The most persuasive argument that I have found for seeing literary theory as part of social theory is that proposed by Anthony Giddens.[35] He directly attacks the Saussurian view that meaning is built in to the codes or sets of differences associated with langue or language system. He emphasises the importance of what he calls talk – day-to-day communication between individuals and groups where signification is saturated in the settings of practical action. "The meanings engendered within language would not exist", he writes, "were it not for the situated, yet reproduced, nature of social practices ... A competent language user has not merely mastered sets of syntactical and semantic rules, but the gamut of conventions involved in 'going on' in day-to-day contexts of social activity".[36]

Talk, then, a combination of linguistic and social factors, is primary and what Giddens calls cultural objects, including written texts, must be considered in that light. Written texts differ from talk in that they can be stored and retrieved, and retained over such long periods of time that when they are read, the social, non-linguistic conventions implicit in their original production are either unknown to the readers, or can only be reconstructed (by what we would call diachronic methods). This inevitably focuses attention upon reading or readers, and entails not only a concentration upon the signifiers but also inevitably results in a multiplicity of interpretations. Now much of this – the stress on reading, the signifiers and the multiplicity of interpretations – has by now become commonplace in Biblical Studies. But Giddens's approach is also a reminder that the act of reading will itself be undertaken within practical situations where interpretation is affected by social and non-linguistic factors; and discussion about texts or reading will imply that all the participants are affected

---

[35] See A. Giddens, "Structuralism, post-Structuralism and the Production of Culture" in A. Giddens, J. Turner (eds.), *Social Theory Today*, Cambridge 1987, 195-223.

[36] Giddens, "Structuralism, post-Structuralism", 215.

in some way by non-linguistic factors. Social theory will help participants to understand these factors, which is why literary theory cannot
do without social theory. And given that at least some types of social
theory also try to understand what it means to be human, and how
cultural objects including art and literature play a part in this, we are
back to where we started – with De Wette's interest in the synchronic
aesthetic interpretation of biblical texts.

K. Spronk   *Culemborg – The Netherlands*

Synchronic and Diachronic Approaches to the Book of Nahum

The unsuspecting reader of "the book of the vision of Nahum the Elkoshite" will be surprised by its literary beauty, the exuberant wealth of word plays and nicely worked out metaphors. However, he or she is also bound to be shocked by the repeated assurance of Yhwh being jealous, avenging and full of wrath. At the end of the previous book He was praised as an incomparable deity who takes away guilt and who lets his anger not rage for ever (Mic.7:18). One could also remember Jonah's complaint that Yhwh is "gracious and merciful, slow in anger, rich in kindness, and regretting evil" (Jon. 4:2) and therefore sparing the wicked but timely repenting city of Nineveh. In the book of Nahum, however, it is clear from the outset that this time Yhwh will not refrain from destroying Nineveh. The same words "slow in anger" are now supplemented by the verdict that "He certainly not leaves unpunished" (Nah. 1:3). And the verb נחם referring to Yhwh's change of heart (regret) in Jon. 4 now returns in the name of the prophet who announces that there will be no comforters נחמים for the devastated city of Nineveh (Nah. 3:7). It is also interesting to compare the final verses. Of all books in the Old Testament only the book of Jonah and the book of Nahum end with a question. Both deal with the same issue. Nahum asks the king of Nineve: "Upon whom has not come your evil continually?", whereas Yhwh says to Jonah: "And I, should I not pity Nineveh that great city, in which there are more than a hundred and twenty thousand persons who do not know their right hand from their left, and also much cattle?" The focus has shifted from the innocent inhabitants of Nineveh to the many, probably equally innocent victims of the Assyrians.

Next to this theological problem regarding the place of the book of Nahum within its canonical context, the question has been raised whether the book is a unity in itself. In the history of research[1] the unity of the book of Nahum was first questioned after the discovery of traces of an acrostic in chapter 1.[2] Since then it is often taken for

---

[1] Cf. K. Spronk, Nic. H. Ridderbos, *Worstelen met een wrekende God: De uitleg van de profetie van Nahum*, Kampen 1995.

[2] By Rev. G. Frohnmeyer, as reported by F. Delitzsch in 1867 in his commentary on the Psalms; cf. the biographical information provided by K. Seybold, *Profane Prophetie. Studien zum Buch Nahum* (SBS, 135), Stuttgart 1989, 74, n.1. Appar-

granted that at least part of chapter 1 was added to the prophecy of
Nahum at a later date.[3] This matter of literary criticism strongly in-
fluences the interpreter's view of the theological message of the book,
as is apparent, for instance, in the studies of Seybold.[4] In his opinion
the book of Nahum consists of soldier's songs, which have been put
into the framework of a traditional religious text. On the other hand
one comes across the meaning of another expert in this field stating that there is "no reason whatsoever to doubt its literary unity."[5]
Many scholars share this opinion,[6] but the same can be said of the
opposite view.[7] Proponents of the one opinion usually simply ignore

---

ently he may have regretted this use of his discovery in historical-critical research;
cf. G. Bickel's remark: "An der weiteren Verwertung dieses schönen Fundes verhin-
derte ihn, als entschiedenen Anhänger Hengstenberg's, aber schon seine Ueberzeu-
gung von der ausnahmslosen Richtigkeit des masoretischen Textes." ("Das alphabetische Lied in Nahum I 2 – II 3", *Sitzungsberichte der Kaiserlichen Akademie
der Wissenschaften*, Phil.-hist. Klasse, V. Abhandlung, Wien 1894, 1-12 (2).

[3]Cf., for instance, K. Koenen, *Heil den Gerechten – Unheil den Sündern: Ein
Beitrag zur Theologie der Prophetenbücher* (BZAW, 229), Berlin & New York
1994, 167-8.

[4]K. Seybold, *Profane Prophetie: Studien zum Buch Nahum* (SBS, 135),
Stuttgart 1989; idem, *Nahum, Habakuk, Zephanja* (ZBK, 24/2), Zürich 1991.

[5]A.S. van der Woude, "The Book of Nahum: A Letter Written in Exile", *OTS*
20 (1977), 108-26, 124, and *Jona – Nahum* (PredOT), Nijkerk 1978, 72-3.

[6]Cf. W.A. Maier, *The Book of Nahum: A Commentary*, Saint Louis 1950, 50-
70; C.-A. Keller, "Die Theologische Bewältigung der geschichtlichen Wirklichkeit
in der Prophetie Nahums", *VT* 22 (1972), 399-419; idem, in: R. Vuilleumier, C.-A.
Keller, *Michée, Nahoum, Habacuc, Sophonie* (CAT, 11b), Neuchâtel 1971, 101-11;
T. Longman III, "The Form and Message of Nahum: Preaching from a Prophet of
Doom", *RTJ* 1 (1985), 13-24; idem, in: T.E. McComiskey (ed.), *An Exegetical &
Expository Commentary: The Minor Prophets*, vol. 2, Grand Rapids 1993, 769-75;
W. Rudolph, *Micha–Nahum–Habakuk–Zephanja*. (KAT, 13/3), Gütersloh 1975,
144-5; B.E.J.H. Becking, "Is het boek Nahum een literaire eenheid?", *NedThT*
32 (1978), 107-24; C.E. Armerding, in: *The Expositor's Bible Commentary*, vol.
7, Grand Rapids 1985, 451-2; R.D. Patterson, M.E. Travers, "Literary Analysis
and the Unity of Nahum", *GTJ* 9 (1988), 45-58; D.L. Christensen, "The Book
of Nahum: The Question of Authorship within the Canonical Process", *JETS* 31
(1988), 51-8, and "The Book of Nahum as a Liturgical Composition: A Prosodic
Analysis", *JETS* 32 (1989), 159-69; M.A. Sweeney, "Concerning the Structure
and Generic Character of the Book of Nahum," *ZAW* 104 (1992), 364-77.

[7]Cf. S.J. de Vries, "The Acrostic of Nahum in the Jerusalem Liturgy", *VT*
16 (1966), 476-81; J. Jeremias, *Kultprophetie und Gerichtsverkündigung in der
späten Königszeit Israels* (WMANT, 35), Neukirchen-Vluyn 1970, 11-55; B. Renaud, "La composition du livre de Nahum: Une proposition", *ZAW* 99 (1987),
198-219, and *Michée–Sophonie–Nahum* (SBi), Paris 1987, 268-9; T. Hieke, "Der
Anfang des Buches Nahum", *BN* 68 (1993), 13-7 and 69 (1993), 15-20; J. Nogalski, *Redactional Processes in the Book of the Twelve* (BZAW, 218), Berlin & New
York 1993, 93-128.

or put aside the other,[8] but some of them appear to be more open-minded, leaving room for the possibility that the assumed editing and re-editing of the text resulted in a well structured final form.[9]

It may have become clear that in the present state of research of the book of Nahum no method is without its problems and that the choice for one approach of the text is also often a choice against the other. The least one should ask from new researchers is to be aware of this and to account for the method used. Such a well-considered way of exegesis, however, does not guarantee that its results will be convincing, in the sense that it gives the impression of justice being done to the text. A well-known example for this is the study by Schulz,[10] which is much quoted but hardly ever with consent.[11] According to Schulz, the contemporary study of the prophetic books is concentrated too much on the person of the prophet and on the prophetic traditions, i.e. on attempting to reconstruct what lies behind the text. Schulz calls for more attention to the books themselves and to the institutions which can be held responsible for their composition. In his opinion we have to think here of the community of the period after the Babylonian exile.[12] The common historical-critical analysis has failed to give this the attention it deserves, because it has let the diachronic analysis prevail over a thorough synchronic approach.[13] Schulz's sharp distinction between a synchronic and a di-

---

[8] In his survey of previous research Seybold does not fail to mention the views of Keller, Rudolph and Van der Woude about the unity of the book (*Profane Prophetie*, 13-6). This does not keep him, however, from starting his own research by simply taking for granted that the book of Nahum is a collection of originally seperate units (*Profane Prophetie*, 19). Moreover, he dismisses Rudolph's approach by calling it a "traditionelle –man muß fast sagen– vorkritische Sicht Nahums" (*Profane Prophetie*, 15). Seybold c.s. in turn, though not mentioned by name, get their share when Patterson judges that the denial of the unity of the book of Nahum "rests on the shakiest of premises." According to him, such views are "arbitrary and without foundation" (R.D. Patterson, *Habakkuk, Nahum, Zephaniah* (The Wycliffe Exegetical Commentary), Chicago 1991, 11-2).

[9] Cf. Renaud, "La composition", 213-4 and Christensen, "The Book of Nahum", 57.

[10] H. Schulz, *Das Buch Nahum: Eine redaktionskritische Untersuchung* (BZAW, 129), Berlin & New York 1973.

[11] Cf. the critical remarks by, amongst others, N.H. Ridderbos, *GThT* 75 (1975), 116-7; Becking, "Is het boek Nahum", 108; Renaud, "La composition", 199-200; Seybold, *Profane Prophetie*, 14-5.

[12] Schulz speaks of "die grundlegende Einsicht (...) daß die alttestamentliche Prophetie Ausdruck gottesdienstlicher Auseinandersetzung mit den Problemen der nachexilischen Zeit ist" (*Das Buch Nahum*, 2).

[13] Schulz speaks of "vorschnellen Rückschlüssen von der 'Unheitlichkeit' des Textes auf (diachrone) Entstehungsprozesse". Characteristic of his own approach

achronic approach should not be seen as a dismissal of the view that texts in the Old Testament can show signs of growth and of editing. It may be confusing when others use the term synchronic to indicate that they reject the historical-critical approach.[14] Schulz on the contrary is very critical. The many irregularities and tensions he finds in the Hebrew text lead him to break it into many bits and pieces. He then rearranges them into new, regular, and in his opinion the original, units. Nevertheless, he concludes that the book in its present state is the work of one post-exilic author who composed out of these now reconstructed units a literary coherent piece of work. According to Schulz this consists of three circular compositions: 1:11-2:11 and 2:12-3:6, framed by a hymn at the beginning and a mocking song at the end.

It seems legitimate to ask where and when the reconstructed supposedly original parts originated. Schulz, however, does not take up this issue, as this would be part of a diachronic approach. He does not want to cross the border drawn by himself. His decision to keep strictly to this one method does not make his conclusions more convincing. As long as these reconstructed parts do not receive their place and time, the dating of the book as a whole in the period after the Babylonian exile remains doubtful. One could say that this synchronic approach has too many hidden diachronic aspects. This is most apparent in the sometimes over-critical attitude towards the text. Just as Schulz wanted to postpone the diachronic approach, he might have left more room for the possibility of the text being a unity all along.

Schulz's study did not have much impact.[15] We now come to two

---

are the following remarks: "Eine längere literarische Entstehungsgeschichte des Textes läßt sich (...) nicht ohne weiteres aus der Disparatheit seiner einzelnen Elementen ableiten. Um eine Abfolge verschiedener Redaktionsstadien ermitteln zu können, muß man zunächst den Kontext auf synchroner Ebene so genau wie möglich analysieren und Kriterien entwickeln, die einen Übergang auf die Ebene der Diachronie gestatten. Auf jeden Fall ist eine strenge Scheidung zwischen den beiden analytischen Ebenen eine für die Redaktionskritik unabdingliche Voraussetzung." (*Das Buch Nahum*, 3) The same plea for the priority of the synchronic approach, postponing the attempt to resolve the problems of a text from a diachronic point of view, can also be found with W. Richter, *Exegese als Literaturwissenschaft: Entwurf einer alttestamentlichen Literaturtheorie und Methodologie*, Göttingen 1971, 35-7.

[14] Cf. Longman, "The Form and Message", 769, stating that his approach "differs in two major ways from traditional form criticism: it is predominantly synchronic rather than diachronic; and it is descriptive rather than prescriptive."

[15] Cf. the Rudolph's remark, *Micha–Nahum–Habakuk–Zephanja*, 147: "Es muß sich zeigen, ob sich eine Darstellung bewährt, die dem Propheten Nahum systematisch das Lebenslicht ausbläst."

studies representing more common views. The first (by Seybold) offers
the diachronic analysis that Schulz avoided, the second (by Sweeney)
shows the respect for the Masoretic text one misses in the work of
Schulz. In line with the work of Jeremias and Renaud, though not
sharing all their conclusions, Seybold attempts to reconstruct the formation of the book.[16] Like Schulz he assumes the existence of originally separate units. Unlike Schulz he did not find them scattered
through the present text. They more or less preserved their original
form. The oldest are three poems found in 3:8-19a; 3:1, 4a; and 3:2
+ 2:2, 4-13. Unlike Schulz he also proposes a date, namely the period
shortly after the capture of Thebes (= No Amon; Nah.3:8) in 663
BCE for the first poem, and about 650 BCE for the other two. According to Seybold only these parts of the text can be attributed with
certainty to the prophet Nahum. They were taken together with the
divine words of threat in 2:14 and 3:5-7, written down c. 615 by an
unknown author. From this edition also stem some smaller additions
(in 3:1,4b; 2:12b; 3:10b,11b and 15). In this form it may have circu-
lated as a pamphlet describing the fall of Nineveh in 612 interpreted
as the fulfilment of Nahum's prophecies. Its title probably was the
first of the two headings in 1:1: "A pronouncement about Nineveh".
The second heading was added with a new edition close to the end
of the Babylonian exile, c. 550, when old prophecies were taken up to
formulate new hopes for the exiles. Seybold finds this indicated in the
two added promises of salvation for Judah (1:12-3 and 2:1, 3). Finally,
around 400, the book of Nahum was made more acceptable from an
orthodox theological point of view by adding the hymn of 1:2-8. The
remaining 1:9-14 are interpreted as fragments which were originally
remarks written in the margin, or in the space below or above the
columns of the text. Seybold also assumes that in the course of the
transmission of the text two pages were exchanged. In this way he re-
constructs a more logical order: originally 2:14-3:17 would have been
followed by the first poem about Nineveh (2:2, 4-13). Only 3:8-19
would be in its original place.

Seybold admits that his suggestions about the order of the pages
and the marginal notes remain hypothetical. The same can be said,
however, of most of his other suggestions. In some respects his reconstruction of the formation of the text may be called brilliant
and not impossible, but it is by no means inevitable.[17] Hieke, who

---

[16] *Profane Prophetie*, 19-34; cf. also the summery in *Nahum, Habakuk, Zephanja*,
11-2 and his article "Vormasoretische Randnotizen in Nahum 1", *ZAW* 101 (1989),
71-85.

[17] Cf. the criticism by H.G.L. Peels, *'Voed het oud vertrouwen weder': De Gods-*

also takes "Spannungen und Brüche" in the text "als Spuren einer Bearbeitung",[18] regards only 1:1, 11, 14 and 2:2, 4-14 as original words of Nahum. Nogalski[19] agrees with Seybold on many points, but he assumes two formative layers. In his opinion an early corpus consisting of most material of chapters 2 and 3 with a clear literary unity was reshaped after the Babylonian exile, adding the theophonic hymn and allusions to Joel (in the locust metaphor in 3:15-17) and Deutero-Isaiah (Isa. 52:7 cited in 2:1).

The next example of recent research will show that a similar amount of scientific creativity as with Seybold, but with more trust in the literary quality of the complete Masoretic text[20] can lead to completely different conclusions. Sweeney argues for a coherent structure in the book written by the prophet Nahum shortly before or shortly after the fall of Nineveh. He does not want to exclude the possibility that some elements, such as the hymn in 1:2-8 and the address to Nineveh in 2:2-3:17, were written separately before that date, but in his opinion any attempt to explain the difficulties of the text as the product of post-exilic redaction "must be abandoned".[21] Sweeney takes up Becking's observation that it is possible to find some order in the difficult verses 1:9-14. The key to the solution of the problem is the right understanding of the change of the second person address forms.[22] The masculine should be interpreted as referring to the oppressor judged by YHWH, the feminine to Judah that will be delivered. Unlike Becking, Sweeney also distinguishes here between the singular forms and the plural form in 1:9. He finds both Judah and Nineveh (or the Assyrian king) addressed here asking what they think

---

openbaring bij Nahum, Kampen 1993, 25, n. 12: "De zwakte van Seybolds werk ligt – afgezien van de soms zeer speculatieve redeneringen – vooral in het feit dat hier de diachronische uitleg de aandacht voor het synchronische tekstonderzoek, dat de prioriteit dient te hebben, geheel verdrongen heeft. Het gevaar dat de door de bijbelse auteur bewust aangebrachte overgangen en spanningen in de tekst worden wegverklaard als redactionele naden, is bij deze vorm van exegese niet denkbeeldig."

[18] "Der Anfang des Buches Nahum", 68, 13.

[19] *Redactional Processes*, 123-8.

[20] Seybold's conclusions are based on a rather low esteem of the Masoretic text, as can be deduced from a number of derogatory remarks, like "Textzerstörungen", "destruktive Beziehung des Textmaterials", "gewaltsamer Einbruch (...) in geradezu schmerzlicher Eindringlichkeit", "Textunfall" (*Profane Prophetie*, 20, 23, 24).

[21] "Concerning the Structure", 376.

[22] Becking, "Is het boek Nahum", 111-4; in his article Becking referred to earlier conclusions by De Vries, "The Acrostic of Nahum", 480; cf. also W.C. Graham, "The Interpretation of Nahum 1:9-2:3", *AJSL* 44 (1927/1928), 37-48, esp. 45.

about YHWH. From the context it is clear that after 2:2 the second person feminine singular refers to Nineveh and the masculine form to the Assyrian king. The different addressees being clarified this way, it is now possible to subdivide the book: the first part (1:2-10) is an address to both Judah and Nineveh concerning their estimation of YHWH; the second part (1:11-2:1) addresses Judah speaking of its deliverance; the final part (2:2-3:19) addresses Nineveh and the Assyrian king announcing their downfall. According to Sweeney this tripartite book can be regarded as a "prophetic refutation speech", based on the fixed form of the disputation genre. The basic elements of this genre, quotation of the opinion to be disputed and its refutation, can be found in all main parts of the book.

These form-critical remarks are primarily based on the exegesis of 1:9 as questioning YHWH's efficacy. It would have been precisely this opinion that is refuted by the prophet's vision. Although the interpretation given of 1:9a is plausible, it must be doubted whether it takes such a central place. Already v. 9b seems to give the answer. One would also expect more direct associations to the view that YHWH is powerless, if the book as a whole was meant to deny this. In a footnote Sweeney offers a more convincing interpretation, based on a refinement of the disputation genre,[23] which distinguishes three basic elements: thesis, counter-thesis, and dispute. According to this pattern Nah.1:2-10 would be the counter-thesis to an implied thesis of YHWH's impotence. Nah.1:11-2:1 and 2:2-3:19 then constitute the dispute directed to Judah and Assyria respectively. The proposed division of the text, however, is not in every respect convincing. Especially in the second part it remains unclear why in the address to Judah one suddenly reads words spoken to the oppressor (1:14). Apparently things are more complicated than Sweeney wants us to be believe. It seems to be more to the point to regard, with Becking, as the governing principle of the unity the paradox that salvation and annihilation are two sides of one and the same judgement by YHWH.[24]

The convincing power of the arguments in favour of the literary unity of the book of Nahum is weakened by the fact that there appears to be so little agreement about its structure. Every new study seems to result in a new division of the text.[25] In this situation one is happy

---

[23] "Concerning the Structure", 375, n.36; based on a suggestion by D.F. Murray, "The Rhetoric of Disputation: Re-examination of a Prophetic Genre", *JSOT* 38 (1989), 95-121.

[24] Becking, "Is het boek Nahum", 122; cf. Hieke, "Der Anfang des Buches Nahum", 16, who speaks of "das antithetische Prinzip".

[25] Only with Keller, in: CAT XIb, 101-2, we find a division close to the one

to hear that someone has found "coded information" in the Hebrew text providing the clue for a proper, indisputable understanding of the structure of the text.[26] According to Christensen this information is provided by the author who must have had future readers in mind. This at first sight hidden information appears to have been preserved well in the Masoretic tradition. The author, probably the prophet Nahum himself, gave an artful summary of his message in an acrostic in 1:2-10. He reworked an originally alphabetic acrostic into a new acrostic. [27] The initial letters and/or words now form two sentences: אני יהוה גאה ולפני חטו[אן, "I am the exalted YHWH and (I am) in the presence of sin." / בשטף עבר כל מלא, "In a flood (I am) bringing a full end completely." The second clue is found by counting 'morae' (syllables, the ones with a long vowel counting double) and syntactic-accentual units (as a rule coinciding with the Masoretic distinctive accents). This leads to a division of the book into two halves: 1:2-2:10 and 2:12-3:19, which have the same length, both in accentual units (170) and according to mora-count (respectively 1036 and 1038). These equal halves frame 2:11. This verse mentioning the destruction of the city and the despair of its inhabitants is regarded by Christensen as "a summation of the book itself". Together with the coded verse of the acrostic it "contains the essential message of the book of Nahum

---

proposed by Sweeney, but it is not the same. Keller divides the third part of the text into eight strophes of comparable length and with different themes: 2:4-6, 7-11, 12-14; 3:1-3, 4-7, 8-11, 12-15, 16-18. Patterson and Travers, "Literary Analysis", 48-9 see the text arranged in a "basic bifid structure": the two parts 1:2-2:1 and 2:2-3:19 are built up in the same way. A theme formulated at the beginning (1:2; 2:2-3) is developed in distinct units (1:3-10; 1:11-2:1 and 2:4-14; 3:1-19). The distinct units in the second part are also interconnected, because they are both closed with a taunt song (2:12-14; 3:8-19) and the mentioning of the (in)activity of messengers (2:14b; 3:19).

[26] Christensen, "The Book of Nahum: The Question of Authorship", 52; cf. also idem, "The Book of Nahum as a Liturgical Composition", 32; idem, "The Acrostic of Nahum Once Again: A Prosodic Analysis of Nahum 1,1-10", ZAW 99 (1987), 409-15; idem, "The Masoretic Accentual System and Repeated Metrical Refrains in Nahum, Song of Songs, and Deuteronomy", in: E.J. Revell (ed.), VIII. International Congress of the International Organization for Masoretic Studies, Chicago 1988 (MasSt, 6), Atlanta 1990, 31-6, especially 32-3.

[27] "The Book of Nahum: The Question of Authorship", 55. Christensen is building here on a suggestion put forward by Van der Woude, "The Book of Nahum", 123, who found in the first letters of each line together with לפני in 1:6a the following sentence: אני גאה ולפני חטיך, "I am the Exalted One and confronting them who commit sin against you". Cf. also Bickel, "Das alphabetische Lied", 3, mentioning his earlier, but now dropped suggestion of reading a new acrostic נונא (Nineveh) in 1:1-2. This would have matched the acrostic אשור in 1:12a, discovered by J. Reider, "The Name Ashur in the Initials of a Difficult Phrase in the Bible", JAOS 58 (1938), 153-5.

in summary fashion".[28] With the help of this counting he also finds a number of metrical patterns distinguishing the smaller units 1:1-10, 12-14; 2:1-10, 12-14a, 14b-3:7, 8-13, and 14-19.

One can understand why Sweeney, who knew the work of Christensen and who could have used some support on strictly formal grounds for his definition of the structure, did not take over or even mention any of the conclusions of Christensen's analysis. First, Christensen seems to be the only one who sees in 2:11 in one way or another the centre of the book of Nahum.[29] Second, the clarity with regard to the numbers of metrical patterns does not coincide with their contents. Third, the reference to the Masoretic accentual system is weakened by the fact that Christensen in a number of cases omits or adds accents. He also mentions the *setumah* and *petuḥah* (after 1:10 and 1:14), but he gives no explanation for the fact that these important Masoretic markers seem to contradict his view of the structure of the text.

This survey and evaluation of recent research on the book of Nahum clearly shows the difficulties of both the diachronic and synchronic approach. Even worse, the two approaches seem to be totally incompatible. The following analysis[30] attempts to bridge this gap by avoiding to choose too soon for one or the other approach. It starts with a synchronic analysis for the simple reason that it is easier to go from here to a diachronic analysis than vice versa.[31] Moreover, it is the best way to understand the Hebrew text as it is transmitted to us. The Masoretic text should be seriously accepted as trustworthy until the contrary can be demonstrated. When it comes to the book of Nahum, this respect for the Masoretic text is corroborated by the

---

[28] "The Book of Nahum: The Question of Authorship", 56.

[29] According to Christensen, "The Book of Nahum as a Liturgical Composition", 166, "numerous commentators" share his interpretation of this verse, but with the exception his own commentary (in *Harper's Bible Commentary*, San Francisco 1988, 716-8, esp. 717) one will look in vain for them.

[30] Thanks are due to Professors Becking, Clines and Van der Woude for their critical remarks during the congress, and especially to Professor De Moor for his support in preparing the final version of this article.

[31] Cf. R. Oost, *Omstreden bijbeluitleg: Aspecten en achtergronden van de hermeneutische discussie rondom de exegese van het Oude Testament in Nederland – Een bijdrage tot gesprek*, Kampen 1986, 121: "From an exegetical-methodical point of view the emphasis ought to be on the structural analysis of the text produced by the final redaction, but this should be carried out within the framework of, and controlled by, historical criticism, which regulates the questions with regard to the text as tradition. Scholars ought to be constantly aware of the fact that the 'given' text is an 'evolved' text."

fact that there appear to be hardly any major textual corruptions[32]
and by the consistent beauty of its language. A first close reading
of the Hebrew text will suffice to understand why the prophet can
be called "poet laureate of the minor prophets".[33] His book begins
with a chiastic structure in 1:2. There is a wordplay with the letters
נ and ק in 1:2-3. Again there is a chiasmus in 1:4. One may note the
alliteration with the letter כ in 1:9-11a. And so on.[34] It would be interesting to know whether similar literary devices are also used on a
larger scale. One can think here of the use of keywords and distant
or external parallelism. For this reason we want to offer here a structural analysis according to the rules of the 'Kampen School.'[35] It is
the aim of this method to give a comprehensive survey of the literary
devices used by the poet to design his/her text.[36] Attention is paid to
all more or less striking elements in the text, like repetition of words,
use of parallel pairs at close range and more distantly, unusual wor-
dorder, abrupt transitions. Many of these elements have been used in
the literary-critical analysis, for instance by Schulz, to divide the text
into chronologically separate layers. In addition to this, the 'Kampen
School' works with formal units and dividers the antiquity of which
has been established beyond all doubt, like the *setumot* and *petuhot*,
dividing accents, etc.[37] In this type of structural analysis it is first at-

---

[32]Cf. D. Barthélemy, *Critique textuelle de l'Ancient Testament*, t. 3 (OBO,
50/3), Fribourg & Göttingen 1992, 784-822.

[33]R.D. Patterson, M.E. Travers, "Nahum: Poet Laureate of the Minor Prophets", *JETS* 33 (1990), 437-44.

[34]See next to the article by Patterson and Travers, the survey by O.T. Allis,
"Nahum, Nineveh, Elkosh", *EvQ* 27 (1955), 67-80, esp. 73ff., and the many ref-
erences to the book of Nahum in W.G.E. Watson, *Classical Hebrew Poetry: A
Guide to its Techniques* (JSOTSup 26), Sheffield 1984.

[35]For a convenient survey of the method and bibliography, see J. Kim, *The
Structure of the Samson Cycle*, Kampen 1993, 118-34; see also J.C. de Moor,
W.G.E. Watson (eds.), *Verse in Ancient Near Eastern Prose* (AOAT, 42),
Neukirchen-Vluyn 1993.

[36]In this regard it can be compared to the work of J.P. Fokkelman on the *Nar-
rative Art and Poetry in the Books of Samuel*, Assen 1981ff. and of D. Pardee,
Ugaritic and Hebrew Poetic Parallelism: A Trial Cut ('nt I and Proverbs 2)
(VT.S,39), Leiden 1988.

[37]See De Moor, Watson (eds.), *Verse in Ancient Near Eastern Prose*, xv. The
'Kampen School' usually follows the colometry of the Masoretes. On the basis of
colometrically written Ugaritic tablets, Hebrew and Aramaic acrostics, colometrically written manuscripts of Qumran and colometrically written poems like Ex.15
and Deut.32 it has been established that the distinctive accents of the Masoretes
can be trusted in about 90% of the cases. In the edition of the Hebrew text by
Elliger in the BHS the division into verses usually (more so than in the previous
BHK-edition) coincides with the Masoretic accentuation. In the transcribed text
below the dividing accents are indicated by the numbers in square brackets. These

tempted to explain them as markers of the structure of the text, which have been deliberately used for this purpose by the poet. Within the limits of this contribution it is not possible to list all literary striking elements and markers.[38] Only the conclusions can be presented here in the form of the text divided into verses, strophes, canticles, subcantos and cantos.[39] As a rule this subdivision on purely formal grounds appears to coincide with the contents. In other words, it should be possible to summarize the units easily.

I.i.1

מַשָּׂא נִינְוֵה [2]   A pronouncement about Nineveh. (1aA)

סֵפֶר חֲזוֹן נַחוּם הָאֶלְקֹשִׁי [1]   The book of the vision of Nahum the Elkoshite. (1aB)

I.i.2

אֵל קַנּוֹא וְנֹקֵם יְהוָה [5]   A jealous and avenging God is YHWH, (2aA)

נֹקֵם יְהוָה וּבַעַל חֵמָה [2]   avenging is YHWH, a lord of wrath. (2aB)

נֹקֵם יְהוָה לְצָרָיו [5]   Avenging is YHWH against his adversaries, (2bA)

וְנוֹטֵר הוּא לְאֹיְבָיו [1]   and reserving (his wrath) is He for his enemies. (2bB)

I.i.3

יְהוָה אֶרֶךְ אַפַּיִם וּגְדוֹל־כֹּחַ [5]   YHWH, He is slow in anger and great in power,
(3aA)

וְנַקֵּה לֹא יְנַקֶּה [2]   but He certainly does not leave unpunished. (3aB)

יְהוָה בְּסוּפָה וּבִשְׂעָרָה דַּרְכּוֹ [5]   YHWH, in whirlwind and storm is his way, (3bA)

וְעָנָן אֲבַק רַגְלָיו [1]   and clouds are the dust of his feet. (3bA)

. . . .

I.ii.1

גּוֹעֵר בַּיָּם וַיַּבְּשֵׁהוּ [5]   He is rebuking the sea and dries it up, (4aA)

וְכָל־הַנְּהָרוֹת הֶחֱרִיב [2]   and all the rivers He makes dry, (4aB)

---

numbers refer to the accents as they are listed in the 'Tabula accentuum' of the BHS.

[38] I hope to publish the full analysis in a commentary on Nahum scheduled to appear in 1996 in the series Historical Commentary on the Old Testament (Kok, Kampen).

[39] For instance, II.A.i.3 is the third strophe of the first canticle of the first subcanto of the second canto. In the Masoretic text this is 1:14. This strophe consists of two verse-lines: a bicolon and a tricolon.

אמלל בשן וכרמל [5] They languish, Bashan and Carmel, (4bA)

ופרח לבנון אמלל [1] and the bloom of Lebanon languishes. (4bB)

I.ii.2

הרים רעשו ממנו [5] Mountains quake because of Him, (5aA)

והגבעות התמגגו [2] and the hills are moving. (5aB)

ותשא הארץ מפניו [5] And the earth raises up before Him, (5bA)

ותבל וכל־ישבי בה [1] and the world and all that dwell therein. (5bB)

I.ii.3

לפני זעמו מי יעמוד [5] Who can stand before his wrath? (6aA)

ומי יקום בחרון אפו [2] And who can withstand the glow of his anger? (6aB)

חמתו נתכה כאש [5] His wrath is poured out like fire, (6bA)

והצרים נתצו ממנו [1] and the rocks are scattered because of Him. (6bB)

. . . .

I.iii.1

טוב יהוה [5] Good is YHWH, (7aA)

למעוז ביום צרה [2] indeed, a shelter in the day of distress, (7aB)

וידע חסי בו [1?] and knowing those who seek refuge in Him, (7bA)

ובשטף עבר [5] and in the torrent He passes by. (8aA=7bB)

I.iii.2

כלה יעשה מקומה [2] An end He makes to her place, (8bA)

ואיביו ירדף־חשך [1] and his enemies He pursues (into) darkness. (8bB)

מה־תחשבון אל־יהוה [5] What do you think up against YHWH? (9aA)

כלה הוא עשה [2] An end He makes, (9aB)

לא־תקום פעמים צרה [1] distress shall not stand up a second time. (9aC)

I.iii.3

כי עד־סירים סבכים [5] For like entangled thorns (10aA)

וכסבאים סבוכים[40] [2] and like winding bindweed (10aB)

אכלו [5] כקש יבש מלא [1] they shall be consumed, like thoroughly dried stubble. (10aC)

---

[40]See for this emendation of the text, based on the LXX and the context, Rudolph, *Micha–Nahum–Habakuk–Zephanja*, 153, and *HAL*, 697.

[5] ממך יצא   From you has come forth (11aA)

[2] חשב על־יהוה רעה   one planning evil against YHWH, (11aB)

[1] יעץ בליעל   counseling wickedness. (11aC)

SETUMAH _____

II.A.i.1

[7] כה אמר יהוה   Thus says YHWH: (12aA)

[5] אם־שלמים וכן רבים   "Though they are complete and so many, (12aB)

[2] וכן נגזו ועברו[41]   even so they shall be cut down and fly away. (12aC)

II.A.i.2

[5] וענתך   And I have afflicted you, (12bA)

[1] לא אענך עוד   (but) I will afflict you no more. (12bB)

[2] ועתה אשבר מטהו מעליך   And now, I will break his yoke from upon you (13aA)

[1] ומוסרתיך אנתק   and your chains I will burst." (13aB)

II.A.i.3

[5] וצוה עליך יהוה   And YHWH commands concerning you: (14aA)

[2] לא־יזרע משמך עוד   "There will be sown from your name no more. (14aB)

[10] מבית אלהיך   From the house of your gods (14bA)

[12?] אכרית פסל ומסכה   I will cut off idol and cast image (14bB)

[1] אשים קברך כי קלות   I will prepare your grave, because you are worthless." (14cB)

PETUḤAH ....

II.A.ii.1

[13] הנה על־ההרים   Behold, on the mountains (1aA)

[5] רגלי מבשר משמיע שלום   the feet of a messenger announcing peace! (1aB)

[8] חגי יהודה חגיך   Celebrate, Judah, your feasts, (1bA)

[2] שלמי נדריך   fulfill your vows! (1bB)

[12] כי לא יוסיף עוד   For never again (1cA)

[8] לעבור־בך בליעל   shall the wicked come over you. (1cB)

[1] כלה נכרת   He is completely cut off. (1cC)

_____

[41] With BHS it is assumed that the ו of וענתך (12bA) should be taken with the preceding עבר. See for this translation Jer.13:24, where עבר is used with קש (cf. Nah.1:10aC!).

II.A.ii.2

עלה מפיץ על־פניך [8] Does a scatterer come up against you. (2a)

נצור מצרה [2] Guard the fortification, (2bA)

צפה־דרך [10] watch the road, (2bA)

חזק מתנים [5] strengthen the loins, (2cA)

אמץ כח מאד [1] fortify the power in the highest degree! (2cB)

II.A.ii.3

כי שב יהוה את־גאון יעקב [5] For YHWH shall restore the pride of Jacob, (3aA)

כגאון ישראל [2] yeah, the pride of Israel. (3aB)

כי בקקום בקקים [5] For destroyers have destroyed them (3bA)

וזמריהם שחתו [1] and their branches they have ruined. (3bB)

. . . .

II.B.i.1

מגן גבריהו מאדם [7] The shield of his heroes is made red, (4aA)

אנשי־חיל מתלעים [5] (his) soldiers are clad in scarlet. (4aB)

באש־פלדות הרכב [8] With the fire of the steel are the chariots (4bA)

ביום הכינו [2] in the day of his preparation (4bB)

והברשים הרעלו [1] and the lances are brandished. (4bC)

II.B.i.2

בחוצות יתהוללו הרכב [5] In the streets the chariots run as mad. (5aA)

ישתקשקון ברחבות [2] They rush in the squares. (5aB)

מראיהן כלפידם [5] Their appearance is like torches. (5bA)

כברקים ירוצצו [1] Like lightning they dash to and fro. (5bB)

. . . .

II.B.ii.1

יזכר אדיריו [5] He remembers his noble ones. (6aA)

יכשלו בהלכותם [2] They stumble in their going. (6aB)

ימהרו חומתה [5] They hasten to her wall (6bA)

והכן הסכך [1] and a mantelet is set up. (6bB)

II.B.ii.2

שערי הנהרות נפתחו [2] The gates of the rivers are opened (7aA)

וההיכל נמוג [1] and the palace collapses. (7aB)

והצב גלתה העלתה [2] And he is put down, she is exposed, raped.[42] (8bA)

ואמההתיה [7] מנהגות   and her maidens are moaning as the voice of doves

כקול יונים [5]   (8bB)

מתפפת על־לבבהן [1]   beating their breasts.(8bC)

. . . .

II.C.i.1

ונינוה כברכת־מים [8] And Nineveh, it was as a pool of water (9aA)

מימי היא [2]   during her days (9aB)

והמה נסים [5] And they are fleeing. (9bA)

עמלו עמדו [8?]   Stand, stand! (9bB)

ואין מפנה [1]   And there is no one who turns back. (9bC)

II.C.i.2

בזו כסף [8] Plunder silver, (10aA)

בזו זהב [2]   plunder gold (10aB)

ואין קצה לתכונה [5] and there is no end to the treasure, (10bA)

כבד [6] מכל כלי חמדה [1]   wealth from all precious vessels. (10bB)

II.C.i.3

בוקה ומבוקה [8] Destruction and devastation (11aA)

ומבלקה [2]   and ruin! (11aB)

ולב נמס ופק ברכים [7] And the heart melts and the knees totter (11bA)

וחלחלה בכל־ותנים [5]   and trembling in all the loins (11bB)

ופני כלם קבצו פארור [1]   and the faces of them all gather a glow. (11bC)

. . . .

II.C.ii.1

איה מעון אריות [5] Where is the lair of the lions (12aA)

ומרעה הוא לכפרים [2]   and the feeding place of the young lions? (12aB)

אשר הלך אריה לביא שם [12] Where the lion went, the lioness was there, (12bA)

גור אריה ואין מחריד [1]   the welp of the lion and there was no one who
made (him) afraid. (12bB)

---

[42] If one does not want to emend the Masoretic text, this seems to be the most likely interpretation: the king is put aside; he is now no more than a powerless spectator (cf. the use of the verb נצב in Ps. 39:6), who has to watch how the queen is raped by the victorious enemy.

II.C.ii.2

אריה טרף בדי גרותיו [5] The lion was tearing for his welps (13aA)

ומחנק ללבאתיו [2] and strangling for his lionesses. (13aB)

וימלא־טרף חריו [5] And he filled his caves with torn flesh (13bA)

ומענתיו טרפה [1] and his lairs with torn animals. (13bB)

II.C.ii.3

הנני אליך [7] נאם Behold, I am against you!, pronouncement of

יהוה צבאות [5] YHWH of hosts. (14aA)

והבערתי בעשן רבך[43] [5] And I will burn in smoke your abundance (14aB)

וכפיריך תאכל חרב [2] and your young lions the sword will devour. (14aC)

והכרתי מארץ טרפך [5] And I will cut off from the earth your prey (14bA)

ולא־ישמע עוד קול and the voice of your messengers will be heard no

מלאככה [1] more. (14bB)

III.A.i.1

הוי עיר דמים [2] Ah, city of bloodshed, (1a)

כלה [7] כחש פרק מלאה [5] all of her a lie, of pillage full, (1bA)

לא ימיש טרף [1] prey never fails to be present. (1bB)

III.A.i.2

קול שוט [5] Sound of whip(s) (2aA)

וקול ראש אופן [2] and sound of rattling wheel(s). (2aB)

וסוס דהר [5] And hors(es) galloping (2bA)

ומרכבה מרקדה [1] and chariot(s) bounding. (2bB)

פרש מעלה [7] Horsemen charging (3aA)

ולהב חרב [10?] and the flame of a sword (3aB)

וברק חנית [5] and the lightning of a spear. (3aC)

III.A.i.3

ורב חלל [8] And a great number of slain (3bA)

וכבד פגר [2] and a heavy mass of corpses. (3bB)

ואין קצה לגויה [5] And there is no end to the bodies. (3cA)

יכשלו בגויתם [1] They stumble over their bodies. (3cB)

. . . .

---

[43]Read with the LXX רַבֵּךְ in stead of MT רִכְבָּהּ, "her chariots."

III.A.ii.1

[5] מרב זנוני זונה   Because of the great number of harlotries of the
harlot, (4aA)

[2] טובת חן בעלת כשפים   good of grace, mistress of sorceries. (4aB)

[5] המכרת גוים בזנוניה   Selling nations with her harlotry (4bA)

[1] ומשפחות בכשפיה   and families by her sorceries. (4bB)

III.A.ii.2

[5] הנני אליך נאם יהוה צבאות   Behold, I am against you!, pronouncement of
YHWH of hosts. (5aA)

[2] וגליתי שוליך על־פניך   And I will lift up your skirts over your face. (5aB)

[5] והראיתי גוים מערך   And I will let nations stare at your nakedness (5bA)

[1] וממלכות קלונך   and kingdoms at your shame.(5bB)

III.A.ii.3

[8] והשלכתי עליך שקצים   And I will throw filth at you (6aA)

[2] ונבלתיך   and I will mock you (6aB)

[1] ושמתיך כראי   and make you a spectacle. (6aC)

. . . .

III.B.i.1

[5] והיה כל־ראיך ידוד ממך   And it shall be that everyone who sees you will flee
from you (7aA)

[5] ואמר שדדה נינוה   and say: Nineveh is devastated. (7aB)

[2] מי ינוד לה   Who will grieve for her? (7bA)

[1] מאין אבקש מנחמים לך   Where can I find comforters for you? (7bB)

III.B.i.2

[5] התיטבי מנא אמון   Are you better than No-Amon, (8aA)

[5] הישבה ביארים   dwelling at the rivers? (8aB)

[2] מים סביב לה   Waters were surrounding her, (8aC)

[5] אשר־חיל ים   whose rampart was the sea, (8bA)

[1] מים חומתה   of the sea her wall. (8bB)

III.B.i.3

[12] כוש עצמה ומצרים   Cush was her strength and Egypt (9aA)

[5] ואין קצה   and there was no end, (9aB)

[5] פוט ולובים   Put and Lubim (9bA)

[1] היו בעזרתך   were your helpers. (9bB)

. . . .

III.B.ii.1

גַּם־הִיא [7] לְגֹלָה הָלְכָה בַשְּׁבִי [5] She too went into exile in captivity. (10aA)

גַּם עֹלָלֶיהָ יְרֻטְּשׁוּ בְרֹאשׁ Her children too were dashed in pieces at the head

כָל־חוּצוֹת [2] of all the streets. (10aB)

וְעַל־נִכְבַּדֶּיהָ יַדּוּ גוֹרָל [5] And for her nobles they cast the lot (10bA)

וְכָל־גְּדוֹלֶיהָ רֻתְּקוּ בַזִּקִּים [1] and all her great men were bound in chains.

(10bB)

III.B.ii.2

גַּם־אַתְּ תִּשְׁכְּרִי [5] You too will become drunk. (11aA)

תְּהִי נַעֲלָמָה [2] You will be dazed. (11aB)

גַּם־אַתְּ תְּבַקְשִׁי מָעוֹז מֵאוֹיֵב [1] You too will seek shelter from the enemy. (11aC)

III.B.ii.3

כָּל־מִבְצָרַיִךְ [5] All your strongholds (12aA)

תְּאֵנִים עִם־בִּכּוּרִים [2] are fig trees, with first-ripe figs. (12aB)

אִם־יִנּוֹעוּ [6] When they are shaken, (12bA)

וְנָפְלוּ עַל־פִּי אוֹכֵל [1] they fall into the mouth of the eater. (12bB)

. . . .

III.C.i.1

הִנֵּה עַמֵּךְ נָשִׁים בְּקִרְבֵּךְ [5] Behold, your people are women in your midst.

(13aA)

לְאֹיְבַיִךְ [5] פָּתוֹחַ נִפְתְּחוּ שַׁעֲרֵי To your enemies the gates of your land are wide

אַרְצֵךְ [2] open. (13bA)

אָכְלָה אֵשׁ בְּרִיחָיִךְ [1] Fire has consumed your bars. (13bB)

III.C.i.2

מֵי מָצוֹר שַׁאֲבִי־לָךְ [5] Water for the siege draw for yourself, (14aA)

חַזְּקִי מִבְצָרָיִךְ [2] strengthen your strongholds! (14aB)

בֹּאִי בַטִּיט וְרִמְסִי בַחֹמֶר [8] Go into the clay and tread the mortar, (14bA)

הַחֲזִיקִי מַלְבֵּן [1] make strong the brick-mold. (14bB)

III.C.i.3

שָׁם תֹּאכְלֵךְ אֵשׁ [2] There the fire will devour you, (15aA)

תַּכְרִיתֵךְ חֶרֶב [5] the sword will cut you down, (15aB)

תֹּאכְלֵךְ כַּיָּלֶק [2] it will devour you like the locust, (15aC)

הִתְכַּבֵּד כַּיָּלֶק [5] } {*numerous like the locust,* (15bA)

הִתְכַּבְּדִי כָּאַרְבֶּה [1] [44]{ *numerous like the grasshopper.* (15bC)}

. . . .

---

[44]These lines have to be regarded as a later addition which disturbs the regular

III.C.ii.1

הרבית רכליך [5] You have increased your merchants (16aA)

מכוכבי השמים [2]   more than the stars of heaven. (16aB)

ילק פשט ויעף {[1] {A locust spreads its wings and flies away. (16b)

מנזריך כארבה [5] Your princes are like grasshoppers (17aA)

וטפסריך כגוב גבי [2]   and your captains as the hords of locusts. (17aB)

החונים בגדרות ביום   Settling in the hedges on a cold day. (17aC)}

קרה{ [5] ⁴⁵

שמש זרחה ונודד [5] The sun rises and they disappear (17bA)

ולא־נודע מקומו אים [1]   and their place is not known. Where are they? (17bB)

III.C.ii.2

נמו רעיך מלך אשור [5] Your shepherds are asleep, king of Assyria, (18aA)

ישכנו אדיריך [2]   your nobles lie down. (18aB)

נפשו עמך על־ההרים [8] Your people are scattered on the mountains (18bA)

ואין מקבץ [1]   and there is none to gather (them). (18bB)

III.C.ii.3

אין־כהה לשברך [5] There is no lessening of your blow. (19aA)

נחלה מכתך [2]   Your wound is grievous. (19aB)

כל שמעי שמעך [7] All who hear the news of you (19bA)

תקעו כף עליך [5]   clap their hands over you. (19bB)

כי על־מי־עברה רעתך   For upon whom has not come your evil

תמיד [1]   continually? (19bC)

In most cases it is not necessary to defend the delimitation of verses, as they are not only indicated by the Masoretic distinctive accents but also supported by the clear internal parallelism and other poetical divices like chiasmus and wordplay. In a number of places, however, there are reasons to question the colometry indicated by K. Elliger in the BHS. Most of the time the Masoretic division appears to be preferable. In an insignificant number of cases I had to express doubt with regard to the correctness of the dividing accents of the Tiberian Masoretes.

Nah.1:1 is usually regarded as a superscript which does not belong to or is a later addition to the following poem. It is, however, clearly a bicolon with two corresponding halves. Within the context of this

---

structure of the poem. See below.

⁴⁵ A later explanatory addition mixing two different metaphors.

book the names of Nineveh and Nahum function as a parallel pair.
The name of the capital of Assyria is used here and in 2:9 and 3:7,
whereas the name of the prophet is only used at the beginning. It is
certainly no coincidence that verb related to the name of the prophet
(nḥm) also returns in 3:7. The superscript is also connected poetically
to the verses immediately following it. The name of the apparent home
town of the prophet parallels the first epithet of YHWH: אל ‖ אלקשִׁי
קנוֹא. The name of the town can be translated as "God is severe",
which forms a good parallel pair with "God is jealous".[46]

With BHS, BHK and against the Masoretic accents we take the
first two words of 1:8 together with the second part of v. 7. This
verse appears to be built up in the same way as the preceding one.
It begins with a positive statement about YHWH (טוב ‖ בו ידע חסי
יהוה). The second cola both describe a dangerous situation (ביום צרה
‖ בשטף) in which YHWH brings relief (עבר[47] ‖ למען). Note also the
chiastic structure of this verse, with participles describing activities
of YHWH at the beginning and at the end. The Masoretes may have
been misled by the uncommon use of the verb עבר. In line with the
more negative meaning in 1:12; 2:1; and 3:19 they connected it with
the description of the judgement in the next verse.

Contrary to the colometry in the BHS Nah.1:9-11 should be regarded as consisting of three tricola. Apparently Elliger denies, at
least for the book of Nahum, the existence of such longer verses. There
can be no doubt, however, that this important device of lengthening
and thus demarcating larger poetic units[48] was also used by this poet.
This is indicated by the Masoretic accents and confirmed by the internal parallelism in v. 10 (סירים ‖ סבבים ‖ קש and כ ‖ כ) and v. 11
(בליעל[49] ‖ רעה). The coherence of this verse is also underlined by the
wordplay: יצא י ‖ יעץ.

The difficult 2:9 is probably better understood when we regard
והמה נסים as the beginning of the second verse which consists of three
short cola, as is indicated by the Masoretes. Such short cola are not

---

[46]Cf. Song of S. 8:6 קשה כשאול קנאה, "jealousy is as severe as Sheol". This lends
support to Allis's suggestion that the name of this town was fictitious ("Nahum,
Nineveh, Elkosh", 76). The poet may have been inspired here by the pronouncement (משא) in Isa. 21 speaking of a "severe vision" (חזון קשה) and a coming
destruction (שדה, v. 2, cf. Nah.3:7!). Less likely is the suggestion of O. Happel,
Das Buch des Propheten Nahum, Würzburg 1902, 6, that it is a misread marginal
note: "Vision of Nahum from אל to קש", viz. from v. 2 until the word קש in v. 10.

[47]Cf. for this use of the verb עבר Am.7:8; 8:2; and especially Mic.7:18, where it
is used opposed to the statement of God keeping to his anger (אף).

[48]Cf. Watson, *Classical Hebrew Poetry*, 177-85.

[49]Cf. the use of these words next to each other in Jud. 20:13 and Prov. 16:27.

exceptional[50] and often they contain one or more imperativi. Again this division is supported by internal parallelism (עמד[52] ‖ פנה[51] ‖ נסה). According to the Masoretes, 2:11 is built up in the same way: a bicolon followed by a tricolon. This time, however, the cola are much longer. This may have to do with the difference in the situation described: v. 9b is about fleeing hastily, whereas v. 11b is about lasting fear. The unity of v. 11 is also supported by the clear internal parallism of "heart, knees, loins, face". There is also a chiastic element, because the "melting" mentioned at the beginning presupposes the heat which can make "faces glow."[53]

The delimitation of strophes can be based on the many markers and cases of external parallelism. For instance, in the second strophe (I.i.2 = Nah. 1:2) the binding element is the use of יהוה נקם. The following strophe is characterized by the name of YHWH as casus pendens in both verses. Another often returning phenomenon is the use of distant parallism: next to the well-known *parallelismus membrorum* per verse, words forming parallel pairs can also be used to bind together larger units. For instance, in strophe I.ii.1 (Nah. 1:4) we find the verb יבש in the first verse and אמלל in the second verse. From Joel 1:10 we learn that these verbs can be regarded as a parallel pair. Similar examples can be found throughout this text. To mention only a few of them: ענה and מוסר (strophe II.A.i.2) can be regarded as connected roots because of Ps. 107:10; זרע and כרת (II.A.i.3) are part of a standard phrase in Isa. 48:19 and Ps. 37:28; מים and טיט (III.C.i.2) form a parallel pair in Isa. 57:20 and Ps. 69:15; and קבץ ‖ רעה (III.C.ii.2) in Isa. 40:11; Jer. 31:10; Ezek. 34:13.

The same phenomenon can be observed on the level of canticles and (sub)cantos. The first canticle is bound together by the use of name of YHWH, which is lacking in the next and then returns in the third canticle. In this third canticle (Nah.1:7-11) we come across the often used poetic device of inclusion. Not only the name of YHWH is found at the beginning and end, but also the parallel pair טוב ‖ רעה.[54] The inclusion by the repetition of the name of YHWH, next to the repetition of איב in v. 2 and 8, and of הוא in v. 2 and 9, strongly

---

[50] Cf. Korpel, De Moor, "Fundamentals of Ugaritic and Hebrew Poetry", in: W. van der Meer, J.C. de Moor (eds.), *The Structural Analysis of Biblical and Canaanite Poetry* (JSOT.S, 74), Sheffield 1988, 7-11.

[51] Cf. Isa.13:14 and Jer. 46:5; 50:1, 6.

[52] Cf. Jer. 46:21 with all three verbs.

[53] Cf. the use of מסס in Isa. 13:7-9.

[54] Also noticed by Armerding, *The Expositor's Bible Commentary*, vol. 7, 452 and 464. See also Pardee, *Ugaritic and Hebrew Poetic Parallelism*, 84; Kim, *The Structure of the Samson Cycle*, 271.

supports the delimination of the first canto, which is also indicated by the Setumah only rarely heeded by modern commentators.[55]

In the second canto we see this inclusion, for instance, in the first canticle (1:12-14) with the phrase "YHWH commands" in the last verse balancing "thus says YHWH" at the beginning, which on the level of the subcanto forms an inclusion with the name of the Lord in 2:3. The first subcanto is also characterized by the repetition of שלם in 1:12 and 2:1 (two times), of עבר in 1:12 and 2:1, of לא עוד in 1:12, 14 and 2:1, and of the particle כי in 1:14; 2:1 and 3 (two times). As a rule 1:12-14 is taken together with 1:1-11, but the connections with 2:1-3 appear to be much stronger.

In canto II the name of YHWH not only marks the first canticle and the first subcanto, it also marks the canto as a whole (cf. "pronouncement of YHWH" in 2:14). Again, this is not the only indication for 1:12-2:14 as a larger unit. One can also note an inclusion by רב (1:12 and 2:14), כרת (1:12, 2:1 and 14), and לא עוד (1:12, 14 and 2:14).

The proposed division in strophes sheds new light on the problem of the different suffixed personal pronouns. At first sight there is a strange intermingling of plural and singular, feminine and masculine. On the level of strophes, however, their use appears to be far more consistent. The suffixes can now be easily determined. The second person masculine plural in 1:9 (strophe I.iii.2) are the enemies of YHWH; the second person feminine singular in 1:11 (I.iii.3) is Nineveh (inclusion with 1:1!); in 1:12-13 (II.A.i.2) the second person feminine singular is Judah; the second person masculine singular in 1:14 (II.A.i.3) is the king of Assyria (inclusion with 3:18!); the second person feminine singular in 2:1 (II.A.ii.1) is Judah, but in the next strophe (2:2) Nineveh again.

Canticle II.A.ii is characterized by the use of names (Judah, Jacob, Israel). The same can be observed in III.B.i (Nineveh, No-Amon, Cush, Egypt, etc.), which supports this delimination of the canticle. Another argument for this division is the inclusion by נחם (3:7) ‖ עזר (3:9).[56] The relation between these verbs also explains the at first sight illogical use of the suffixed second person pronoun[57]: "*your* helpers" corresponds to the question "where can I find comforters *for you*", whereas Nineveh is referred to in the third person before.

---

[55]Exceptions are E. Achtemeier, *Nahum–Malachi* (Interpretation), Atlanta 1986, 6-7 and R.J. Coggins, in: R.J. Coggins, S.P. Re'emi, *Israel Among the Nations: A Commentary on the Books of Nahum, Obadiah, Esther* (ITC), Grand Rapids 1985, 7.

[56]It can be regarded as a break-up of a standard phrase; cf. Ps. 86:17.

[57]Cf. the emendation proposed in the BHS.

Other examples of external parallelism binding together canticles can be found in 2:4-5 (II.B.i): אש ‖ לפידם ‖ ברק[58]; in 2:6-8 (II.B.ii): אדיריו ‖ אמהתיה (inclusion by mentioning opposite classes of people) and חומתה ‖ שערים;[59] 2:12-14 (II.C.ii): the metaphor of the lion's family; and 3:1-3 (III.A.i): פגר ‖ דמים.[60]

Especially on the level of canticles and strophes the poem as a whole shows a well-balanced structure:

(Sub)cantos	Canticles	Strophes	Verses
I	3	3+3+3	17
II.A	2	3+3	12
II.B	2	2+2	8
II.C	2	3+3	12
III.A	2	3+3	12
III.B	2	3+3	11
III.C	2	3+3	12

Canto I is a hymn singing of Yhwh as an avenger and a judge. It can be compared to poems like Pss. 94 and 97. This first canto disturbs the numerical balance. The poet must have had his reasons for this. He probably was forced – as will be demonstrated below – to admit this slight imbalance because he had to work with already existing material. He was able to adapt the length of the canticles, but he did not force it as a whole into his own structure.

The second canto describes the judgement of Nineveh by the avenging God of Israel. His pronouncement forms the inclusion of the canto. In between we find a vision of the judgement taking place. This beautifully agrees with the double heading in 1:1 announcing a pronouncement and a vision.

The third canto is a reaction to this judgement in the form of an ironic elegy, which is expressed at the beginning and end. It also takes up elements of the judgement and vision of the previous canto.

The cantos are clearly interrelated. The first canto is tied to the following cantos by the repetition of a number of words, some of which can be labelled as key-words; especially אש (1:6; 2:4; 3:13, 15), טוב (1:7, 3:4,[61] 8), מעוז (1:7; 3:11), עבר (1:8, 12; 2:1; 3:19). A number of words appears throughout the book as marking larger units: the particle כי is usually found at the end of canticles and subcantos (1:10, 14; 2:1, 3

---

[58] Cf. the use of these words within one verse in Ezek. 1:13 and Dan. 10:6.

[59] Cf. Isa. 60:18; Jer. 1:15; 51:58; Ezek. 26:10.

[60] Cf. Isa. 34:3.

[61] It should also be noted that it is used here together with בעל. This can be related to Yhwh being called בעל as well in 1:2.

(2x), 19); the verb אכל is always found at the end of the cantos (1:10; 2:14; 3:12, 13, 15); the same can be said of רעה (1:11 and 3:19).[62]

The cantos are connected as a chain. Its links are בליעל (1:11; 2:1), טרף (2:14; 3:1), קול (2:14; 3:2), and חרב (2:14; 3:3). In this connection one should also note the "pronouncement of YHWH of host" (2:14) being taken up in the first subcanto of canto III (3:5). This relation is underlined by the similar structure of the respective canticles (II.C.ii and III.A.ii).

Cantos II and III are interrelated in many ways.[63] There is an inclusion indicated by the repetition of רב (1:12 and 3:16),[64] שמע (2:1aA and 3:19bA), הרים (2:1 and 3:18), חגי (2:1) ‖ תקע כף (3:19),[65] עבר (2:1 and 3:19). Within this inclusion the cantos appear to be built up in the same way: the wickedness described with a methaphor (lion/harlot), followed by words of YHWH announcing the way in which He shall deal with this wickedness.

	Canto II	Canto III
The attacking army	2:4–5	3:1–3
כשל	6	3
גלה	8	5
מים	9	8
אין קצה	10	9
Weakness	11	11–13
Comparison with animals	12–13	15

All this leads to the conclusion that the book of Nahum is a well-structured literary unity. During the structural analysis, however, we also came across some indications of redactional activities. We noticed that in length and structure the first canto deviates from the second and third. This canto is also characterized by the traces of a partial alphabetic acrostic. Most of the letters forming the alphabet are still more or less in place: *alef* in 2aA, *bet* in 3bA, *gimel* in 4aA, *he* in 5aA, *waw* in 5bA, *zain* in 6aA, *chet* in 6bA, *tet* in 7aA, *yod* in 7bA, *kaf* in 8bA, *lamed* in 9aC), and *mem* in 11aA. This can be

---

[62]This was also noticed by Achtemeier, *Nahum–Malachi*, 6.

[63]Cf. also A. Chouraqui, *La bible traduite et présentée: Les douze prophètes*, Paris 1976, 22; Armerding, *The Expositor's Bible Commentary*, vol. 7, 470-1.; Achtemeier, *Nahum–Malachi*, 21 and 27-8; Patterson, Travers, "Literary Analysis", 48-9; and Nogalski, *Redactional Processes*, 123.

[64]In these places רב is opposed to the parallel pair denoting the "flying away" of the many: עבר (1:12) ‖ נדד (3:17bA); cf. Jer.9:9.

[65]Cf. for the interpretation of this expression as an indication of celebration Ps. 47:2.

no coincidence,[66] but it is neither a coincidence that it took so long before it was discovered again. Apparently the poet had no intention to preserve it. The analysis of the text thus far also gives no reason to assume that the Hebrew text of this book was ill-preserved. Therefore, it is most likely that the poet adapted an existing acrostic song[67] and that traces of the original song are found until the letter *mem*.[68]

The history of research shows that it is not fruitful to attempt to restore the original poem. Some conclusions can be drawn, however, from the way in which the poet of Nah. 1 revised this earlier text. He appears to have expanded the first strophe with variations on the themes of נקם (v. 2b) and יהוה (3a).[69] In this way he has emphasized the message about YHWH as an avenger. For the same reason his name was also repeated before the original beginning of the second strophe (בסופה). In v. 4 the original word beginning with *dalet* was replaced by a word repeated at the end of the verse.[70] This repeating of the same word within short range can be regarded as typical of the poet's style, because it is also found in the expanded first part of the poem (1:2) and in the following verses as well (1:12; 2:9, 10, 13; 3:2, 10, 11, 14, 15). In v. 6 the original unusual order of words, with זעמו at the beginning of the verse, was changed. In v. 7b the copulativum *waw* was added, apparently to underline the relation between the two verses forming one strophe. Coming to the end of the first canto the poet again expanded the original poem in the *kaf*- and the *lamed*-strophes. Just as he did before with his description of YHWH as an avenger, the poet now payed extra attention to YHWH "making an end" by repeating כלה in the second of the added cola 9aA and 9aB.

---

[66]M.H. Floyd, "The Chimerical Acrostic of Nahum 1:2-10", *JBL* 113 (1994), 421-37, rightly criticizes the fact that in modern research too often the hypothesis of an originally complete acrostic has been turned into a fact. He goes too far in his criticism, however, when he assumes that the acrostic is only in the mind of some of the readers and not at all in the text.

[67]Cf. Ridderbos, in: Spronk, Ridderbos, *Worstelen met een wrekende God*, 38; A. van Selms, "The Alphabetic Hymn in Nahum 1", in: A.H. van Zyl (ed.), *Biblical Essays: Proceedings of the Twelfth Meeting of "Die ou-testamentiese werkgemeenskap in Suid-Afrika"*, Potchefstroom 1969, 33-45; esp. 40; Van der Woude, *Jona – Nahum* (PredOT), 80; Achtemeier, *Nahum–Malachi*, 6; and J.J.M. Roberts, *Nahum, Habakkuk, and Zephaniah: a Commentary*, Louisville 1991, 48.

[68]Cf., without taking over their suggestions to emend the text, the BHK and G.B. Gray, "The Alphabetic Psalm in Nahum", *The Expositor* 5th Series, vol. 8 (1898), 207-20.

[69]See on the phenomenon of expansion (and contraction) see Korpel, De Moor, "Fundamentals", *passim*.

[70]Comparison with Isa.19:4-8, which also speaks of rivers drying up, renders it likely that the original verb was דלל, "become small", because here, in v. 6, it is used in the same context as the verb אמלל.

The original text is found again in 9aC and in 10aC. The metaphor of
the "dried stubble" is expanded in 10aA-B. Finally, the *mem*-strophe
seems to be expanded by adding 11aB repeating and precising the
already added 9aA.

This adaption of (part of) an already existing acrostic hymn should
not be ascribed, as is done by many modern authors,[71] to later editors
of the book of Nahum, but to the prophet/poet himself. In stead of
assuming that the book of Nahum was connected in this way to the
books of Micah and Joel, it is more to the point to regard the related
passages in Joel (cf. 2:13 and 4:21), just like Jonah, as a reaction to
the message of Nahum. There are clear parallels with Mic. 7, but these
are not clear enough to assume the deliberate adding of words and
phrases to "stitch together" these two books. The more simple and
likely solution is that Nahum was inspired by his predecessor, just
as he in his turn was an inspiration to Habakuk: cf. Hab. 1:8f. and
2:12 with Nah. 2:4 and 3:1ff.; Hab. 3:6, 10 with Nah. 1:5; Hab. 3:8-10
with Nah.1:4; Hab.3:16 with Nah.1:7[72]; cf. also the hymn at the end
of Habakuk with the opening hymn in the book of Nahum; and finally their related headings underlined by the command to Habakuk:
"write down the vision" (2:2; cf. the use of ספר in Nah.1:1).

In this connection a remark should also be made about the well-
known relationship between Nah. 2:1 and Isa. 52:7. Many scholars
assume that Nahum borrowed from the Second Isaiah.[73] This implies
that at least this part of the book of Nahum would have been written
in or after the Babylonian exile. A closer look, however, at these
verses shows that it is the other way around. The first words of Nah.
2:1, "Behold on the mountains the feet of a messenger", have been
altered slightly in Isa. 52:7: "*How lovely* on the mountain are the feet
...". And the phrase "announcing peace" is expanded in Isa. 52 to
"announcing peace, bringing good news, announcing salvation". The
easiest way to explain these differences is that the poet of Isa. 52
rewrote the verse of Nah. 2, qualifying and clarifying it.[74]

---

[71]Cf. R.C. van Leeuwen, "Scribal Wisdom and Theology in the Book of the
Twelve", in: L.G. Perdue *et al.* (eds.), *In Search of Wisdom: Essays in Memory
of J.G. Gammie*, Louisville 1993, 31-49, especially 47-9; J. Nogalski, "The Redactional Shaping of Nahum 1 for the Book of the Twelve", in: P.R. Davies and
D.J.A. Clines (eds.), *Among the Prophets* (JSOT.S, 144), Sheffield 1993, 193-202,
esp. 199-200.

[72]Cf. J.P.J. Olivier, "The Concept of *Day* in Nahum and Habakuk", in: Van
Zyl (ed.), *Biblical Essays*, 71-4

[73]Cf., for instance, Jeremias, *Kultprophetie und Gerichtsverkündigung*, 43; Renaud, "La composition", 205; Nogalski, *Redactional Processes*, 97-8.

[74]Cf. A.S. van der Woude, "Hoe de Here naar Sion wederkeert ... Traditio-

Things appear to be different with Nah. 3:15-17, where many scholars assume a corruption of the original text because of the unexpected inconsistent use of metaphors.[75]. This is supported now by our structural analysis: precisely this part of the poem disturbs its regular structure. The additions (15bB-C and 16aB-17aC) may have been inspired by the metaphor of the grashopper in the book of Joel and can be related, therefore, to the editing of the Book of the Twelve Prophets as a whole. The analysis of the poetic structure of the book of Nahum, however, shows that it is not likely that this editing was accompanied by so much reshaping of the books of the prophets as is assumed by Nogalski.[76] This editing should be seen in the first place as a well-considered attempt to place the twelve books in the right order. Their present shape makes them look like one of the major prophets, not only in length but also with regard to the thematic order: starting with a collection of words of doom directed to their own community, followed by prophecies against foreign nations and concluded with words of hope for restoration.[77] It was only logical to place the book of Jonah, which is in many aspects a reaction to the prophecy of Nahum, before Nahum. A story about the salvation of Nineveh would have made no sense after the description of its definitive destruction. In some places, however, the apparent chronological order must have been broken deliberately. On the basis of chronology the prophecy of Zephaniah should have been placed between Micah and Nahum. Apparently it was inserted after Habakuk because of the similarities between Micah and Nahum and between Nahum and Habakuk. In stead of attributing these similarities to later editorial

---

historische overwegingen bij Jesaja 52:7-8", in: H.H. Grosheide a.o. (eds.), *De Knecht: Studies rondom Deutero-Jesaja aangeboden aan prof.dr. J.L. Koole*, Kampen 1978, 188-196, esp. 190-1; cf. in general on the view that the Second Isaiah may have borrowed from Nahum, or at least knew him: J.L. Helberg, "Nahum–Jonah–Lamentations–Isaiah 51–53", in: Van Zyl (ed.), *Biblical Essays*, 46-55, esp. 53-5; U. Cassuto, "On the Formal and Stilistic Relationship Between Deutero-Isaiah and Other Biblical Writings", in: U. Cassuto, *Biblical and Oriental Studies*, vol. 1, Jerusalem 1973, 141-77, esp. 168-71; R.J. Coggins, "An Alternative Prophetic Tradition?", in: R.J. Coggins *et al.* (eds.), *Israel's Prophetic Tradition: Essays in Honour of Peter R. Ackroyd*, Cambridge 1982, 77-94, esp. 82ff.

[75] Cf. amongst others Jeremias, *Kultprophetie und Gerichtsverkündigung*, 43 and Nogalski, *Redactional Processes*, 124-6.

[76] Cf. his *Literary Precursors to the Book of the Twelve* (BZAW, 217), Berlin & New York 1993 and *Redactional Processes*; cf. also Van Leeuwen, "Scribal Wisdom".

[77] Cf. R.J. Coggins, "The Minor Prophets – One Book or Twelve?", in: S.E. Porter *et al.* (eds.), *Crossing the Boundaries: Essays in Honour of Michael D. Goulder* (BiIntS, 8), Leiden 1994, 57-68.

activities, it is more likely to assume that the prophets themselves partly took their inspiration from predecessors.

It can be concluded that the diachronic analysis clearly benefits from an elaborate synchronic analysis which gives the text the chance to prove its coherence. Beginning the diachronic analysis too soon, because of little trust in the Masoretic text and/or the wish to find out the truth about the famous acrostic, does more damage than good to the interpretation of the well-structured book of Nahum. Methodologically, it is interesting to see how a sound synchronic approach paves the way for a responsible diachronic analysis.

Eep Talstra *Free University, Amsterdam – The Netherlands*

Deuteronomy 9 and 10
Synchronic and Diachronic Observations[1]

0. Does *Kampen* Mean Two Camps?

By way of introduction I quote a short dialogue taken from Chaim Potok's novel *In the Beginning*.[2] Two Jewish boys discuss the decision made by one of them to take up what is called 'secular' biblical studies at a university.

"Will you publish?"	"Yes."
"Books and papers?"	"Yes."
"About this piece of the Torah being from this date and that piece from that date? Things like that?"	"Yes."

(...)

"It's the Torah of Moses, Davey. With all my heart I believe that. If you teach anything else, you destroy it."

Can one teach the Torah of Moses and also teach about several fragments of the text coming from one period of history and other fragments coming from an different period? During a considerable period of time scholars in Biblical research have applied methods of structural and of historical textual interpretation in a mutually exclusive way. Exegetes usually makes choices here. This can easily be observed by comparing various studies of the Deuteronomy chapters that are the topic of this contribution. These studies are either of a synchronic type, i.e. guided by stylistical or biblical-theological questions, such as the work of Polzin,[3] Sailhamer[4] or O'Connell[5] (to mention just a few). Or these studies are of a diachronic type, i.e. guided by histori-

---

[1] This contribution is dedicated to the memory of my teacher and promotor prof. dr. Martin Jan Mulder, professor of Old Testament at the University of Leiden, who died June 24, 1994.

[2] Chaim Potok, *In the Beginning*, 1975 (edition Fawcett Crest: New York 1990), 419.

[3] R. Polzin, *Moses and the Deuteronomist: A Literary Study of the Deuteronomic History*, part 1: Deuteronomy, Joshua, Judges, New York, 1980.

[4] J.H. Sailhamer, *The Pentateuch as Narrative: A Biblical-Theological Commentary*, Grand Rapids 1992.

[5] R.H. O'Connell, "Deuteronomy ix 7–x 7,10–11: Panelled Structure, Double Rehearsal and the Rhetoric of Covenant Rebuke," *VT* 42 (1992), 492-509.

cal or hermeneutical questions, such as the work of Aurelius,[6] García López[7] or Vermeylen.[8]

Concerning Deut. 9 and 10, various proposals on its interpretation do not seem to interact at all with the methods or the results of others. And if so, it is only done in a rather negative mode. Even when in Old Testament scholarship it is repeatedly stated that the synchronic and diachronic types of research should be used on a basis of complementarity,[9] in the actual research, the validity of this claim hardly has been tested.

In contrast to previous interactions, the titles of several contributions of this conference are promising. They use the word 'and' rather then the word 'or' used in formulating the question that is the theme of this conference: 'Synchronic or Diachronic?'. So the answer to this question really seems to be open. Will this debate in 'Kampen' end up in two 'camps' or not?

The challenge of this moment is clear. The use of 'and' rather than 'or' implies that a number of biblical scholars agrees with the claim that synchronic and diachronic do not represent mutually exclusive types of textual interpretation. But, if that is the case, biblical scholarship might be expected to be able to establish one comprehensive method to allow for the application of both approaches to texts in a complementary way. This raises other questions. If both synchronic and diachronic types of interpretation can be applied to the same texts, in which order would one have to apply them? Are the methods dependent on each other for information in some way? A simple plea for plurality of methods may be a good starting point, but methodologically, it is not convincing.

1. Admiration and Irritation

The *first question* that needs to be answered is: if indeed a majority of scholars is willing to agree that diachronic and synchronic methods are not mutually exclusive, then what causes the debate on these matters to become so sharp from time to time? In my view, the ten-

---

[6]E. Aurelius, *Der Fürbitter Israels: Eine Studie zum Mosebild im Alten Testament* (CB.OT, 27), Stockholm 1988.

[7]F. García López, "Analyse littéraire de Deutéronome V-XI", *RB* 84 (1977), 481-522; *RB* 85 (1978), 5-49.

[8]J. Vermeylen, "Les sections narratives de Deut 5-11 et leur relation à Ex 19-34," in: N. Lohfink (ed.), *Das Deuteronomium: Enstehung, Gestalt und Botschaft* (BEThL, 68), Leuven 1985.

[9]In *The Prayer of Solomon: Synchrony and Diachrony in the Composition of I Kings 8,14-61* (CBET, 3), Kampen, 1992, I have collected a number of examples, see 20, 84 n. 5, 257ff.

sion between the two approaches is to be attributed mainly to the fact that both synchronic and diachronic methods continue to concentrate very much on the *authors*, rather than on the *linguistic materials* we actually have, i.e. the textual compositions. Too much of the methodological debate, therefore, seems to be a battle about the assumed or denied qualities and skills of authors:

–   Is the author of Deut. 9 and 10 a highly trained artist, deliberately using complicated composition techniques in order to impress the readers and to guide the reading process of the audience? This is implied in the qualifications used by O'Connell[10] and others for the compositional skills demonstrated by the author of Deut. 9 and 10: 'deliberate', 'designed to', 'strategy' and 'striking'. Synchronic, rhetorical analysis seems to be based on *admiration*: each piece of text has been put in its proper place. No one could have done a better job with this text than this author.

–   Is the author an amateur historian who manipulated his sources in creating a new document and, happily, was clumsy enough to leave a number of traces in the texts to stimulate his modern professional readers to do a better job? See the observations by Aurelius[11] on scholarly "*Verwirrung und Irritation*" when the plot of Deut. 9 and 10 does not seem to fit standards of modern historiography. Diachronic analysis seems to be based on *irritation* originating from lacks of consistency observed in the text. If I were the author of this text, I would have done a better job. My suggestion is, therefore, that both methods still have too much in common, in their literary, author-centered interest, to be able to start a fruitful discussion about their respective claims on *textual* analysis. The *author* either passes the exam or fails. But what about the text? This tendency to start with the author rather than with the text can be demonstrated by comparing, at this point, various approaches to the study of Deut. 9 and 10.

Literary criticism tends to restrict itself to the question of whether the presentation of the desert period in Deut. 9 and 10 does justice to preceding texts in the Pentateuch. One sees the text as a poor imitation of the materials in the books of Exodus and Numbers. What historical information lies behind the text? How did the author use his sources and how has his theology modified the textual material? Thus the start of the inquiry is from a comparison with Exod. 32-34 rather

---

[10]O'Connell, "Deuteronomy ix 7–x 7,10–11", 499-500, 506; Cf. C.J. Labuschagne, *Deuteronomium*, deel 1b, (PredOT), Nijkerk 1987, 185-6.

[11]Aurelius, *Der Fürbitter Israels*, 45-6: "*Verwirrung und Irritation*"; "*wenig natürliche Pause*" "*Ärgerlich*".

than from the structure of the Deut. text itself. Driver,[12] to mention
just one non-extreme example, presents a synoptic table to compare
Deut. 9-10 with Exod. 32-34. He is then surprised to find that the
intercession prayer in 9:25ff reflects the occasion of Exod. 34:9, but is
using the text of Exod. 32:11ff. Examples of much stronger reactions
in terms of irritation rather than of surprise about problems with the
plot in Deut. 9f. are mentioned in Aurelius' work and by Lohfink.[13]

Form critical analysis takes as its starting point the contrast between
two genres used in these chapters: historiographical elements (the
stay at Horeb and the journey in the desert) and parenetical elements (preaching about the covenant) in the text. In the work of N.
Lohfink,[14] this has lead to admiration of the work of the author. In
Lohfink's view, the author used an existing story on covenant break
at Horeb, added an introduction to it in parenetical style (9:1-8), inserted more cases of rebellion in 9:22-24 and structured the text not
in terms of historical plot, but in terms of theological argumentation.
Based on the repetition of the phrases on '40 days and 40 nights'
Lohfink found five strophes in the text. His admiration concerns the
combination of theological and stylistic skills of the author. That the
concentration is on the author, indeed, one can see in Lohfink's more
or less psychological reflections as to why and how the author expanded the original story.[15] This approach partly has been continued
in the analysis by F. García López[16] who, in his literary analysis,
refers to both genres and redactions.

Rhetorical criticism tends to explain *all* details of the text as *inten-
tionally* constructed by an artistic writer, using his skills to compose a
text that should be able to persuade the readers of the theological insights presented with the text. All observed data, mainly lexical data,
are seen as intended by the *author* for some kind of rhetorical effect.
On a number of occasions, O'Connell[17] criticizes Lohfink for having
overlooked some lexical patterns and for his evaluation of 9:1-8 as a

---

[12]S.R. Driver, *A Critical and Exegetical Commentary on Deuteronomy* (ICC),
Edinburgh ³1901.

[13]N. Lohfink, *Das Hauptgebot: Eine Untersuchung literarischer Einleitungsfra-
gen zu Dtn 5-11* (AnBib, 20), Rome 1963, 207ff.

[14]N. Lohfink, *Das Hauptgebot*, 216ff.

[15]In his contribution to *Die Botschaft und die Boten: Festschrift für H. W.
Wolff*, Neukirchen-Vluyn 1981: "Kerygmata des Deuteronomistischen Geschichtswerks", 87-100, Lohfink elaborated his view of the composition of Deut. 9ff., but
he did not substantially change it; 100, n. 44.

[16]F. García López, "Analyse littéraire".

[17]O'Connell, "Deuteronomy ix 7–x 7,10–11", 494, n. 3; 495, n.4.

text of later origin. To O'Connell,[18] the text exhibits an assymmetrical organization that is used as an effective tool for manipulating its reader. Lexical repetitions, chiasms, inclusions, etc. are present, but they are deliberately not used in fully balanced patterns. This implies that a model of symmetry is taken to be a default pattern, which is the one to be expected by a reader. Any deliberate deviation from this pattern is evaluated as even more effective by definition. O'Connell's article is filled with evaluative remarks such as 'rhetorical strategy', 'deliberate', 'designed', 'intended'.

The question remains whether these rather complex patterns of lexical material really are able to leave with the reader the impression of a highly structured text as long as it remains unclear whether grammatical, linguistic observations can support this.

Numerical composition techniques as applied by Labuschagne,[19] clearly demonstrate admiration of the authors, be it for, again, another set of skills. This method holds that counts of words, clauses or clause constituents registered in the texts should not be regarded as a coincidence, rather they can be identified as deliberately constructed numerical patterns. Numerical patterns are literary devices used by the author to structure the text. Redactional activity is not excluded by Labuschagne, but it is seen as governed by the same technique: new material with additional numerical patterns are inserted skillfully into the text.

Narrative Analysis combines textual structure and biblical theology. Sailhamer[20] describes the text of the entire Pentateuch as an intended unity which allows the reader to describe its structure and its theology as a well organized whole. Sailhamer analyzes Deut. 9:1-10:11 as an *"illustration from Israel's past"*, taking Deut. 10:10-11 as a first conclusion of the Horeb episode and 10:12-22 as an admonition that is based on the preceding illustrations from the past.

One may conclude that the various methods *make* themselves incompatible, because they try to make statements on the same domain, i.e. about the author.

Personally I experience great difficulties when I have to evaluate these various methods.
– There is no reason to reject in advance the observations they make in the texts, even when these appear to be contradictory. But clearly,

---

[18] O'Connell, "Deuteronomy ix 7–x 7,10–11", 497, 503.

[19] C.J. Labuschagne, *Deuteronomium*, deel 1b.

[20] J. H. Sailhamer, *The Pentateuch as Narrative*, 8ff., 34ff., 442ff.

it is impossible to explain all observations only by assuming a writer's strategy to cover them all.

– We lack a more comprehensive method able to assign a certain order, or a hierarchy, to the data observed and indicating at what level of argumentation they might have power of argument. That is the reason why a simple plea for plurality of methods is sympathetic as well as unconvincing.

– My proposal is to search for an order of the methods applied. To do so, we need a closer look at the material they all share: the language material. Linguistic analysis should allow us to make statements, both about the *text* and its possible effects on the reader, and the text and the possible origins of its composing parts.

2. The Position of Linguistic Observations

The debate between diachronic and synchronic reading has become so intense because scholars do not sufficiently distinguish observations they make at the level of the linguistic materials from claims they make concerning authors, their theology or their composition techniques. If this statement is correct as an answer to the first question formulated in the previous section, then the *second question* to be answered now, is on the position of linguistic observations in our methods of literary analysis. Of course, exegetes concentrate both on what is *outside or behind* the text (author, history, history of literary forms), and on what is *in* the text, i.e. the linguistic signs that are there to guide the process of reading. The discussion on methods will not change that fact. Rather, the debate between diachronic and synchronic reading invites us to reconsider the balance of the linguistic, literary and historical observations. It is the *order* of the observations in the text and of the data behind the text that counts.

My suggestion is to postpone the questions on extra-linguistic information, such as: what did the author have in mind when writing the text? What historical knowledge, sociolinguistic genres or rhetorical patterns the author used? What may have been the theology from which a particular text has been composed? Important as these questions are in terms of diachronic literary interpretation, in terms of method they are secondary ones. The first analysis should be from the perspective of the process of reading: what happens to the reader when reading this text? Or, to put it more technically: what linguistic markings can be found in the text to give guidance to the process of reading? To what extent can one construct the world of the text with the help of syntactic categories, grammatical relations and lexical data?

Now one should be aware of the fact that the linguistic knowledge used by a modern reader to understand ancient texts, is also historical knowledge. For that reason it is important to avoid a debate on synchronic and diachronic as if it were a debate on 'a-historical' versus 'historical' textual interpretation. Rather it is a debate on the order in which 'linguistic' and 'non-linguistic' data are used in textual analysis.

The linguistic data, in fact, are common to both methods of reading and should be analysed in their own rights much more intensively because they give access to both the textual structure and the world behind the text.

Thus, in my view, the debate is not on synchronic *versus* diachronic method. Rather the debate is on the *order* of methods. The entrance to the text is to be made by a process of synchronic reading using the linguistic (grammatical and lexical) data in the first place. This first step will also give further access to the text both for rhetorical and for diachronic research.

3. The Method Proposed

In continuation of the method proposed in my book on Solomon's Prayer,[21] I also want to argue with this paper for a clear order in the complementary application of methods.

The *first* claim is that synchronic analysis has priority over diachronic analysis. The synchronic analysis searches for both the syntactical and the lexical markers of a textual structure. Within the synchronic analysis observations of 'form' are prior to conclusions of syntactic 'function', syntactical observations have priority over lexical ones, which, in their turn, are prior to stylistic observations.

The *second* claim is that this linguistic and structural research provides the information needed to enter the diachronic analysis as a necessary second step. There is no need to base diachronic analysis on the readers' 'irritation', or on what traditional critical scholarship prefers to call '*Spannungen und Wiedersprüche*', because diachronic questioning can start positively on the basis of linguistically observable patterns and on changes of patterns in the text.

Third, this proposal implies that ideally a text be analysed twice: following the order synchrony – diachrony. I will try to contribute to both types of textual analysis, applying them to the text of Deut. 9 and 10, in order to test the method proposed.

The next sections, therefore, should be read as a test of the validity

---

[21] Talstra, *The Prayer of Solomon*, Chapters 0, 2, 4.

[שְׁמַע] [יִשְׂרָאֵל]   Dtn09,01
[אַתָּה] [עֹבֵר] [הַיּוֹם] [אֶת הַיַּרְדֵּן]   Dtn09,01
[לָבֹא]   Dtn09,01
[לָרֶשֶׁת] [גּוֹיִם]   Dtn09,01
[גְּדֹלִים וַעֲצֻמִים] [מִמֶּךָּ]   Dtn09,01
[עָרִים]   Dtn09,01
[גְּדֹלֹת וּבְצֻרֹת] [בַּשָּׁמָיִם]   Dtn09,01
[עַם גָּדוֹל וָרָם (בְּנֵי עֲנָקִים)]   Dtn09,02
[אֲשֶׁר] [אַתָּה] [יָדַעְתָּ]   Dtn09,02
[וְ] [אַתָּה] [שָׁמַעְתָּ]   Dtn09,02
[מִי] [יִתְיַצֵּב] [לִפְנֵי בְּנֵי עֲנָק]   Dtn09,02
         ...   ...

Fig. 1: Computer-assisted grammatical analysis.

of the claims listed. Accordingly, the process of synchronic reading of Deut. 9 and 10 will be described first (section 4) and after that the process of diachronic analysis of the text (section 5).

The starting point is a proposal of the textual structure that is based on an analysis of syntactic and lexical data. Computer–assisted grammatical analysis is used to produce first a segmentation of the text into phrases and clauses. See fig. 1.

A second set of computer programmes is used to establish a hierarchy of clauses in the text with the help of morphological, syntactical and lexical arguments.[22] This procedure results in a text syntactic segmentation of the text: main clauses, dependent clauses, direct speech, narrative sections, embedded direct speech, etc.

An abbreviated version of this textual hierarchy is presented in fig. 2. Synchronic and diachronic textual analysis is based on these linguistic data.

---

[22]This article, of course, is not intended to discuss the nature of these rather experimental procedures. The programmes experimented with make more or less adequate proposals on clause connections. The user, who is invited to agree or to disagree with machine-made proposals is forced by these procedures to try to reach a high level of consistency in the text-syntactical decisions made. See: E. Talstra, "Hebrew Syntax: Clause Types and Clause Hierarchy", in: K. Jongeling *et al.* (eds.), *Studies in Hebrew and Aramaic Syntax presented to Professor J. Hoftijzer*, Leiden 1991, 180-93; E. Talstra, "Text Grammar and Computer: The Balance of Interpretation and Calculation", in: *Actes du Troisième Colloque International Bible et Informatique: 'Interprétation, Herméneutique, Expertise'*, *Tübingen 26-30 août 1991*, Paris & Genève 1992, 135-49.

		I. D1
imperative+vocative	[שמע] ⁞יִשְׂרָאֵל⁞	Dtn09,01
weqatal	[ו] [וידעת] [היום]	Dtn09,03

		II.a D1
imperative	[זכר]	Dtn09,07
qatal(2s)	[את אשר] [הקצפת] [את יהוה (אלהיך)] [במדבר]	Dtn09,07
	[למן היום]	Dtn09,07
ptc+qatal(2p)	[ממרים] [הייתם] [עם יהוה]	Dtn09,07
		II.a.1. D1
W-X-qatal(2p)	[ו] [בחרב] [הקצפתם] [את יהוה]	Dtn09,08
		II.a.1.1.N1
wayyiqtol	[ו] [ויתאנף] [יהוה] [בכם]	Dtn09,08
	[ו] [ואשב] [בהר] [וארבעים יום / ו ...]	Dtn09,09
	[לחם] [לא] [ואכלתי] ...	Dtn09,09
wayyiqtol ...	[ו] [ואתנפל] [לפני יהוה] ... [וארבעים]	Dtn09,18
	[ו] [וישמע] [יהוה] [אלי] [גם] [בפעם ההוא]	Dtn09,19
		II.a.1.1.N§
W-X-qatal	[ו] [באהרן] [התאנף] [יהוה] [מאד]	Dtn09,20
		II.a.1.2.N§
ptc+qatal(2p)[את..]	[ו] [ובתבערה] /ו/[במסה /ו..] [מקצפים] [הייתם]	Dtn09,22
		II.a.1. D1
ptc+qatal(2p)+sf.1/2p	[ממרים] [הייתם] [עם יהוה] [מיום] [ידעתי] [אתכם]	Dtn09,24

		II.b. N1
wayyiqtol(1s)	[ו] [ואתנפל] [לפני יהוה] [את ארבעים היום...] אשר..	(=18) Dtn09,25
		II.b.1. N§
X-qatal	[בעת ההוא] [ואמר] [יהוה] [אלי]	Dtn10,01
		II.b.2. N§
W-X-qatal	[ו] [בני ישראל] [נסעו] [מבארת בני יעקן] ..	Dtn10,06
		II.b.3. N§
X-qatal	[בעת ההוא] [הבדיל].. [את שבט הלוי]	Dtn10,08
		II.b. N§
W-X-qatal(1s)	[ו] [ואנכי] [עמדתי] [בהר] [כימים הראשנים]	Dtn10,10
wayyiqtol	[ו] [וישמע] [יהוה] [אלי] [גם] [בפעם ההוא]	(=19) Dtn10,10

		III. D1
macrosyntactic marker+vocative	[ו] [ועתה] ⁞יִשְׂרָאֵל⁞	Dtn10,12
	[מה] [יהוה (אלהיך)] [שאל] [מעמך]	Dtn10,12
	[כי אם] לְיִרְאָה ...	Dtn10,12
	[ו] [ואהבתם] [את הגר]	Dtn10,19

Fig. 2: Deut. 9-10: Grammatical structure and lexical repetitions.

4. Synchronic Reading of Deuteronomy 9 and 10

Synchronic reading of a text-linguistic type intends to explore linguistic clues and does not lay a primary weight on non-linguistic information from outside the text. One of these non-linguistic points would be the observation of different literary genres, such as parenetical sections versus narrative sections on history.[23] Priority given to literary decisions in these matters can be demonstrated to have disturbed, on occasion, linguistic observations of textual structure.

From a syntactic point of view, the composition of chapters 9 and 10 as a whole is in direct speech. (This is not to deny the close connection of chapter 10:12ff. to chapter 11 in the context of the book of Deuteronomy. But, for the debate on synchrony and diachrony the text of chapter 9 and 10 is sufficient.) Using the terminology of Schneider's Grammar[24] one may say that the *main* level of communication of these texts is of a *discursive* type (D1). The reader is confronted with a larger speech that is structured by three expressions at the main level of communication: imperative + vocative שְׁמַע יִשְׂרָאֵל in chapter 9, verse 1 (section I), a second imperative זְכֹר in verse 7 (section II) and a continuation with וְעַתָּה יִשְׂרָאֵל in chapter 10:12 (section III).

The first and the last section are dominated by Qetol/Yiqtol and WeQatal clauses. These sections do not change from 'discursive' into 'narrative' verbal forms (with only one exception, i.e. the use of Qatal with a following Wayyiqtol in 10:15, a *"Sprosserzählung"*[25]).

Section II, however, does change from Qetol to Qatal and Wayyiqtol clauses. In terms of *grammar*, the larger part of this section presents itself as a *narrative* text. It is, on the basis of this observation that exegetes tend to deal with section II separately, as a more or less independent narrative in terms of *literary* analysis. Then one decides to read it as a story that is repeating important parts of the Sinai episode from the book of Exodus, but changing its plot. In my view, this separate treatment of section II is incorrect. Section II is part of the larger direct speech section. The narrative (in terms of grammar) parts inserted into the main line of communication (9:8-21 and 9:25-10:10 (N1)) should not be read in isolation because they are structurally well prepared by syntactic means, such as the continuation of 1st and 2nd person verbs and suffixes. Using the syntactic

---

[23]Cf. the discussion of Lohfink, García López, Vermeylen and the criticism formulated by Aurelius.

[24]W. Schneider, *Grammatik des Biblischen Hebräisch*, München 1982.

[25]This is the label Schneider, *Grammatik*, 200, uses for a short narrative excursus in a discursive text. The suffix כֶם– in 10:15 reveals that the addressee of the text has not changed.

clues one can read them as a set of background narratives with the status of argumentation in the discourse. The exegetical discussion of these chapters has too often detached section II from its context. It is, however, not just some deuteronomistic comment to the Horeb story in Exodus, rather it plays a role in the argumentation of the entire speech by Moses in chapters 9 and 10. Thus, one should not, in advance, separate the sections 9:1-6 and 10:12-22 from the section 9:7-10:11. From the reader's point of view, the text can be considered one composition.

Apart from the 'differences' of genre there are other points where the reader may have questions on the structure of the text. In these cases, priority given to linguistic observations may be helpful too. For example,

– The text of 9:25ff. – is this a mere repetition of verse 18? Is it a rehearsal deliberately used to protract the process of reading, as O'Connell[26] puts it? Is it a separate message because of the intercession prayer that follows here instead of in verse 18?

– Four times we have a reference to the period of "40 days and 40 nights" (9: 9, 18, 25 and 10:10). Is this a mere redundancy in the composition of these chapters? Is it disturbing the narrative order and only confusing to the reader? Or is it meaningful in the rhetoric of the speech?

– The rather unexpected statements on Aaron's death and the special position of the tribe of Levi (10:6ff.). They only seem to disturb Moses' account of the Horeb episode. Do the linguistic clues give any indication of their function in this text?

Syntactic and lexical data can be used to answer questions on the position of these phenomena in the text. These linguistic data gave reason to divide section II further into two parts as presented in *Figure 2*. From this text-grammatical proposal on textual structure, one now procede to describe its content and the effects of the linguistic data on the reader:

II.a.

The imperative זכר in verse 7 takes up the imperative שמע in 9:1. Deut. 9:7b-9:24 is structured by a frame made of two statements about Israel's rebellious behaviour (9:7 and 9:24), two statements about the places where Israel provoked the Lord (9:8 and 9:22) and two state-

---

[26] O'Connell, "Deuteronomy ix 7–x 7,10–11", 501ff. The rhetorical function of 9:25ff (his section B') is to protract the account deliberately. Its effect should be 'frustration' on the side of the reader about the redundancy in the story, which reflects all the efforts God had to make in giving the tablets of law twice to Israel.

ments about the anger of the Lord (9:8 and 9:20). These frames, by
their use of 2nd person verbal forms and suffixes, make clear that basically this section is not a narrative on history, but still is part of the
communication in direct speech, adressing the audience directly. Section II.a. comments upon Israel's rebellious acts, and it is illustrating
the expression of verse 9:6 (section I): עַם קְשֵׁה עֹרֶף, that is repeated
in the words of the Lord, in 9:13. We hear the Lord speaking of שַׁחֵת
in 9:12 and we see Moses act in favour of Israel and of Aaron, but we
do not hear any of the words of his intercession. Section II.a. refers
to two periods of 40 days and 40 nights in the Horeb episode (verse
9 and 18 (+ כראשנה)), the second one being the periode of Moses' intercession. In addition to this, however, section II.a. mentions various
other occasions of Israel's rebellious acts in the desert period. The
frame in 9:7,24 states the theme: ממרים הייתם. It is said in 9:19 that
God listened to Moses, but after that the examples of rebellion only
continue. So section II.a. seems to deny any definitive effects on Israel
resulting from Moses' acts of intercession.

II.b.

Section II.b., 9:25-10:11, picks up the intercession theme. The text
is framed by two statements that are in fact repetitions of two lines
from the preceding part II.a. Verse 9:25a repeats 9:18a. Verse 10:10b
repeats 9:19b. Both statements of this frame as well as other statements in II.b. are in first person singular, indicating that we can read
this text as another part of the direct speech section. In section II.b.
we hear the text of Moses' intercession (זכר in 9:27 is addressed now to
the Lord, not to Israel as in 9:7) and at the end (10:10) the conclusion
that the Lord did listen to Moses. And now it really is a conclusion
that is not being overruled afterwards, such as was the case in section
II.a.

The syntactic form of the two references to the 40 days and nights
in combination with the fact that they are part of the frame of this
section (in 9:25 and 10:10) also indicates, that this text is not a poorly
composed repetition, but specially takes up a theme from the preceding section. See the use of the definite article in 9:25 and the אשר clause
that follows, indicating that this information is already 'known' to the
reader. (cf. Deut. 1:46 29:15). The definite article refers to those 40
days as mentioned before (i.e. in verse 18 where the article is not
used). Deut. 10:10 also refers to 9:18 in using the phrase ראשנים + כ
+ definite article which takes up the phrase כראשנה from verse 18.

Within the frame of the two statements about Moses' intercession,
the larger part of section II.b. is composed of smaller paragraphs in
10:1, 6, 8 and 10, all of them being introduced by (W-) X-Qatal

clauses. So the grammatical structure of these paragraphs in section II.b. already makes clear that this is something else than a mere repetition of the Sinai story that already was part of the preceding section II.a. These references to other episodes of Israel's time in the desert mirror the places of rebellion mentioned in section II.a. The Lord's answer is to be experienced from these episodes: new tablets are made and now stored in the ark; Aaron died, but he has a successor and his tribe, the sons of Levi, is given a special task also concerning the ark. See also the remark on the land "rich of water" in 10:7 which parallels Deut. 8:7: ארץ נחלי מים.

After the report of these episodes, Moses *concludes* (W-X-Qatal): *So* (as you also can see from several episodes of our history:) *when I stood on the mountain, the Lord evidently was prepared to listen to me*. (The verb שמע (10:10) now also refers to the Lord, not to Israel as in 9:1). *Clearly He did not intend to destroy* (שחת) *you* (compare 10:10 and 9:12,26).

From the reader's perspective one may conclude that section II.b. takes up a detail, i.e. two lines from section II.a., re-uses them and enlarges them, as a photographer does, to explain the very fact of Israels existence as a decision of God made visible in several episodes of the desert periode. These experiences are mentioned in the text between the two framing statements about Moses' intercession. Gods reaction to the intercession can be read from the itinerary experiences.

Labuschagne[27] rightly concludes: this position in the textual composition makes Moses' intercessory prayer into a prayer for Israel in view of the entire period of exodus and conquest, rather than with reference only to the Horeb period.

However, Labuschagne[28] does not locate the intercession prayer on the mountain. He connects 10:10 only to the preceding verses 9:25-29, not to section II.a. The expression עמד + ב Labuschagne translates with "I stood at/near the mountain", not with "on". This would not be necessary if one reads section II.b. as an enlarged repetition of 9:18-19. In my view the use of ב in 10:10 explicitly refers to the situation of 9:18, which means it reiterates an intercession that took place *on* the mountain. See also the similar expression ועמדת בהר לפני יהוה in a related text, 1 Kgs. 19:11. The W-X-Qatal clause in 10:10 Labuschagne interpretes as emphasizing the "I". It is Moses' personal conclusion marking the importance of the intercession. In my view, it is also the conclusive statement of the entire section II.b. *and* a. by

---

[27]Labuschagne, *Deuteronomium*, deel 1b, 210, 212.
[28]Labuschagne, *Deuteronomium*, deel 1b, 230.

the speaker, Moses: the fact that we are here now, is due to the fact
that in the end God listened to me and did not want to destroy us.

The other W-(X-)Qatal clauses introducing separate paragraphs
of section II.b. are hardly referred to in commentaries as to their
text-grammatical functions. Labuschagne mentiones the third person
address of the W-X-Qatal clause of 10:6,[29] not the grammatical clause
type.

Taking the synchronic observations together it can be concluded that
section II of the text consists of two segments that describe a contrast:
II.a. depicts Israel as a rebellious people, demonstrating this from a
number of examples and occasions of which Horeb clearly is the most
crucial one. Other examples are taken also from the desert period. Together they result in *a negative itinerary*. It is reported that at Horeb
Moses prostrates and prays, but no intercession words are mentioned.
The section ends with statements of even more rebellion.

II.b. reports the intercession by Moses. Gods reaction to it is not in
direct speech, but is clarified by experiences also taken from the desert
itinerary. This enables Moses to conclude: clearly God did not want
to destroy us. The examples result in *a positive itinerary* in the desert
period.

The synchronic reading of Moses's speech means that one should not
test the text in terms of any narrative plot, but rather in terms of
the line of argumentation. Thus, also section II, in my view, is clearly
structured. It also clarifies the argumentative structure of section I-III
as a whole.

After section I, where שמע and זכר are addressed to Israel, and
section II, where שמע and זכר have been practiced by the Lord, section
III can now conclude with a request addressed to Israel: fear, love and
obey.

I.   Hear and remember, entering the land was not your own justice.
II.a.   The negative itinerary of a rebellious people.
II.b.   The intercession and Gods reaction in the positive itinerary.
III.   Now, therefore, Israel, react with love, fear and obedience.

An evaluation of more refined methods of rhetorical analysis such as
those applied by O'Connell and by Labuschagne should be possible
within this linguistically defined textual structure. The same is true
for diachronic analysis, the topic of the next section.

---

[29]Labuschagne, *Deuteronomium*, deel 1b, 222: 10:6-9 and 9:18-20 are a secondary insertion.

5. Diachronic Reading of Deuteronomy 9 and 10

Diachronic reading can start from observations made in the process of synchronic reading on textual structure, lexical material and the balance of actors. Results of synchronic analysis present the questions to be answered by diachronic analysis:

Shifts in the plot of section II. In our case, it means that one can ask questions about the return to the intercession at Horeb in 9:25ff. Many places of rebellion in the desert are mentioned in the text. But only with respect to the Horeb episode is a full description given: the text of the intercession, new tablets, and the introduction of the ark. The Horeb intercession is presented as the crucial event. Other cases of rebellion, even events that came after Horeb, are just mentioned and are not brought to a solution. In 10:10f. Moses again brings the reader back to Horeb, not to the end of the desert period. From this one may ask whether the text is concerned with Israel's conflict with God at Horeb (the greater part of section II) or whether it is on Israel's relationship with God in general? (section I and III). This raises the question: has additional material been inserted into the Horeb episode to make it a report on Israel's rebellion in general?

Shifts in grammatical marking, such as in the number of the second person address by verbs and pronouns. Singular is used in section I; section II has it only in 9:7 and 10:9,10, other cases of second person speech in this section are in plural; section III again has singular verbs and a change to plural in 10:15-19. Equally important is the observation of different clause types, especially the W-X-Qatal and X-Qatal clauses, indicating separate paragraphs in the wayyiqtol sections of both II.a. and II.b.

Also part of the grammatical markings are the shifts of linguistic text types (*"Sprechhaltung"*[30]). The text exhibits direct speech sections, labeled 'parenetic' in literary analysis (section I and III) and wayyiqtol-dominated sections, called 'narrative' both in grammatical and in literary analysis (section II). Scholars that claim a different background of different text types differ in opinion as to the question of whether 'parenetic' texts have been inserted into 'narrative' texts or the reverse.

Shifts and consistency in lexical material. Section I and II share remarks on Israel being קשה ערף. Section I uses ירש seven times and section II ends with the same verb in verse 11. On the other hand only section II uses לוחת seven times and does so twice, both for the first and for the second set of tablets. The text uses both שחת and

---

[30]Schneider, *Grammatik*, 183ff.

שׁמד. For these words and for other lexical material (e.g. אָרוֹן, הִתְפַּלֵּל) a comparison is possible with linguistic material of other texts, e.g. Exodus, Deuteronomy, or Kings.

Exegetical proposals of the diachronical type use the registration of these shifts in various combinations. The observation on the shift of plot, however, is usually mentioned: the plot of the text does not seem to be internally consistent and it does not fit the parallel texts in Exodus. This certainly implies that a debate on diachronical method is a necessary next step: (how) do scholars use the other observations, on grammar and lexicon, to account for the difficulties found in the textual organization?

The commentary of Driver[31] is a clear example of a procedure that compares *sources* and authors' intentions. Driver observes that the text of Deut. 9:7ff. is similar in style to Deut. 1-3, arguing that this combination of texts is based *"upon the narrative of JE of which it is a free reproduction"*. In a separate table, running from 9:9 to 10:11, Driver lists the parallels between the story in Exod. 32-34 and the Deuteronomy story. From the comparison of these texts, problems become visible with respect to plot and sequence. Compare Driver's comment on 9:25-29: *"The Writer reverts here to the occasion mentioned in verse 18 (i.e. Ex. 34:9,28a), for the purpose of emphasizing (...) the (...) intercession*. He finds it "remarkable" to see that the terms of the intercession do not agree with those of Ex. 34:9, but with the earlier intercession Ex. 32:11-13, whereas the situation cannot be the one of Exod. 32:11-13, because that intercession was made *before* Moses' first descent from the mountain.

The problem with 10:10 that repeats 9:18 and does not fit the plot (*"does not describe the sequel of v.5"*), is also solved by referring to the author's intention: *"emphasizing again the earnestness of Moses' intercession"*. Verse 6-7 Driver considers a fragment of an itinerary that was inserted later, interrupting Moses' discourse.

Later diachronic studies reflect the form critical type of analysis. The starting point is the observation of different *genres* in the book of Deuteronomy: law, parenesis and history writing. The question arises, how do we explain the presence of these genres together in one composition and which of them was part of the original background (*Sitz im Leben*) of Deuteronomy? This approach expresses itself by continual comments on the question whether narratives have been inserted into an original parenetic setting of the deuteronomic Tora or the reverse.

---

[31]Driver, *A Critical and Exegetical Commentary on Deuteronomy*, 111ff.

The analysis by Lohfink, who holds that an original Horeb story has been expanded by an parenetical introduction, already has been referred to in section 1.

The research of Minette de Tillesse[32] relies on the grammatical observation of the shift in number. He suggests that the plural sections are made by Dtr, who is to be identified with Noth's history writer. Deut. 9:7-10:10 as a whole is considered a plural section, made by Dtr, and inserted into a parenetic text formulated in singular. In his conclusion, Minette de Tillesse distinguishes between an earlier text, in singular, introducing dtn law, with a Sitz im Leben in '*rituel*' and a text in plural situated in exilic, dtr. theological thinking.

In later studies the combination of form criticism and redaction criticism becomes increasingly more complicated. García López[33] relativizes the distinction of parenetical and narrative genres in Deut. 9 and 10, yet he instead mentions more different text types from which the final text was constructed. He describes the narrative parts as later dtr. insertions.

In more recent research the prominence of form critical argumentation has come to an end. Vermeylen applies a different type of textual criticism, namely a redactional analysis that aims at the identification of redactions by their theology. Vermeylen agrees with a remark made by Lohfink[34] who stated that an inventory of language would hardly help. All dtr. redactions take their material from the same style of the same dtr. school. So it would be better to speak of the various kerygmata to be identified. In this way Vermeylen describes several layers in the text. The first layer, dating from the beginning of the exile (575), presents the dtn lawcode with a narrative introduction: Deut. 5, 9 and 10. The text has been re–edited by two redactions adding parenetic texts: Dtr560 (exilic) and Dtr525/520 (return from exile).

Methodologically more convincing is the position held by Aurelius[35] who also critizes the form critical type of research but continues to test the linguistic features of the literary layers detected. To put form criticism before literary criticism, in his view is, "*wenig hilfreich*". He argues that all textual material should be analysed by the same method without making any distinction of genre in advance. In search for original layers of the text Aurelius concentrates on cer-

---

[32]Minette de Tillesse, "Sections 'tu' et sections 'vous' dans le Deutéronome", *VT* 12 (1962) 29-87.

[33]García López, "*Analyse littéraire*", part I: 482 n. 6; part II: 5, n. 92.

[34]Lohfink, "Kerygmata des Deuteronomistischen Geschichtswerks", 89.

[35]Aurelius, *Der Fürbitter Israels*, 28.

tain formulations of Deuteromomy, such as the עם קשה ערף, that can
be found in verse 7 and 13, i.e. in sections of different genres.[36] He
distinguishes[37] a pre-exilic text as a first layer that concentrates on
Moses' intercession, a praying Moses who is comparable to Amos in-
tercessing on behalf of Israel. Later came a dtr. edition of the text connecting it to Horeb (after the fall of Jerusalem) and an exilic edition
concentrating on the 'tablets' and the 'law'. The itinerary fragments
are considered *"Späte Zusätze"*, added from a different perspective. So
the order of reworking the text demonstrates the interest of several
generations in different theological themes. Also the problems with
the plot Aurelius solves by referring to redactional theology. The repetition of 9:18 in 9:25 and the repetition of 9:19b in 10:10b continues
a story that is interrupted by 'Aaron' (9:20) and the other places of
rebellion (9:22f). The text clearly concentrates on the value of the
intercession, not on chronology.

A Proposal

When comparing current diachronic methods and proposals one can
conclude: the differences of method seem to be a matter of where to
start the textual analysis. Do scholars compare a text with its assumed
sources, do they search for the original genre and *Sitz im Leben* of the
earliest format of the text or do scholars ask for redactional activity
to be recognized from parallel texts elsewhere or from a specific type
of theology?

My proposal is to follow the order of observations mentioned in the
beginning of this section. Consider the results of the synchronic analysis, i.e. evaluate the plot found, and establish possible shifts in the
organization of the text. Start with the grammatical material and after that analyse the lexical material within the observed grammatical
framework. This means searching for both lexical consistency within
the text and for linguistic parallels with other texts.

The general questions about the shift in the plot have already been
listed at the beginning of this section. From there one may turn to
the grammatical and lexical observations to establish their possible
contribution to the shifts of the plot.

The W-X-Qatal clauses have a special function in framing section
II.a and in structuring section II.b. In II.a. they are mainly in the
plural: verse 7, 8, 22-24. These clauses and verses with התאנף, מרה,
קצף have strong parallels with other texts in the DtrH (Samuel and

---

[36] Cf. Aurelius, *Der Fürbitter Israels*, 13, 25.

[37] Aurelius, *Der Fürbitter Israels*, 47-8.

Kings).[38] If one excludes these textual elements, the result is a text
that restricts itself to the Horeb episode. Also the W-X-Qatal clauses
and the short paragraphs on Aaron that they introduce (9:20 and
10:6f.) can be excluded, because the intercession for Aaron interrupts
the actions of Moses destroying the tablets (17) and the calf (21).
Moreover the verbs used in verse 20, התאנף and אתפלל, can also be
connected to dtr. texts in Kings.[39] The verses 18 (אתנפל) and 19 (וישמע)
can be explained as copies from 9:25 and 10:10 that have been inserted
by the redactor who composed the plural frame in 9:8f. and 9:22f.
By copying these lines, the redactor was able just to mention Moses'
intercession and bring the Horeb episode to a preliminary close before
introducing the other locations of the desert period.

My assumption is, that if one leaves out the redactional texts
mentioned, one finds the first dtn. layer of the text as indicated in
fig. 3 at the end of this article. This text restricts itself to the Horeb
episode and addresses the audience in singular. It can be read as one
piece of text arguing about ישראל, ירש and ארץ, and informs its reader
about the first set of tablets, the intercession and the second set of
tablets.

The dtr. redaction that composed the framing texts and inserted
the other texts mentioned, created the sections II.a. and II.b. The
effect being that Moses' prayer in verse 25ff. should be read as an
intercession that regards the entire desert period.

Repetitions of lexical material in the texts of these two layers may
confirm their identification:
The first redaction of the text uses seven times ירש in section I; seven
times the first set of לוחת and seven times the new set of לוחת in section
II; three times עם קשה ערף and three times שחת in section I and II.
This textual layer can be seen as part of the pre-exilic composition
of the book of Deuteronomy. It lacks the strong parallels with other
texts of the DtrH, as the next redaction does. It is interesting to note
that the wording of Moses' conclusion of the Horeb episode לא אבה
יהוה השחיתך has been used in the Book of Kings, 2 Kgs. 8:19 and 13:23,
texts that can be regarded as part of a pre-exilic version of the Book
of Kings.[40] Compare also the reference to the tablets and the ark in
1 Kgs. 8.

---

[38] See the collection of parallel materials presented by Minette de Tillesse, "Sections 'tu' et sections 'vous' dans le Deutéronome", 56ff.

[39] Cf. Minette de Tillesse, "Sections 'tu' et sections 'vous' dans le Deutéronome",
57, 60, and compare *The Prayer of Solomon*, 218ff., where the parallels with the
dtr. redaction of the dedication prayer are discussed.

[40] Cf. Talstra, *The Prayer of Solomon*, 224-5.

The text of the first, dtn. composition ends in 10:11 with again יִרַשׁ
and a suffix marking a second person singular which fits the singular
address of the start clause in 9:7. This first layer is a paranetic text
that is arguing with the help of narrative paragraphs. It comments
upon the texts of Exod. 32-34 and concentrates on one episode in the
desert: the mountain, the tablets, stubbornness of Israel and the gift
of the land.

The second dtr. redaction introduces sections in second person
plural and ties the text much closer into the larger context of the books
Deuteronomy to Kings and can be regarded as part of the exilic DtrH.
The intercession passages use dtr. terminology. The combination of
the words חטא, התאנף, התפלל, שמע is an exception in Deuteronomy,
but can be found, together with the combination of שלח, עם, נחלה, in
the dtr. edition the dedication prayer in 1 Kgs. 8:44-51.[41] By listing
the other cases of rebellion (מרה) and by copying the התפלל and שמע
clauses from 9:25 and 10:10 to 9:18f., this redaction created a new
structure of the text: section II.a. was composed from existing and
from new material and was separated from what was now becoming
section II.b. The intercession formulated in II.b argues along the same
lines as Solomon's prayer does: Israel is your עם and נחלה (1 Kgs.
8:51). The more general, negative evaluation of Israel's history, based
on more occasions than Horeb alone, also parallels the tendency of
the two last petitions in 1 Kgs. 8.

In the third layer the 'deuteronomic editor' (I am adopting here the
terminology employed by Mayes[42]) inserted the tradition of Aaron's
death, his successor and the task of the Levites (10:6-7 and 10:8-10).
This can be argued by observations of plot (the interruption of the
Horeb period of the new tablets) and of grammar and lexicon (W-X-
Qatal, introducing new paragraphs with new material; no markers of a
dialogue). In this edition the text also is giving its definitive ordering.
By these insertions the order of *negative and positive itinerary places*
was composed.

With respect to the position of section III, Deut. 10:12ff., I accept
the argumentation by Mayes, García López[43] and several other commentators that this part of the text also belongs to the later edition.
Mayes points out the remarkable resemblance to the text of Deut. 4:1-

---

[41] Cf. Talstra, *The Prayer of Solomon*, 218, 224f. on the dtr. redaction that
added petition VI and VII into the structure of seven petitions using terminology
for 'sin' and 'intercession' that parallels the prayer of Moses in Deuteronomy 9.

[42] A.D.H. Mayes, *The Story of Israel between Settlement and Exile: A Redactional Study of the Deuteronomic History*, London 1983.

[43] Mayes, *The Story of Israel*, 34; García López, "Analyse littéraire", 194.

40 in terms of grammar, the use of both singular and plural second person address and in terms of lexical material. The transition from the preceding text to 10:12 is the same as the transition from Deut. 1-3 to 4: ועתה ישראל.

The result of the diachronic analysis in this section, is a proposal that is close to the position held by Mayes. Additional is my attempt to analyse the first layer, the one that according to Mayes[44] was used by DtrH, the Dtr. historian, in creating the edition that in my analysis was called the second layer. A difference is that I do not think that the material extended by DtrH was only parenetical. In Mayes' description a basic parenetic layer between 9:1 and 10:11 was supplemented by the Dtr historian, in order to connect the theme of 'the possession of the land' with 'the law given at Horeb'. DtrH. not only composed the framework in Deut. 1-3; 31 and 34, but also the Horeb texts: Deut. 5 and 9f. According to Mayes, the parenetic layer to which DtrH. added his 'history' was the original introduction to the deuteronomic law. In my analysis references to the tablets and 'the mountain' already were part of that first deuteronomic layer. See fig. 4 at the end of this article.

6. Conclusions

–   In the attempts to establish an operational order of exegetical methods the position of linguistic and non-linguistic data is crucial. It is in the first place the language material that allows a reader to enter the world of the text.

–   The analysis of linguistic routines needs to have its position prior to the analysis of literary techniques such as the definition of genre or the description of rhetorical patterns and compositional calculations. What can be explained with reference to general linguistic routines, is not be explained by referring to an individual author or a particular style.

–   Synchronic analysis has procedural priority over diachronic analysis. Synchronic analysis concentrates on the question, how a text can be read on the basis of linguistic knowledge and knowledge of rhetorical patterns, admitting that in the case of ancient texts this is historical knowledge.

–   Diachronic analysis concentrates on the question, how and when a text has been produced. It can begin with the results of synchronic analysis in structure and shifts of plot or grammar and lexicon. It proposes segments of text that have linguistic material in common and

---

[44]Mayes, *The Story of Israel*, 34.

it proposes a relative chronology of the segments of the text. Eventually it applies to the text an hypothesis on its historical contexts, its authors and its audiences.

This contribution is more about *how* methods could be used in a complementary way, than it is about *why* such a thing should be done at all. Hermeneutically speaking, I would suggest that the reading of the Bible in our culture, both as an ancient book and as the source text of faith, simply provokes the debate on structure and message, as well as on claims of truth and history. My test of a complementary use of exegetical methods may be read as a reaction to fears and reservations expressed regularly in our time towards historical research: would not Moses suffer more from diachronic analysis than from synchronic analysis? I strongly doubt it. The debate on methods is a challenge to academic theology to confront the texts of one's religious tradition with *all* analytical instruments developed in literary and biblical scholarship. Perhaps one could best start from another reaction Chaim Potok reports on in his novel[45] that was mentioned at the beginning of this contribution. It is the reaction of Rav Sharfmann to David Lurie's decision to enter secular biblical scholarship:

> *"Lurie, if the Torah cannot go out into your world of scholarship and return stronger, then we are all fools and charlatans. I have faith in the Torah. I am not afraid of truth."*

---

[45] Chaim Potok, *In the Beginning*, 415.

direct speech, imperative addressed to Israel   [וישמע] [וישראל]   Dtn09,01

.....

e.g. (ארץ +) ירש 7x   [ולרשת] [ואת ארצם]   Dtn09,05
Israel - קשה   [וכי] [עם קשה ערף] [ואתה]   Dtn09,06

2nd imperative   [זכר]   Dtn09,07
wrath of the Lord (2sg)   ... [הקצפת] [את יהוה] ..   Dtn09,07

at the mountain   [ב-עליתי] [וה-ההר]   Dtn09,09
לוחת 7X   [ולקחת] [ולוחת האבנים (לוחת הברית)]   Dtn09,09
40 days   [וו] [ואשב] [בהר] [וארבעים יום / וארבעים לילה]   Dtn09,09

.....

God: Israel - שחת (pi.)   [וכי] [וישחת] [עמך]   Dtn09,12
Israel - קשה   [וו] [והנה] [עם קשה ערף] [הוא]   Dtn09,13
    [......] [ועגל מסכה]   Dtn09,16

Moses: [וו] [ואתפש] [ובשני הלחת] ... [וו] [ואשברם]   Dtn09,17
    [וו] [ואת העגל] ... [ולקחתי]   Dtn09,21
    [וו] [ואתנפל] [לפני יהוה] [וארבעים (ה)יום / ו ...]   Dtn09,25
40 days

Prayer: Do not destroy   [ואל] [וישחת] [עמך] [....]   Dtn09,26
Israel - קשה   [ואל] [ותפן] [ואל קשי העם הזה]   Dtn09,27

God: new tablets   [ובעת ההוא] [ואמר] [ויהוה] [ואלי]   Dtn10,01
לוחת 7X   [ופסל] [ולך] [ושני לוחת אבנים] [וכראשנים]   Dtn10,01
    [וו] [ועלה] [ואלי] [וההרה]   Dtn10,01
ark   [וו] [ועשית] [ולך] [וארון עץ]   Dtn10,01

God listened   [וו] [וישמע] [ויהוה] [ואלי] [וגם] [ב ...]   Dtn10,10
no intention to destroy   [ולא] [ואבה] [יהוה] [השחיתך]   Dtn10,10
sfx: 2sg

God:
ארץ + ירש   [וו] [וירש] [ואת הארץ]   Dtn10,11

Fig. 3: Deut. 9-10: Diachrony: first, dtn. composition.
Deut. 9:1-6; 7*-17*; 21; 25*-28*; 10:1-5; 10-11.
(selected texts)

general location: in the desert   במדבר   **Dtn09,07**

frame 1   [ממרים] [והייתם] .. [ולמן היום]   **Dtn09,07**

frame 2: Horeb, main location of rebellion
        [ו] .. [בחרב] [והקצפתם] [את יהוה]   **Dtn09,08**
frame 3: wrath   [ו] [יתאנף] [יהוה] [בכם]   **Dtn09,08**
        [להשמיד] [אתכם]   **Dtn09,08**

dtr. terminology, e.g.   (16) חטאתם (14) ואשמידם (12;16) סרו מהר

inserted copy from 9, 25: intercession located at Horeb
      [ו] [ואתנפל] [לפני יהוה] [כראשנה] [וארבעים יום]...   **Dtn09,18**

dtr. terminology, e.g.   (19) קצף; השמיד (18) חטאתכם

inserted copy from 10,10 to conclude intercession at Horeb
       [ו] [וישמע] [יהוה] [אלי] [גם] [בפעם ההוא]   **Dtn09,19**

frame 3: second case of wrath and intercession
        [ו] [ובאהרן] [התאנף] [יהוה] [מאד] [להשמידו]   **Dtn09,20**
          [ו] [ואתפלל] [גם] [בעד אהרן] ..   **Dtn09,20**
     dtr. terminology, e.g.   (21) חטאתכם

frame 2: other locations of rebellion
     [ו] [ובתבערה /ו /במסה /ו /ב...] [ומקצפים] [והייתם] ...   **Dtn09,22**
         [ו] [ובשלח] [יהוה] [אתכם] [מקדש_ברנע]   **Dtn09,23**
frame 1, repeating verse 7
     [ממרים] [והייתם] [עם יהוה] [מיום] [דעתי] [אתכם]   **Dtn09,24**

effect: the intercession (25ff.) regards entire desert period

dtr. terminology, e.g.   (26,29) [עמך /ו /נחלתך] (25) להשמיד

reference to the second period of 40 days
     [ו] [ואנכי] [עמדתי] [בהר] ... [וארבעים יום] ..   **Dtn10,10**
re-introduces the conclusion: God listened

Fig. 4: Diachrony: second, dtr. composition.
New composition by inserting new frames.
(selected texts)

H. G. M. Williamson   *Oxford – United Kingdom*

Synchronic and Diachronic in Isaian Perspective

In recent years the book of Isaiah has moved to centre stage in the discussion of the relative merits of synchronic and diachronic exegesis of biblical literature in ways that would have been unthinkable as little as a generation ago. Until then, and for reasons which it is not necessary to rehearse again here, the basic threefold division of the book as established by Duhm[1] was accepted by virtually all critical scholars. Central to this consensus was the agreement that Isaiah 1-39 and 40-66 should be treated in complete isolation from each other. The major areas of disagreement with regard to our present concern focussed on the diachronic analysis of Proto-Isaiah (though this was mainly a matter of detail rather than of principle), the unity or otherwise of Isaiah 56-66, and the nature of the relationship of these latter chapters to Isaiah 40-55. Only with regard to Deutero-Isaiah was there sufficient confidence in the existence of a unified composition from both the literary and the historical points of view for what we now think of as synchronic concerns to be raised.[2]

No one familiar with even a fraction of the recent literature on Isaiah will fail to recognize how quickly this brief characterization has become outdated.[3] It is now a commonplace to read studies of verbal, thematic and structural links between the parts;[4] chapters

---

[1] B. Duhm, *Das Buch Jesaia* (HK, 3/1), Göttingen 1892.

[2] The commentary by J. Muilenburg is probably best known in this regard: "The Book of Isaiah, Chapters 40-66", *IntB*, vol. 5, Nashville 1956, 381-773.

[3] Cf. R. Rendtorff, "The Book of Isaiah: A Complex Unity. Synchronic and Diachronic Reading", *SBL.SP* (1991), 8-20.

[4] See, for instance, C.T. Begg, "Babylon in the Book of Isaiah", in: J. Vermeylen (ed.), *The Book of Isaiah* (BETL, 81), Leuven 1989, 121-5; R.E. Clements, "The Unity of the Book of Isaiah", *Interp.* 36 (1982), 117-29; R.E. Clements, "Beyond Tradition-History: Deutero-Isaianic Development of First Isaiah's Themes", *JSOT* 31 (1985), 95-113; R.E. Clements, "Patterns in the Prophetic Canon: Healing the Blind and the Lame", in: G.M. Tucker *et al.* (eds.), *Canon, Theology, and Old Testament Interpretation: Essays in Honor of Brevard S. Childs*, Philadelphia 1988, 189-200; R.J. Clifford, "The Unity of the Book of Isaiah and its Cosmogonic Language", *CBQ* 55 (1993), 1-17; G.I. Davies, "The Destiny of the Nations in the Book of Isaiah", in: J. Vermeylen (ed.), *The Book of Isaiah*, 93-120; J.H. Eaton, "The Origin of the Book of Isaiah", *VT* 9 (1959), 138-57; C.A. Evans, "On the Unity and Parallel Structure of Isaiah", *VT* 38 (1988), 129-47; J. Jensen, "Yahweh's Plan in Isaiah and in the Rest of the Old Testament", *CBQ* 48 (1986), 443-55; D.G. Meade, *Pseudonymity and Canon: An Investigation into the Relationship of Authorship and Authority in Jewish and Earliest Christian Tradition*, Grand Rapids 1986, 26-42; R. Rendtorff, "Zur Komposition des Buches Jesaja",

33,[5] 35,[6] 36-9,[7] and 40[8] have all been intensively studied with regard to their function as hinges or 'mirror texts' within the whole; the role of the opening and closing chapters of the book as introduction and closure as well as the relationship between them have attracted particular attention;[9] the redaction of one section in the light of another has also produced fruitful results;[10] and the older, familiar approach to composite texts by way of relecture has been raised to new heights of sophistication in order to take account of these newer developments.[11]

VT 34 (1984), 295-320; R. Rendtorff, "Jesaja 6 im Rahmen der Komposition des Jesajabuches", in: J. Vermeylen (ed.), *The Book of Isaiah*, 73-82; and J.J.M. Roberts, "Isaiah in Old Testament Theology", *Interp.* 36 (1982), 130-43.

[5]See W.A.M. Beuken, "Jesaja 33 als Spiegeltext im Jesajabuch", *EThL* 67 (1991), 5-35.

[6]See O.H. Steck, *Bereitete Heimkehr: Jesaja 35 als redaktionelle Brücke zwischen dem Ersten und dem Zweiten Jesaja* (SBS, 121), Stuttgart 1985.

[7]E.g. P.R. Ackroyd, "Isaiah 36-39: Structure and Function", in: W.C. Delsman *et al.* (eds.), *Von Kanaan bis Kerala: Festschrift für Prof. Mag. Dr. Dr. J. P. M. van der Ploeg O.P.* (AOAT, 211), Neukirchen-Vluyn 1982, 3-21 = *Studies in the Religious Tradition of the Old Testament*, London 1987, 105-20; E.W. Conrad, "The Royal Narratives and the Structure of the Book of Isaiah", *JSOT* 41 (1988), 67-81; J.W. Groves, *Actualization and Interpretation in the Old Testament* (SBL.DS, 86), Atlanta 1987, 191-201; A. van der Kooij, *Die alten Textzeugen des Jesajabuches: Ein Beitrag zur Textgeschichte des Alten Testaments* (OBO, 35), Freiburg & Göttingen 1981, 17-8; R.F. Melugin, *The Formation of Isaiah 40-55* (BZAW, 141), Berlin 1976, 177-8; C.R. Seitz, *Zion's Final Destiny: The Development of the Book of Isaiah: A Reassessment of Isaiah 36-39*, Minneapolis 1991; K.A.D. Smelik, "Distortion of Old Testament Prophecy: The Purpose of Isaiah xxxvi and xxxvii", *OTS* 24 (1986), 70-93.

[8]E.g. R. Albertz, "Das Deuterojesaja-Buch als Fortschreibung der Jesaja-Prophetie", in: E. Blum *et al.* (eds.), *Die Hebräische Bibel und ihre zweifache Nachgeschichte: Festschrift für Rolf Rendtorff zum 65. Geburtstag*, Neukirchen-Vluyn 1990, 241-56; C.R. Seitz, "The Divine Council: Temporal Transition and New Prophecy in the Book of Isaiah", *JBL* 109 (1990), 229-47.

[9]E.g. P.R. Ackroyd, "Isaiah i-xii: Presentation of a Prophet", in *Congress Volume: Göttingen 1977* (VT.S, 29), Leiden 1978, 16-48 = *Studies in the Religious Traditions of the Old Testament*, 79-104; W.A.M. Beuken, "Isaiah Chapters lxv-lxvi: Trito-Isaiah and the Closure of the Book of Isaiah", in: J.A. Emerton (ed.), *Congress Volume: Leuven 1989* (VT.S, 43), Leiden 1991, 204-21; G. Fohrer, "Jesaja 1 als Zusammenfassung der Verkündigung Jesajas", *ZAW* 74 (1962), 251-68 = *Studien zur alttestamentliche Prophetie (1949-1965)* (BZAW, 99), Berlin 1967, 148-66; R. Lack, *La Symbolique du Livre d'Isaïe: Essai sur l'image littéraire comme élément de structuration* (AnBib, 59), Rome 1973; L.J. Liebreich, "The Compilation of the Book of Isaiah", *JQR* n.s. 46 (1955-1956), 259-77; *JQR* n.s. 47 (1956-1957), 114-38; A.J. Tomasino, "Isaiah 1.1-2.4 and 63-66, and the Composition of the Isaianic Corpus", *JSOT* 57 (1993), 81-98.

[10]See especially J. Becker, *Isaias: Der Prophet und sein Buch* (SBS, 30), Stuttgart 1968; M.A. Sweeney, *Isaiah 1-4 and the Post-Exilic Understanding of the Isaianic Tradition* (BZAW, 171), Berlin 1988.

All the modern approaches to the study of Isaiah mentioned so far have in common, however, that they still work on a fundamentally diachronic model. In some cases, it is true, this is somewhat hidden from view in that no attempt is made to explain the literary-historical processes by which these associations across the traditional boundaries of the book have come about, but it is unlikely that any of the scholars referred to would in principle deny the possibility of so doing, even if they would remain sceptical about our ability now to follow this through in detail. Others, however, are more confident, and the work of Steck is especially instructive in this regard.[12] Indeed, there is a certain irony in the fact that hand in hand with his interest in the growth of the book of Isaiah as a whole goes a strong advocacy of the redactional fragmentation of Isaiah 40-55, once regarded as the only truly unified section of the book. It is thus clear that for some, at least, final unity is achieved only at the expense of even more rigorous and radical diachronic division of the book's constituent parts.

Most recently, however, a few voices have been raised to urge the case for a truly synchronic study.[13] This is by no means a return to authorial unity, nor is it a simple extension of redaction criticism. It is, rather, a genuinely post-critical enterprise, one which does not deny that the book has grown up over an extended period of time, but which despairs of our ever being able to reconstruct this process and which further denies that it is of value from the point of view of sound method even to attempt to do so. The only two certainties are the text as it now exists and myself as its reader interacting with it in order to create meaning. This does not, of course, make me an infallible reader, since it is open to you to persuade me that yours makes so much better sense that I choose to adopt it too, but the interpretative key lies here in the present act of reading, not there in the historical process of the text's production or of its first reception. Synchronic in this sense, however, has nothing whatsoever to learn from the diachronic perspective, so that there is no way in which the relationship between

---

[11] See, for instance, K. Nielsen, *There is Hope for a Tree: The Tree as Metaphor in Isaiah* (JSOT.S, 65), Sheffield 1989, where the focus of attention is restricted to Isaiah 1-39.

[12] Steck, *Bereitete Heimkehr*; O.H. Steck, *Studien zu Tritojesaja* (BZAW, 203), Berlin & New York 1991; O.H. Steck, *Gottesknecht und Zion: Gesammelte Aufsätze zu Deuterojesaja* (FAT, 4), Tübingen 1992.

[13] See especially E.W. Conrad, *Reading Isaiah*, Minneapolis 1991; P.D. Miscall, *Isaiah*, Sheffield 1993; B.G. Webb, "Zion in Transformation: A Literary Approach to Isaiah", in: D.J.A. Clines *et al.* (eds.), *The Bible in Three Dimensions: Essays in Celebration of Forty Years of Biblical Studies in the University of Sheffield* (JSOT.S, 87), Sheffield 1990, 65-84.

the two can be discussed. But since the focus of this conference is precisely on the relationship between the two (at least, so I assume, since there would be little value in simply trumpeting the virtues of one approach at the purely theoretical level over the other; if that were the intention, there would be little point in doing so within the narrow focus of the 'Old Testament' guild), it follows that such purist synchronous approaches must be ruled out from the start. I shall therefore not deal with them further here but concentrate rather on the questions which the more recent mainstream studies of the book as a whole have thrown up in regard to the traditional critical concerns with rigidly diachronic analysis.

In order to give further focus to the discussion, I shall concentrate in what follows on the first chapter of the book. For several reasons this passage should prove instructive. First, it is widely believed to combine authentic material by the eighth century prophet with later additions of various periods, some probably quite late, so that it may be said to provide in a nutshell the problems posed by the book as a whole. Secondly, it has frequently been studied in association with the concluding section of Trito-Isaiah, thus giving prominence to its potentially significant function in the final shaping of the book. Thirdly, rhetorical features in the text, usually associated with synchronic analyses, have been variously isolated in order to arrive at different demarcations of the extent of the composition. Fourthly, it includes, of course, the superscription to the book in 1:1, whose interpretation is both an issue in itself and a problem in view of the comparable heading in 2:1. Finally, having just devoted a monograph to the composition of chapters 2-55 with diachronic and synchronic questions particularly in mind,[14] it is inevitable that I should now move back to give some attention to the topic of chapter one. I shall try to show that a properly synchronic reading depends on a prior, rigorous diachronic analysis (as opposed to many which mix the two in a half-hearted manner in the service of some alternative agenda), and then conclude with some cursory and preliminary reflections on what this might mean for the task of the commentator.

The problems in treating this chapter, as just enumerated, may be illustrated by surveying a few recent, representative studies with particular attention to questions of method. In seeking to determine the extent of "the first pericope in the book of Isaiah", Willis works on the basis of what at first sight would generally be regarded as a

---

[14]H.G.M. Williamson, *The Book Called Isaiah: Deutero-Isaiah's Role in Composition and Redaction*, Oxford 1994.

conventional diachronic analysis.[15] Against a wide variety of alternative proposals, he argues that 1:2-20 is a single oracle delivered by the prophet Isaiah near the end of his long ministry, and that this fact is sufficient to account for the passage's apparently summarizing nature to which several other scholars have drawn attention. He arrives at this conclusion on the basis of rhetorical and form-critical arguments. Thus he notes, for example, the apparent *inclusio* formed by כי יהוה דבר in verse 2 and כי פי יהוה דבר in verse 20, the use of catchwords between sections, the repetition of vocabulary in most parts of the passage, and the fact that, contrary to what is often stated, the prophet is the speaker throughout. As to form, he argues that it is a lawsuit, though the somewhat circular nature of his argument here is clear from his conclusion that "This is not to affirm that all these elements are present in every lawsuit, or that they are all absolutely necessary to the lawsuit genre, but that in the right circumstances it is possible for them to be part of the lawsuit" (p. 74). Such judgments are difficult to evaluate when there is no other passage which takes the same form as this one.[16]

Negatively, Willis proceeds in a similar manner. Thus, against Mattioli's suggestion that the whole chapter is a single unit (also a lawsuit) in three parts, marked by the summons to hear in verses 2, 10, and 24,[17] Willis replies that to start a new division at verse 24 would

---

[15] J.T. Willis, "The First Pericope in the Book of Isaiah", *VT* 34 (1984), 63-77. Willis includes abundant references to earlier work on the chapter.

[16] See the discussion of the problems relating to the identification of a *rib*-pattern in Isaiah 1 in J.W. Whedbee, *Isaiah and Wisdom*, Nashville & New York 1971, 28-35, E.W. Davies, *Prophecy and Ethics: Isaiah and the Ethical Traditions of Israel* (JSOT.S, 16), Sheffield 1981, 40-61, and S. Deck, *Die Gerichtsbotschaft Jesajas: Charakter und Begründung* (FzB, 67), Würzburg 1991, 95-7. A further difficulty is posed by the disagreement over whether the form should be sought in verses 2-20, as Willis suggests (so also J. Vermeylen, *Du prophète Isaïe à l'apocalyptique: Isaïe, I-XXXV, miroir d'un demi-millénaire d'expérience religieuse en Israël*, Paris 1977-1978, 42-9), or in verses 2-31 (so, for instance, B. Gemser, "The *Rîb-* or Controversy-Pattern in Hebrew Mentality", in: M. Noth, D. Winton Thomas (eds.), *Wisdom in Israel and in the Ancient Near East* (VT.S, 3), Leiden 1955, 120-37 [130]), or in 2-3 alone (so, for instance, K. Nielsen, *Yahweh as Prosecutor and Judge* (JSOT.S, 9), Sheffield 1978, 27-9), or even in 2-3+10-20 (J. Harvey, *Le plaidoyer prophétique contre Israël après la rupture de l'alliance: étude d'une formule littéraire de l'Ancien Testament* (Studia, 22), Paris & Montreal 1967, 36-42), or in 2-3+21-31 (S. Niditch, "The Composition of Isaiah 1", *Bib* 61 (1980), 509-29). H. Wildberger seems unclear on the subject; contrast his concluding summary of chapter 1, *Jesaja 1-12* (BK 10/1), Neukirchen-Vluyn 1980², 73-4 (= *Isaiah 1-12: A Commentary*, Minneapolis 1991, 78-80), with his discussion of the individual units in the preceding commentary.

[17] A. Mattioli, "Due schemi letterari negli oracoli d'introduzione al libro d'Isaia:

destroy the chiastic structure of verses 21-26, that the occurrence
of איכה at verse 21 indicates the start of a new genre (unlike הוי in
verses 4 and 24), and that the recurrence of themes and words across
the whole chapter need not be an indication of unity since "Isaiah
may have used the same words or spoken on the same subjects to
different audiences on different occasions, and his oracles may have
been arranged in their present order later because they contain the
same words or ideas" (p. 66). This random mixing of historical and
rhetorical considerations, some of which seem to be used in different
ways according to whether they support or challenge Willis's theory,
gives the impression of the cart driving the horse.

Finally, it is instructive to notice what is not dealt with. Although
early on it is conceded that 1:2-20 may have been incorporated by
the final editor of the book of Isaiah "because of its relevance to
his own generation and circumstances, and thus adapted to his own
theological purposes" (p. 64), no attempt is made to read the passage
in this light. No serious attention is paid to the last part of the chapter
– its date, method of incorporation and effect on the interpretation
of what precedes – nor does Willis have anything to say about the
links which other scholars have pointed out with the closing chapters
of Isaiah or on why this *ex hypothesi* late oracle of Isaiah should have
been placed first in the book. Thus Willis's method makes eclectic use
of both diachronic and synchronic considerations, but it does so only
on the micro level of the pericope itself. This, however, is inconsistent,
since, being literary, such considerations ought also to operate on the
macro level of the wider book. His agenda is set rather by a purely
historical concern (and in this, of course, he is by no means alone), but
his arguments are not all by any means best suited to that purpose.

A more purely synchronic reading of this chapter is attempted by
Gitay as part of his study of Isaiah 1-12 in terms of Isaiah's rhetoric.[18]
He too regards the first address as comprising 1:2-20,[19] while the second covers 1:21-2:5. He is critical of standard diachronic analyses with
their appeal to later, editorial insertions: the method, he says, is "a
victim of the sporadic-fragmented reading of the prophetic discourse,
which presupposes that each short paragraph conveys an independent utterance. Thus there is no reading of the whole, which may
shed light on the meaning and the function of the vision according to

---

Is. 1,1-31", *RivBib* 14 (1966), 345-64.
    [18]Y. Gitay, *Isaiah and his Audience: The Structure and Meaning of Isaiah 1-12*
(SSN, 30), Assen & Maastricht 1991.
    [19]See also his "Reflections on the Study of the Prophetic Discourse: The Ques-
tion of Isaiah i 2-20", *VT* 33 (1983), 207-21.

Isaiah's total prophetic perspective" (p. 39). In contrast, Gitay strives valiantly to make coherent rhetorical sense of each larger unit, with careful attention to the definition of the limits of each address, to the development of the argument through each part and to the rhetorical devices which the prophet employed.

A difficulty arises from our point of view, however, from the fact that Gitay reads the text firmly within what he supposes to be its historical setting. With what to most scholars will appear to be inadequate justification, he does not allow that any part of Isaiah 1-12 is of later origin than the eighth century. Were he to operate on the literary level alone, his procedure might be allowed, but he is clear that he is discussing the historical Isaiah and his contemporary audience. Furthermore, this raises particular difficulties when it comes to exclusively literary elements within the text itself. Thus, for instance, his handling of the second heading in 2:1 seems to confuse literary and historical concerns. With Ackroyd,[20] he regards the heading, not as the mark of an independent collection, but as a device to strengthen Isaiah's prophetic authority (p. 41); it is not then clear, however, how it can have operated with "a clear rhetorical function". If, as Gitay asserts, "The heading stresses that Isaiah, and not his contemporary Micah ... saw the vision", we are clearly moving into the area of later literary, if not scribal, concerns, rather than of contemporary oral presentation. Finally, the decision to complete the unit at 2:5 seems arbitrary from a literary perspective. As most commentators recognize, the use of catchwords in 2:5 with verses 2-4 on the one hand and 2:6 on the other points to the verse's function as a redactional join between units,[21] suggestive again of literary activity. In short, Gitay's synchronic analysis fails on its own terms because it does not adequately take into account features of the text itself which point to diachronic literary development.

So far, two studies of Isaiah 1 have been presented which focus respectively on a diachronic and on a synchronic approach but which introduce elements from the other in a manner which leads to their undoing. Quite different, but leading to contrasting conclusions, are two articles which were published alongside one another in a recent issue of the *Journal for the Study of the Old Testament*.[22] Both are interested in the relationship between Isaiah 1 and the concluding chapters of the book as a whole (though in Carr's case this is only

---

[20]P.R. Ackroyd, "A Note on Isaiah 2_1", *ZAW* 75 (1963), 320-1.

[21]Cf. *The Book Called Isaiah*, 144-6.

[22]D. Carr, "Reaching for Unity in Isaiah", *JSOT* 57 (1993), 61-80; Tomasino, "Isaiah 1.1-2.4 and 63-66".

a part of his concern), but they approach the topic from different perspectives.

Tomasino's article is a sophisticated study which seeks to take the connections between these two parts of the book to new levels of precision. With a careful attention to detail which cannot be summarized here, he argues that 1:2-2:4 are paralleled in structure and to some extent in vocabulary in 63:7-66:23 (though chapter 65 is excluded). At the same time, however, he maintains that 1:2 and 1:31 are resumed at 66:1 and 66:24. His explanation of these observations is that the closing chapters of the book were developed in two stages. The first patterned 63-64 and most of 66 on 1:2-2:4 (which still lacked the heading in 2:1). A later redactor, however, knew of, or himself added, the heading in 2:1, and so treated chapter 1 as a separate unit in framing chapter 66 in a similar fashion. It was this second redactor who also added chapter 65.

Without wishing to detract in any way from Tomasino's stimulating discussion, which deserves a far closer analysis than can be offered here,[23] we need to ask in the present context how this affects our reading of chapter 1, even though Tomasino's concern is primarily with chapters 63-66. He proposes three possible diachronic explanations. Either Isaiah 1 has been composed with 63-66 in mind, or 63-66 has been composed with chapter 1 in mind, or both have been composed by the same author. Surprisingly, however, in ruling out the first possibility it emerges that he is working with a rather rigid definition of the word 'composed', namely (in my own paraphrase) 'written from scratch'. The connections between Isaiah 1 and the rest of Proto-Isaiah are sufficient for him to conclude that "Isaiah 1 was not composed separately from the rest of Proto-Isaiah and then transported to its present position". The possibility that chapter 1 represents a later, redactional assemblage of mainly Proto-Isaianic material, as has been proposed by Barth, among others,[24] is not discussed.

This leads to a second problem, namely Tomasino's unsatisfactory treatment of the headings in 1:1 and 2:1. The former he dismisses as "of little relevance at this place in our study" (p. 84), even though he

---

[23]I would simply note in passing that there are some inevitable uncertainties in arguing for the structure of one section of the book being based upon another; as Tomasino candidly admits (n. 7), Vermeylen used a similar approach to conclude that Isaiah 1:1-2:5 served as a pattern for Trito-Isaiah as a whole; see Vermeylen, *Du prophète Isaïe à l'apocalyptique*, 504-11.

[24]H. Barth, *Die Jesaja-Worte in der Josiazeit: Israel und Assur als Thema einer produktiven Neuinterpretation der Jesajaüberlieferung* (WMANT, 48), Neukirchen-Vluyn 1977, 217-20; cf. R.E. Clements, *Isaiah 1-39* (NCeB), Grand Rapids & London 1980, 28.

is clearly working with one of the latest phases in the book's development. The latter heading is clearly even more of an embarrassment to him, for he wants to do without it in the form of the text known to his first redactor but to bring it in as justification for his second redactor treating chapter 1 as a separate unit. His comment that "Apparently, by this author's day, the secondary introduction had already been inserted at Isa. 2.1 (or perhaps the author made the insertion him- or herself)" (p. 97) is merely a consequence of his redaction-critical conclusions based on the ending of the book and does nothing to explain why 2:1 was added at all, nor what function it serves in the present form of the book. Thus, whatever the merits of Tomasino's study of chapters 63-66, he does little in the end to help us with either a synchronic or a diachronic reading of chapter 1. To reach satisfactory conclusions on the basis of these methods, it may be concluded, both passages under examination need to be studied in their own right as well as in combination; otherwise, as we have seen, there is the danger that the diachronic conclusions drawn from one passage (in this case 63-66) will be misused by way of a synchronic cross reference to the other passage (in this case, chapter 1) in order to prejudice the results of a diachronic analysis of that other passage, with all the consequences which flow from that for a fully satisfying reading.

The second article to which I have referred supports this conclusion to some extent, even though its main focus lies elsewhere. In a discussion entitled "Reaching for Unity in Isaiah", Carr examines the relationship between particular passages which some have suggested lend the book an overall unity and the rest of the material in Isaiah. His principal conclusion is that although these passages certainly attest a redactional concern to draw together the various parts of the book, "no editor intervened deeply enough into the book to make it all conform to an overall conception" (p. 78). Rather than attesting what Carr calls a macrostructural perspective, these late editors worked at the margins, introducing their material at the opening and close of sections in order to invite a particular reading of the whole while nevertheless respecting the integrity of the material which they inherited. In many cases this material includes passages which run counter to the later editors' dominating perceptions. For modern scholars to attempt to force the whole book into a synthesis on the basis of these redactional passages can never, therefore, be more than partially successful. Their limited impact on the growth of the book as a whole needs to be respected.

I take Carr's discussion to be a significant word of caution against overenthusiastic practitioners of synchronic readings of Isaiah. With regard in particular to the relationship between chapters 1 and 65-66, for instance,[25] he notes first the verbal and thematic links which have been proposed by others and then enters the following caveats: the suggestion that Isaiah 1 functions as an introduction is contradicted by its failure to anticipate many crucial elements in the book which follows; even more important, there is "a fundamental conflict between the exhortatory focus of 1.2-31 and the rhetorical presuppositions of other parts of the book, particularly Isaiah 65-66" (p. 73), in which the groups of sinners and righteous have already been determined; and in development of this point, whereas chapter 1 focusses on the consequences of future decisions in order to influence them, the final chapters describe the consequences of decisions that have already taken place. He thus concludes that the two passages attest diverging conceptions of the Isaianic tradition. "This is not just a thematic conflict, but a conflict in rhetorical aim, a conflict that makes it difficult for 1.2-31 and 65-66 to function cohesively as a paired introduction and conclusion to the book as a whole" (p. 75).

What lessons are to be learned from this analysis of a few of the recent studies of Isaiah 1? First, that we need to be clear about the questions we are asking of the text and to adopt appropriate methods for their solution. The confusion of synchronic and diachronic approaches apparent in the work of some scholars needs to be avoided by a clearer definition of aim. Secondly, it makes a difference in this context whether we intend to read the text forwards or backwards, so to speak.[26] That is to say, a historical reading, most naturally associated with diachronic concerns, tends to read the text forwards, isolating what may be ascribed to the earliest levels, studied against their historical background, and then looking in turn at what may have been added later. This, of course, has validity in its own right, though it involves an inevitable element of the hypothetical and fails to account for a number of elements in the text which seem to be designed to reach beyond such issues. Conversely, a synchronic approach may be said to read the text backwards, looking at it only in the light of all that follows. Untempered by diachronic safeguards, however, this strategy runs the risk, as Carr has made clear, of riding roughshod over parts of the evidence at our disposal in its over-enthusiasm to force everything into its mould. Finally, whichever approach is adopted, care must be taken to do full justice to each element of the text in its own right in the first instance, and not to allow

---

[25] The other passage to which he devotes particular attention is Isa. 35-40.
[26] Cf. Rendtorff, "The Book of Isaiah: A Complex Unity".

other considerations drawn from elsewhere to distort or minimize the significance of any given feature in the passage itself.

A problem which has been noted with regard to several of these studies is their unsatisfactory treatment of the headings in 1:1 and 2:1. In some cases they are deliberately ignored while in others their witness is overridden or taken insufficiently seriously because they seem to conflict with the wider case being argued. In the present context, however, there is a strong argument to be made for taking them as a starting point. Few will doubt that they are a literary or scribal feature, presupposing the existence of a text which they are designed to introduce. They ought, therefore, to tell us something about a late, if not the final, shape which has been given to at least this part of the book. By the same token, they point towards the fact that the book has developed over the course of time. They are thus the most promising single element in the text for a discussion of the relationship between synchronic and diachronic readings.

Both approaches have been applied to them in the past, but surprisingly rarely in combination. Broadly synchronic concerns may be said to characterize discussions of how much of the text each heading is designed to introduce[27] and of how they relate to the headings in other prophetic books,[28] while diachronic analysis has tended to focus on the small differences in wording between the two headings, together with the comparable one in 13:1, in order to determine the order in which they were written.[29]

In *The Book Called Isaiah* (see especially pp. 162-164), I have suggested that a more fruitful approach (which can only be summarized here) is to contrast the broadly comparable form of heading in 1:1, 2:1 and 13:1 with the completely different form in 6:1 and 14:28. This latter pair obviously belongs together, the first three words in each case being identical: "In the year of the death of king X". In 6:1, the king mentioned is Uzziah, and in 14:28 Ahaz. This suggests that the two headings introduce respectively material dating to the reigns of Jotham and Ahaz on the one hand and Hezekiah on the other. Now, since on a purely historical reading of Isaiah 1-39 it is widely agreed that the two major periods of the prophet's ministry centred on events in the reigns of Ahaz and Hezekiah,[30] and since, fur-

---

[27] E.g. Sweeney, *Isaiah 1-4*, 27-32.

[28] Cf. G.M. Tucker, "Prophetic Superscriptions and the Growth of a Canon", in: G.W. Coats, B.O. Long (eds.), *Canon and Authority: Essays in Old Testament Religion and Theology*, Philadelphia 1977, 56-70; D.N. Freedman, "Headings in the Books of the Eighth-Century Prophets", *AUSS* 25 (1987), 9-26.

[29] E.g. Vermeylen, *Du prophète Isaïe à l'apocalyptique*, 37-42.

[30] No word of Isaiah is explicitly related to the reign of Jotham, though 6:1

thermore, the genuinely Isaianic material in 1-12 is for the most part
related to the earlier period while the material relating to Hezekiah's
reign is predominantly to be found in later chapters, it seems reasonable to conclude that the earliest form of the book which gathered
together all the prophet's own sayings was arranged according to this
two-period schema.[31]

As already pointed out, the headings with which we are here primarily concerned take a completely different form. Though all three
share certain distinctive features in common, 2:1 and 13:1 are the
most closely comparable: "The word *which Isaiah the son of Amoz
saw* concerning Judah and Jerusalem" (2:1), and "The oracle about
Babylon *which Isaiah the son of Amoz saw*" (13:1). They both introduce material which is unlikely to derive from Isaiah himself but
which I have argued stem from the Deutero-Isaianic redaction of the
book which (together with other material and some rearrangement
of already existing passages) structured the earlier written deposit of
Isaiah of Jerusalem along rather different lines from that attested by
the earliest form of heading. On this view, the late exilic form of the
book of Isaiah began at 2:1, and up to this time there is evidence that
the editors still felt a certain freedom radically to reshape the book
to serve their new interests in a manner which Carr has shown was
not shared by the later redactors.

The position just summarized is only a small part of an extensive
theory regarding a significant phase in the composition of the book
of Isaiah, and I appreciate that it has yet to be evaluated by other
scholars. It is clearly diachronic, though it seeks to press the methods
appropriate to that form of study further than has been usual until
now in explanation for the development of the book as a whole. If
it is even broadly along the right lines, it offers a natural account
for the occurrence of a heading in 2:1, something which, as we have
seen, has proved a stumbling block to other diachronic analyses. In

---

implies a date in his reign for the famous temple vision. The situation is further
complicated by the fact that the length of his reign as given in 2 Kgs. 15:33
is thought to be mistaken on both textual and chronological grounds, and some
scholars have even gone so far as to suggest that he died before Uzziah; for discussion, see J. Hughes, *Secrets of the Times: Myth and History in Biblical Chronology*
(JSOT.S, 66), Sheffield 1990, 209-22. He dismisses the possibility that the figure
includes a coregency with Uzziah during the period of the latter's leprosy on pp.
104-5.

[31] This should not, of course, be taken to mean that all the material in these
two major sections was correctly placed chronologically (though in fact most of it
appears to have been), since the editor may also have used thematic considerations
in some cases and may simply not have known the correct dates in others.

development of that conclusion, it now becomes clear that Isaiah 1 must have been given its present location at a later stage, in what may be roughly categorized as the Trito-Isaianic period.[32] The presence of material often thought on other grounds to derive from this period at the end of the chapter (verses 27-8 and 29-31) is thus almost to be expected.

The form of heading in 1:1 seems to support this conclusion. Although it is clearly more closely related to 2:1 and 13:1 than to 6:1 and 14:28, it differs from them both in ways which go far beyond the manner in which they themselves differ from each other. The addition of the list of kings suggests the influence of the form of heading found in a number of other prophetic books, the name of the prophet is moved forward into a more prominent position, and the first word, חֲזוֹן, 'vision', is most probably chosen on the basis of the cognate verb חָזָה, 'saw',[33] which occurs in both the other comparable headings and which, being less specific than either דבר or מַשָּׂא, may have been considered more suitable for an introduction to the complete book. These differences are fully compatible with the suggestion that 1:1 was written by a different hand than 2:1 and 13:1 while yet having been influenced by them. They could not themselves establish the case, of course, but they fit well with that conclusion reached on other, stronger grounds.

So far, I have argued on an exclusively diachronic basis, and on the same basis an analysis of the independent units within chapter 1 itself would conclude, as the overwhelming majority of commentators has always held, that part, at least, of the contents of the chapter derives from the eighth century.[34] Exactly how much need not concern us

---

[32] Other material in Isa. 1-39 which almost certainly derives from this period includes at least 4:2-6; 11:10; parts of the oracles against the nations; 24-27; and 34-35.

[33] For a discussion of this root, see H.F. Fuhs, *Sehen und Schauen: Die Wurzel ḥzh im Alten Orient und im Alten Testament: Ein Beitrag zum prophetischen Offenbarungsempfang* (FzB, 32), Würzburg 1978, although he takes a very different diachronic approach to its use in Isaiah from that advocated here.

[34] For a recent defence of this conclusion with regard to 1:4-9, see J.A. Emerton, "The Historical Background of Isaiah 1:4-9", in: S. Aḥituv, B.A. Levine (eds.), *Avraham Malamat Volume* (ErIs, 24), Jerusalem 1993, 34*-40*. He discusses in particular the contrary opinions of O. Kaiser, *Das Buch des Propheten Jesaja, Kapitel 1-12* (ATD, 17), Göttingen 1981[5] (= *Isaiah 1-12: A Commentary* (OTL), London 1983[2]); O. Loretz, *Der Prolog des Jesaja-Buches (1,1-2,5): Ugaritologische und kolometrische Studien zum Jesaja-Buch*, Altenberge 1984; W. Werner, *Eschatologische Texte in Jesaja 1-39: Messias, Heiliger Rest, Völker* (FzB, 46), Würzburg 1982; and Vermeylen, *Du prophète Isaïe à l'apocalyptique*. The most recent advocate of this approach is B. Gosse, "Isaïe 1 dans la rédaction du livre

for the present, since it is the general principle about the nature of the chapter which needs to be borne in mind for the purpose of this methodological study.

At the same time, there are obviously consequences of the highest significance for a synchronic study. The most important point is that the whole of chapter 1 has been assembled as a single unit at a late phase in the development of the book. If, as is apparent, the chapter is made up of several originally independent elements, however delimited, it becomes immediately clear that it is illegitimate to seek to group some of those elements together as a unit for interpretation in isolation from the others. Contrary to the approach of so many scholars, the redaction of the whole chapter is what must concern the synchronic reader, for in the present form of the book no part of it was ever meant to be read in isolation from any other part. Secondly, since we have concluded that this redaction was undertaken late in the process of the formation of the book of Isaiah, it follows that the reader who would be true to the redactor's intention (if I may still be allowed to talk in such terms) should undertake his or her interpretation from the standpoint of one who is being introduced to more or less the whole of the book of Isaiah.[35] In other words, a truly diachronic analysis, as opposed to so many half-hearted attempts which are found in commentaries limited to Isaiah 1-39 alone, demands a reading which both takes the whole chapter as the unit for interpretation and which does so in the light of the book as a whole.

It goes beyond the limits of the present discussion to attempt such a reading here. I would simply suggest that it is likely to look very much like that which Sweeney offers, "an exhortation to the people to choose righteousness" (p. 133). Although Sweeney does not reach his conclusions along precisely the same lines as those for which I have argued, there are many points in common between our two approaches. Furthermore, taking Carr's observations seriously, we should also conclude that this chapter is not intended as an introduction to the book in the sense of offering a summary of its major themes and concerns so much as a prologue in which the reader is challenged to adopt a responsive attitude to the book which is to follow.

---

d'Isaïe", *ZAW* 104 (1992), 52-66.

[35]Details concerning whether particular passages may have been added elsewhere to the book even later may remain undecided here. Clearly, it would ideally be necessary to determine in particular how much, if any, of the closing section of the book presupposes knowledge of the first chapter, or conversely whether knowledge of the way the book concludes influenced the compiler of chapter 1 in his arrangement.

I conclude by drawing attention in a preliminary manner to a few consequences which arise naturally from my analysis for the writing of a modern critical commentary on this chapter. (I exclude, of course, such necessary issues as textual and linguistic analysis, discussion of *realia*, and so on, which are affected to only a lesser degree by the present discussion.) First, as will be obvious, to limit the parameters for the interpretation of this chapter to Isaiah 1-39 alone is insufficiently critical, for it does not follow the consequences of a rigidly diachronic analysis through to their logical conclusion. The commentator should not impose an arbitrary chronological cut-off point midway through the period during which the book of Isaiah was being compiled for the assemblage of the 'main' part of the chapter and then relegate any later element to the status of a subsequent addition or appendix. Each part needs to be interpreted first as a contribution to the whole.

Secondly, since I am in agreement with those who believe that substantial parts of the chapter were originally written long before the time when the chapter was assembled, care will need to be taken to distinguish between the main thrust of each paragraph, which is what the final redactor will have concentrated on, and individual details which, if pressed, might be found not to fit so well with his overall concern. This is really only a small example of the general principle described by Carr. A synchronic analysis which fails to take account of this point in an attempt to make every word or feature fit neatly into a watertight package runs the danger of distorting the text and of returning to the diachronically inadmissable conclusion of authorial unity, whether early or late.[36]

Thirdly, the consequences of our conclusions for a historical reading need to be carefully considered. The method of composition outlined above has concluded that material which originally stood elsewhere in the Isaianic corpus has been assembled in the present chapter to serve a new purpose, and the possibility has been allowed that a small amount of new material has been added to it at the same time. While there need thus be no objection to the attempt to locate and explain the early material in its historical context, the limitations of this procedure will need to be made clear. Apart from the uncertainties surrounding any historical reading of the Old Testament, which

---

[36] As noted above, a distinction needs to be drawn here between earlier redactors who still exercised freedom to intervene radically in the text they were working with and those who came later and worked only 'at the margins'. Chapter 1 seems to fall into the latter category, and so requires commentary of a different sort from the material which begins at chapter 2.

have been much emphasized in recent years, there are in this case
the additional problems that we can have no certainty about where
each paragraph may once have stood[37] and hence what its wider literary context may have been, that we have no certain knowledge
whether any of the smallest units in the chapter were already joined
before they were given their present setting or whether all the verbal
and thematic links between them are the work of our final redactor,
and that we cannot be sure, in consequence, to what extent he may
have intervened in the texts being assembled in order to make them
flow more smoothly as a new unity, thereby distorting their original shape.[38] In other words, contrary to the impression which most
commentaries give, greatest uncertainty confronts a historical reading
and greatest security a synchronic reading understood on the terms I
have outlined. A truly critical commentary should make such degrees
of probability apparent to its readers.[39]

Finally, some progress has been made for a commentary on the
heading in 1:1, but one major difficulty remains outstanding. In terms
of what the heading is meant to introduce, we may conclude that it
combines the functions of an introduction to the book as a whole and
to chapter 1 in particular, as Sweeney has rightly affirmed. To suggest that it serves as an intermediate heading, to chapters 1-12, for
instance,[40] is inadmissable. But what does the focus on the individual prophet in a specified historical period mean as an introduction
to either a book or even a chapter which probably includes material
from a far later period? Although this is a question for hermeneutics
rather than a discussion of literary methods, I can only suppose that
the answer must be sought in terms of giving the widest possible interpretation to the initial word חזון, 'vision',[41] which, I have suggested,
was chosen deliberately as being less specific than either דבר or משׂא.

[37]For some tentative suggestions about this, see Barth, *Die Jesaja-Worte in
der Josiazeit*, 220, n. 48; I have noted similar problems with regard to some other
passages in chapters 2-12 in *The Book Called Isaiah*, 132, 137-40, and 153.

[38]Cf. E. Robertson, "Isaiah Chapter 1", *ZAW* 52 (1934), 231-6, for an attempt
to sort out some of these problems from within the general standpoint advocated
here. The fact that many would demur from several of his conclusions only rein-
forces the hypothetical nature of the exercise.

[39]Cf. E. Ben Zvi, "Isaiah 1,4-9: Isaiah, and the Events of 701 BCE in Judah: A
Question of Premise and Evidence", *SJOT* 1991/1, 95-111.

[40]So, for example, G.B. Gray, *A Critical and Exegetical Commentary on the
Book of Isaiah I-XXVII* (ICC), Edinburgh 1912, 1.

[41]Cf. D.R. Jones, "Exposition of Isaiah Chapter One Verses One to Nine", *SJTh*
17 (1964), 463-77.

Ellen J. van Wolde   *Tilburg – The Netherlands*

Telling and Retelling:
The Words of the Servant in Genesis 24

1. Introduction

When I was in the United States recently, I met a lady who works for a government agency that trains teachers in intercultural education programmes. She told me that it is not so difficult to make 'newcomers' or 'immigrants' (Asians, people from South-America) aware of their own cultural orientation, but that it was particularly difficult to make native Americans aware of the fact that their European, white, and male view is also culturally determined. They consider their own view as 'culturally neutral', as 'objective', and not as subjective or culturally determined.

In my view a similar thing also happens in Old Testament studies. In the last fifty years, the historically critical exegesis has gradually become 'standard' to such an extent that its practitioners consider it to be 'subject neutral' or 'objective science'. Or to use a linguistic term: they consider their view of science as 'unmarked'. Thus there are still people who can only regard the diachronic approach as scientific and objective, and dismiss other, often synchronic views as subject-oriented and unscientific. I remember how an exegete, trained and working in the historic-critical tradition, said to me, after having read my article about the reader as a central factor in determining the meaning of a text: 'Yes, you are absolutely right. Each synchronic reading is subjective. That's why I prefer diachronic exegesis; it refers exclusively to the text.'

Apart from this criticism of subject-orientedness, diachronic exegetes usually formulate other questions and objections to synchronic study of the Hebrew bible. The general diachronic censure is that synchronic research is a-historical and that synchronicity has degenerated into a-chronicity. They say: how can synchronists think they can understand texts that have been written so many centuries ago without any historical research? Together with this reproach of a-chronicity, the objection of ana-chronicity is expressed and the question is asked of whether the synchronic indiscriminate application of the modern literary strategies as plot, theme and characterisation etc. does not lead to an anachronistic interpretation and a distorted picture of that literature? In short, a-chronicity and ana-chronicity, in addition to

subject-orientedness, are the most significant objections of the dia-
chronists to synchronic study of texts.

In spite of all this, people from the other camp within Old Testament studies continue to carry out synchronic research. They even
think that their field is flourishing greatly. From this quarter, the 'old'
diachronic research is observed with wonder: how is it possible that
in diachronic research the prehistory of the text and text fragments
are focused on, and the final product is hardly considered? The diachronic criticisms of the Pentateuch, for example, are based on the
assumption that the Pentateuch cannot be understood as a single,
unified work. It is based on the hypothesis that a historical growth
and causal relationships can explain the repetitions, fractures and
contradictions in the texts, and that the growth in sources could be
described.[1]

The synchronic exegetes have a number of questions on this point.
If such diachronic criticism arises from the desire to understand texts
of the Hebrew Bible, it is difficult to understand why the scholars are
mainly dealing with the pre-existing fragments or layers and why they
are hardly dealing with the final assemblage. They try to make sense
of the textual elements, why not try to make sense of the final result?
Also, synchronic exegetes often voice the objection of anachronicity in
this context. Is it not anachronistic to presuppose a kind of unity in an
old text that is similar to our modern idea of unity? Is not diachronic
text interpretation greatly one-sided, since a text must be entirely coherent, may not contain repetitions or fractures, and must completely
satisfy the expectations of present-day exegetes? Moreover, are the
images formed about authors or redactors not equally constructions
invented by readers, and therefore constructions of the exegetes who
study the text?[2] Another point of criticism made by synchronists
is that the diachronic approach overemphasizes imperfection as the
point of departure: for if the text were perfect by diachronic standards,
it would be impossible to trace sources and redactors. In short, the
objections of synchronic exegesis to diachronic exegesis involve frag-
mentedness and an overappreciation of an unverifiable prehistory of
the fragments, and an inadequate and anachronistic treatment of the
text.

---

[1]See for a accurate description of diachronic methods: J. Barton, *Reading the
Old Testament: Method in Biblical Study*, Philadelphia 1984, 1-60.

[2]F. van Dijk-Hemmes, *Sporen van vrouwenteksten in de Hebreeuwse bijbel*
(Utrechtse Theologische Reeks, 16), Utrecht 1992, 33-45.

2. Chronicity

Thus, one of the key concepts in this discussion appears to be the concept of time (chronos) or chronicity. Indeed the one criticizes the other on account of an achronistic or anachronistic approach and the other criticizes the one on account of reducing time to a hypothetical genesis of hypothetical sources or layers and an anachronistic view of text unity. This leads to the question: Is there a possible approach in which the synchronic aspect is not achronistic or anachronistic, and in which the diachronic aspect does not restrict time to steps in a hypothetical process of development and does not impose a constructed coherence upon a text? I would like to take the opportunity to cut across the achronistic idea in so far as it is bound up with a synchronic approach, without lapsing into the fragmented through-the-ages approach of diachronic research.

As readers and as exegetes we cannot proceed differently than by taking the directly perceptible as a starting point: the linguistic and literary elements of a Hebrew text (in its final wording and as it has been handed down by the massoretes). But these directly perceptible lines soon point to something outside the text, namely to the Hebrew language system. The relation between this language system and its taking concrete shape in a Hebrew bible text will therefore be central in the analysis. However, with this language system and its concrete shape in a context, the reader or hearer of the text also come into view, for both language system and text point to the intended reader and the functioning in a particular historical community of readers. By studying the text in relation to the language system and to the reader, the a-chronistic aspect of this (more or less synchronic) approach is removed. The chronistic aspect of the study then consists of the text in one temporal phase, namely the final phase, being studied in relation to the language (and culture) system of that time and to the reader community of that time.

The relationships between these three parts, the text, the Hebrew language system and the intended reader, require some explanation. Elsewhere I have supplied an analysis of the relation between Hebrew bible text and Hebrew language system as concerns semantic aspects.[3] This analysis showed that the relation between text and language system in Hebrew is completely different from a similar relation in for instance English or Dutch. Biblical Hebrew has a small number of roots.[4] The roots generally consist of a sequence of three conso-

---

[3] E. van Wolde, "A Text-Semantic Study of the Hebrew Bible, Illustrated with Noah and Job", *JBL* 113/1 (1994), 19-35.

[4] The term 'root' is used here in the sense of a 'stable consonant sequence'

nants, which is also a small number. A sequence of vowels in combination with these consonant-sequences indicates a certain morphological function. So the three consonants can be part of an adjective,
a noun, or a verb. In other words, several different morphological and
grammatical functions can be fulfilled by the same three-consonantal
root.[5] In addition to these three characteristics, the Hebrew language
system has another striking feature: a common consonant sequence
in different words often has completely different meanings. This polysemic feature sometimes even leads to roots denoting contradictory
meanings.[6] As a matter of fact, markers in the Hebrew language system are fewer than and differ from from those in the Indo-European
languages. Because of the smaller number of roots there is greater
need for additional specification in the text, in the textual relationships. In a language like English the opposite applies. The English
lexicon is larger and more specified and therefore requires less specification in the textual relationships. Because the Hebrew language
system is, from a semantic point of view, so general, the relationships
in the text are necessary to specify the general, context-independent
and polysemic possibilities. The meanings of words in Hebrew bible
texts and their semantic structures are therefore to be determined
not so much on the basis of dictionaries but rather on the basis of
contextual relations, since the interaction between language system
and text is different from the one in our Indo-European languages.

The result is also that the relation to the reader is a different
one. The text is aimed at readers/hearers who know this language
system and take this relation between language system and text as a
point of departure. Because the roots in the Hebrew language system
have a number of different meanings, combinations of these roots
in the texts result in a strong increase in the number of possible
meanings. The reader makes a selection from the very large number

---

and not in the sense of 'root meaning'. See J. Barr, *The Semantics of Biblical
Language*, London 1961, 100-6; J. Barr, "Did Isaiah Know About Hebrew 'Root
Meanings'?", *ET* 75 (1964), 242.

[5] Cf. J. Sawyer, "Root-Meanings in Hebrew", *JSSt* 12 (1967), 42.

[6] This phenomen is called *'addad*. See: T. Nöldeke, *Wörter mit Gegensinn (Addad): Neue Beiträge zur semitischen Sprachwissenschaft*, Strassburg 1910, 67-108;
R. Gordis, "Studies in Hebrew Roots of Contrasted Meaning", *JQR* 27 (1936-37),
33-58; J. Barr, *Comparative Philology and the Text of the Old Testament*, Oxford
1968, 173-7; D. Cohen, *Études de linguistique sémitique et arabe* (Janua Lin-
guarum Series Practica, 81), Den Haag & Paris 1970, 101-4; R. Meyer, *Gegensinn
und Mehrdeutigkeit in der althebräischen Wort- und Begriffsbildung*, Berlin 1979;
H.-P. Müller, "Polysemie im semitischen und hebräischen Konjugationssystem",
Or. 55 (1986), 365-89; J. Hospers, "Das Problem der sogenannten semantischen
Polarität im Althebräischen", *ZAH* 1/1 (1988), 32-9.

of possibilities on the ground of the textual markers as well as on the basis of the assumed resemblance between text and reality. The reader has his or her own part to play here: the more context-independent a word, the greater the necessity for both text and language user to establish relationships. Thus the text presupposes an active reader: the intended reader is able to interact actively with the text to make it function in his or her life and community. This intended reader is therefore a product of his/her time, it is the reader who the author or redactor had in mind.

Summarizing, the proposed research studies the interaction between language systems, text and reading community. This study is synchronic in so far as it is based on the text in one phase of final wording and one point in time and is chronistic as far as it studies the text in relation to the dated language system and the intended (contemporary) audience. In order to illustrate this form of synchronic research, extended with 'chronicity' and to clarify the differences with the usual diachronic and synchronic views, let us look at Genesis 24.

3. Telling and Retelling in Genesis 24 in a Diachronic Perspective

In Genesis 24 Abraham orders his servant to find a wife for Isaac in his native country. There, the servant meets Rebekah when she is drawing water from the well, and asks her father and her brother for her hand. After they have given their permission, Rebekah leaves for the country to which the servant will lead her. The story ends with Rebekah's arrival in the Negev, where Isaac takes her as his wife. Apart from the fact that this story of the meeting at a well of a man and a girl who is to become the wife of his master's son, is told and retold in Genesis, the story itself is also conspicuous for its repetitions.

In diachronic research the repetitions are conceived of as indications of fractures in the evolution of the text: the text in Genesis originated in the continuous retelling, so that it contains a great deal of overlap and many contradictions. While source criticism proceeds by breaking up the text into sections that one author could have written, form criticism detects elements and suggests that they belong to different genres which functioned in different historical contexts, and redaction criticism explains the repetitions in the text as products of various redactors. These three forms of diachronic text analysis start with the repetitions in the bible text and study, each in their own way, this process of retelling.

In studying Genesis 24 scholars therefore concentrate on the repe-

titions and frictions in the texts. Gunkel[7] enumerates all irregularities
in Genesis 24: Rebekah has more servant girls to accompany her in
verse 61, while in verse 59 she only takes her nurse; Rebekah's family members say nothing (50b) or comply with the servant's request
(50a, 51), they ask Rebekah (57) and they don't (50 and 51), Rebekah leaves twice (61a and 61b); twice Laban goes to the man at the
well (29 and 30), twice the servant gives Rebekah a wedding present
(22 and 53); the servant asks Rebekah two questions (23a and 23b)
and she answers twice (24 and 25); at the repetition in 47 the second
question is omitted; Abraham thinks it is possible that the mission
will fail (5, 6 and 8; 39 and 41) and is otherwise fully convinced that
YHWH will prosper the journey (7b, 40); the servant's destination is
indicated twice (10) as is the time (11b), Rebekah's descent is also
reported twice (15 and 24). According to Gunkel, these repetitions
and contradictions point to two independent reviews or story layers.

Gunkel was preceded by a generation (Dillmann, Wellhausen, Holzinger)[8] that regarded Genesis 24 as a unity despite its inconsistencies.
However, with Gunkel there was an increase in the number of historical-critical exegetes who distinguished two sources in this text, such
as Smend, Skinner, Procksch, Eissfeldt and Eichrodt.[9] The following
generation of diachronic exegetes, Volz, Noth, Von Rad, Zimmerli,
Speiser, Van Seters and Roth,[10] again regard the text as a unity.
Westermann,[11] whose comment has become a kind of standard work
for diachronic exegesis of Genesis, acknowledges the inconsistencies in
Genesis 24, but studies the phenomenon of telling and retelling not

---

[7]H. Gunkel, *Genesis*, Göttingen [3]1903 ([9]1977), 244-61 (244-5).

[8]A. Dillmann, *Genesis* (KeH), Leipzig 1875, [6]1892; J. Wellhausen, *Die Composition des Hexateuch*, Berlin 1876/77, [4]1963; H. Holzinger, *Genesis* (KHC),
Freiburg, 1898.

[9]R. Smend, *Die Erzählung des Hexateuch auf ihre Quellen untersucht*, Berlin
1912; J. Skinner, *Genesis: A Critical and Exegetical Commentary* (ICC), Edinburgh 1910, [3]1930; O. Procksch, *Kommentar zur Genesis* (KAT), Gütersloh
1923, [3]1924; O. Eißfeldt, *Hexateuch-Synopse*, Leipzig 1922 (Darmstadt [2]1962); W.
Eichrodt, *Die Quellen der Genesis von neuem untersucht* (BZAW, 31), Giessen
1916.

[10]P. Volz, *Der Elohist als Erzähler: Ein Irrweg der Pentateuchkritik* (BZAW,
63), Giessen 1933, 47-59; M. Noth, *Die Überlieferungsgeschichte des Pentateuch*,
Stuttgart 1948 (Darmstadt [3]1966); G. von Rad, *Das erste Buch Mose: Genesis*
(ATD), Göttingen [1]1949, [2]1968; W. Zimmerli, *1. Mose 12-25: Abraham* (ZBK),
Zürich 1976; E.A. Speiser, *Genesis* (AncB), Garden City 1964; J. Van Seters,
Abraham in History and Tradition, New Haven & London 1975, 242-8; W.M.W.
Roth, "The Wooing of Rebekah: A Tradition-Critical Study of Genesis 24", *CBQ*
34 (1972), 177-87.

[11]C. Westermann, *Genesis*, 2. Teilband: Genesis 12-36 (BK), Neukirchen-Vluyn,
1981, 462-80.

so much within Genesis 24, but rather in comparison with Genesis 29 and Exodus 2:15-22.[12] In his view, one and the same event is at the root of these three texts, namely the family story that is part of the oral tradition: as a result three variants have emerged.

> Gn 24 in der uns übergelieferten Form ist die Umgestaltung dieser älteren Erzählung unter einem neuen Gesichtspunkt, dem der Führung Gottes. Wir haben hier einmal die seltene Möglichkeit, die spätere Umgestaltung von der älteren Erzählung unterscheiden zu können, jedoch nicht in einer Quellenscheidung. Diese ist hier fehl am Platz, weil Gn 24 in seiner jetzigen Form literarisch einheitlich ist. (...) Diese in sich einheitliche Darstellung als Gottes Fügung ist etwas der einfachen Familienerzählung gegenüber Eigenständiges. Das zeigt sich auch darin, daß die Zeichenbitte in Gn 29 und Ex 2 keine Entsprechung hat sondern nur dazu dient, die Begegnung als Fügung Gottes dar zu stellen. Die Umgestaltung zur Führungsgeschichte konnte erst in einem zeitlich weiten Abstand von der alten Familienerzählung entstehen. (...) Es ist dann ausgeschlossen, Gn 24 dem Werk des J zuzurechnen, sofern man ihn im 10. oder 9.Jh. ansetzt. (Westermann, *Genesis*, 2.Teilband, 469-70)

According to Westermann, Genesis 24 thus distinguishes itself from the other two stories because of the central theme: divine providence.[13]

4. A Text-Semantic Approach: The Main Theme in Genesis 24

Although Westermann studied the main theme of Genesis 24 in comparison to Genesis 29 and Exodus 2, other, synchronistically oriented,

---

[12]K.T. Aitken, "The Wooing of Rebekah: A Study in the Development of the Tradition", *JSOT* 30 (1984), 3-23 (10-20), follows Westermann and his comparative study, adding some new elements to it.

[13]Aitken, "Wooing of Rebekah", 3, summarizes these diachronic studies of Gen. 24 in a slightly different way: "The story of the wooing of Rebekah (Gen. 24) is commonly viewed as a 'late connective piece' bordering on, if not belonging to, the literary stage in the formation of the Patriarchal tradition. It is thereby implied that it had no independent *Sitz im Leben* or history of transmission but came into being to function as a bridge between originally seperate tradition cycles within the structure of the emerging Patriarchal history as a whole. In support of this view it is argued that (1) the story is composed in the 'discursive' style, judged to be later than the 'saga' cycle of early Patriarchal narratives, (2) it shows a knowledge of other traditions in their literary or near literary form through links to such themes as the call of Abraham and the birth of Isaac in Sarah's old age, (3) the genealogical relationships assumed (...) presuppose the Jacob tradition and the final stage in the genealogical ordering of the once independent Patriarchal figures."

exegetes[14] such as Aitken (1984) and Sternberg (1985), detect on the basis of a text-internal approach a similar emphasis on the contribution of God in finding the right wife for Isaac. Most of them see God's guidance as the text's main theme.[15] Even though everyone recognizes the servant's efforts, divine providence is still experienced as determining their success. Indeed, Rebekah is the bride chosen by God, and led by God the servant merely takes the course he must follow. In this view, the reactions of Laban and Bethuel are likewise actually 'acts of providence'. Sternberg formulates this explicitly in the conclusion of his analysis of Genesis 24:

> Where God has 'spoken' through the design of events, there remains little room for human speech. (...) Like all the other limited participants –the reader included– the Mesopotamians (i.e. Laban and Bethuel) undergo a process of discovery that brings home to them God's management of the world. (Sternberg, *Poetics*, 151-2)

Isn't this strong emphasis on providence in literature rather one-sided? It is striking that Sternberg remarks about a text in which so much is said, especially by the servant: 'here God has spoken, there remains little room for human speech'. Is it not precisely the acting as well as the speaking of the people in this story that form the requirements for changes to take place? Haven't exegetes overemphasized the theological element in their interpretation of Genesis 24? In order to answer these questions, I would like us to have a closer look at one text-semantical line, that is, the relation between לקח and הלך in Genesis 24.

The story of Genesis 24 opens (verses 1-9) with a conversation between Abraham and his servant. This dialogue results in the servant swearing Abraham an oath; it also records the servant's mission and the aim of his journey.

---

[14]B. Jacob, *Das erste Buch der Torah: Genesis*, Berlin 1934; N. Leibowitz, *Studies in the Book of Genesis*, Jerusalem 1972; B. Vawter, *On Genesis: A New Reading*, Garden City 1977; Aitken, "Wooing of Rebekah"; R. Alter, *The Art of Biblical Narrative*, New York, 52-54; M. Sternberg, *The Poetics of Biblical Narrative: Ideological Literature and the Drama of Reading*, Indiana 1985, 131-52; S.P. Jeansonne, "Images of Rebekah: From Modern Interpretations to Biblical Portrayal, *BR* 34 (1989), 33-52.

[15]Aitken, "Wooing of Rebekah", 10: "The theological and interpretative framework which gives the story its meaning thus devolves upon the themes of divine pronise and dive guidance: Yahweh's guidance of the servant towards the successful execution of his mission and thereby towards the fulfilment of Yahweh's promise."

Abraham said:	Put your hand under my thigh,	
	and I will make you swear by YHWH,	
	the God of the heaven and the God of the earth,	
	that you will not take a wife for my son [from here],	לקח
	but will go to the land of my birth	הלך
	and take a wife for my son Isaac.	לקח
The servant said:	What if the woman does not want to go after me,	הלך
	shall I then let your son return to the land,	לא שיב
	from which you came?	יצא
Abraham said:	On no account must you let my son return there!	לא שיב
	YHWH, the God of heaven, who took me	לקח
	from my father's house,	
	He will send his messenger before you	שלח
	and you will take a wife for my son from there.	לקח
	And if the woman does not want to go after you,	הלך
	you shall then be clear of this oath to me.	
	But do not let my son return back there.	לא שיב

The oath that the servant must swear, covers going (הלך), taking
(לקח) as well as not letting [Isaac] return (לא שיב): the servant and the
woman must go, and Isaac may on no account return to Abraham's
land of birth. This is clearly expressed by the repetition of the words
לקח (four times) and הלך (three times) in four verses. The content of
Abraham's command is unequivocal: the servant must go, the woman
must want to go after him, and Isaac who has no say in the matter,
must not return to the country which Abraham himself has left. It is
remarkable that both Abraham and the servant stress the fact that
the woman herself must want to go. It is equally remarkable that
Abraham himself refers back to YHWH's 'taking'. Just like YHWH
took him from that country, the servant must 'take' a woman from
the same country. This elucidates the relation between Genesis 12:1
and this text:

לֶךְ־לְךָ מֵאַרְצְךָ וּמִמּוֹלַדְתְּךָ וּמִבֵּית אָבִיךָ אֶל־הָאָרֶץ אֲשֶׁר אַרְאֶךָּ   12:1

אֶל־אַרְצִי וְאֶל־מוֹלַדְתִּי תֵּלֵךְ וְלָקַחְתָּ אִשָּׁה לִבְנִי לְיִצְחָק   24:4

יְהוָה אֱלֹהֵי הַשָּׁמַיִם אֲשֶׁר לְקָחַנִי מִבֵּית אָבִי וּמֵאֶרֶץ מוֹלַדְתִּי . . .   24:7
הוּא יִשְׁלַח מַלְאָכוֹ לְפָנֶיךָ וְלָקַחְתָּ אִשָּׁה לִבְנִי מִשָּׁם

By phrasing his command to his servant in this way, Abraham constitutes a resemblance between himself and the woman from his father's
house:[16] in 24:4 he uses the words ארץ and מולדת in addition to הלך and
לקח, and in 24:7 he even associates YHWH's לקח of him with the לקח

---

[16] Gen. 24:28 says that Rebekah hurries to her mother's house. This is striking
because untill now only the term father's house was used (by Abraham). It is the
more conspicuous because the mother, who has no name in the story, will not
occur at all. The father and the brother of Rebekah have names and are acting
as characters. Even in 24:15 where Rebekah was presented as the one "who was
given birth to Bethuel", the mother has no name.

of the woman by the servant, a situation in which YHWH will render assistance.[17] Just as previously Abraham 'was taken' and himself had to go to a country which he did not know, thus the intended woman is now 'taken' and she must be willing to go to a country and a man she does not know (24:8).

The remainder of Genesis 24 covers the execution of the order. The servant immediately leaves for Aram Naharaim and the city of Nahor; in this context the word הלך is used twice (24:10). The journey itself, though it must have taken a great deal of time and energy, is not described, since the next verse narrates that towards evening the servant made his camels kneel down by the well outside the city. He begins to talk to himself and the narrator extensively reports his thoughts. Both here and later in the text, it becomes increasingly clear that the narrator prefers spoken text to actions such as travelling and the like. The servant has scarcely finished speaking (to himself), when Rebekah, who was born to Bethuel, the son of Milcah the wife of Abraham's brother Nahor, comes out (יצא) with her jar on her shoulder (24:15). This event is followed in 24:16-20 by a rapid succession of actions by Rebekah, formulated by the narrator in a pizzicato–like series of *wayyiqtol* forms (וַיֹּאמֶר, וַיָּרָץ, וַתָּעַל, וַתְּמַלֵּא, וַתֵּרֶד, וַתֵּרֶד, וַתֹּאמֶר, וַתְּכַל, וַתַּשְׁקֵהוּ, וַתֵּרֶד, וַתְּמַהֵר, וַתֹּאמֶר) Rebekah goes down to the well, fills her pitcher and comes up; she hurries again, lowers her pitcher, draws water, hurries again, fills her pitcher, hurries back to the well, waters the camels.[18] In a dialogue between the servant and Rebekah it becomes clear who she is, and while she hurries to her mother's house, the servant praises YHWH who led him to the house of Abra-

<hr>

[17] Cf. Roth, "Wooing of Rebekah", 179: "The same emphasis is apparent in the Yahwist's choice of words for that which both Abraham and Rebekah leave behind: 'their country' (12:1/24:4), 'their kindred' (12:1/24:4) and 'their father's house' (12:1/24:38)."; Aitken, "Wooing of Rebekah", 9: "The first relative clause (of 24:7) qualifying 'Yahweh' makes retrospection to the 'call' of Abraham in Genesis 12.1-3 and the second to the divine promise of the gift of the land, especially as formulated in 12.7 and 15.18."

[18] Cf. Alter, *Art of Narrative*, 54: "In four short verses (Gen. 24:16, 18-20) she is the subject of eleven verbs of action and one of speech, going down to the well, drawing water, filling the pitcher, pouring, giving drink. One might note that the two verbs of rushing and hurrying (*ruts* and *maher*) generally reserved for the bringing of the news of the stranger's arrival are here also repeatedly attached to Rebekah's actions at the well, and the effect of rapid bustling activity is reinforced by the verbatim recapitulation of this moment with its verbs (verses 45-46) in the servant's report to Laban." Sternberg, *Poetics*, 138, compares Rebekah's hurry with Abraham's: "It echoes nothing less than Abraham's model hospitality, "He ran to meet them ... Abraham made haste into the tent ... Abraham ran to the tent ... he made haste to prepare it" (18:2-7); and the elevating analogy stamps her as worthy of the patriarch himself."

ham's brother. The word הלך does not occur in this context, because
it is only used in Genesis 24 in the sense of 'going and leaving behind
home and country'.

After Rebekah's report to her father and brother, Bethuel, Laban and the servant have a conversation. After having told them who
his master is and that he has greatly prospered, the servant repeats
the details of Abraham's command to him, and in the process he
uses the words לקח and הלך three times. All the same, the servant
does change some of the particulars in his account of the conversation with his master:[19] in 24:7 Abraham said that YHWH took him
(לקח) from his native land, while in 24:40 the servant does not mention this to Laban and Bethuel. Instead, he says that Abraham said
that he 'goes with YHWH'. Maybe he is afraid to offend them: YHWH
'took' Abraham and not Bethuel. He implies that Abraham's leaving was his autonomous decision. The servant flatters the family by
changing Abraham's instructions to go to his מולדת (birthplace), and
uses instead the words בית אב (father's house) and משפחה (family),
emphasizing familial and tribal connections. Nor does the servant repeat that Abraham said that Isaac was to return to Abraham's birthplace on no account, indisposed as he is to antagonize them with this
piece of information, too. The servant concludes his grandiloquent
request for Rebekah's hand with the words "to take (לקח) the daugh-
ter of my master's brother to his son" (24:48). In the conversation
between Abraham and the servant, the condition was discussed that
the woman had to be willing (24:5,8). Towards Laban and Bethuel he
implies that it depends on whether they, Rebekah's family members,
consent to let her go. However, Rebekah's acquiescence eventually
proves to be necessary to prevent postponement or cancellation of
her journey to Canaan (24:58). Subsequently, the servant repeats his
considerations and the conversation with Rebekah. While in verse 22
he gave the lady presents after she had given him drink, that is: before
he asked her name, he now suggests to Laban that he asked her name
first and then gave the presents, as if he gave her something because
she was related. All these small variations hint at the fact that the
servant's speech is diplomatic: he appeals to the family tie, vaguely

---

[19] G.W. Savran, *Telling and Retelling. Quotation in Biblical Narrative*, Indiana
1988, gives in his very interesting study an analysis of the formal aspects and
functions of direct speech and quotations in the Hebrew bible. In this context he
also deals with Gen. 24 (45-51). "As narrator of the retelling, the servant controls
the story (...). The servant accomplishes his task by means of a variety of subtle
changes introduced into his retelling of the story in vv. 34-49, and it will be helpful
to view these differences as reflexes of the active/passive axis."

speculates on Laban's and Bethuel's greed, and acts as if the power of decision is all on their side (irrespective of what the woman wants). The repetitions and contradictions which Gunkel observed and which diachronistically oriented exegetes tried to explain in a causalistic-historical way are very functional within the text from a literary point of view. The mechanism of telling and retelling apparently does not have to be explained by hypotheses about the development process. Telling and retelling, the repetitions and fractions are functional in a literary perspective.

After this strategic argument of the servant, Laban and Bethuel immediately react with: קַח וָלֵךְ, take and go (24:51). Yet somewhat later they try to postpone Rebekah's departure: "You go first, the girl will remain here for another ten days or so" (24:55). It is unclear whether they are trying to cancel the affair, since the presents have already been given. There is also the possibility that this is a way to extort more gifts. The servant urges instant departure, so that Laban and Bethuel propose to let Rebekah decide for herself. Rebekah reacts positively. Her reply is the acme of brevity: אֵלֵךְ, I'm going. This sums up the essence of the story: to go or not to go, that is the question. The narrator continues: "she and her companions followed the man. The servant took (לקח) Rebekah and went (הלך)." The servant goes and takes, but Rebekah herself has voiced her will to set out.[20] This circumstance increases the similarity between Abraham and Rebekah: Abraham was taken by YHWH and Rebekah by the servant from his/her native land and kindred, and both agree to go. Both react to the 'taking' by means of 'setting out themselves' and in both of them that option is chosen without reserve, despite the uncertain future that awaits them.

At the very end of the story, after the return journey (that is described as little as the outward journey) the story concludes in verse 67: Isaac 'takes' (לקח) Rebekah and she becomes his wife and consoles him for the death of his mother. The story that began with an order from Abraham to his servant to go and take a wife for his son, here finds its completion: the deceased mother is succeeded by a young woman who holds the promise of new life in the future.

Thus, the entire story seems to depend merely on the setting out and taking of people. But the individual choice of the servant and of Rebekah to go and the personal decision of the servant and of Isaac

---

[20]Sternberg, *Poetics*, 151 stops his analysis of Gen. 24 after Laban and Bethuel gave their permission. Rebekah's own consent and will to go is for him a neglectable part of the story (although the text itself states three times that the woman has to express her consent to go with the servant).

to take, only highlight the active side of people in this process. In addition, a passive or receptive side, or, put differently, an active contribution on the part of YHWH is also required. In particular the people in this story who set out, evince their awareness of the fact that they are dependent on YHWH's contribution. He will prosper their way. This is what Abraham calls YHWH's support ("he will send his messenger before you", 24:7), and the servant himself repeatedly speaks of YHWH's help: הִצְלִיחַ דַּרְכִּי, YHWH has made my journey successful (cf. 24:21,40,42,56). Laban and Bethuel, however, hardly mention it. Accordingly, 'to go your way' and 'YHWH's guidance on that way' are closely connected for people who set out. A successful journey requires somebody's personal choice to go: there is no way without setting out. Not only divine guidance, nor people's plain going, but the interrelated combination in particular, forms the essence of this story. In my view this pattern of mutual effort is the main theme of Genesis 24.

5. A Text-Semantic Approach:
The Words of the Servant

The words of the servant emphasize this theme in a particularly ingenious way. In his diplomatic argument the servant heaps embedded discourse upon embedded discourse (especially in verses 43 and 44): telling and retelling become a tool in his hands to secure his aim. This phenomenon of heaping embedded discourse upon embedded discourse is found in more places in the Hebrew bible.[21] Genesis even contains the highest number of speeches with verifiable quotations (forty-nine). But Genesis 24 is unique in the amount of embedded direct speeches or discourses it contains.[22] There are ten separate speeches in 24:2-27, all of which are repeated by the servant in one long monologue (24:34-39). The speech of the servant to Laban and Bethuel in 24:34-51 is as follows:

34. He said: (...)
42.   "I came today to the spring
         and I said:
             "YHWH, God of my master Abraham
             may you prosper the journey
             on which I go!

---

[21] For Genesis see H. White, *Narration and Discourse in the Book of Genesis*, Cambridge 1991; for a general description of the narratives in the Hebrew Bible, see Savran, *Telling*.

[22] Savran, *Telling*, 46.

43.   Behold,
    I am standing by the spring of water;
    and it will happen that the young woman
    who comes out to draw
    to whom I shall say:
      "Please, let me drink a little water from your jar."
44.   and she will say to me:
      "You may drink
      and I will also draw for your camels."
    She is the woman
    whom YHWH has appointed for my master's son."
45.   Before I had finished speaking in my heart,
    Behold,
    Rebekah came out with her jar upon her shoulder,
    and went down to the spring
    and drew.
    And I said to her:
      "Please, give me to drink."
46.   And she made haste
    she lowered her jar from her shoulder
    and said:
      "Drink,
      and I will also water your camels."
    So I drank
    and she watered the camels too.
47.   And I asked her
    and said:
      "Whose daughter are you?"
    She said:
      "The daughter of Bethuel, son of Nahor,
      whom Milcah bore to him."
    I put a ring on her nose and bracelets on her hands,
48.   and I bowed low
    and brought homage to YHWH
    and blessed YHWH, the God of my master Abraham,
    who has led me on the right way
    to get the daughter of my master's brother for his son
49.   And now,
    if you mean to treat my master with true kindness,
    tell me;
    and if not,
    tell me also,
    and I will turn to the right or the left."

50.   Then Laban and Bethuel answered
      and said:
          "The thing/word issues from YHWH;
          we cannot speak to you bad or good.
51.   Behold,
          Rebekah is before you.
          Take her
          and go!
          Let her be the wife of your master's son,
          as YHWH has spoken."

It is clear that the servant heaps embedded discourse upon embedded discourse. In verse 43 and 44 he makes an agreement with YHWH: "if the girl says 'drink', then I know that you have chosen this girl." And lo and behold, the girl says 'drink', and the servant thanks YHWH for his success. Subsequently, he tells this to her family: "I said to YHWH: 'If the girl says to me '...', then I know 'This is the woman (הוא אשה) whom God has marked out for Isaac'; it happened, therefore I know now that YHWH wishes this girl as wife for the son of my master." The servant lets Rebekah's words parallel his wish and his agreement with YHWH. He lets, consequently, his business depend on Rebekah's words, and lets God depend on his agreement, and in that way he makes his words a business of God's. He is successful in this persuasion procedure, for the family members acknowledge it: these are the words of YHWH, this business is a business of YHWH. The servant's construction of embedding discourses serves his end of trying to convince Rebekah's kinsmen that his words agree with the words and the business of YHWH. The embedded form of speech within the action reflects the close connection between word and deed. Therefore, the embedded way of speaking embodies the rhetorical if not manipulative force of the servant's argument. It is not only God who is acting, but also the servant who makes his words coincide with God's deeds. Savran summarizes the speech–quality of the servant as follows.

> The servant narrates at such length not to bring out his role in shaping events, but to demonstrate that ineluctable divine providence which has pointed everything toward Rebekah as the chosen woman. These two paradoxical factors –the servant's narrative authority and the centrality of divine providential authority– constitute the axis upon which the story rotates. (...) As narrator of the retelling, the servant controls the story, yet he must tell a story that emphasizes his own lack of power and God's controlling hand. (Savran, *Telling*, 46)

On the textsemantic level, the rhetorical qualities of the servant, syntactically expressed by the embedded way of speaking and quoting, are expressed by one word: דבר. In the Hebrew language system the word דבר refers both to 'word' and to 'thing'. Genesis 24 uses this semantic possibility and lets דבר refer to both meanings at the same time. The correlation between the two is essential for the functioning of this word in the speech of the servant. Indeed, the words of the servant correspond to the thing (business) of YHWH, as is revealed both by his own words, and by the first and last words of Laban and Bethuel (24:50–51): "מֵיהוָה יָצָא הַדָּבָר, this thing/word issues from YHWH, we cannot speak to you bad or good; כַּאֲשֶׁר דִּבֶּר יְהוָה, as YHWH has spoken." The words of the servant are equated with the words and with the wishes of YHWH. In Hebrew this can be expressed by one word, דבר, because דבר means 'word' as well as 'thing'.

The words of the servant illustrate that words are equated with things, and in a similar way the whole text breathes a vision on the coherence of everything. The distinct correlation between the going of Abraham and the going of Rebekah (expressed by the words הלך) and the leading or guiding by God. The servant must go on his way, but only YHWH can make his way a success (הִצְלִיחַ דַּרְכִּי; 24:21,40,42,56). They are the two sides of the same coin: God can only make someone's way a success if that person him/herself sets out. By the embedding of speech in speech, the servant reflects the same idea. The entire pattern of narratives, speeches and embedded speeches can be interpreted as an indication of underlying correlations and of patterns of meaning, one of which is the close connection between the words and the things of people and of YHWH, as is reflected by the functioning of the word דבר in the words of the servant.

6. Conclusion

In the debate about diachronicity and synchronicity I proposed, at the beginning of this paper, to pay more attention to chronicity in a synchronic method, without relapsing into fragmentation and a through-the-ages approach characteristic of diachronic analysis. Recognizing the chronistic aspect does not mean that a text or text elements are explained in terms of a straightforward causal connection (in the sense that phenomena are explained as being the result of prior cause), but rather that the text is studied as functioning within a particular time and culture, in relation to a particular language system and reader. For instance, in Genesis 24 the polysemy of the Hebrew language system proves to be of vital importance: the double meaning of דבר in this language enables the correlation of the servant's words and

YHWH's business to play a central part. This is also connected with the culture in which words and things are not perceived as separate, as we have been want to do since the Enlightenment. If words and things are interdependent, the narrator or the character can postulate a thing as real, as being present, by narrating something and the narrated event can happen at the moment of reading or hearing. In that case texts are not only words, but words as well as things, that become reality through reading.

This is bound up with another aspect of Hebrew. As everybody knows, there are many embedded narrators' texts in the Hebrew bible. Recently, scholars[23] have recognized that the Hebrew verbal system is also based on the distinction between narrative and embedded discourse.[24] In a language and in texts in which embedding of direct speech is so important, the intended reader will be confronted with discourses embedded in narratives and he or she will understand the repetitions and variations in these discourses. Accordingly, a diachronic approach which attempts to attribute repetitions and variations to divergent sources or describe them separately per redactor, makes insufficient allowance for the specificity of the Hebrew language system on the one hand and for the actual text construction and the

---

[23] W. Schneider, *Grammatik des Biblischen Hebräisch*, München 1974, [6]1985, and in his tradition of research E. Talstra, "Text Grammar and Hebrew Bible. I: Elements of a Theory", *BiOr* 35 (1978), 169-74; idem , "Text Grammar and Hebrew Bible. II: Syntax and Semantics", *BiOr* 39 (1982), 26-38; idem, "Text Grammar and Biblical Hebrew: The Viewpoint of Wolfgang Schneider", *Journ. of Transl. & Textling.* 5 (1992), 269-97; A. Niccacci, *The Syntax of the Verb in Classical Hebrew Prose* (JSOT.S, 86), Sheffield 1990.

[24] In this Hebrew text syntaxis the verbs are described as follows. The narrator uses (after a beginning with *wayyehi*, or a time specifier or a *qatal* form), the *wayyiqtol* form to indicate the actions of a person. In addition, the narrator may briefly suspend the description of actions and interrupt the story-telling in order to supply background information; the narrator then describes the circumstances that form the background to the action, using a *non-wayyiqtol*-form: mostly a nominal sentence (a sentence without a verb or a sentence with a participle or an infinitive) or a verbal sentence with a *qatal* form. In the case of a discourse, a person recounts the sequence of actions in direct speech and thereby uses mostly *yiqtol* forms (according to Niccacci; Schneider considers the *qatal* form as the form of the direct speech; I follow Niccacci here) or modal forms like imperative, cohortative or iussive. The character may also suspend the description and interrupt his/her account of events to supply background information. He/she then uses mostly *non-yiqtol* forms or a nominal sentence or a verbal sentence with a *qatal*-form. In other words, in the recounting of actions or in the presentation of foreground information, the narrator and the personage are distinguished from each other by divergent verbal forms; in the presentation of background information, the narrator and the personage use the same verbal forms which relate to the circumstances and mostly appeal to the general knowledge of the reader.

intended reading community on the other. To put it another way, it is precisely because the Hebrew biblical texts contain so much embedded speech and because the Hebrew language system is partly based on the distinction between narrative and discourse that the reader is involved with the text in a different way from, for example, modern English, modern Hebrew or Dutch literature. In these modern texts the narrator, in addition to direct descriptions, also gives many indirect accounts of thoughts and feelings of characters (amongst other things in indirect and free indirect speech). A direct recounting of the words of a character involves the reader far more directly with the perceptions and words of that particular character.

These factors, the embedding of direct speech and observation, the polysemy, the absence of distinction between words and things, the frequent occurrence of repetitions and variations, achieve that the intended reader is involved with the Hebrew text in a way which differs from that of the contemporary reader. Recognition of the particular time frame of the biblical texts and the Hebrew language leads us to a chronistic synchronic reading in which the relation of the text to the Hebrew language system and the intended reader is central.

Index of Authors

Index of Biblical Texts

OUDTESTAMENTISCHE STUDIËN

Edited by J.C. de Moor

15. *The Priestly Code and Seven Other Studies.* 1969. ISBN 90 04 03099 9
17. *The Witness of Tradition.* Papers Read at the Joint British-Dutch Old Testament Conference Held at Woudschoten (Holland), September 1970. 1972. ISBN 90 04 03343 2
18. LABUSCHAGNE, C.J.; LEEUWEN, C. VAN; MULDER, M.J.; BRONGERS, H.A.; JONGELING, B.; DEQUEKER, L.; BOER, P.A.H. DE. *Syntax and meaning.* Studies in Hebrew Syntax and Biblical Exegesis. 1973. ISBN 90 04 03785 3
19. *Language and Meaning.* Studies in Hebrew Language and Biblical Exegesis. Papers Read at the Joint British-Dutch Old Testament Conference Held at London, 1973. 1974. ISBN 90 04 03943 0
20. *Instruction and Interpretation.* Studies in Hebrew Language, Palestinian Archaeology and Biblical Exegesis. Papers Read at the Joint British-Dutch Old Testament Conference Held at Louvain, 1976. 1977. ISBN 90 04 05433 2
21. ALBREKTSON, B.; et al. *Remembering All the Way...* A Collection of Old Testament Studies Published on the Occasion of the Fortieth Anniversary of the Oudtestamentisch Werkgezelschap in Nederland. 1981. ISBN 90 04 06305 6
22. WILDE, A. DE (ed.). *Das Buch Hiob.* Eingeleitet, übersetzt und erläutert. 1981. ISBN 90 04 06372 2
23. *Prophets, worship and theodicy.* Studies in Prophetism, Biblical Theology and Structural and Rhetorical Analysis, and the Place of Music in Worship. Papers Read at the Joint British-Dutch Old Testament Conference Held at Woudschoten, 1982. 1984. ISBN 90 04 07035 4
24. *Crises and Perspectives.* Studies in Ancient Near Eastern Polytheism, Biblical Theology, Palestinian Archaeology and Intertestamental Literature. Papers Read at the Joint British-Dutch Old Testament Conference Held at Cambridge, U.K., 1985. 1986. ISBN 90 04 07873 8
25. WOUDE, A.S. VAN DER (ed.). *New avenues in the study of the Old Testament.* A Collection of Old Testament Studies Published on the Occasion of the Fiftieth Anniversary of the Oudtestamentisch Werkgezelschap and the Retirement of Prof. Dr. M.J. Mulder. 1989. ISBN 90 04 09125 4
26. WOUDE, A.S. VAN DER (ed.). *In Quest of the Past.* Studies in Israelite Religion, Literature and Prophetism. Papers Read at the Joint British-Dutch Old Testament Conference, Held at Elspeet, 1988. 1990. ISBN 90 04 09192 0
27. BOER, P.A.H. DE; DUIN, C. VAN. *Selected Studies in Old Testament Exegesis.* 1991. ISBN 90 04 09342 7
28. SMELIK, K.A.D. *Converting the Past.* Studies in Ancient Israelite and Moabite Historiography. 1992. ISBN 90 04 09480 6
29. DIRKSEN, P.B.; VAN DER KOOIJ, A. (eds.). *Abraham Kuenen (1828-1891). His Major Contributions to the Study of the Old Testament.* A Collection of Old Testament Studies Published on the Occasion of the Centenary of Abraham Kuenen's Death (10 December 1991). 1993. ISBN 90 04 09732 5
30. HOUTMAN, C. *Der Himmel im Alten Testament.* Israels Weltbild und Weltanschauung. 1993. ISBN 90 04 09690 6
31. PEELS, H.G.L. *The Vengeance of God.* The Meaning of the Root NQM and the Function of the NQM-Texts in the Context of Divine Revelation in the Old Testament. 1995. ISBN 90 04 10164 0
32. LUGT, P. VAN DER. *Rhetorical Criticism and the Poetry of the Book of Job.* 1995. ISBN 90 04 10326 0

33. EYNIKEL, E. *The Reform of King Josiah and the Composition of the Deuteronomistic History*. In preparation.
34. MOOR, J.C. DE (ed.). *Synchronic or Diachronic?* A Debate on Method in Old Testament Exegesis. Papers Read at the Ninth Joint Meeting of Het Oudtestamentisch Werkgezelschap in Nederland en België and the Society for Old Testament Study, Held at Kampen, 1994. 1995. ISBN 90 04 10342 2